REVOLUTIONARY IDEOLOGY
AND CHINESE REALITY

Volume 47, Sage Library of Social Research

SAGE LIBRARY OF SOCIAL RESEARCH

REVOLUTIONARY IDEOLOGY &

CHINESE REALITY

Dissonance under Mao

PAUL J. HINIKER
Introduction by **ITHIEL de SOLA POOL**

Volume 47
SAGE LIBRARY OF
SOCIAL RESEARCH

 **SAGE PUBLICATIONS**　　Beverly Hills　　London

For information address:

SAGE PUBLICATIONS, INC.
275 South Beverly Drive
Beverly Hills, California 90212

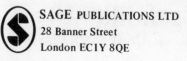

SAGE PUBLICATIONS LTD
28 Banner Street
London EC1Y 8QE

Printed in the United States of America

Library of Congress Cataloging in Publication Data

Hiniker, Paul J.
    Revolutionary ideology and Chinese reality.

    (Sage library of social research ; v. 47)
    Includes bibliographical references.
    1. Communism—China.   2. Communication in politics—
China.   3. Dissonance (Psychology)   I. Title.
HX388.5.H55   301.6'333   77-7484
ISBN 0-8039-0834-2
ISBN 0-8039-0835-0 pbk.

FIRST PRINTING

CONTENTS

*To my mother
in memory of my father*

INTRODUCTION

China's Cultural Revolution was, in Hiniker's phrase, a "transitory phenomenon." But though it lasted a brief two years, and though it has now been buried in the inevitable "routinization of charismatic movements," its significance is permanent. From time to time there are brief episodes that compress within themselves the dynamics of history with such force that their story is written for ages after, over and over again. Such were the days of the shot heard round the world in 1775, or of the drums of August in 1914, or the ten days that shook the world in 1917. The Cultural Revolution in China in 1966-1968 was such a time.

It is too soon for us to know what the end significance of that era of political madness may be. It may be noted in the history books as an odd aberration, like the flagellants, and Hussites, and Anabaptists, who dramatically reflected the tensions of their times and gave a foretaste of bigger revolutions to come. It may become a folk story for billions of children in China, drained by orthodoxy of much of its significance—a story like that of Robin Hood. Or it may, like the Paris Commune, become part of the mythos of a revolutionary secular religion for generations to come.

Hiniker does not try to predict what the Cultural Revolution will become in the eyes of history. He tries to explain how that remarkable event came about. He traces it back to another almost equally remarkable movement, China's "Great Leap Forward" in 1958-1959. Hiniker traces for us how he sees the linkage; it is not for the preface to tell you the plot before you start. But one cannot help but comment on the fact that the linkage is through the psychology of one man.

Mao Tse Tung impressed himself on the face of the world. With the megalomania that mankind seems to tolerate in what get labeled as great men, he acted out his fantasies on the broad stage of history—and what fantasies they were! In the Great Leap Forward he tried to merge the millions of Chinese families and the hundreds of thousands of Chinese villages (with all the strong cultural heritage that supported the autonomy of those traditional units) into some 26,000 communes averaging 5,000 households each. Not only were these cooperative working units, but collective dining halls were also to replace eating in the home. In the Cultural Revolution eight years later, Mao took on in conflict the ruling Communist party of a totalitarian country; with the aid of the army and mobs of students he deposed its top leaders and tried to reverse its course. He could not achieve his chiliastic goals, but remote as the results from his aims, he succeeded in remaining in power till his death. He has been canonized by those who are leading China in quite different directions.

Mao's efforts and behavior are what Hiniker tries to help us understand. To do so is an interdisciplinary exercise. It requires an understanding of the psychology of the individual, as well as of the social system in which he operated, and also of the detailed history of modern China. That is perhaps what is most interesting in this book, and what will make it hardest for members of the different disciplinary audiences to accept.

Sinologists are often not receptive to the attempts of psychologists or sociologists to apply their bag of tools to the subject matter of China. One can understand why. It is extraordinarily hard for anyone who is not a professional China specialist to perceive at all accurately what is going on in that tightly closed inner kingdom. It was always hard for anyone who did not give the years it takes to learn Mandarin, and in this era of a secretive Communist regime it is even harder. So not only has China been a closed domain, but also Sinology.

Hiniker, in this book, should satisfy historians with his detailed reporting of the obscure events in China in the 1950s and 1960s. At the same time he brings to bear psychological insights and a lot of the quantitative apparatus of sociologists. One can hardly accuse him of the glibness that has plagued some of psychohistory. It is, of course, true that there is no way to put a dead historical figure on the couch. That is a problem not just for psychohistory, but for any kind of history. Historians must inevitably make much of whatever evidence there is. The test is whether the available evidence has been explored as thoroughly and meticulously as possible. This book seems to me to meet that test.

Despite the problems, there is a growing though still small social science literature on China. Hiniker refers, among others, to Lucian Pye's book on Mao, to Richard Solomon's book on Chinese national character, and to Ezra Vogel's study of Canton.[1] This is a literature to which Hiniker now contributes and which one hopes will grow. One of the problems of social science is, after all, the predominant focus on a single case, namely what we call Western civilization. The inadequacy of such a limited base of observations has long been recognized, and indeed a whole discipline, anthropology was set up to study the diversity of human societies. But on the one hand anthropology tended to focus on small societies. On the other hand comparative studies partitioned off in a discipline of their own did not provide an adequate corrective to the parochialism of the other social science disciplines.

The study of modern China by political scientists, psychologists, and sociologists is a welcome development. China is a big society, a great society, and an extraordinarily different society. What is particularly interesting in Hiniker's results is that despite the differences, what he finds is a confirmation of hypotheses about human behavior under stress, paralleling historical results from a variety of situations in the West.

Ithiel de Sola Pool

NOTE

1. Lucian W. Pye, *Mao Tse Tung: The Man In The Leader*, New York: Basic Books, 1976; Richard H. Solomon, *Mao's Revolution and the Chinese Political Culture*, Berkeley: University of California Press, 1971; Ezra F. Vogel, *Canton Under Communism*, New York: Harper and Row, 1971.

ACKNOWLEDGMENTS

This book was written with the encouragement and support of persons too numerous to mention, but a number must be given specific credit. First of all, the forbearance of my wife, Lisa, and my children, Linda and Peter during the long hours away from the family, which writing this book required, has earned by heartfelt appreciation. The members of my family, nuclear and extended, deserve credit for their support. In the course of developing the thesis of the book, valuable comments, criticisms and support were forthcoming from many of my former teachers and colleagues in social science. Leon Festinger, Frederick Frey, Doris Graber, William Parish, Ithiel de Sola Pool, and Lucian Pye deserve special mention in this regard. Without the intrepid comments of my students, the book would have been the lesser; without the assistance of Vincent King, William Kwan, and Jerome S.H. Wang, the data base would have been smaller; without the support of my friends, the book would not have been written.

Several institutions provided support for this study. The Center for International Studies at MIT deserves special credit for funding the initial research that paved the way for the eventual book. As the seed of the idea germinated, additional support in terms of writing time was provided by my employers at Michigan State University. The University of Chicago, the University of Illinois at Chicago Circle and the Universities Service Center in Hong Kong also provided facilities for completing this work. The interpretations expressed in this book are my own, however, and should not be attributed to any of these institutions. For the errors and shortcomings, I bear final responsibility.

PREFACE

This book is not an exhaustive history of Maoist Communism. It represents a quest for explanation rather than description. The book is an effort to use some derivations from an established social science theory, that of cognitive dissonance, to explain the motivation underlying the Great Proletarian Cultural Revolution (GPCR) in China. Although rival approaches have been advanced to account for this event, e.g., the concept of "struggle for power," they find it most difficult to account for the extremist methods employed in the movement, which are well documented here. This is especially true of the reluctance of the Maoists to compromise their ideals in the face of apparent failure and obvious criticism. The theory of cognitive dissonances specified here in the concept of ideological polarization accounts well for the major characteristics of the Cultural Revolution as well as other important historical movements, seven of which are summarized. The increase of ideological proselyting, growth of an exculpating rationalization, and severe split along the lines of prior commitment within the movement following a failed prophecy is a well documented paradigm in the history of many social movements.

In the modern Chinese case, the phenomenon is well documented from the 1950s through the 1970s by chronological analysis of Mao's speeches and party documents, content analysis of the party press and magazines, scaling of politburo members' ideological commitments, background analysis of the changing politburo composition, and survey analysis of adult media exposure and communications behavior. The combined results are quite confirmatory of the explanatory utility of the dissonance-derived concept of ideological polarization, and quite devastating to the view of the Cultural Revolution as just another enigmatic "power struggle." The massive proselyting for the thought of Mao Tse-tung (TMTT) that occurred in the wake of the Great Leap failures is otherwise difficult to explain. Although other explanations of the Cultural Revolution are indeed possible, it is our view that the dissonance-reduction interpretation is one that deserves serious consideration along with them in the tentative search for valid generalizations that characterizes the spirit of scientific inquiry.

PROLOGUE

*The social myth of the early Christians was the second coming of Christ
and the reign of the saints in the new Jerusalem. The second coming of
Christ never took place, and the reign of the saints was a delusion. Yet
faith in these things converted millions of people. It enabled thousands
of martyrs to endure the most excruciating tortures with expressions
of joy upon their lips. It overthrew an ancient and widespread system
of religion, backed by all the physical force of a world-empire. It
changed a poor, despised Jewish sect into the most powerful theocracy
in history. This faith may be considered totally absurd. Yet without it
Christianity would have had no history—no existence.*

*The great red leaders—Lenin, Trotsky, Kalinin, and others—are not
to be thought of as ordinary statesmen or politicians, governed by the
usual motives of gain or expediency. Essentially they were evangelists
preaching the gospel of St. Marx.*

—Lyford P. Edwards,
The Natural History of Revolution,
1927

One thousand *Li* above the sea, the atmosphere is cold and clear in this year,
1970 A.D. Revolving here in majestic dynastic cycles, the weight of three
emperors ensphered in the heavens sails supersonically through the universe,
shines down on earth, and softly speaks, "Tung Fang Hung!" The east is red.

As the white clouds part before the east wind, the metallic strains of the
emperors' chorus are more clearly apprehended by the gazing populace below. The verses now seem to split the atmosphere; they fly crashing momen-
tarily into each naked and crazed psyche:

The east is red,
Rises the sun,
China has brought forth a Mao Tse-tung.
He plans blessings for the people,
He is the great savior of the people.

As the satellite whirls on and over the horizon, the strains of the chorus diminish in amplitude for awhile, but the people around Canton city know that later on this April day the shining sphere, and shouting emperor, will recycle again ... and again. The peasants stoop in unison, pick up their wooden plows and hoes and shuffle resignedly in makeshift military formation toward dilapidated commune plots awaiting the spring's planting. The brown soil is warm and the morning mist moistens the bare feet as the peasants plod on.

One of the peasants, Lao Chiang, lags behind the others. He is reflecting on the readings and discussion at the political study session last night. They have been more frequent lately, and last night the session went on for nearly three hours. The cadre reread the legend of "The Foolish Old Man Who Removed the Mountains" and then they all discussed over and over some passages from *Quotations of Chairman Mao.* Chiang is trying to gather his thoughts. As he thinks, he recollects some of the things his cousin in Canton has told him of what he has learned from the Red Guards as they stormed through the streets a few years ago. Let us listen to some of the things related by Chiang's cousin.

Chairman Mao is the charismatic leader of these youths and the omnipotent party which they were attacking. Chairman Mao maintains supreme authority as the great leader of the monolithic party organization, great helmsman of the ship of state, and great commander. Yet, one of his major principles of leadership is, "To rebel is justified." It was Chairman Mao who encouraged the *tatzepao* (large character poster) medium in August of 1966 with his own *tatzepao* which read: "Bombard the headquarters." As commander of the armed forces Mao sometimes had his People's Liberation Army put down popular uprisings such as those occurring in Canton or Shanghai, or had his paratroopers fight his infantry, such as occurred at Wuhan. Although Mao is the great helmsman of the ship of state, until 1966 the government really was run by Mao's subordinate and archenemy, a Chinese by the name of Khrushchev (alias Liu Shao-ch'i), who had subsequently confessed his sins on revisionism and proclaimed himself a supporter of Mao's thought. Liu's policies as head of state were "left in form but right in substance." Despite the fact that Liu had led the government back to economic stability, since "the three hard years," his following in the party and government consisted of "ghosts and monsters" who had been "waving red flags to oppose red flags." While Liu had been "pointing at the mulberry bush and reviling the locust tree," his followers had been spreading "poisonous weeds." Liu's followers had been "using ancient things to satirize the present" instead of "remembering bitterness and thinking of sweetness"; they had attempted to bribe the workers with bonuses and wage increases instead of mobilizing them for extensive democracy. Such were the confusing events in China of the mid-sixties.

If one's mind boggles before this recent Chinese scene, one need not feel alone. This dissonant clash of symbols compels the attentive to listen the more intently. Many learned observers of contemporary China have put together some of the pieces. What has transpired in Communist China during the Great Proletarian Cultural Revolution has been a power struggle between Mao Tse-tung and Liu Shao-ch'i. Admittedly, it was a very odd kind of power struggle, for there were no Stalinist-style bloody purges or Kruschchev-Beria style political infighting. It even bore little similarity to the Chinese purge of Kao and Jao in the Manchurian region during the midfifties. Liu even claimed to be a Maoist; and Mao went far beyond the party to recruit supporters for his cause from the nation's youth as well as its army.

If it was a power struggle then, what was its origin, what were the issues involved—just personalities and their personal followings? What were the alignments of groups behind the opposed leader, who had more support and from what groups? It has been asserted that Mao's major following was in the People's Liberation Army and that Liu's major following was among the party bureaucrats. But Mao's support cut across these constituencies. A power struggle between two leaders implies that there is competition for political positions and for political supporters. But Mao has always retained the number one position in the Chinese Communist party since his selection as chairman in the mid-1930s. There was indeed a power struggle for positions in the politburo in the fall of 1966, the greatest political reshuffling in the politburo since Mao came to power in 1935; but those who were promoted were the ones who had been most vociferous and active in supporting the massive Great Leap failure seven years earlier, and those who were demoted or purged were the ones who had presided over the economic recovery.

If the Cultural Revolution is to be explained solely as a power struggle, how does one account for the passionate displays of ideological ferver? Why was there so much fanfare over the Thought of Mao Tse-tung? It was necessary to declare in the leading national newspaper what appeared in *People's Daily* on June 19, 1967: "Every sentence uttered by Chairman Mao is truth. Mao Tse-tung's thought is universal truth tested in revolutionary practice and is living Marxism-Leninism at its highest stage in the present era."

Why has a nationwide cult of the Thought of Mao Tse-tung developed in China and why did a smaller but similar cult make its appearance in 1960? Were such displays of fervor designed to increase Mao's base of political support? Why was it that during the Great Leap Forward, Mao proclaimed art

and literature to be the second; and then after the Great Leap failure, he proclaimed that all art and literature should be for the working people, and
classical art anathema? Does one broaden one's base of political support by
becoming more restrictive in one's policies?

Why was there more proselyting in the nation's press for the Thought of
Mao Tse-tung after the Maoist Great Leap failed than while it was being
planned and implemented? Does one broaden one's base of political support
by propagandizing for the principles and plan of a movement that has recently caused several years of suffering and misery to the population? Why in the
midst of economic recovery, were people compelled to spend more time in
political study than prior to economic well-being? Why were more of the
propaganda campaigns before the Great Leap targeted upon the bourgeois
rightists and most of the campaigns after the Great Leap failure targeted upon
the proletariat?

If it was solely a power struggle, how does one account for the Maoists'
persistent prediction of the success of the People's Communes which were
effectively diminished as unfeasible to one hundredth of their original size
in the early 1960s? Why did Mao praise the use of his dialectics to improve
the playing of table tennis and the growing of watermelons? Were these
actions designed solely to increase Mao's political support?

More than some cynical struggle for position and power, what transpired
in China's Cultural Revolution was a great upsurge in Maoist proselyting
coupled with the polarization of Chinese polity and society about that ideology. A single example of the army's involvement in Maoist faith healings
should serve to illustrate not only the presence but indeed the centrality of
the quasi-religious, ideological component of the Cultural Revolution. The
following account of the army's activities was published in a popular national
magazine in 1969:

> In August last year, revolutionary medical workers of the Peoples Liber-
> ation Army no. 208 Hospital relying on the invincible Mao Tse-tung
> thought, succeeded in curing Chang Kuei-chih, a young woman worker
> who had been paralyzed for four years and diagnosed by the reaction-
> ary bourgeois medical "authorities" as "incurable." . . . The Hospital's
> Party committee considered that in order to cure the "after-effects" of
> infantile paralysis, it is necessary first of all to cure the ideological
> "after-effects" on the medical workers of the poison of the counter-
> revolutionary revisionist line pushed by the big renegade Liu Shao-ch'i
> in medical and health work. . . . They solemnly pledged to the great
> leader Chairman Mao.

> "Chairman Mao! Ah, Chairman Mao! We are the people's army, loyal
> fighters defending your revolutionary line. The people's needs are our

fighting order. We are determined to restore more sick class brothers
to health so that they can closely follow you in making revolution."

Enduring acute pain, they tried the big acupuncture needles out on
their own bodies. Their thighs became swollen, and their eyes were
red after sleepless nights. But the revolutionary medical workers armed
with Mao Tse-tung thought regarded this as pleasure and happiness.
They said: "To defend Chairman Mao's revolutionary line, we are willing to acupuncture our legs to pulp."[1]

This modern secular parable concluded with the assertion that after repeatedly acupuncturing their own bodies, the cadres led the "overwhelming
majority" of the hospital's 6,000 patients to marked improvement, enabling
them to "stand up" and take part in Mao's revolution. Thus one is to conclude that suffering for the sake of Mao's Thought does bring an earthly
reward, the claim of the archrenegade notwithstanding. The millennial over-
tones are clear.

Indeed, the recent struggle was more of an inquisition within a crusade
than a mere jostling for position. Why in 1965 did Mao publicize the text of
his previously confidential 1956 speech "On the Ten Great Relationships"?
Why were the mass media filled with quotations from Mao Tse-tung? Why
the appearance of millions of Red Guards? Why the attempt to apply Mao's
Thought to all of life's endeavors? Why the extreme ideological rigidity of
the Maoist leadership in the face of moderating policies? Why the increasingly
virulent hatred of the Soviets as well as domestic class enemies? Why the
spreading of peoples' wars to the developing nations? Why the spreading of
Mao badges to other areas such as Burma, Hong Kong, Macau? Why this
ideological polarization? What is the motive force behind it all?

To attempt an explanation which is not ad hoc, one needs a bit of historical perspective and a theory about ideological social movements. Our
assertion is that the recent Chinese turmoil was the result of an ideologically
based social movement that experienced a sharp failure more than six years
before. The Great Proletarian Cultural Revolution of 1966-1969 was due to
the failure of the Great Leap Forward circa 1959. When the Great Leap failed,
it split the leadership of the party and spawned a new kind of ideological
social movement, one of semireligious proselyting for a doctrine in distress.

The Historical Paradigm of Ideological
Polarization

Throughout recorded history groups of committed men reacting to social
strain have had lasting impact in changing social values. Such has never been
accomplished without the use of ideology; but ideology has nowhere been

entirely right. Everywhere utopia is vacant. Still it is avidly pursued. The phenomenon of increased proselyting by intransigent members of an ideological movement coupled with increased rejection and derogation of disbelievers, which we have observed as central to Mao's Great Proletarian Cultural Revolution, is curious indeed; but it is not unprecedented in history. Such ideological polarization is observable throughout centuries of recorded history of medieval Europe. Norman Cohn has provided a number of fascinating case histories of these movements.[2]

Shortly after the year 1000 A.D. a form of extreme ideological commitment similar to that recently recommended and practiced by the acupuncturing P.L.A. soldiers for the sake of Mao Tse-tung Thought became a prevalent phenomenon. Then it was practiced with flails by the hermits in monastic communities such as Camaldoli for the sake of Christ's teachings.[3] By the late fourteenth century the practice of self-flagellation for the sake of religious beliefs had reached massive proportions. The significance of the practice is summed up in the words of a fourteenth-century friar who, one midwinter's night

> shut himself up in his cell and stripped himself naked . . . and took his scourge with the sharp spikes, and beat himself on the body and on the arms and on the legs, till blood poured off him as from a man who had been cupped. . . . He stood there bleeding and gazed at himself. It was such a wretched sight that he was reminded in many ways of the appearance of the beloved Christ, when he was fearfully beaten. Out of pity for himself he began to weep bitterly. And he knelt down, naked and covered with blood, in the frosty air, and prayed to God to wipe out his sins from before his gentle eyes.[4]

After such a self-inflicted experience what hot cognition could contradict the friar's conviction? The friar provides a medieval example of the modern committed ideologue. He did not stand alone. Multitudes were similarly engaged in the collective *imitatio Christi* in hope of redeeming the world of its sin and its sinners. The ideology to which the multitudes were committed rested on two fundamental tenets. First of all, secular and religious authorities alike were held responsible for the misery of the masses. In the most important of the movements, the flagellants of Thuringia, the members repudiated both the emperor of the Holy Roman Empire and the Church of Rome, even to the extent of exhorting the common people to stone the local clergy. Second, they believed that with their aid these despised authorities would shortly be overthrown and replaced with the millennial kingdom in which "grouped around their Emperor-God, the flagellants would form an angelic choir and would be called sons of princes."[5] To this end many monks underwent the baptism of blood inflicted by their charismatic leader, Konrad

Schmid, a baptism that was necessary to gain membership in the movement; and subsequently they sold all their belongings, refused to work, and professed that their very salvation depended on their attitude toward Schmid. Membership in the movement swelled in concert with outbreaks of the plague which was sweeping Europe at the time. The social strain induced by the raging plague and the sweeping Inquisition made multitudes of miserables. During a particularly severe epidemic of 1368, Konrad Schmid prophesied that the last judgment would be held and the millenium begin the following year.

But the millenium failed to take place as prophesied. Furthermore, it is reliably reported that Konrad Schmid, the Emperor-God himself, was burnt at the stake by the forces of the Inquisition. New-found facts notwithstanding, the committed followers of Konrad Schmid went undaunted by the disconfirmation of his prophecy. Though some recanted, beginning in 1370 his movement spread posthumously and with a new intensity.

Following 1369, the polarized movement spread first over Germany, then south into France, Spain, and Italy, finally threatening the Pope in Rome at the end of the century. Immediately southwest of Thuringia, the Bishop of Würzburg forbade flagellation in 1370. In 1372 the Pope had to urge the Inquisition in all Germany to put down the flagellants. But the movement continued underground popping into public with the peasant and artisan demonstrations in Heidelberg, intensifying in Erfurt with the slaughter of incredulous Jews. New disciples saw visions of the approaching Last Days. In 1396, St. Vincent Ferrer lead flagellant processions through France, Spain, and Italy in opposition to the impending reign of Anti-Christ. In 1399, an Italian peasant led a flagellant movement that covered all of Italy, finally descending with a procession on Rome. He was rebuked and burnt by the Pope. But still it was in Thuringia that the polarized movement thrived most intensely. After the turn of the century and more than eight decades after Schmid's prophecy was disconfirmed, the Thuringian flagellants maintained Schmid's doctrine intact and persisted in his predictions that Anti-Christ would soon be overthrown, that the Last Days would soon come to pass, and that they would be presided over by none other than Konrad Schmid, now resurrected!

As the Thuringian flagellant movement dropped underground into durable secret enclaves during the fifteenth century, another movement was being born just two hundred miles southeast of the flagellant movements fourteenth-century birthplace. The pattern exhibited by the Taborite movement as it took shape is familiar.[6]

Severe strain wracked Bohemian society after the onset of the fifteenth century. King Wenceslas, brother of the Holy Roman Emperor Sigismund, ruled a native Bohemia increasingly influenced by an alien German minority.

Among the higher clergy, especially, the aliens held sway. What is more, the clergy, under the authority of a corrupt Pope John XXIII, was wantonly worldly. Abetted by economic pressures of increasing inflation, urban unemployment, and repeal of peasant's rights to the land, it was not long before the corrupt forces of Rome became fused in the natives' eyes with the alien German minority as oppressive representatives of Anti-Christ. This belief was crystallized by a vivid personal example. When John Huss, a popular local preacher against church corruption, was sommoned in 1414 to appear before the Ecumenical Council at Constance, while guaranteed safe conduct by the Emperor, he was arrested and, refusing to recant, burnt as a heretic. This by the same council that had just deposed the Pope for simony, murder, sodomy, and fornication. The population of Bohemia was incensed. Under pressure from Emperor and Pope, the King then removed all Hussite councilmen from the government. The populace rose, stormed the townhall and threw the new councilors from the windows. In August 1419, King Wenceslas died of the shock. The natives were thus strengthened in the belief in their own efficacy. For several months the Taborites sustained savage persecution aimed at their extermination. Revolutionary ideology waxed stronger. It blamed the Roman church and the alien Germans for the natives' misery and promised the eventual triumph of the natives. The millenarian ideology was articulated by Martin Huska, the leader of a number of former priests. He and his priests publicly prophesied that the millennium was at hand: Between the tenth and fourteenth of February, 1420 every town and village would be destroyed by fire like Sodom before them; only those who fled to the five Taborite mountain strongholds would be spared the wrath of God. Multitudes of the poor burnt their homes, sold their belongings, moved their families to the mountains, and threw their money at the feet of the preachers.

When mid-February arrived and the millennium failed to appear, the movement polarized: Some dropped from the movement in disbelief, but others felt their fervor increase. In February, immediately *following* the disconfirmation, a significant new community was constructed just twenty miles to the east and named for the nearby mountain dubbed Mount Tabor the year before. Formed by radical priests and highly committed followers, the new community became the radical center of the movement and set itself about inaugurating the elusive Golden Age for all Christendom. Within its walls, the followers were utterly convinced that while the earth was being cleansed of sinners, Christ would descend upon the mountain and replace the unworthy Emperor Sigismund. He would rule over the millenial realm where saints would live together in an abundant community of love, devoid of suffering. The book learning of the clergy would come to be regarded as vanity as the church, itself, withered away. Outside its walls were those marked for extermination as sinners, and hosts of Anti-Christ grew to include not only active opponents but also "anyone, of whatever status, who did not actively help them in 'liberating the truth' and 'destroying sinners.' "[7] They proselyted Europe with their doctrine striking fear into the hearts of authorities in France and Spain as well as Germany. In 1430 Taborite armies penetrated as far as Leipzig, Bamberg, and Nuremberg in their joint mission of proselyting potential believers and exterminating disbelievers. As late as 1434, speakers at Taborite assemblies in Bohemia persisted in the besmirched prophecy of the Second Coming; but, rough beast that it was, it slouched toward New Jerusalem to be born.

If a resurrected Martin Huska could have climbed atop Mount Tabor and cast a timeless gaze to the northwest, he would have spied old Erfurt, scene of Schmid's fourteenth-century flagellants, and glancing just 150 miles further see the site of the sixteenth-century Anabaptists at Münster, Jan Bockelson's New Jerusalem. Severe social strain prevailed in this area of Germany. By the third decade of the sixteenth century the Lutheran Reformation had broken the church's monopoly on authority. The authorities were threatened as the Catholic world view began to crumble. By the end of the decade, the German peasants' war had ended in defeat for the peasants with perhaps a hundred thousand dead and those living feeling threatened in their rights by the rise of the princes. In 1529 the Black Death devastated Westphalia, the crops failed, and the price of rye trebled the following year.[8] To top it off, an extra tax was levied to support resistance to the Turkish invation in the eastern part of the empire. In 1530 the Bishop of Münster attempted to sell his bishopric. The town revolted.

A now familiar ideology arose in new clothes to explain the strain. It was Anabaptism. Among its tenets were the twin notions that the worldly authorities, princes and priests alike, were responsible for the sufferings of the good, and that the good, mostly artisans and peasants, would overthrow the authorities and establish the millennium. The movement also contained a strong does of communalism. Besides adoption of its tenets, that which initially committed believers to the movement was, as with the flagellants, designed in its name. Anabaptists were rebaptized adults. Such rebaptism designated a kind of voluntary separation from the unredeemed world; more importantly under prevailing social conditions, it branded the believer as opponent of the powers that were and designated him as a target of ferocious persecution and possible execution.

In 1533 one of the peripatetic prophets of the movement, Melchior Hoffman, predicted the dawn of the millennium on the fifteenth centennial of the death of Christ, in the town of Strasbourg. The millennium failed to materialize. Instead Hoffman was imprisoned by Strasbourg authorities to live out his days in a cage in the town tower. The mantle of the sullied prophet passed on to a Dutch baker, Jan Matthys, who far from shirking began promptly in 1534 to proselyte for a more militant form of Anabaptism. In one hand he took up the sword against the ungodly; in the other he sent forth apostles who, inspired by the Holy Spirit, baptized multitudes throughout Europe. Two such apostles reached Münster and within a week had baptized 1,400 receptive citizens.[9] As the original pair of apostles moved on to proselyte other towns, they sent two new apostles in their stead. One of their replacements was the charismatic Jan Bockelson, who was destined to rule Münster's 10,000 citizens for a year as their King.

Surviving one severe disconformation, indeed thriving upon it, the radicalized Anabaptists persisted in their prophecy and soon proceeded to another. In February 1534, the swollen Anabaptist population revolted, occupied the town hall and extracted from the town council legal recognition of the principle of freedom of conscience. Indigenous Lutherans moved out and Anabaptists moved in from as far away as Frisia and Brabant, recomposing the majority. The Dutch prophet Matthys, himself, arrived. It was then prophesied that the rest of the earth would be destroyed by Easter, but Münster would survive and become the New Jerusalem. At the prophet's command, Lutherans and Catholics were jeered and expelled from town amid blows of the Anabaptists. It became a capital offense to be unbaptized. By March there were no 'unbelievers' left; only 'brothers' and 'sisters' remained in the chosen community within which all wealth and property were pooled and held in common. Communal dining halls were established. All books, save the Bible, were burnt. The New Jerusalem had begun; the Bishop went about raising an army of mercenaries to besiege it. When Easter arrived, the armed prophet, turned dictator, Matthys, received a divine command to make a sortie from the town, upon which he believed God would drive off the Bishop's besiegers and liberate the town. Before the Easter sun set, he and his handful of companions were cut to pieces. The prophet's mantle passed to Bockelson. Upon Matthys' death it was revealed to Bockelson that the town needed a new, even more stringent constitution since the former had been devised by man not God. Bockelson and twelve elders assumed life and death authority over all matters, spiritual and material, public and private.

In August of 1534, Bockelson's charisma waxed as a result of a victory over the Bishop's forces. To a subordinate prophet, Dusentshur, it was revealed that Bockelson was to be King of the New Jerusalem and Messiah of the world. Befitting the new state, the streets of Münster were appropriately renamed, the coinage reminted, and Bockelson newly attired in robes with a sceptre. It became the sacred duty of the citizenry to purify the world of evil in preparation for the Second Coming. In such preparation, those outside the walls and not marked with the sign of the Anabaptists were to be killed as a matter of duty. Within the walls of Münster, anyone who "persisted in sinning against the recognized truth must be brought before the King and sentenced to death."[10] Several inhabitants were so executed, some for mocking the doctrine of preachers. Despite these totalitarian strictures, the size of the town did not dwindle after the defeat of the Bishop's forces. Foregoing the opportunity to defect, they believed in the New Jerusalem.

In June 1535, the Bishop's forces finally destroyed the town but not the movement. All the leaders of Anabaptism in Münster perished, but Anabaptism did not. It arose again in militant form in 1567 when Jan Willemson gathered some 300 militants, including survivors of Münster, and set up another New Jerusalem in Westphalia, an episode which lasted a dozen years until Willemson and his followers were captured and executed. Anabaptism survives even today in pacific form in such communities as those of the Mennonites and the Hutterites.

In these three capsule histories of ideological polarization in revolutionary movements, a common paradigm is present. In the face of severe social strain, a revolutionary ideology often develops which serves to explain that strain in terms of culpable social agents while promising relief through their demise. Perplexed people join movements under a leader who commits them to action on the basis of the ideology. Whenever convinced and committed members are faced with severe disconfirmation of their ideologies, rather than disintegrating, the ideological movement polarizes. Increasingly intransigent members increase their proselyting while rejecting and derogating growing numbers of disbelievers. The movement splits. The fellow-traveler falls away. The true believer becomes all the more uncompromising, takes on new ideological commitments, and persists in ideological prophecy. This recurrent phenomenon is not restricted to remote religious movements.

More familiar than these three medieval microcosms of revolution are the classic revolutions of Britain (1640), France (1789), and Russia (1917). These secular revolutions also displayed symptoms of the phenomenon of ideological polarization resulting from similar preconditions. In his famous study of the classic revolutions, Crane Brinton points to the importance of social strain and ideological conviction for a successful revolutionary take over, and then he details a recurrent phenomenon which *follows* the seizure of state power by revolutionaries.[11] Among the victors, and following a series of troubles, power passes from the moderates of the movement to the extremists who proceed to implement a "reign of terror and virtue" in the concerted but doomed attempt, once and for all, to close the gap between human aspiration and human nature.[12] In 1648, after several years of civil war, the Independents (including persistent Anabaptists as well as Puritans) through Cromwell's New Model army wrested power from the moderate Presbyterians who had taken over in 1640 from King Charles I. In late 1793, after the Great Fear and the September Massacres, the Jacobins under

Robespierre wrested power from the moderate Gironde, who had taken over in 1789 from the Bourbons. In the fall of 1918, after continuing civil war the Bolsheviks under Lenin seized power from moderate Mensheviks who had taken over in 1917 from the last of the Romanovs. In all three cases the temporary moderate rulers were faced with the difficult tasks of restoring economic normalcy and of renovating the institutions of rule, and utilizing them to conduct domestic affairs while simultaneously conducting foreign or civil war. In the eyes of the extremists they failed. The moderates are men who "do not really believe a heavenly perfection is suddenly coming to men on earth"; they are all for "compromise, common sense, toleration, comfort."[13] Even so they could not cope. Increasingly arrayed against them were the extremists who insisted that "the moderates were trying to stop the revolution, that they had betrayed it, that they were as bad as the rulers of the old regime—indeed much worse since they were traitors as well as fools and scoundrels."[14] The extremists themselves are men who "combine in varying degrees, very high principle and a complete contempt for the inhibitions and principles which serve most other men as ideals"; they "are not philosopher-kings but philosopher-killers" possessing "enough of the prophet's fire to hold followers who expect the New Jerusalem around the next corner."[15] In short, they are the ideologically committed; and they are unsatisfied.

When the extremists eventually gain power, as they did in these three cases, they institute a "reign of terror and virtue." During this reign the social atmosphere becomes supercharged with a heady mix as an organized one or two percent of the population enforces its ideology on the remaining ninety-eight. In London clarions of the Second Coming blared beside the thud of the scaffold. In Paris Festivals of Reason were celebrated in the glint of the guillotine. In Moscow proletarian communes arose from the caustic smoke of the firing squad. Everywhere the renamed streets were alive with galvanized crowds. Brinton outlines seven characteristics of the reign of terror and virtue that are common to the three classic revolutions. They are all examples of ideological polarization. During this period, the extremists proselyted in their ideology both at home and abroad: An intrepid Puritan, Admiral Blake, spread the gospel to foreign lands claiming "All kingdoms will annihilate tyranny and become republics"; the Jacobins announced that they were bringing the blessing of freedom to all the people of the earth; the Bolsheviks set about their great task as apostles of worldwide revolution. The extremists all were utterly convinced that they would inevitably succeed in their mission. They had a utopia and believed they would soon attain it. They were convinced that they were members of an elect group and that unbelievers were sinners. They became increasingly hostile to the competing ideology of organized Christianity; they displayed outward signs, symbols, and rituals to designate their membership in the movement. They were universalist in aspiration, but never in accomplishment.[16]

Thus Brinton's characteristics of the "reign of terror and virtue" present in the British, French, and Russian revolutions provide more vivid examples of the concept of ideological polarisation, instances of which were also found in the three medieval millennial movements examined. In the earlier movements, ideological polarization was preceded by the clear disconfirmation of a millennial prophecy. If one considers the initial revolutionary take over as an implicit prophecy of the imminent realization of the movement's utopia, then retarding or retrogressing events that occur after the take over provide similar but less unambiguous ideological disconfirmations.

For a successful revolutionary movement in charge of a state, the reign of terror and virtue does not last forever. It is invariably supplanted by the Thermidorean reaction. Brinton discovered in all three classic revolutions "a similar moral let down, a similar process of concentration of power in the hands of a 'tyrant' or 'dictator,' a similar seeping back of exiles, a similar revulsion against the men who had made the Terror, a similar return to old habits in daily life."[17] In short, the reign of terror and virtue ends when committed ideological leaders and policies are replaced by ideological moderation and tolerance. The English terror ended in April 1654 when Cromwell dissolved the Rump parliament; the French terror ended in July 1794 when Robespierre fell to corrupt Jacobins, themselves replaced by Napoleon five years later; the Russian terror ended in 1921 when Lenin switched from the radical egalitarian policies of War Communism to the retrogressive practices of the New Economic Policy, although Stalin's subsequent first five year plan showed some but not all the signs of a recrudescence of the terror.

In addition to the reigns of terror and virtue in the classic revolutions, a number of familiar twentieth-century movements have displayed similar periods of ideological polarization. In 1919 the reign of terror and virtue in the Russian Revolution spawned an international proselyting movement, the Comintern, which endured until 1943. Pool and Leites have noted the exceptional resilience of the Comintern in the face of ideological frustration.[18] They analyzed the Comintern's reaction in their official publication, *Imprecorr*, to frustrations brought about by failed strikes and electoral defeats. A major conclusion of their content analysis is that left periods (especially the six and one-half years dating from the failed Austrian uprising of July 15, 1927, and including Stalin's disruptive first five year plan) differ significantly from right periods (especially the preceding Russian Thermidor, 1921-1927, and the succeeding years, 1934-1939). The left-period communications were characterized by greater "cumulation," i.e., relevant issues were treated in terms of the extremes of goodness or badness with few mixed descriptions; greater restrictiveness was invoked in considering any nonparty groups as revolutionary allies, and less "self-indulgent" rationalizations were employed, indicating a preference for "self-deprivational" commitment. It is noteworthy that the left period was associated with very severe purges in the Russian party. It was not a time of compromise by leftists. If one assumes that the left period was the time when the salience of the quest for Communist utopia was strong, then it is not surprising that the movement's defeat reactions of the left period are more characteristic of ideological polarization.

In the 1920s, the Nazi movement led by Adolph Hitler developed a millennial ideology to account for the strains of defeat in war and economic instability which wracked Germany. In *Mein Kampf*, Hitler blamed the strain on the non-Germanic Jews whose evil ways and foreign Bolshevism had rotted the fiber of Aryan racial greatness. Were the Germans to regain their true character, European society would be revitalized in a new thousand-year Third Reich, perpetuating German glory. Millions of Germans committed themselves to Hitler's ideology in opposition to leftist causes. By 1933 Hitler was elected and appointed Chancellor of the Weimar Republic.

In *Mein Kampf* Hitler had prophesied that German territorial expansion would include East Europe and Russia which was "ripe for dissolution, [and] the end of the Jewish domination in Russia will also be the end of Russia as a state."[19] In a concerted attempt to realize his millennial prophecy, Hitler unequivocally committed himself and his army to a five-month blitz victory over Russia to commence in the summer of 1941.[20] On October 3, 1941 he publicly stated that Russia was defeated and "will never rise again."[21] By January 1942, the German army had suffered over a million casualties and had still failed to capture Moscow. Hitler's longstanding millennial prophecy had demonstrably failed by the end of 1941.

Hitler's movement did not wither in the winter of 1941-1942; it polarized. Hitler's immediate reaction to the failure of his prophecy was not to diminish his conviction but to renew his ideological fervor. He increased proselyting for his Aryan ideology and reasserted his conviction in the millennial prophecy, assuming personal command of a second invasion of Russia in 1942. He turned increasingly to the advice of his more committed Nazi followers, rejecting that of growing numbers of waverers especially in the military high command. He urged his followers on to renewed activity in the task of extermination of the Aryan's Jewish nemesis.

The history of Hitler's Germany in early 1942 is replete with signs of polarization of the movement. In the beginning of 1942, a Thirty-point program for a National Reich church was promulgated. It ordered the removal of all crucifixes and Bibles from the church altars and declared among its articles that "the Führer's *Mein Kampf* is the greatest of all documents. It . . . not only contains the greatest but embodies the purest and truest ethics for the present and future life of our nation."[22] Hitler, himself, delivered three major national addresses in early 1942 culminating in his victory speech before the Reichstag on April 26. The Reichstag replied by elevating Hitler's pronouncements above all extant law and clothed the Führer with six additional supreme titles:

> The Führer must have all the rights demanded by him to achieve victory. Therefore—without being bound by existing legal regulations—in his capacity as Leader of the Nation, Supreme Commander of the Armed Forces, Head of the Government, and Supreme Executive Chief, as Supreme Justice and Leader of the Party—the Führer must be in a position to force, with all means at his disposal, every German . . . to fulfill his duties.[23]

Hitler became the incarnation of virtue; his opponents, unmitigated evil. Hitler increasingly restricted his range of advisors to only the truest believers in his Aryan faith. The Nazis' "grand inquisitor," Heinrich Himmler, and his blood-pure SS political soldiers rose in influence, and Himmler himself attained the added position of Minister of Interior the following year.[24] The professional generals declined in influence. Indeed, in the spring of 1942 a growing opposition group solidified among the generals and acknowledged General Beck leader of a task force to assassinate the Führer.[25] So great was the military purging spurred by the failed Russian invasion that by war's end only four high commanders retained their positions in the total of seventeen field marshalls and thirty-six full generals.[26]

Himmler's renewed ideological commitment was to expunging the Jewry as a precondition to the establishment Hitler's New Order. Just outside Berlin, on January 20, 1942, the Final Solution was formally decided: The eleven million Jews thought to live in the greater Reich were scheduled for systematic total extermination.[27] In Berlin, swastika-festooned streets distracted the senses from the surrounds.

A Dissonance Theory of Ideological Polarization

In our brief examination of several historical movements, we have uncovered a common social phenomenon. Whether it is called an upsurge in revolutionary millenarianism or a reign of virtue and terror, the general phenomenon is ideological polarization. It is everywhere manifested as increased ideological proselyting by members of a social movement coupled with rejection and derogation of growing numbers of disbelievers. It entails the urging of further action commitments on believers while proscribing any actions that would compromise ideological tenets. Middle-of-the-roaders cease to be tolerated, as the purging of uncommitted members from the movement and the heightened search for empirical confirmation of ideological tenets progresses. Support for an exculpating rationalization for failures of the movement is avidly sought. The question is what causes such ideological polarization. The answer is individual attempts at dissonance reduction in the social context. To make our answer meaningful we will first examine the general conditions for dissonance arousal and reduction, further focus upon the same in the social context, and finally consider the special case when the dissonance involves ideological beliefs held by members of a social movement. This approach will provide us with an explanation of ideological polarization, of which Mao's Cultural Revolution is an instance.

Our basic premise is that human behavior abhors the existence of serious cognitive inconsistencies.[28] If a man's beliefs, attitudes, and behaviors did not fit together, confusion would reign and his behavior become disoriented. According to Festinger's formulation, when cognitions do fit well with each other to the extent of one psychologically implying the other, they are deemed consonant. Other cognition having nothing to do with each other are pairwise irrelevant. Pairs of cognitive elements which are neither consonant nor irrelevant are dissonant.

In particular, two cognitive elements are in a dissonant relation if, considering these two alone, the obverse of one element follows from the other. The existence of dissonance is uncomfortable. The more important the dissonant elements involved, the greater the pressure to reduce the dissonance.[29] There are three major ways in which dissonance may be reduced: (1) by changing one or more of the elements involved in dissonant relations; (2) by decreasing the importance of the elements involved in dissonant relations; (3) by adding new cognitive elements that are consonant with already existing cognition. It should be pointed out that if the first two options are foreclosed by strong commitments to one's own preexisting opinion, and by the dissonant information being undeniable, then all one can do is attempt to bolster one's original position.

In the social context, other persons provide both a source of dissonance arousal and a medium for dissonance reduction. Social disagreement dissonance is aroused whenever some person holds one opinion and simultaneously knows that another person whom he considers generally like himself, holds a contrary opinion. Such dissonance becomes greater the more similar the other person, the more discrepant his opinion and the more numerous and important are other cognitions dissonant with one's opinion. As dissonance increases, so do the pressures to reduce that dissonance. There are three ways of reducing dissonance in the social context: (1) changing one's own opinion in response to disagreement; (2) influencing those who disagree to change their opinions; (3) making those who disagree noncomparable to oneself.[30]

In general, when the magnitude of dissonance is low, it is reduced in the social context by changing one's own opinion or by influencing those who disagree most extremely to change their opinion. However, when dissonance is increased, the group process switches from the converging politics of compromise and consensus to the escalating politics of polarization: One no longer is willing to change one's own opinion, one avoids those who deviate extremely in opinion, *derogates* them and renders them personally noncomparable; in addition, one seeks contact with those expected to support one's own opinion and proselytes those who disagree only moderately with one's own view. The combination of these behaviors is social *polarization* around the opinion. Furthermore, for one who is strongly committed to an opinion which becomes involved in a dissonant relationship with undeniable evidence or with the unwavering opinion of like persons, the politics of polarization is always the sole recourse for dissonance reduction in the social context. Thus, as opinion variance within a group increases, the magnitude of dissonance experienced by group members also increases and spurs the polarization. When the opinion item involved in such a dissonant relationship is a committed ideological belief, ideological polarization naturally ensues.

Ideological beliefs constitute a special case in human cognition. Especially relevant to the understanding of ideological polarization are two fundamental tenets present in all revolutionary ideologies.[31] These may be termed Manichean blame and apocalyptic hope. Manichean blame asserts that the forces of evil are responsible for the misery of the good. Apocalyptic hope asserts that the forces of good will overcome the forces of evil. This is the general formula of the revolutionary myth. From these two tenets the utopian corollary follows easily. When the good of society are miserable, a group of the bad must be responsible; since the bad are the cause of all social ill, when they are destroyed, society will function devoid of evil in a new utopian state. Revolutionary ideology thus provides a tight bundle of internally consonant cognitions. Particular revolutionary ideologies substitute particular groups for the forces of good and evil. Millenarians saw the believing poor as followers of Christ and the corrupt authorities as followers of Anti-Christ whose overthrow would occur with the Second Coming; some Marxists see the industrial proletariat as the chosen of history, and the exploiting capitalists as the damned whose overthrow will bring the classless society.[32] Sophisticated modern revolutionary ideologies also include special tenets on the strategy and tactics, by which the good may assure their triumph. Such tenets are absent in more primitive revolutionary ideologies.[33] All revolutionary ideologies initially promise a transformation of society which is both imminent, and total.[34]

In view of the simplistic nature of the two fundamental tenets of revolutionary ideology, one wonders how they come to be adopted by persons in the first place. It is noteworthy that the tenet of Manichean blame is almost never wholeheartedly adopted by persons under conditions of social normalcy, but only when severe sociopsychological strain exists.[35] Only when society is a blooming buzzing confusion, when people are shaken loose from their normal social ties and habits, in short when people are experiencing large amounts of dissonance among important beliefs, attitudes, and behaviors does such an ideological tenet gain wide acceptance. It would appear that Manichean blame helps to introduce some consonance into the whirl of cognitions by explaining, after a fashion, the existing social strain while exempting the abused self from painful blame.[36] Fellow faithful provide support for the new view. This projection of blame, this devil theory explanation of one's own misery, this *Weltanschauung* cleaving the world into unmixed good and evil, with one's self included among the good, provides for one's self and one's fellows a cognitively balanced picture.[37]

The tenet of Manichean blame would seem to provide the beginnings of a primordial world view, to which men regress under stress. It is only natural that one's self is good; it is only natural that one's friends are also good; it is only natural that one's friends like one's friends and dislike one's enemies; it is only natural that one's friends benefit one and that one's enemies harm one. Hence it is only natural that oneself and one's friends are good while harmed and disliked collectively by one's enemies. It is only natural, then, that the forces of evil are responsible for the misery of the good.[38] Such is the enticement of the tenet of Manichean blame. Once adopted collectively by members of a particular social movement, the belief is easily maintained by mutual social support. The main danger of falsification arises when the movement has achieved a successful revolutionary take over and eliminated its enemies. Then the internal blame for social strain can only be attributed to their ghosts. If some members of the movement itself must be blamed for the strain, then dissonance with the ideology obtains. There is no dissonance in disagreeing with one's enemies, only consonance; there is strong dissonance in disagreeing with one's close fellows. As the explained "evil" subsides, as selves drop from the movement to more specialized action in the social routine, the tenet loses its immediate support, its relevance and its meaning. What belief remains is likely to be ritualized rather than alive.

If the tenet of Manichean blame is adopted, then a cherished belief in social justice will suffice to dictate the validity of the tenet of apocalyptic hope. It seems only just that goodness and happiness belong together; happiness peacefully coexisting with wickedness is dissonant. Common sense tells us that any imbalance represents but a temporary state of strain: The wicked may have their field day now, but eventually they will be punished and the good rewarded.[39] This concept of social justice has been expressed by Heider in the following proposition:

$$\text{lot p: lot of o = value p: value of o}$$

where p and o stand for a person and another.[40] First of all it follows that if p and o have equal value then any discrepancy in their fortunes is clearly imbalanced and hence tension-filled. Moreover, considered in conjunction with the tenet of Manichean blame, if the good are miserable and the bad not, even greater injustice prevails. Justice can be achieved only by reversing the fortunes of the good and the evil. Such a state of affairs will transpire when the forces of good overcome the forces of evil. Thus justice guarantees the success of the exploited good.[41] Once adopted by members of a social movement, the tenet of apocalyptic hope is readily maintained by mutual social support, by a kind of terrestrial collective faith. Without being directly discarded by the members of a movement, this tenet also may be ritualized if it ceases to be relevant to the voluntary activities of individual members. It also may be disconfirmed if it is too clearly specified. However, taken together in the throes of social strain the admixture of apocalyptic hope and Manichean blame provides a powerful compound for collective social action when adopted and acted on by members of particular groups.

Characteristic of the revolutionary movements we have examined is the promulgation and acceptance of a millennial or utopian prophecy. This prophecy unequivocally specifies in time and detail the realization of the tenet of apocalyptic hope. Whether it predicts a particular final exterminatory struggle against the "great ones,"[42] or the onset of the "egalitarian millennium,"[43] or what is more modern, "a world shorn of all its deficiencies,"[44] it does provide a new incentive for concerted action by members of the movement. The prophecy of utopia provides a future opportunity to gain empirical evidence in ultimate consonance with the ideology. If the prophet is bothered by dissonance, successful prophecy provides possibility of relief. However, the prophet wields a twin-edged sword: The utopian prophecy also renders the ideology vulnerable to sudden disconfirmation. The adoption of the prophecy, the conviction of realization of the impossible dream, is all the more tempting to those who have personally undergone the experience of "utter change" in their own lives. The true converts are more susceptible to credence than the hangers-on within the movement. Those who have become intoxicated by involvement in the prior real growth and accomplishments of the movement are more susceptible.[45] This consideration brings us back again to the concept of social strain.

The existence of social strain is a precursor to widespread adoption of revolutionary ideology. Strain provides the *explicandum* of ideological tenets as well as the force which disrupts former opinions and behavior patterns to make way for the new. While there are various definitions of social strain,[46] at a minimum such strain is composed of situations or events that compel people to new information and behaviors that are dissonant with important beliefs or values held. Especially important are relatively immutable beliefs about the self. Revolution is preceded by cries of indignation.[47] In a contrived social environment, though reform begins with an assault upon the ego, the authorities seeking to introduce private guilt and its public form shame, to pave the way for conversion in an oriental version of "hellfire and brimstone."[48] In the laboratory, self-esteem is lowered by experimenters to render persons more vulnerable to opinion change.[49] In society, various events may similarly affect the experiences of large numbers of people so as to create a shared dissonance with personal beliefs. Widespread famine, flood, or epidemic serve to disrupt normal social intercourse, introducing a fear of annihilation dissonant with the belief in self-preservation. Government defeat in warfare and the ensuing submissive behavior of the defeated serve to humble all selves that identify with the legitimate nation state. Severe and sudden economic deprivation, especially that entailing group-splitting, self-demeaning unemployment, can serve to alter radically the ways of life of large numbers of people such that they are collectively forced to engage in unaccustomed self-demeaning activities. In theory, even a sharp upward shift in economic well-being may bring about new information and activities dissonant with cherished expectations for the self and similar others.[50] The keynote then is sharp personal change; such change inflicts pain.[51]

Personal commitment to the revolutionary ideology is the key to the nature of the revolutionary movement. Whatever the nature of the compelling strain, once members of revolutionary movements have adopted the tenets of the ideology they may still vary in their degree of commitment to the tenets of the ideology and to the utopian prophecy. Medieval Christians varied in their state of "grace"; modern Communists vary in their degree of "progressiveness" or "redness." All movements display outward signs to designate the commitment of their members. In general, individuals vary in ideological commitment when they vary in the extent to which they have engaged in behaviors which pledge or personally bind themselves to ideological tenets.[52] Kiesler has outlined five characteristics which serve to make a behavior and its implied belief more personally binding: (1) The more explicit, the more public, and the less ambiguous or deniable the act, the more committing. (2) The more important the act, the more sacrifice, suffering or effort expended, the more committing. (3) The more irrevocable the act, the less undoable, the more committing. (4) The more frequent the act, the more committing. (5) The more voluntary the act, the less coerced, the more committing.[53] Thus the member of a movement who freely decides to make frequent, explicit public statements for the sake of his belief in the utopian prophecy while risking years of punishment by the authorities is ipso facto a highly committed ideologue. He has internalized his belief. It is obvious that the more committed the ideologue, the more resistant he is to change his beliefs.[54]

Not all members of movements can be considered equally committed in the strength of their beliefs. If one considers the person who infrequently performs ambiguous, unimportant acts under intense social pressure, one has a picture of the ritualized believer. Such a person, whose ideological acts are so divorced from himself would be said to lack true conviction. Remove the outside forces on him and his views would snap back like a rubber band. In sum, he is a ritualized believer, precisely because he lacks personal commitment. His behavior, thus determined by outside social forces, has elsewhere been termed seeming compliance.[55] It follows that he is not very resistant to change in his belief and behavior. His belief will shift if and when the prevailing social forces shift. It is likely that the behavior of a complier has little personal meaning to himself and that he has compartmentalized his behavior, seeing little linkage between it and other beliefs he calls his own.

Yet a third path to ideological behavior and belief which does not spring voluntarily from one's own thought or action and yet is not forced upon one by others is that which procedes indirectly via voluntary identification with another.[56] It follows from considerations of social disagreement dissonance that if one considers oneself generally like another, if one "identifies" with another, pressures arise to agree with his opinions. If opinion adoption halts with verbal emulation of the other, the opinion can be changed by a loss of attraction to the other person or group of persons. However, if identification with an attractive other leads one voluntarily to engage oneself in committing ideological behaviors, then the opinion becomes more resistant to change and approaches the stability of internalization. The identifier approaches the committed believer. This is precisely the function of the charismatic leader present in all successful social movements. Besides lending credence to the tenet of apocalyptic hope by his "signs" and successes in prophecy and warfare, he serves to commit members to new actions in consonance with the tenets of the movement through identification with him.[57] Such a leader provides a personal model for the personal commitment of followers. Like brothers and sisters they follow footsteps of the father. When an actor accepts the commands of an authority as legitimate solely because of the extraordinary personal character of that figure, he is obeying by virtue of his identification. Should such an authority pass from the scene, replacing his authority with that of another is obviously most difficult. Only his symbols remain to be shared by his followers. Personal role models are also provided by movements below the level of the leader. Thus martyrs are movement members who provide models for committing behavior while lending further credence to the belief in Manichean blame. Commitment to the ideology is greatly augmented through voluntary engagement by the insurgents in the use of force for the sake of their beliefs, thereby usurping and antagonizing the powers of the old government in one fell swoop. Moreover, ruthless repression by the authorities creates martyrs, and both are consonant with belief in Manichean blame. Both bind selves to the movement, and both are likely to lead to the escalation of commitment.

Having reviewed some central proposition in the theory of cognitive dissonance, having examined the nature of dissonance arousal and reduction in the social context, and having joined these general propositions to more specific beliefs and behaviors involved in ideological movements, we are in a position to gather some conditions for the rise and decline of revolutionary movements.

A revolutionary movement is a group of individuals who are convinced of and committed to a revolutionary ideology containing tenets of apocalyptic hope and Manichean blame. Unless a routinized society is disrupted by severe social strain, no revolutionary movement of appreciable size will develop. Furthermore, ceteris paribus, the size of a social movement is directly proportional to the intensity and extensiveness of the experienced social strain with which the ideology is consonant.[58] As such strain subsides, so does the salience of the ideology; hence the ideology is less likely to evoke new action commitments from its adherents and more likely to become ritualized as society is reroutinized according to more mundane commitments of its members. Thus the observed paradigm for the adoption of revolutionary ideology consisting of widespread social strain and confusion, followed by conviction regarding an explaining ideology, followed by action commitments to that ideology under the aegis of a charismatic leader, is one that is in full accord with dissonance theory. However, the less obvious application of dissonance theory, relates not to the initial growth phase of revolution but to the later stages. It applies directly the question of what occurs when the utopian prophecy falls short of fulfillment. What happens to the ideological movement when it is demonstrated that the forces of the movement will *not* overcome the forces of evil and establish utopia as promised? Under specified conditions the result is not the diminishment of ideology, but ideological intensification and polarization. The general propensity of the committed believer to intensify his belief upon disconfirmation is well documented in laboratory and field studies of opinion change as well as in the narrative of history.[59] As depicted in the following diagram, the differentiating condition among the members of the movement is personal commitment.

Consider the case of the movement member who is convinced of and committed to the tenets of Manichean blame, apocalyptic hope, and the realization of the latter through the utopian prophecy. When unequivocal evidence of disconfirmation occurs, he experiences cognitive dissonance between his ideological beliefs and his knowledge of the disconfirmation. Since the evidence of disconfirmation is important and undeniable, his options for reduction of his dissonance are only two: He can diminish his conviction

Ideological Polarization Resulting from Disconfirmation

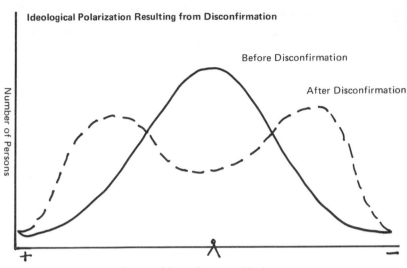

Degree of Commitment to Ideology

and commitment to the ideology or he can strive to increase his cognitions, behavioral, informational, or social, that are consonant with the ideology. If the member's commitment to the ideology is relatively low, the disconfirmation will diminish his ideological conviction and serve to further lower his future action commitments. If his commitment is relatively high, he cannot diminish his conviction, rather he will select the other option striving to bolster his cognitions consonant with the ideology, thereby reducing but never completely eliminating the magnitude of cognitive dissonance he experiences between the ideology and his undeniable knowledge of the disconfirmation. His behavior is very different from that of the uncommitted. He may engage in new forceful actions of his own which are consonant with the ideology, thus escalating his commitment. He may, for example, persist in ideological predictions whose empirical outcomes he expects will be consonant with the ideology. He will seek an exculpating rationalization of the failure which is consonant with the evidence of disconfirmation while also consonant with the integrity of the ideology. Also, in the social context, the committed ideologue cannot reduce the social disagreement dissonance brought on by the disconfirmation through changing his own conviction, he can only hope to reduce it by proselyting others whom he expects will accept his own conviction, and by making those who persist in ideological disagreement with him noncomparable to himself by disparagement. Those despairing of apocalyptic hope may themselves become the new targets of Manichean blame, for now more than ever people are perceived in the strict Manichean terms of the ideology. They either support the movement wholeheartedly or they oppose it. The apparent power struggle within the movement is derivative of a more basic motive: Around the movement sinners abound, while inside more culpable heretics are purged in the new passion for unanimity. In sum, by the disconfirmation, the movement itself is polarized and cleaved along the lines of prior commitment to the ideology: The less committed become even less so, the more committed become even more so; the ideology itself becomes the most salient issue in membership. The boundaries of the movement blur as the remaining radical core seeks social support external to the original membership. Ideological polarization sunders the movement with virtuous enlightenment and terrifying thunder.

Ideological polarization cannot continue indefinitely. A movement which successfully gains control of a state apparatus legitimizes its rule in terms of the ideology by protecting its citizens from the movement's enemy and by moving the society forward toward its promised utopia. But eventually the committed ideologues are themselves forced by socioeconomic exigencies to engage in behaviors inconsistent with the ideology and to accept colleagues in the leadership of the movement who are less than unsullied. The movement fractionalizes as policy is made on nonideological bases in the spirit of compromise. The radical proselyting and ideological derogation diminish. The polarization ends.

The movement in power is invariably faced with certain socioeconomic exigencies.[60] With the actual decline of the internal enemy, a rationale for failures and a source of unity is lost to the movement. With the decline of the enemies' wealth as a source of booty, the movement is forced to develop its own regular financial base in the pursuit of its utopia. The latter necessitates the formation of a regular division of labor under the movement's control for the sake of efficient production: Managers are raised above egalitarian workers; functional specialties are differentiated from each other. The expanded division of labor leads ineluctably to a division of opinion based upon the regularized and specialized commitments.

These exigencies have certain consequences for the nature of the ideological movement. In staffing the new hierarchies, personnel are now more frequently sought on the basis of special technical skill than general ideological commitment. In the search for predictable regularity, the spontaneity and voluntarism sought in the early movement member gives way to more formalistic membership criteria and ritualistic procedures. As consequence of the division of opinion, the original exclusive, intolerant "priesthood of all believers" becomes fractionalized and more tolerant of its membership as well as its subjects. To accommodate these differences, the committed ideologues lose influence in the leadership of the movement and moderates purged in the period of polarization are usually readmitted to the leading circles in the spirit of amnesty and compromise. The members of the move-

ment formerly bound by ideologically intolerant mechanical solidarity become more organically intertwined in a more regularized society.

Ideological Polarization and the
Chinese Cultural Revolution

We shall pause here to paint the changing Chinese landscape with a broad
brush in preview.[61] China entered the stage of twentieth-century history in
a state of turmoil. The Opium War and subsequent defeats had humiliated
the ancient middle kingdom from outside; the abortive Taiping Revolution
had gutted her inside. The Ch'ing dynasty fell in 1911. Severe social strain
plagued the populace as Sun Yat-sen's paper republic went up in flames
before the torches of local warlords. The Chinese Communist party was born
into Sun's Kuomingtang in 1921 as contact was made with the proselyting
Comintern. An adapted Marxist view of China's problems was adopted by
many for diagnosis and cure. Domestic landlords and foreign imperialists
were proclaimed the main disease agents. After the Communist party split
from the Kuomingtang in 1927, an exponent of peasant insurrection, Mao
Tse-tung, emerged as the leader of the beleaguered Chinese Communist party
in 1935. Pursued by the divorced Kuomingtang, he and his followers completed an heroic Long March to the remote area of Yenan. Principally in this
austere area, Mao and his disciples set about constructing the Chinese variant
of Marxist utopia, in theory as well as practice. They rectified the party
organization according to Mao's ideas in 1942-1944. These strenuous efforts
met with considerable success. The movement grew as intellectuals and peasants flocked to Yenan from the jaws of the Japanese invasion of 1937. After
defeating first the Japanese imperialists in 1945 and then their temporary
Kuomingtang allies in bloody civil war, Mao's party captured the Chinese
mainland in 1949. They again set about the tasks of consolidating power,
fostering economic development and achieving the socialist transformation
in China, but now for the entire nation. They borrowed a Soviet model of
development for their moderate first five year plan in 1953. In 1957, midst
some measured success and much social strain, the Soviet model was rejected.
Mao and his followers pushed through his Yenan-modeled Great Leap for
China's utopian second five year plan, while simultaneously conducting an
anti-rightist campaign against laggards.

The Great Leap Forward of 1958 was an ideological social movement
predicated upon Marxism-Leninism and the Thought of Mao Tse-tung. From
this ideology it followed that the Great Leap would rapidly move China
closer to true communism and economic wealth. Some so prophesied. In
China, at the time of the Great Leap there were a number of persons perched
high in the party hierarchy who were convinced of the validity of the Maoist

ideology and committed to the success of the Great Leap movement; but their public prophecy was clearly disconfirmed. When in 1959 it became apparent that the Great Leap Forward had failed, a terrible dissonance was created in the minds of the convinced and committed Maoists. On the one hand the Maoist ideology predicted the success of the movement in bringing China closer to communism; on the other hand, increasing amounts of empirical evidence indicated that the Great Leap was instead moving China closer to economic stagnation, social disorganization, and political chaos. Rather than admitting the incorrectness of their ideology, and giving up their faith in the Great Leap movement, the convinced and committed Maoists became all the more ideological as ideological polarization set in.

The committed Maoists rationalized the Great Leap failure as partially due to sabotage by class enemies and tried to organize a campaign to reform them. The Maoists immediately clustered together and began to seek social support for their views among the persons they viewed most likely to be supportive of their ideology: the soldiers, the nation's youth, and the large proletarian masses. They revived the Yenan heritage of the People's Liberation Army. They fostered future Red Guards. They conducted new communistic experiments such as the Tachai production brigade. They sent apostles of Maoism to other developing nations. They attempted to create the new socialist man in China. By amassing social support for the validity of their ideology—by recruiting others who professed their belief—the inconsistency between the Great Leap promise and the evidence that the Great Leap had failed became less painful for the convinced and committed Maoists. However, as the Maoists persisted in proselyting to acquire social support for their shaken ideology, they alienated those individuals who were initially unconvinced of the validity of the ideology for achieving economic growth and the socialist transformation, and uncommitted to its sanctioned Great Leap movement. The latter group—especially the intellectuals located in the party and government bureaucracies—became increasingly anti-Maoist in the face of continued Maoist proselyting. When some intellectuals publicly asserted the revisionist philosophy that in the course of social development "two could combine into one," the Maoists insisted on the dialectical opposite, "one divides into two": Class struggle is sharp, literary characters are either unmixed Manichean heroes or class enemies; no ideological compromise is permitted. Polarization of politics around the Maoist ideology as an issue increased.

As the anti-Maoists subtly voiced their opposition, they disturbed the social support of the Maoists and spurred them on to greater ideological commitment and greater proselyting efforts. The opponents of Maoism became targets of Maoist reform. Class enemies were discovered high *inside* the party. Throughout the 1960s, increased Maoist proselyting increased both

Maoist social support and voiced opposition to the Maoists. The dual effects of the proselyting mutually reinforced each other to further increase Maoist proselyting. Viewed from the Maoist perspective, the process would end with the elimination of inconsistencies between ideology and reality. With the popular acceptance of the Maoist ideology, the reformation or purge of the Maoist critics and the reimposition of Maoist Great Leap and People's Commune practices in China's domestic policy, social and empirical support for the ideology would be complete.

The story of this book is the interpretation of the relation between the pervasive Great Leap debacles and the Cultural Revolution. In Part I an examination of the preconditions for Maoist proselyting is undertaken. This includes an assessment of the state of Maoist conviction and commitment prevailing in China at the time of the Great Leap Forward as well as an assessment of the doctrinal disconfirmation that occurred with the Great Leap failure and the initial social support accorded the Maoists. Part II traces the time course of Maoist proselyting in the mass media and political campaigns from its inception in late 1959 to the Cultural Revolution of 1966. In the process, evidence of mounting opposition to the Maoists is documented. Part III examines the polarizing effect on Chinese society of the Maoist proselyting campaigns through 1969 at three levels and the attempts to reinstitutionalize an even more radicalized version of the Maoist vision. It examines the splitting of Maoist support among the masses, within the mid-level cadres, and the unprecedented politburo purges; it examines persistent radical attempts to revive the rural People's Communes. Finally, the Epilogue examines the significance of the current thermidor which has soothed the Chinese masses in the wake of the raging Cultural Revolution, with the moderating breeze of the tenth party congress of 1973 and the subsequent demise of the politboro radicals in 1976.

NOTES

1. "Overcoming the sequelae of infantile paralysis," *China Pictorial*, No. 9, 1969, pp. 32-35.

2. Norman Cohn, *The Pursuit of the Millennium*. New York: Oxford University Press, 1970, passim.

3. Cohn, op. cit., p. 127.

4. Ibid.

5. Ibid., p. 144.

6. Ibid., pp. 205-222.

7. Ibid., p. 213.

8. Ibid., p. 257.

9. Ibid., p. 260.

10. Ibid., p. 275.

11. Crane Brinton, *The Anatomy of Revolution.* New York: Vintage, 1965, especially pp. 122 and 132. The American Revolution, though also studied by Brinton, was admittedly of a different sort than the three we consider here. It was essentially a territorial and nationalistic revolution targeted upon a colonial power; and it did not display a victory of extremists over moderates nor a subsequent reign of terror and virtue of any magnitude. One might speculate that an expelled foreign enemy makes for both a less socially divisive revolutionary take-over and a slippery scapegoat for postrevolutionary difficulties. Such postcolonial revolutionary objectives are both more limited and better delimited.

12. Brinton, op. cit., p. 122.

13. Ibid., p. 146.

14. Ibid., p. 122.

15. Ibid., p. 157.

16. Ibid., pp. 191-197.

17. Ibid., po. 235-236.

18. Nathan Leites and Ithiel do Sola Pool, "Interaction: The response of communist propaganda to frustration," in Harold D. Lasswell and Nathan Leites, et al., *Language of Politics.* (1949) Cambridge, Mass.: MIT Press, 1965, pp. 334-381.

19. Alan Bullock, *Hitler, A Study in Tyranny.* New York: Harper and Row. Revised Edition, 1962, p. 650.

20. Ibid., pp. 597-599. See also p. 650.

21. William L. Shirer, *The Rise and Fall of the Third Reich.* New York: Simon and Schuster, 1960, p. 854.

22. Ibid., p. 240.

23. Bullock, op. cit., p. 675.

24. Daniel Lerner, "The Nazi elite," in Harold D. Lasswell and Daniel Lerner, *World Revolutionary Elites: Studies in Coercive Ideological Movements.* Cambridge, Mass.: MIT Press, 1965, pp. 278-279.

25. Shirer, op. cit., p. 908.

26. Ibid., p. 903.

27. Ibid., p. 965.

28. Leon Festinger, *A Theory of Cognitive Dissonance.* Evanston, Ill.: Row Peterson, 1957, passim.

29. The total magnitude of dissonance which exists between two clusters of cognitive elements depends on the weighted proportion of all relevant relations between the two clusters which are dissonant, each dissonant or consonant relation being weighted according to the importance of the elements involved in that relation. The presence of dissonance gives rise to pressures to reduce that dissonance, the amount of pressure depending on the total magnitude of dissonance. See Festinger, op. cit., pp. 16-18.

30. Ibid., pp. 177-183.

31. See Cohn, op. cit., p. 21; and Brinton, op. cit., pp. 48-49. See also Neil Smelser, *A Theory of Collective Behavior.* New York: Free Press, 1962, p. 348; and William Gamson, *Power and Discontent.* Homewood, Ill.: Dorsey, 1968, p. 42. The latter is especially important for the concepts of political trust and political efficacy.

32. Smelser, loc. cit.

33. E. J. Hobsbawm, *Primitive Rebels.* New York: W. W. Norton, 1959, pp. 57-65. This book also updates Cohn's case studies with nineteenth and twentieth century movements.

34. Cohn, op. cit., p. 15.

35. See Brinton; Cohn; and Smelser, op. cit. See also Ted Gurr, *Why Men Rebel.* Princeton, N.J.: Princeton University Press, 1970. The latter is especially important for the concept of relative deprivation.

36. Smelser, op. cit. See also Clifford Geertz, "Ideology as a cultural system," in David Apter, *Ideology and Discontent.* Glencoe, Ill.: Free Press, 1964. The latter is especially important for the role of ideology in providing "templates" for action programs.

37. Fritz Heider, *The Psychology of Interpersonal Relations.* New York: John Wiley, 1958. Heider developed the original formulation of cognitive balance.

38. Heider, op. cit. See also James Stoessinger, *Nations in Darkness: China, Russia and America.* New York: Random House, 1971, esp. pp. 184-197. The latter is especially important for applications of cognitive balance to international relations.

39. Heider, op. cit., p. 235.

40. Ibid., p. 289.

41. Gamson, op. cit., p. 42.

42. Cohn, op. cit., p. 286.

43. Ibid., p. 285.

44. Hobsbawm, op. cit., p. 57.

45. Ibid., p. 61.

46. Ibid.

47. See Geertz; Gurr; and Smelser, op. cit.

48. Brinton, op. cit.

49. Carl Hovland, et al., *Personality and Persuasibility.* New Haven, Conn.: Yale University Press, 1959.

50. Bernard Grofman and Edward Muller, "The strange case of relative gratification and potential for political violence: The V-curve hypothesis," *American Political Science Review,* Vol. 67, June 1973, pp. 514-539, esp. pp. 535-537. See also Edward Muller, "A test of a partial theory for political violence," *American Political Science Review,* Vol. 66, September 1972, pp. 928-959.

51. For historical observations on the disruptive effects of rising economic status, see Brinton, op. cit., pp. 250-264. See also Alexis de Tocqueville, *The Old Regime and the French Revolution.* New York: Doubleday, 1965.

52. Charles Kiesler, *The Psychology of Commitment.* New York: Academic Press, 1971, pp. 25-33.

53. Kiesler, op. cit.

54. Ibid., p. 32.

55. Paul Hiniker, "Chinese reactions to forced compliance: Dissonance reduction or national character," *Journal of Social Psychology,* Vol. 77, 1969, pp. 157-176. See also Herbert Kelman, "Processes of opinion change," *Public Opinion Quarterly,* Vol. 25, 1961, pp. 57-57.

56. Kelman, loc. cit.

57. Max Weber, "The basis of legitimacy," in Talcott Parsons, *Max Weber: The Theory of Social and Economic Organization.* New York: Free Press, pp. 324-329, see also pp. 358-373 on charismatic authority.

58. See Gurr; and Smelser, op. cit. See also Anthony Wallace, "Revitalization movements," *American Anthropologist,* Vol. 58, 1956, pp. 264-281. The other important factor in movement size is, of course, the degree of realism attached to the belief in apocalyptic hope. If the felt efficacy of movement members is zero, then the movement should not grow. It is analytically appealing to view Manichean blame and apocalyptic hope as combining multiplicatively rather than additively in supporting social movements.

59. For a laboratory experiment which demonstrates how more highly committed subjects intensify their behavior and belief upon receiving disconfirmatory communications, see Kiesler, op. cit., pp. 65-73. See also the report of the experiment by D. Marlowe, R. Frager, and R. Nuttal, "Commitment to action-taking as a consequence of cognitive dissonance," *Journal of Personality and Social Psychology,* Vol. 2, 1965, pp. 864-868. For a field study demonstrating the same phenomenon, see Kiesler, op. cit., pp. 74-89. For a pioneering field study showing details of the intensification of proselytizing occurring with disconfirmation in a modern millennial movement, see L. Festinger, H. Riecken, and S. Schachter, *When Prophecy Fails.* New York: Harper and Row, 1964, esp. pp. 3-42, 216-229.

60. For a useful summary of the pressures toward institutionalization of social movements, see Smelser, op. cit., pp. 359-360.

61. For an excellent compilation of historical documents and analyses of China from the eighteenth century to the present, see Franz Schurmann and Orville Schell, *The China Reader.* New York: Vintage, 1967, Vols. 1, 2, 3, deal respectively with Imperial China, Republican China and Communist China.

PART I

PRECONDITIONS: THE PROPHECY

Turning and turning in the widening gyre
The falcon cannot hear the falconer;
Things fall apart; the center cannot hold;
Mere anarchy is loosed upon the world,
The blood dimmed tide is loosed, and everywhere
The ceremony of innocence is drowned;
The best lack all conviction, while the worst
  are full of passionate intensity,
Surely some revelation is at hand; . . .

William Butler Yeats
"The Second Coming "

Chapter 1

CONVICTION AND

THE BLOOM OF CONFUSION

Out of the incredible turmoil and humiliation that engulfed twentieth-century China, the Chinese Communist party was born at a meeting which began on July 1, 1921 in the French concession in Shanghai. The twelve delegates attending the first national party congress represented some fifty party members in China at the time. They were advised in their deliberations by a pair of world revolutionaries from the Comintern. Among the delegates was a twenty-seven year old teacher and labor organizer from Changsha, Mao Tse-tung.

Mao was formerly a student of Li Ta-chao and heavily influenced by Ch'en Tu-hsiu, and former assistant librarian at Peking University. Five years after the first congress, writing as a leading member of the Chinese Communist party (CCP) growing within the bosom of the Kuomintang (KMT), Mao published his first article. It identified in Marxist terms the social source of China's strain. The concluding words of Mao's "Analysis of the Classes in Chinese Society" read as follows:

> To sum up, it can be seen that our enemies are all those in league with imperialism—the warlords, the bureaucrats, the comprador class, the big landlord class and the reactionary section of the intelligentsia attached

to them. The leading force in our revolution is the industrial proletariat. Our closest friends are the entire semi-proletariat and petty bourgeoisie. As for the vacillating middle bourgeoisie, their right wing may become our enemy and their left wing our friend—but we must be constantly on our guard and not let them create confusion within our ranks.[1]

Thus the imperialists, the landlords and their allies were designated as the cause of China's misery and the archenemy of the chosen proletariat and their semi-proletarian allies. Furthermore, the imminent struggle was not merely probable but apocalyptic since "the two major forces, revolution and counter revolution are locked in final struggle."[2] Hence, Mao reasoned, the "intermediate forces" were "bound to disintegrate quickly."

Mao's prediction quickly proved prophetic as the next year the organized expression of the vascillating national and middle bourgeoisie, the KMT under Chiang Kai-shek's "rightist" leadership, turned on the Communists, now swollen to 50,000 within his party, and decimated their ranks eight times over. Among the 10,000 survivors many despaired, but Mao persisted in revolutionary hope. In a letter to Lin Piao at the beginning of 1930, he likened the imminent revolution to "a child about to be born, moving restlessly in its mother's womb."[3] He asserted that it was "inevitable" that the red forces would grow and the white (KMT) forces decay through internal contradictions.[4] As a means of hastening the inevitable, he urged the adoption of the policy he shared with Chu Teh of employing guerrilla tactics to establish rural "base areas," while augmenting the regular red army troops by recruiting local activist "red guards" from the villages up through the counties.[5]

Mao had publicly championed the strategy of forming rural base areas before the split with the KMT.[6] After the split, Mao led an unsuccessful autumn harvest uprising in Hunan, was captured by the KMT, escaped, and established his first revolutionary base in Chingkangshan on the Hunan-Kiangsi border. For his precipitous and unsuccessful revolt he was also dismissed from the Communist politburo. However the sixth party congress was held in Moscow during the summer of 1928 and endorsed the policy of establishing rural base areas or "soviets" along with the more orthodox concept of fostering urban insurrections. By the end of 1930, the rural base area concept gained predominance over that of urban insurrection and a vindicated Mao Tse-tung controlled the largest base, located in southern Kiangsi to which he and Chu Teh had marched with the battered remains of the principal units of the red army early in 1929. With the formation of several "soviets" in China, each of which redistributed land with one hand and built its army of peasants with the other, the Chinese Soviet Republic was established in December 1931 with its central government located at Juichin and headed by Mao Tse-tung. Under the strategy of rural soviets the CCP grew to 300,000 by 1934 in strife-torn China.

In late 1933 Chiang Kai-shek launched his fifth bandit extermination campaign aimed at the Communists. His new policy of encirclement succeeded in strangling members of Mao's Kiangsi soviet by the autumn of 1934. The surviving 120,000 members pulled themselves from the vortex in October and embarked on the epic Long March.

Even in retreat Mao's Communists did not so much flee from the enemy as march toward a new northeastern site of the promised land, Yenan. The year-long feat involved trudging some 6,000 miles over five snow-capped mountains and into steaming jungles, wading through clinging marshlands and across rapid rivers, foraging for wild vegetables in myriad forests and sleeping some nights huddled and exhausted beneath the open sky, but some nights still afoot. The treacherous trek traversed twelve of China's provinces, in many of which battles were pitched with provincial troops and those of Chiang Kai-shek. For Mao's forces fought as they marched, burning out landlords and redistributing property as they passed through villages, fomenting class struggle and finding new converts to replace those lost to the cruel elements. In the midst of the Long March, Mao was elected chairman of the politburo. When he marched into Yenan, he commanded but a quarter of his original forces; but these 30,000 followers of Mao now contained more strongly committed ideologues.

Shortly after enduring the incredible hardships of the Long March, an undaunted Mao Tse-tung composed the lyric poem "Snow," in the winter of 1936, gazing outward from the dark caves of Yenan:

> This is the scene in the northern land;
> A hundred Leagues are sealed with ice,
> A thousand Leagues of whirling snow. . . .
> Lured by such great beauty in our landscape
> Innumerable heroes have rivaled one another to bow in homage.
> But alas, Ch'in Shih Husang and Han Wu Ti
> Were rather lacking in culture,
> T'sang T'sei Tsung and Sung T'ai Tsu
> Had little taste for poetry,
> And Genghis Khan
> The favorite son of heaven for a day
> Knew only how to bend his bow to shoot great vultures.
> Now they are all past and gone.
> To find heroes in the grand manner,
> We must look rather in the present.[7]

Mao the man, was just such a hero now harkening to the call of history echoing about his snow-bound cave. This remarkable new leader of the CCP then characterized by Edgar Snow as a man possessing a "deep sense of personal dignity" compounded with the "power of ruthless decision" and by Agnes Smedley as an "aesthete above all else," reserved and aloof, now set earnestly about his messianic mission.[8] While he urged guerrilla war with his enemies, Chiang's Kuomintang and from 1937 the invading Japanese, he simultaneously conducted the "Sinification of Marxism" among his followers.

During the Yenan era (1936-1945), Mao wrote the majority of the articles now assembled in the four volumes of his *Selected Works*. Mao spearheaded his native ideological movement with important theoretical essays in the summer of 1937. In July he delivered "On Practice," in August "On Contradiction." These two works portrayed a world of perpetual flux and constituted cornerstones of Mao's theory of "permanent revolution." Later in 1940, Mao produced another theoretical essay entitled "On Dialectical Materialism" and yet another in 1943, his famous "mass line" treatise "On Methods of Leadership." Let us summarize some of the basic principles in Mao's revolutionary ideology.

Revolutionary Ideology and the Thought of Mao

The thought of Mao Tse-tung as codified during the Yenan era and further explicated thereafter can be analyzed into four central tenets, the first pair of which are particular formulations of general revolutionary tenets of apocalyptic hope and Manichean blame and the second pair of which are uniquely Maoist expressions of the means by which the revolutionaries can accelerate their triumph. The thread which runs through all four tenets of Mao's thought is dialectics or the theory of contradictions. According to this dialectic, history is seen as moving inexorably toward its culmination in the Marxian classless society through the resolution of internal contradictions between one force and its opposite. The principal historical contradiction exists between social classes, between the exploited and the exploiters who inflict their misery. The two classes are locked in apocalyptic struggle.

The party, of course, is the organized expression of the forces of the exploited and chosen class, the "proletariat." It achieves its historical mission of accelerating history by augmenting its own forces, while locating and reducing internal contradictions and maximizing contradictions within the enemy class. Contradictions between the party and its enemy are "antagonistic" and are reduced by forceful annihilation of the enemy. When the enemy is relatively strong, the guerrilla strategy and tactics apply. When it is weak, superior force suffices. Contradictions among the party, its "people," and its allies are nonantagonistic and not to be reduced by force. Among the chosen class, vertical contradictions between leaders and led are reduced by "mass line" practices. Horizontal contradictions between one interest or opinion group and its opponent are significantly reduced by role interchanges according to the tenet of the "omnicompetent worker." Through the skillful location and reduction of significant contradictions, with nature, within allies, and between enemies, society moves forward faster towards its historical culmination.

To render a complete exposition of the thought of Mao Tse-tung would require an exegesis of the text of the Maoist bible, the four volumes of the *Selected Works of Mao Tse-tung,* and an analysis of the recent Maoist catechism, *Quotations from Chairman Mao Tse-tung.*[9] Shrinking before the enormity of such a task, we will concentrate on the four central themes of Maoism for achieving the socialist transformation. They deal respectively with historical progress, social integration, political leadership, and economic construction. Each has been illustrated with quotations from works that Mao produced during the Yenan era.

1. RESOLVING HISTORICAL CONTRADICTIONS: DIALECTICAL PROGRESS

History inevitably moves in the direction of the proletarianization of society according to a dialectical resolution of internal contradictions:

> Changes in society are due chiefly to the development of the internal contradictions in society, that is, the contradictions between the productive forces and the relations of production, the contradiction between the old and the new; it is the development of these contradictions that pushes society forward and gives the impetus for the supersession of the old society by the new.[10]

According to the Maoist faith, a revolutionary can intervene in the inevitable historical stream of things by correctly applying his consciousness of the truths of Marxism-Leninism to social change, not to alter the course of history, but to speed it up by the correct methods of resolution of given historical contradictions. In general contradictions are reduced by "struggle," by pitting one thing against its opposite; particular forms of "struggle" are appropriate to particular forms of contraduction. To illustrate Mao's thesis on the resolution of basic contradictions:

> Qualitatively different contradictions can only be resolved by qualitatively different methods. For instance, the contradiction between the proletariat and the bourgeoisie is resolved by the method of socialist revolution; the contradiction between the great masses of the people and the feudal system is resolved by the method of democratic revolution; the contradiction between the colonies and imperialism is resolved

by the method of national revolutionary war; the contradiction between the working class and the peasant class in socialist society is
resolved by the method of collectivization and mechanization of agriculture; contradiction within the Communist Party is resolved by the
method of criticism and self-criticism; the contradiction between society and nature is resolved by the method of developing the productive
forces. . . . The principle of using different methods to resolve different
contradictions is one Marxists-Leninists must strictly observe.[11]

A Marxist pragmatist might agree with the principle of historical dialectics,
but be less convinced of the broad utility of contradiction analysis (of
dialectics) to solve all social problems. Such a Marxist would be more concerned with detailed analyses of particular social problems provided by the
specialized competences of expert social planners. Such pragmatic Marxists
were to provide opposition to Mao's efforts to achieve China's socialist
transformation.

2. SOCIAL INTEGRATION: THE CLASS STRUGGLE

In a socialist society, as in all precursors to Communist utopia, there still
exist class differences which must be eliminated by struggle in the progress
towards communism. At Yenan Mao wrote that "In class society everyone
lives as a member of a particular class, and every kind of thinking, without
exception, is stamped with a brand of class."[12] That the class struggle had
still not ended in Communist China by 1957 is borne out by the following
Maoist analysis:

In China although the main socialist transformation has been completed
with respect to the system of ownership and although the large scale
and turbulent class struggles of the masses characteristic of the previous
revolutionary periods have in the main come to an end there are still
remnants of the overthrown landlord and comprador classes, there is
still a bourgeoisie and the remoulding of the petty bourgeoisie has only
just started. The class struggle between the proletariat and the bourgeoisie, the class struggle between the different political forces and the
class struggle in the ideological field between the proletariat and the
bourgeoisie will continue to be long and tortuous and at times will even
become very acute. The proletariat seeks to transform the world according to its own world outlook and so does the bourgeoisie. In this
respect, the question of which will win out, socialism or capitalism is
still not really settled.[13]

The social contradictions existing at that time were many:

Under present conditions, the so-called contradictions among the people include contradictions within the working class, within the intellectuals; contradictions between working and peasant class and other toiling people with the national bourgeoisie; contradictions within the national bourgeoisie class, and so on. Our government is truly a government that represents the people. But there are certain contradictions between it and the popular interest and collective interest with individual interest, the contradiction of democracy and centralism, the contradiction of leader and led, the contradiction of bureaucratism of some workers in state agencies with the masses. There is also a contradiction among the people. In general, contradictions among the people are contradictions on a foundation of basic harmony of the people's interest.[14]

The contradictions among the people were seen as nonantagonistic and to be resolved by the means of democratic struggle or persuasion following the formula of "unity—criticism—unity" and attempting to "cure the illness in order to save the man." The contradictions between the people and the enemy were seen as antagonistic and to be resolved by coercive struggle involving use of force. One of the main characteristics of the capitalist world outlook as opposed to the socialist viewpoint was the pursuit of self-interest as opposed to collective interest. A pragmatic Marxist might contend that the class struggle is essentially eliminated by the revolutionary take over and that small vestiges of "capitalism" evidenced in the pursuit of self-interest are relatively unimportant. In any case, the business of class struggle takes time and is disruptive of the coordinated functioning of planned economic development.

3. POLITICAL LEADERSHIP: THE MASS LINE

Correct political leadership is implemented by cadres who apply general ideological principles to the specific local problems and ideas of the masses.

In his work on leadership in 1943, Mao amplified his leadership principles of "linking the general with the particular" and "mass line."

In all practical work of the party all correct leadership is necessarily "from the masses to the masses." This means: take the ideas of the masses (scattered and unsystematic ideas) and concentrate them (through study turn them into concentrated and systematic ideas), then go to the masses and propagate and explain these ideas until the masses embrace them as their own, hold fast to them and translate them into action and test the correctness of these ideas in such action. Then once again concentrate ideas from the masses and once again go to the masses so that the ideas are persevered in and carried through, and so on and over and over again in endless spiral with the ideas becoming more correct, more vital and richer each time. . . . Such is the Marxist theory of knowledge.[15]

On the other hand, correct political leadership is definitely not implemented by a large central bureaucracy, staffed with specialists and careerist officials issuing commands ignoring the wishes of subordinates or promulgated on the basis of particularistic interests independent of the ideological general line. Mao's continued opposition to bureaucracy as an instrument of political leadership is illustrated by the following quotation from his 1957 address:

> In a big country like ours it is nothing to get alarmed about if small numbers of people should create disturbances; rather we should turn such things to advantage to help us get rid of bureaucracy.[16]

A pragmatic Marxist, less concerned with the mobilization of mass enthusiasm, might take pride in a large efficient central bureaucracy staffed with specialists and meting out the plans of the center. Despite revolutionary Leninist admonitions against bureaucracy it is certainly a hallmark of Stalinist development efforts and Khrushchev's communism.

4. ECONOMIC CONSTRUCTION: THE OMNICOMPETENT WORKER

Economic construction is rapidly achieved by large-scale mobilization of the broad masses to heterogeneous production tasks. To a significant degree, people are seen as interchangeable between production tasks; motivation is relatively more important than skill; with sufficient motivation and correct ideological leadership, the unleashed energy of the masses can rapidly surmount any production obstacle.

One of Mao's Yenan writings asserts his conviction that a proper change in relations of production unleashes significant new productive energy in working men:

> I have obtained data from various places in northern and central China, all of which show that after rent reduction the peasants take much greater interest in production and are willing to organize mutual aid groups like our labor-exchange terms here, in which the productivity of three persons now equal that of four in the past. That being the case, 90 million people can do as much as 120 million.[17]

Another passage from the same article asserts that a change to less specialized, more egalitarian methods of production enhances productivity not only for peasants and manual workers, but also for government officials, soldiers and others:

> Thus it can be seen that in the context of guerrilla warfare in rural areas, those army units and government and other organizations which undertake production for self-support show greater energy and activity in their fighting, training, and work, and improve their discipline and their unity both internally and with civilians. . . . Once we master it, no material difficulty can daunt us.[18]

The selfsame philosophy of the omnicompetent worker was carried over in Mao's attempt to spur productivity in postliberation China. In urging the importance of collectivization on Chinese society Mao reasserted his Yenan philosophy in 1955:

> The wealth of society is created by the workers, peasants, and working intellectuals. If they take their destiny into their own hands follow a Marxist-Leninist line and take an active attitude toward solving problems instead of evading them, there will be no difficulty in the world which they cannot overcome.[19]

That Marxist dialectics are central to economic planning is evidenced in the following Maoist analysis of the economy preparatory to the initiation of the Great Leap Forward. The passage deals with Mao's speech on "The Ten Great Relationships" written in April 1956 and summarized by Liu Shao-ch'i in May 1958 at the second session of the eighth party congress. The core of this summarization of the employment of Maoist dialectics for economic development is as follows: (1) the relation of industry and agriculture, of heavy and light industry; (2) the relation of coastal and inland industry; (3) the relation of economic construction and diverse construction; (4) the relation of state, cooperative, and individual; (5) the relation of center and region; (6) the relation of Han and minority people; (7) the relation of party and nonparty; (8) the relation of revolution and counterrevolution; (9) the relation of right and wrong within and without the party; and (10) the international relationship.[20] The dialectical nature of this outline for China's second five year plan is self-evident. Liu went on to characterize the lingering Yenan mentality underlying this plan by asserting that the general spirit of the report was that all positive factors must be mobilized, all usable forces mobilized in the struggle to make the country a modernized, rich, and powerful socialist country as rapidly as possible.[21]

A pragmatic Marxist opponent might have relied less on the Maoist faith in the efficacy of the mobilization of mass enthusiasm for economic development. He might shy away from the labor-intensive ideas to more capital-intensive ideas such as are present in the Russian model of economic development, and in China's first five year plan which mimicked this model. He might place more faith in the use of educated specialist, rationalized bureaucracy, and central planning, and seek slow but steady progress with the use of financial incentives rather than ideological exhortations.

During the Yenan era, the application of Mao's dialectics to the Chinese revolution met with much success. Mao's own doctrine of dialectical progress found considerable support. In the Yenan rectification (cheng-feng) campaign of 1942-1944, Maoist dialectics in the form of articles authored by Mao or central committee resolutions drawn up under his guidance provided more than two-thirds of the eighteen documents originally selected for study. Parallel to the campaign, Mao reorganized the important Central Party School to promote the intensive study and promulgation of his works among a growing number of supporters. At the end of the Yenan era, the delegates of China's Communist party now numbering over one million members, controlling nineteen liberated areas containing one hundred million people, not only reelected Mao Chairman of the politburo at the seventh party congress but also inscribed the thought of Mao Tse-tung in the party constitution next to Marxism-Leninism as providing guidelines for all their actions. Under the banner of Mao they marched on to defeat the Japanese imperialist enemy in the same year; four years later four million party members flying the banner of Mao defeated the Kuomintang class enemy and established the Chinese People's Republic containing one half billion Chinese citizens.

At Yenan, significant innovations were made in the methods of resolving social contradictions. While it is true that the class struggle theme of the Communists was played down compared with the years preceding the Japanese invasion, the crisis conditions of struggle against a fearsome enemy were clearly operative in the war against Japan. Within the "people" egalitarian ideas were pursued with a continuation of moderated land reform practices and with the first concerted attempts at mass education of the peasantry, seeking goals of widespread literacy and employing means of unified work-study programs.

In 1943 Mao propounded his mass line principle for resolving political contradictions. This principle was fleshed out with the following leadership innovations first implemented at Yenan: the first "to the village" (hsia hsiang) campaign, the first campaign to simplify administration, the introduction of "dual rule" under party leadership, the direct popular election of political leaders, the concerted thought reform of errant cadres, the injunction for all political cadres to engage in productive labor, the first "labor hero" emulation campaigns, and the propaganda technique of disseminating Communist ideals through traditional vehicles such as folk songs and stage plays.

Innovations were also made in methods for the resolution of economic contradictions. At Yenan, the "production war" was conducted by decentralized leadership who employed labor-intensive schemes in mass mobilization style. The ideal of the omnicompetent worker emerged at this time as did the principle of soldiers participating in agricultural production. As PLA soldiers worked the fields, field hands played soldier as members of the "People's Militia," a paramilitary organization of two million members by the end of the Yenan era. The first amateur steel smelting began under Communist leadership in Yenan in keeping with the slogan to develop economic self-sufficiency. What is more, the first appearance of basic-level agricultural cooperatives utilizing the concept of "mutual aid teams" occurred during the Yenan era. The similarity of the foregoing social, political and economic innovations to the practices of the Great Leap era is indisputable.[22]

From Prerevolutionary Conviction to Postrevolutionary Confusion

Six years after coming to power on the mainland, Chairman Mao could look back and point to significant accomplishments.[23] Over 90 percent of those employed among China's 600 million citizens were now engaged in socialist enterprise. Following an initial bloody two years of land reform in which over a million landlords and counterrevolutionaries were executed, peasant families were coaxed into small mutual aid teams and then these were amalgamated into larger collectives with the socialist upsurge in the countryside of 1955-1956. Following a period of recovery from the civil war and then three more years of China's wartime involvement in Korea, China's industrial establishments were gradually nationalized through a system of joint state-provided control; and with the final surge of 1955-1956, fewer than 10 percent remained in the private hands of members of the national bourgeoisie. The socialist transformation of agriculture and industry was essentially complete.

The economy, itself, had grown considerably under the imported Soviet plan initiated in 1953. The central government planners who employed this capital-intensive model, with Russian assistance, saw successive and impressive 6 percent annual increments in the gross domestic product through 1956.[24] Industry itself underwent the most rapid growth, more than double the rate of the rest of the economy.[25] China was well on the way to modernization.

The party, now grown to ten million members, held firm control on the new government which administered this economic development. According to Mao's own 1949 formulation "On the People's Democratic Dictatorship," the government operated under the leadership of the working class, through

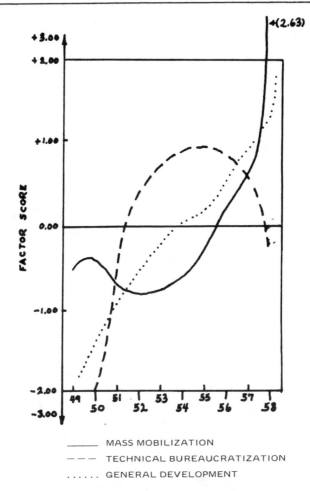

_____ MASS MOBILIZATION

− − − TECHNICAL BUREAUCRATIZATION

. . . . . . GENERAL DEVELOPMENT

A total of seventy-three variables were included in the factor analysis. The top ten variables in loading on the mass mobilization factor included the following five: agricultural collectivization, party members per adult, number of different magazine titles, rural telecommunication facilities, and non-Communist imports per capita. The top ten variables in loading on the technical bureaucratization factor included the following five: percentage of government bureaucrats not engaged in productive labor, proportion of the GNP in the central government budget, number of movie theatres, number of professionally trained medical personnel, and total medical personnel.

NOTE: Adapted from Paul J. Hiniker and R. Vincent Farace, "Approaches to National Development in Communist China: 1949-1958," **Economic Development and Cultural Change,** Vol. 18, No. 1 (October 1969), p. 70.

Figure 1.1: **DOMINANT NATIONAL DEVELOPMENT STYLES DURING THE FIRST DECADE**

the Communist party, and was based on a close alliance with the peasantry, and with the other classes among the people, the urban petty bourgeoisie and the national bourgeoisie.[26] This four-class bloc composed the "people" who practiced democracy among themselves and dictatorship over the reactionaries. The first national people's congress so echoed in its constitution in the fall of 1954. The party had brought a new unity and a new order to China.

However, as Mao surveyed the Chinese scene in 1956 and 1957, the new order was not without contradictions. There was considerable political and economic strain in Mao's China even though, in the main, the class enemy had been slain. Who now to blame? Mao found contradictions among the "people" as well as contradictions between them and vestiges of the class enemy. Like a vermiform appendix, the taint of the class enemy could still exist and be diseased in any body; its reptilian form was not relegated to some extinct species in the evolution of history. In socialist China, Mao became the arbitrary diagnostician of the body politic and an increasingly ruthless surgeon.

The first to be excised were rightist bureaucrats while lesser evils were exorcised from other retarding rightists as Mao "treated their illness to save the men." In April of 1956 Mao delivered his address to the politburo on "The Ten Great Relationships" which contained his diagnosis and proposed cure for the ailments of postliberation China.[27] The main points of his dialectical analysis found relatively too much emphasis on heavy industry, as opposed to agriculture and light industry, too much central ministerial control of factories, too much emphasis on centralized government administration, too much repression of the non-Communist "minority" parties, and the viewpoints of other nonparty people, and too much uncritical aping of certain "foreign nations." In sum, Mao found that the progress of the socialist revolution under the Soviet-modeled first five year plan was too foreign, too repressive, too bureaucratic, and, above all, it was too slow. It was an increasingly technical-bureaucratic approach to national development. Mao's proposed remedy was his revolutionary Yenan model of mass mobilization (see Figure 1.1). Out of his dialectics came the recommendation that the central party and government bureaucracy be cut by two-thirds, and this indeed provided internal enemies and opposition on the politburo.[28] When the eighth party congress was convened in the fall, many members chaffed at Mao's call for a rectification movement aimed at bureaucratic cadres and lower-level party leaders. By the end of the congress, the thought of Mao Tse-tung had been removed from the text of the new party constitution.

Following Mao's April 1956 proposal to liberalize the expression of nonparty opinion and his May speech introducing the slogans, Lu Ting-yi, Director of the propaganda department of the party central committee, announced the opportunity for people to speak out according to Mao's new policy to "Let one hundred flowers bloom; Let one hundred schools of thought contend." The public response was initially cautious, but it was spurred on by news of Mao's February 1957 speech before the supreme state conference "On the Correct Handling of Contradictions Among the People."[29] In it Mao distinguished between the two types of social contradictions, criticized the party and government bureaucracy, and spoke again of liberalization and mass mobilization. He publicly admitted there had been strikes of workers and students and peasant disturbances in 1956, but categorized them in the main as contradictions within the people whose "root cause" was bureaucracy.[30] He admitted that there were unfair wage differentials which discriminated against peasants to the benefit of many government cadres and some workers, and proposed more equality.[31] And he spoke out against those who opposed the full development of agricultural collectivization and those whose "understanding of [the objective laws of development of socialist economy] is relatively inaccurate," but considered even these to be contradictions among the people.[32]

Mao's words were supported by the deeds of the central committee in April when they announced the beginning of a rectification movement within the party to encourage the control of bureaucratism and the acceptance of public criticism.[33] It was now aimed high, at cadres from the municipal level to the top.

But when the intellectuals spoke out in the spring of 1957, they overstepped the bounds of criticism. In May they did not restrict themselves simply to criticizing bureaucracy, they went so far as to criticize the government's function of rule, the sham coalition government, the socialist transformation of agriculture, and even Mao's own Yenan line on literature, which urged them solely to extol the proletarian hero. What was mainly murmured in 1956, rose to a clamor in May of 1957 and demonstrated that the party's campaign of thought reform of the intellectuals of 1951-1952 had been unsuccessful.[34]

In May with an address to the party entitled "Things Are Changing," Mao reacted by moving left to criticize the right:

> There are all kinds of people within the Communist Party. The majority of them are Marxists. They also have shortcomings, but not serious ones. Some people possess the erroneous ideology in the form of dogmatism. Most of these prople are loyal to the Party and the state although their method of viewing problems is marked by one-sidedness of the "Left". With this kind of one-sidedness overcome, they will take a big step forward. Some people possess the erroneous ideology in the form of revisionism or Right opportunism. These people are more dangerous because their ideology is a reflection of the bourgeois ideology within the Party; they yearn for bourgeois liberalism and negate every-

thing, and they are connected in a thousand and one ways with bourgeois intellectuals in society.[35]

Thus Mao found a confusing mixture of social contradictions prevailing in
postliberation China. The class enemy had been slain, but still there was
strain. By May 1957, not all party members could be considered true allies
of the revolution; some were linked with nonparty rightists in harboring
revisionist ideology. So far the social tensions within the party were not so
deep as to demand classifying any leading party member as an antagonistic
"enemy of the people"; so far actual purging was not necessitated for the
option of reducing social disagreement dissonance by persuading the extreme
right opinion deviates was not yet obviated. The party leadership remained
intact under Mao's formula of "unity-criticism-unity." Mao, himself, remained relatively confident of the validity of his revolutionary ideology,
despite the fact that some of his close party colleagues could not yet agree
with his proposed course for continuing the revolution. The Great Leap
Forward and associated large-scale antirightist campaign would demonstrate
the truth of his position to the more moderate and the skeptical.

In June 1957, with the publication of Mao's revised speech on correctly
handling contradictions among the people, the party policy turned from
tolerance to intense persuasion. Public blame for the deepened strain of
economic recession and large-scale unemployment was diverted from the
party and focussed on the disruptive intellectuals. In July, *People's Daily*
labelled the critics not as tenders of blooming flowers but as evil spirits and
demons who spread poisonous weeds. They became the "rightists" and the
new bloom of flowers was to be socialist culture. Their fate was to become
targets of the antirightist campaign of late 1957-1958. They were portrayed
in the press as having tried to undermine socialism and do away with the
leadership of the proletariat. Individual leaders were singled out and subjected
to accusations by the press and at numerous meetings by their peers until at
last they confessed their "crimes." Concurrently, the party carried out the
rectification campaign in their own ranks against liberal and rightist tendencies. In 1958 the rightist witch hunt deepened and ideological remolding
sessions were carried out in the major cities and universities, and large numbers of persons were transferred downward to learn mass culture, collective
spirit, and labor appreciation from peasants and workers. Mao's literary line
of Yenan was reasserted with its emphasis on the political and class nature
of literature, the party interpretation of socialist realism, and the necessity
of popularization.[36]

As Mao had stated in his February speech, ascertaining who were the allies
of revolution and who were the enemy was a confusing task in 1957:

Quite a few people fail to make a clear distinction between these two different types of contradictions—those between ourselves and the enemy and those among the people—and are prone to confuse the two. It must be admitted that it is sometimes easy to confuse them.[37]

Being on the side of the allies became increasingly crucial to the survival of those uncommitted to Maoist ideology in the succeeding year. As vestiges of the "class enemy" were skewered, China moved toward Mao's apocalyptic Leap Forward.

NOTES

1. Mao Tse-tung, "Analysis of the classes in Chinese society" (March 1926), *Selected Works* (SW), Vol. I. Peking: Foreign Language Press, 1967, p. 19. The semiproletariat includes: (1) the overwhelming majority of the semiowner peasants; (2) the poor peasants; (3) the small handicraftsmen; (4) the shop assistants, and (5) the pedlars. The "rural proletariat" includes farm laborers hired on a temporary basis. The industrial proletariat includes only two million workers mainly in mines, railways, shipbuilding, maritime transport, and textiles. In the future we shall lump together all these categories as "proletarians." (Hereafter *SW*.)

2. Ibid., p. 14.

3. *SW*, Vol. I, p. 127.

4. *SW*, Vol. I, p. 119.

5. *SW*, Vol. I, pp. 118, 124.

6. Mao Tse-tung, "Report on an investigation of the peasant movement in Hunan" (March 1927), *SW*, Vol. I, pp. 23-59. For a brief account of party history, see Franklin W. Houn, *A Short History of Chinese Communism*. Englewood Cliffs, N.J.: Prentice-Hall, 1957, passim.

7. See Stuart Schram, *Mao Tse-tung*. New York: Simon & Schuster, 1969, pp. 175-179.

8. See Schram, op. cit., p. 205.

9. The "Little Red Book," *Quotations from Chairman Mao*, was first published in May 1965, by the general political department of the PLA under the auspices of Lin Piao in hundreds of thousands of copies for distribution in the army and later reprinted with an introduction by Lin Piao in 1966 for mass distribution among the civilian populace.

10. "On contradiction" (August 1937), *SW*, Vol. I, p. 314.

11. Ibid., pp. 321-322.

12. Mao Tse-tung, "On practice" (July 1937), *SW*, Vol. I, p. 296.

13. Mao Tse-tung, *On the Correct Handling of Contradictions Among the People* (February 27, 1957). Peking: Foreign Languages Press, 1960, pp. 51-52.

14. Ibid.

15. Mao Tse-tung, "From some questions concerning methods of leadership" (June 1, 1943), *SW*, Vol. III, p. 119.

16. Mao Tse-tung, "On the correct handling of contradictions among the people," op. cit. See also the translation in Robert R. Bowie and John K. Fairbank, *Communist China 1955-1959: Policy Documents with Analysis*. Cambridge, Mass.: Harvard University Press, 1962, p. 292.

17. Mao Tse-tung, "We must learn to do economic work" (January 1945), *SW*, Vol. III, p. 191.

18. Mao Tse-tung, *SW*, Vol. III, p. 194.

19. Introductory note to "The party secretary takes the lead and all the party members help run the co-operatives" (1955), *The Socialist Upsurge in China's Countryside*. Peking: Foreign Languages Press, 1957, pp. 1-26.

20. Mao Tse-tung, "The ten great relationships," as summarized by Liu Shao-ch'i and quoted in Franz Schurmann, *Ideology and Organization in Communist China*. Berkeley: University of California Press, 1966, p. 77, as taken from *Jen Min Shou-tse*, 1959, p. 21. See also "On ten major relationships," as recirculated to party committees on December 27, 1965, and printed by the "Facing the Sun" column of the teachers and workers department of the Peking College of Economics on December 22, 1966, and translated in "Collection of statements by Mao Tse-tung (1956-1967)," *Current Background* No. 892, October 21, 1969, pp. 21-34. (Hereafter *CB*.)

21. Ibid.

22. For an excellent summary of the ideological and practical innovations of Yenan, which we have relied upon here, see Mark Selden, "The Yenan legacy: The mass line," in a Doak Barnett, ed., *Chinese Communist Politics in Action*. Seattle: University of Washington Press, 1969, pp. 99-151.

23. Alexander Eckstein, "The pattern of economic performance" in *Communist China's Economic Growth and Foreign Trade*. New York: McGraw-Hill, 1966, pp. 41-86.

24. Liu Ta-chung, "The tempo of economic development of the Chinese mainland, 1949-65," in Joint Economic Committee of the U.S. Congress, *An Economic Profile of Mainland China*. New York: Praeger (Special Studies in Economic Development) 1968.

25. Robert M. Field, "Chinese Communist industrial production," in Joint Economic Committee, op. cit.

26. Mao Tse-tung, "On the people's democratic dictatorship" (June 1949), *SW*, Vol. IV, pp. 417-423.

27. *CB*, No. 892, loc. cit.

28. Ibid., pp. 25, 29.

29. Mao Tse-tung, "On the correct handling of contradictions . . ." op. cit., passim.

30. Ibid., pp. 59-61.

31. Ibid., p. 38.

32. Ibid., pp. 34, 69.

33. Editorial, *Jen-min Jih-pao* (People's Daily) May 19, 1957, as cited in Merle Goldman, *Literary Dissent in Communist China*. Cambridge, Mass.: Harvard University Press, 1967, pp. 189-190. (Hereafter *JMJP*.)

34. Goldman, op. cit., pp. 157-202. Goldman's chapter, "Writers bloom in the Hundred Flowers Movement," provides a very literate analysis of the period, and we have relied on it here.

35. Mao Tse-tung, "Things are changing" (May 1957, translated in *CB* No. 891, October 8, 1969, p. 24.

36. An excellent account of Mao's effort to mobilize discontent during this period is provided by "The anti-rightist drive against the writers, 1957-1958," in Goldman, op. cit., pp. 203-242.

37. Mao Tse-tung, "On the correct handling of contradictions. . . ." op. cit., p. 21.

Chapter 2

PROPHECY AND THE POTENTIAL
OF DISCONFIRMATION

Ideologies are notoriously difficult to disconfirm. Much more than empirically testable scientific theories, they depend for their viability on the degree of social support they can muster from groups of people. Perhaps the viability of these great simplifiers depends upon this quality. Nevertheless, the thought of Mao Tse-tung provided itself with a testing ground, a physical embodiment of the great Maoist vision, the Great Leap Forward.

In heralding the People's Communes movement, the Maoists readvanced the central phantasy of revolutionary eschatology which has reappeared down through the ages; but in China of the late 1950s, the realization of this millennial phantasy was prophesied to assume a particular concrete form. This form was embodied in the official "Commune Resolution" of August 1958.[1] In keeping with this myth, the nation was depicted as having been dominated by an evil, demonic power, "the reactionary capitalists," who were to blame for inflicting intolerable sufferings on the people; outraged by their oppression, the awakened chosen people of "500 million" politically conscious peasants led by the "poor and lower-middle peasants," were to rise up and overthrow their oppressors, and inherit rightful dominion over their society, which would now flower in the utopian abundance of true "communism." In the opening words of the resolution:

Large, comprehensive people's communes have made their appearance, and in several places they are already widespread. . . . An unprecedented advance has been made in agricultural capital construction since the advocates of the capitalist road were fundamentally defeated economically, politically and ideologically. This has created a new basis for practically eliminating flood and drought, and for ensuring the comparatively stable advance of agricultural production.[2]

Not only were the communes predicted to put an end to flood, drought and famine, but also to usher in a utopian communist society in which "the differences between workers and peasants, town and country, and mental and manual labor . . . will gradually vanish, and the function of the state will be limited to protecting the country from external aggression but will play no role internally."[3] Thus both the oppressive relations of authority and the acrimonious differences between social groups would steadily decline in the new society. Furthermore, the resolution concluded with the promise that true communism was not remote but *imminent* through the communes:

It seems that true attainment of communism in China is no longer a remote future event. We should actively use the form of the people's communes to explore the practical road of transition to communism.[4]

Although the millennial prophecy is somewhat muted in the exposition of the resolution, the archetype is clearly present. The specific means by which these apocalyptic events were to come to pass were carefully articulated through Maoist dialectics. To observe the actual dependence of the Great Leap Forward of 1958 on the thought of Mao Tse-tung, let us reexamine the relationship of the four tenets to the actual policies of the Great Leap Forward.[5]

Empirical Predication

CONTRADICTIONS AND THE TEN GREAT RELATIONSHIPS

The economic, social and political organization of the Great Leap Forward can be shown to be dialectically reasoned out as evidenced in Maoist documents. The basic policy guidelines for the Great Leap Forward were provided by the "Ten Great Relationships" of April 1956, and the Maoist article, "On the Correct Handling of Contradictions Among the People" of February 1957. Both of these are authored by Mao Tse-tung. The Great Leap Forward in comparison to the previous first five year plan, was an economic plan in which the predestined proletariat and their party representatives were in command of the economy rather than the central government bureaucrats, the

institutional managers, the bourgeois, or the intellectuals. There was concurrent with the Great Leap and following the Hundred Flowers campaign,
a thought rectification movement aimed at outspoken intellectuals (including
the "surrender your hearts to the party" campaign aimed at rightists and
intellectuals), which removed many bureaucrats and intellectuals from effective control of the economy while they were undergoing reform. In addition,
while "rightists" underwent reform, proletarians and party cadres ran the
economy.

SOCIAL INTEGRATION AND CLASS TRANSFORMATION

To reduce the contradictions between the proletariat and nonproletarians,
i.e., to help eradicate class differences, several movements were initiated to
transform nonproletarians into proletarians and to raise the skill levels of
proletarians. Besides the sending of officials to lower levels and the sending
of intellectuals to the countryside, "peasant universities" were established
to raise the educational level of the peasants; students were sent to the
countryside to teach the peasants technical skills such as blast furnace construction; a "three unification movement" was waged aimed at mutually
transforming workers, technicians, and cadres while molding them together
into single work teams.

The most dramatic attempt rapidly to bring forth communism, with its
classless society and its material plenty, was the establishment of the rural
People's Communes. The communistic aims of the People's Communes are
well described in the "Commune Resolution" promulgated by the central
committee of the Chinese Communist party on August 29, 1958, following
the enlarged session of the politburo held in the resort town of Pei Tai-ho.
In this resolution it is stated that "people's communes are the best form
for the attainment of socialism and gradual transition to communism."
The resolution goes on to describe the end state towards which the communes are leading:

> Some years after that [transition to socialism] the social product will
> become very abundant; the communist consciousness and morality of
> the entire people will be elevated to a much higher degree; universal
> education will be achieved ... ; the differences between worker and
> peasant, between town and country, between mental and manual labor
> ... and the remnants of unequal bourgeoise rights ... will gradually
> vanish; and the function of the state will be limited to protecting the
> country from external aggression; and it will play no role internally.[6]

In December of 1958, 26,000 communes averaging 5,000 households each
and encompassing the entire Chinese peasantry were in existence, having been

formed during 1958 by the amalgamation of 740,000 agricultural producers' cooperatives. Clearly, the communes were to represent a radically new leap towards communism, with a much larger social unit for sharing of the tools of production and the rewards of consumption than ever provided by earlier agricultural cooperatives. The Communist ethic was put into practice in many commune units. Within the commune as a whole, work was demanded as goods were distributed in some communes according to the maxim, "From each according to his ability, to each according to his needs." With the communes the peasant mode of production was organized to be more similar to the factories of the urban proletarians with special units for fertilizing, harvesting, and seeding. Communal innovations were made for health care, child care, food preparation and distribution, through the establishment of "happiness homes" for the aged, cooperative nurseries for the young, and communal mess halls for all. Indeed, the peasants were instructed to build small scale industry of their own, the most notorious examples being the backyard blast furnaces. In slack seasons peasants were organized to aid in construction work such as the building of dams and sent to aid factory workers in the cities. The military took an active role in organizing militia units in every commune, and peasants engaged in a "war against nature" with an enthusiasm and discipline never before witnessed in China's countryside. Students, intellectuals, and bureaucrats alike were sent to the countryside to teach the peasants techniques of industrial production and to learn from the peasants the love of the soil and manual labor. An attempt was made to organize urban housewives, the old, and the unemployed into urban communes for small-scale production such as textiles and handicrafts. Besides being an attempt at increasing China's economic productivity, the commune movement was clearly an attempt to reduce class and occupational differences and transform all Chinese into true proletarians.

The growth of people's communes provided for Mao the organizational proof that his ideology was the correct way rapidly to bring true communism to China. The instrumentality of the people's communes for the rapid realization of communism in China was an article of faith buttressed with scriptural evidence through the esoteric research of several of Mao's writers during 1958. It was pointed out by one of these writers, Fan Hung, that in his *Principles of Communism,* Engels himself had predicted that the "citizens' commune" would be the basic social unit of the future society of full communism. Other Chinese theorists discussing Mao's people's communes in 1958 pointed to several features of his plan, designated as "buds of communism," which would put China ahead of the Soviet Union:

(1) the twofold system of "free supply" (distribution "according to need") and of wages (distribution still "according to work");

(2) the public mess halls, nurseries, kindergartens, and rural "housing estates";

(3) ownership by "all the people," i.e., the state, in rural areas;

(4) integration of *hsien* (township) government with the commune;

(5) establishment of a commune militia; and

(6) elimination of the difference between town and country, worker and peasant, mental and manual labor.[7]

As scriptural precedents for most of these concepts the Chinese theorists in 1958 cited many classical texts, including the following: *Lectures at Elberfeld* (Engels, 1845); *Principles of Communism* (Engels, 1845); *Communist Manifesto* (Marx and Engels, 1847-1848); *Anti-Dühring* (Engels, 1891); *Critique of the Gotha Program* (Marx, 1875); *Preface to Civil Wars in France* (Engels, 1891); *Report on the Rural Poor* (Lenin, 1903); *State and Revolution* (Lenin, 1917); *A Good Beginning* (Lenin, 1919); *Anarchism or Socialism?* Stalin, 1906); *Dizzy with Success* (Stalin, 1930); and *Economic Problems of Socialism in the U.S.S.R.* (Stalin, 1952). Even the primordial ideas of the "utopian socialists" dating from the sixteenth century, including those of Thomas More, Morelly, Babeuf, Saint-Simon, Fourier, and Owen, were cited by the Chinese theorists in their effort to establish the communist orthodoxy of communes.[8]

Having enshrined the commune concept in classical orthodoxy, the Chinese theorists proceeded to celebrate the creative innovations in this framework wrought by Mao's people's communes. First of all, Mao's commune was unique because it had a wider functional competence in political, social, economic, and military fields than any previous commune concept. Mao's multifunctional commune concept was presented by Chen Po-ta as "a conclusion drawn from the experience of actual life."[9] Chen asserted that whereas Marx, Engels, and Lenin "could not provide each country and nation with a detailed plan," in China, Mao had solved this problem "courageously and with extraordinary brilliance." Second, Mao's people's commune concept was unique in the manner in which the collective ownership system was transformed into a system of "all people's" (i.e., state) ownership.[10] Finally, Mao's people's commune was unique in the application of the principle of "uninterrupted revolution" to the problem of agricultural cooperativization and collectivization under socialism.[11] In particular, both with the establishment of people's communes in 1958 and with the prior establishment of agricultural producers cooperatives in 1955, Mao applied the principle of developing progressively higher levels of collective relations of production in advance of industrialization and mechanization. Both moves were clear-cut departures from Lenin, and both were based upon a distillation from

Mao's unique Chinese experience. By further collectivizing the means of production, Mao hoped to unleash new productive energy and thereby increase productivity.

The organizational proof of Mao's ideological prophecy, the people's commune, was imminent in 1958: One of Mao's writers, Ho Ch'ien, even went so far as to state that the transition to full state ownership would be "completed in 3 or 4 years in some areas, while other areas might require 5 or 6 years, or a bit more."[1][2]

Great things were publically prophesied to ensue shortly after the full establishment of the people's communes. On September 3, 1958 an editorial in *JMJP* predicted that

> it [the commune] will become the basic unit in the future communist society, as thinkers from many outstanding utopian socialists to Marx, Engels, and Lenin—had predicted on many occasions.[1][3]

Furthermore commune-sustained utopia was imminent. In China in the 1960s enormous political changes would soon be wrought as a result of the full establishment of communes:

> the function of the state will [in at most six plus "a few years"] be limited to protecting the country from external aggression; it will play no role in domestic affairs.[1][4]

By the end of 1958 the sprouts of utopian communism, the people's communes, were fully rooted throughout all China; but events of the subsequent year were to belie the millennial predictions.

POLITICAL LEADERSHIP AND THE MASS LINE

To reduce the contradictions between leaders and followers posed by the growth of a large central bureaucracy during the first five year plan, a policy of political decentralization was enacted. Hundreds of thousands of government officials were "sent down to lower levels"; many large factories previously under central government control were put under provincial government or local control; in small factories the civilian manager gave way to the party secretary in operational as well as political control. As the size of the central government bureaucracy diminished, the size of the party grew to accommodate a need for expanded grass roots leadership. Leadership passed to local party committees at the expense of central government ministries. In conjunction with government decentralization and the expansion of grass roots cadres in direct contact with the masses, the ideological central party line was brought directly to the cadres and the masses by a wide expansion in local mass media such as institutionally controlled loudspeakers, locally published newspapers and magazines, and commune-run mobile cinema teams, to exhort the people to greater efforts.

ECONOMIC CONSTRUCTION AND MASS MOBILIZATION

In order to reduce the contradictions between society and nature, the leadership demanded enormous application of human effort to soil and matter for production's sake. The Maoist spirit of "mass mobilization" of all usable forces in the struggle to make the "country a modernized, rich, and powerful socialist country as rapidly as possible" was evidenced in the first of the Maoist "Three Red Banners," namely the Great Leap Forward. One instance of a Great Leap production target was the 1958 campaign for smelting steel in indigenous furnaces to produce 10,700,000 tons of steel during the year, a target that was raised over 2 million tons above that set by an enlarged meeting of the politburo held at Peitaiho during late August 1958. The second of the "Three Red Banners" used as slogans during the Great Leap period was the people's communes which were to be instrumental in achieving these high production targets. The third of the Three Red Banners was the general line coined by Mao Tse-tung to urge the people to catch up with Great Britain in industrial production. It was adopted as the general line for building socialism at the second session of the eighth CCP central committee during May 1958. The general line was "to build socialism by exerting the utmost efforts and pressing forward consistently to achieve greater, faster, better and more economical results." As we have seen, the characteristics of the mode of production used to achieve these astronomical targets involved massive mobilization of the labor force, constant exhortation by mass media and grass roots cadres to renewed production efforts, sacrifice of personal desires to the collective interest, militaristic discipline, indiscriminate application of all-purpose laborers to production tasks, the simultaneous development of agriculture and industry, decentralized government authority and budgeting, and an increased share of the gross national product reinvested in capital goods. With this massive mobilization of human energy, how many Great Walls could Mao have wrapped around China?

Clearly, then, the Great Leap Forward was predicated upon the thought of Mao Tse-tung and represented an enormous commitment of prestige, self-sacrifice and human effort by the leadership and the masses rapidly to bring communism to China through the resolution of economic, social, and political contradictions. What better explanation can one provide for the style and enormity of this movement? If the Great Leap Forward were to fail to attain the specifics of its objectives, one can imagine the implications for the credibility of the thought of Mao Tse-tung.

Whereas the Chinese revolution had provided one empirical test of the validity of the thought of Mao Tse-tung, the Great Leap Forward movement, employing the same basic principles, provided another. Whether the Great Leap, employing Maoist tenets and practices, was moving China closer toward communism could be empirically judged in a number of ways. Economic production achievements provided a test. Did the Maoist radical organization of people's communes in the countryside result in higher figures for grain production? Did the assemblage of backyard blast furnaces result in greatly expanded steel production? Did overall industrial production rise as a result of Maoist movements? Indices of public opinion and morale also provided a test. Did the Great Leap movement result in more harmonious relations between leaders and followers? Did it result in more harmonious relations between proletarians and bourgeoisie or among the various social classes in general? Did the sending of hundreds of thousands of upper-level cadres to work at lower levels serve to promote harmonious integration with the masses? Did the employment of grass roots media of communication serve to raise the level of morale of the peasants and integrate them with the rest of society?

Millenarianism and the Mind of Mao

I have observed this nation of ours for seven or eight years. I see great hope in our nation. Especially during the past years, it can be seen that the national spirit of our 600 million people has been more than buoyant as compared to the past eight years. Through the great debate of extensive contending and extensive blooming, we have clarified our problems and understood our tasks. We will catch up with Britain in about fifteen years. Promulgation of the forty articles of the [twelve-year] Agricultural Development Program has greatly encouraged the masses. We can now do and have confidence in many things that were impossible before. . . .

Our nation has awakened, like we wake up in the morning; awakened, after having overthrown the feudal system of past millenniums; awakened, after having changed the system of ownership. We are now engaged in rectification and have achieved victory in the antirightist campaign.

Our country is poor and blank: the poor own nothing, and the blank is like a sheet of white paper. It is good to be poor, good for making revolution; when it is blank, one can do anything with it, such as writing compositions or drawing designs; a sheet of white paper is good to write compositions on. . . .

Thus, our nation has this zeal for endeavor. To catch up with Britain, we will have to produce 40 million tons of steel, our present output being some 5 million tons; 500 million tons of coal, our present output being some 100 million tons; we will have to develop 450 billion kwh of electric power generating capacity, our present capacity being 40 billion kwh, and therefore it must be increased tenfold. It will take a decade to carry out the forty articles of the Agricultural Development Program. It may not take ten years; some say five years, others say three years, it would seem that it may take eight years to complete the program. . . .

There are two kinds of leadership, or work style, involved in achieving socialism. For instance, one the question of cooperativization, some advocated quick action, others—slower action. I consider the former better. Strike the iron when it is hot; better to get it done in one stroke than drag on. Between rectification and no rectification, I choose rectification. And in order to carry out rectification, it is better to effect extensive contending and extensive blooming. . . . I advocate the theory of uninterrupted revolution.[15]

Thus spake Mao Tse-tung on January 28, 1958 in ushering in China's new millennium before the assembled supreme state conference.

The year of the Great Leap Forward, 1958, opened with verbal adulation and enthusiastic implementation of the great Maoist vision. On the occasion of the first anniversary of Mao Tse-tung's address of February 27, 1957, "On the Correct Handling of Contradictions Among the People," one hundred and eighty eminent philosophers, economists, and historians met under the auspices of the China Academy of Sciences to discuss the significance of the thought rectification campaign approved by the central committee of the Chinese Communist party on November 1, 1957 "to remold the old thoughts of the intellectuals and enhance the socialist awakening of the students.[16]

In 1958 most of China's intellectuals and higher party cadres were made aware of the fact that the Great Leap Forward represented a testing ground for the utility of Maoist dialectics in bringing forth the true communist era in China. The knowledge of this dependency was well expressed by two leading intellectuals at the 1958 conference sponsored by the Chinese Academy of Sciences to discuss the significance of this intensive thought rectification campaign. Ai Szu-chi one of the leading exponents of modern Chinese Marxist dialectics, pointed to the "Great Leap Forward" during the previous six months and made the point that "incessant disclosure and elimination of contradictions between socialist relations of productive forces constitutes a motivating force for social development under socialism." Another intellectual, Hsu Li-chun, described Mao's theory on "contradictions among the people" as a creative contribution to Marxist-Leninist theory and said that its correctness had been proved by the results of the rectification campaign and the "current production upsurge," which it had made possible. He gave warning that any departure from Chairman Mao's "creative theoretical works" would make it impossible to "formulate the general line of socialist construction in our country." According to this interpreter, "Chairman Mao had esteblished the best examples of upholding the dialectical materialist world outlook and of developing the subjective motivating nature of the masses of people."[17]

Later in the year, on the first anniversary of the open publication of Mao's "contradictions" treatise, the masses of people were made aware, if more dimly than the intellectuals, of the authorship and theoretical significance of China's Great Leap Forward. On June 18-19, 1958 nationwide ceremonies, discussion meetings, and press activity commemorated Mao's "contradictions" speech as one of "great historical significance."[18] In conjunction with this public adulation of Mao's "contradictions" speech, on June 19, 1958, China's leading national newspaper, *Jen-min Jih pao* (People's Daily) enthusiastically proclaimed 1958 "The Great Year." The great Maoist vision was in the process of becoming China's reality.

The implementation of the Maoist vision steadily increased throughout the year 1958 and greatly affected the life of every individual inhabiting the Chinese mainland. The escalating popular enthusiasm for the Great Leap on the part of party cadres and common folk is well illustrated in an account of the movement in Canton City and its rural environs in Kwangtung Province during 1958.[19] In January the Kwangtung Provincial Twelve Year Program for Agricultural Development was published. Initially it called for an average increase in grain production of 8 percent per year from 1955 to 1962, and for increasing the average rice yield per month from the 400 catties of 1955 to 700 catties by 1962 and 900 by 1967. Only three weeks later, at the January 28 conference on agriculture, the enthusiastic Kwangtung party cadres more than tripled their aspiration level for grain increases to 26 percent per year during the period 1955-1962, and set their minds to doubling the number of catties of rice produced per month in just one year—1958—instead of five.[20]

Paralleling their escalating agricultural aspirations were industrial targets. At the October 1957 party congress, the party cadres had set a 5.8 percent increase over that year's industrial production as their goal for Canton City in 1958. In the initial heat of Great Leap enthusiasm generated at the January planning conference, the goal was adjusted upward to 12.4 percent. A few days later at the municipal party committee meeting, the local party honchos were not to be outdone in their display of enthusiasm: They reset the target for 1958 industrial production to 15 percent over 1957, nearly triple the original increase target. In February the vice-mayor of Canton

City, Chiao Lin-i, personally pronounced a production target of 33.2 percent for 1958, more than doubling the wager laid down by the Canton municipal party committee just ten days before. Furthermore, he guaranteed that within five years, Canton's industrial production would double. Finally, in early March, the mayor himself, Chu Kuang, endorsed the slogan that "within five years Canton will be an industrial city."[21]

Slogans of impending utopia resounded from the mouths of people around Canton City in the spring of 1958. The common folk talked of "Bitter struggle for three years leads to 1,000 years of happiness." Cadres demonstrated the success of the recent thought rectification movement by agreeing to raised production targets for their fiefs and by mouthing slogans of new personal goals for themselves: "Within a year or two, become a specialist; within three to five years, become an insider; within five to ten years, become an engineer."[22]

The summer was filled with mass mobilization efforts as new waves or cadres flooded the countryside. Peasants were conscripted to engage in massive construction projects such as dam construction for irrigation and hydroelectric power. At the summer's end, the PLA carried the "everyman a soldier" campaign, with its military slogans to the villagers for the new "war against nature." In August the drive to produce steel through conventional methods and local furnaces for a possible war over Taiwan was heated up in the face of attempted Soviet restraint. On August 11, the *New China News Agency* published the report of Chairman Mao's August 6 visit to the experimental Chi-Li-ying people's commune of Honan privince whereupon Mao, gazing at the vigorous new commune, endorsed the words of We Chih-p'u, First Secretary of the Honan party committee, "Where there is one, there will surely be many." On August 29, following the enlarged politburo plenum at Peitaiho begun on August 16, *People's Daily* carried the editorial "Long Live the People's Communes" to the minds of its Canton readers.[23] Before the end of the month, all the remaining private plots of the peasants were appropriated by the newly formed Kwangtung people's communes. Much of this land was used to supply the new communal mess halls which sprouted around the provinces along with cooperative nurseries for children. By November 1, just two months after the movement began in the province, 98.5 percent of the peasants were reported members of 790 multipurpose communes formed from 25,450 agricultural cooperatives.[24] The era of Mao Tse-tung had at last come to pass.

In fact, Mao had wholeheartedly committed himself and his ideology to the Great Leap Forward as a testing ground for its utility in ushering in the communist transformation of China. By autumn of 1958, Mao and the thought of Mao Tse-tung had become the prophet and the prophecy of communist utopia for China. At the peak of the Great Leap Forward, on

National Day 1958, Mao's prophecy of imminent communist utopia, was spread across the pages of China's leading national newspaper:

Today is the era of Mao Tse-tung, heaven is here on earth. . . . Chairman Mao is a great prophet. . . . Each prophecy of Chairman Mao has become a reality. It was so in the past; it is so today.[25]

NOTES

1. "Resolution on the establishment of people's communes in the rural areas" (central committee of CCP, 8/29/58), *Peking Review* No. 29, September 16, 1958, pp. 21-23. (Hereafter *PR*.)

2. Ibid., p. 21.

3. Ibid., p. 22.

4. Ibid., p. 23.

5. For a brilliant analysis of the Great Leap Forward as a dialectically reasoned, physical embodiment of the thought of Mao Tse-tung, see Franz Schurmann, *Ideology and Organization of Communist China*. Berkeley: University of California Press, 1966, pp. 73-104.

6. "Resolution on some questions concerning the people's communes" (Sixth plenary session of the eighth central committee of the Communist party of China). Peking: Foreign Languages Press, 1958, pp. 25-26, as quoted in John Wilson Lewis, *Leadership in Communist China*. Ithaca, N.Y.: Cornell University Press, 1963, pp. 262-263.

7. See Arthur A. Cohen, *The Communism of Mao Tse-tung*. Chicago: University of Chicago Press, 1964, pp. 168-187, esp. p. 174. We have relied heavily here upon his excellent chapter on "Transition to communism: People's communes" in order to underline the importance of people's communes as visible means of bringing communism to China.

8. See *On Communist Communes,* compiled in book form by the Basis Department of Marxism-Leninism of the Chinese People's University, Part 3 (Peking, July 1958), as cited in Cohen, op. cit., p. 175.

9. Ch'en Po-ta, "Under the banner of Mao Tse-tung," *Hung Ch'i* No. 4, July 16, 1958, as cited in Cohen, op. cit., p. 176. (Hereafter *HC.*)

10. Fan Hung, *Marx, Engels, Lenin, and Stalin on the Theory of Communism* (Peking, April 1959), pp. 42-51, as cited in Cohen, op. cit., p. 177.

11. Chin Liao-chou, "Disseminate the ideology of Communism," *Hsueh-hsi* No. 19, October 10, 1958, as cited in Cohen, op. cit., p. 178.

12. Ho Ch'ien "Communism is not a mystery," *Hsueh-hsi* September 10, 1958, as cited in Cohen, op. cit., p. 168.

13. "Hold high the red flag of people's communes and march on," editorial, *JMJP* September 3, 1958, as cited in Jan S. Prybylla, *The Political Economy of Communist China*. Scranton: International Textbook Co., 1970, p. 286.

14. Ibid.

15. "Speech at supreme state conference" (January 28, 1958), as translated in *Chinese Law and Government* Vol. 1, No. 4, Winter 1968-1969, pp. 10-14. (Hereafter *CLG*.)

16. See H. Arthur Steiner, "The curriculum in Chinese socialist education: An official bibliography of 'Maoism'," *Pacific Affairs*, Vol. 31, No. 3, September 1958, pp. 286-299.

17. See Ralf Bonwit, "Communist China's Leap Forward," *Pacific Affairs*, Vol. 31, No. 2, June 1958, pp. 170-171.

18. See H. Arthur Steiner, op. cit., p. 291.

19. For a thoroughly documented description and first-rate analysis of the implementation of the Great Leap Forward in Canton City and its rural environs, see Ezra F. Vogal, *Canton Under Communism*. Cambridge, Mass.: Harvard University Press, 1969, pp. 218-270.

20. Ibid., p. 233.

21. Ibid., pp. 234-236.

22. Ibid., p. 236.

23. Ibid., p. 245.

24. Ibid., pp. 248-249.

25. *JMJP*, October 1, 1958, as quoted in Richard L. Walker, "Chairman Mao and the cult of personality," *Encounter*, June 1960, p. 34.

Chapter 3

PERSONAL COMMITMENT AND
THE YENAN HERITAGE

Having examined some of the basic precepts from the thought of Mao Tse-tung that underlay the design and implementation of the Great Leap Forward movement and having noted the potentialities for empirical disconfirmation of the doctrine that were inherent in that movement, it is important to the thesis of this book that we undertake an examination of those individuals who were convinced of and committed to the Maoist doctrine and the associated Great Leap movement prior to the fall of 1959. Who were the ones that were convinced of and committed to the belief that the Maoist Great Leap Forward would lead China rapidly closer to communism? Who were the ones that, for the sake of this belief, had taken important actions that were difficult to undo? Who had unalterably pledged themselves to Mao's prophecy? We shall examine these questions at three levels of the Chinese political system: The politburo of the central committee of the Chinese Communist party; the ranks of middle-level party, government, and military cadres; and the great masses of the Chinese population.

The most powerful group in the triad of rule institutionalized by the party by the late fifties was the 26 man politburo of the central committee (CC) of the CCP. The CC is elected at the national party congress, and it in turn elects the politburo. The seventh congress was held in Yenan in 1945 and the eighth in Peking in 1956. Within the party, lower-level cadres obey higher levels according to the principles of democratic centralism. In 1957 the committee and branch structure of the 13 million man party organization thoroughly penetrated the provinces, cities, and counties into the basic levels where the 400 million adults were organized into socialized factories, schools, business enterprises, agricultural collectives, and government offices. Flanking the party politburo in civil society is the government cabinet, the state council, composed of the premier and vice-premiers elected from 49 central government ministers and commission heads. Leading government officials are elected at semiregular national people's congresses. The first congress was held in 1954. Flanking the politburo in the military sector is the People's Liberation Army (PLA) whose leaders receive party directives through the Military Affairs Commission (MAC) of the party. The chairman of the politburo exercises extraordinary power through the leading representatives of the government and the military who hold concurrent memberships on the politburo. Let us examine the degree of commitment to Mao's Great Leap and commune program of these 26 powerful men at the time of decision to engage in this radical endeavor.

Commitment in the Politburo

As chairman of the politburo, Mao was extremely committed to his Great Leap program. At Yenan he had codified his dialectics into the thought of Mao Tse-tung and urged them on his colleagues in the rectification campaign of 1942-1944. In the mid-fifties, he was active in reiterating his Yenan philosophy by spurring the collectives for the socialist transformation of agriculture. This is indicated by his writings in "The Socialist Upsurge in China's Countryside" in 1955. Then he forcefully urged the stepping up of agricultural collectivization:

> When the ties hampering the forces of production are thus loosened, production will develop much more rapidly. . . . Most first-stage cooperatives that have been in existence about three years basically meet the requirements. The Party organizations in every province, city and autonomous region should look into the situation and, with the agreement of the masses, arrange for the establishment of experimental higher-stage cooperatives during 1956 and 1957.[1]

In 1956 and 1957, as we have seen, Mao applied his dialectics to the task of achieving national development while opposing bureaucratism and conservatism in his speeches "On the Ten Great Relationships" and "On the Correct Handling of Contradictions Among the People." In 1958, Mao endorsed a more detailed plan for even more extreme agricultural collectivization. In his draft of the "Sixty Work Methods," he applied his dialectics to the test of designing China's socialist transformation and exuded confidence as he urged them on his colleagues. Mao went so far as to provide an explicit criterion for testing the validity of his or any plan:

> Among our cadres, quite a number of people probably do not understand this simple truth: the thought, idea, plan and method of any hero can only be the reflection of the objective world. His raw material and semi-processed products can only come from the practice of the masses of the people or his own scientific experiments . . . whether or not this finished product manufactured by the human brain is fit for use or correct has yet to be tested by the masses of the people.[2]

Risky though it was, Mao was so confident of the future success of this Great Leap movement, that in January he proposed that he relinquish one of his posts, the chairmanship of the People's Republic, by years end, since the nation was "in a time of peace."[3] Apparently, the Great Leap Forward was to be Mao's last great act.

The extreme form of agricultural collectivization personally endorsed by Mao was the people's commune. In August 1958, *People's Daily* reported Mao's wishes to the Chinese masses. When T'an Ch'i-lung, (Shantung) provincial secretary, reported that Pei-y'uan hsiang in Li-ch'en hsien was preparing to set up large collective farms, Chairman Mao said, "It is better to set up people's communes. Their advantage lies in the fact that they combine industry, agriculture, commerce, education and military affairs. This is convient for leadership."[4] While criticizing Stalin's *Economic Problems of Socialism* in his speech at Chengchow in mid-November 1958, Mao again personally endorsed the people's communes as facilitators of the Great Leap Forward and as the foundation of future communism in China:

> In addition to the rectification movement and the breakdown of the bourgeois legal power ideology, China has the people's commune, which makes it even easier to attain greater, faster, better, and more economical results. . . . The commune is the best organizational form for the two transitions, from the socialism of today to complete ownership by all the people, and from the latter to communism. When the transitions are completed in the future, the commune will serve as the basic level structure of the communist society.[5]

So great was Mao's belief in the efficacy of the commune that he prophesied great production achievements to accrue. In his speech before directors of various cooperative areas at the end of November 1958, Mao personally predicted enormous increases in grain production to result from Great Leap commune formation. Citing the 1958 output level at 375 million metric tons (double the 1957 figure), he predicted that the 1959 figure would show a 40 percent increase, and that three years hence the 1958 output, itself, would double.[6]

Not every party leader was agreed with Mao's Great Leap and commune program in 1958. Many members of the politburo were apparently skeptical of the utopian movement. The existence of significant political opposition to Mao's communes is evidenced by the fact that the initial Honan Sputnik Commune experiment of April 1958, which had also been personally endorsed by Mao, had not even been mentioned in the party resolution on agriculture adopted at the second session of eighth party congress in May. "This [Honan Sputnik Commune] was, in essence, already the start of the movement for people's communes. But people were not yet aware of the significance of the development. Only after Comrade Mao Tse-tung gave his directive regarding the people's communes did they begin to see things clearly, comprehend the reasoning of this new form of organization that has appeared in the vast rural and urban areas, and feel more confident and determined to take this path."[7]

Other members of the politburo varied in their commitment to Mao's thought through 1958. Active participation on behalf of Maoist dialectics in the Yenan rectification campaign, abstention from engaging oneself in bureaucratic position and behavior during the first five year plan, and early public endorsement of Mao's radical agricultural collectivization program had afforded members of the 1958 politburo important opportunities to commit themselves personally to the thought of Mao Tse-tung and its implied programs. Only some members availed themselves of all opportunities. Besides Mao, three other members of the twenty-six man politburo had actively supported the spread of Mao's dialectics through the Central Party School in the Yenan rectification campaign and had subsequently abstained from holding high bureaucratic office during the Soviet-modeled first five year plan. These three committed Maoists, Lin Piao, Ch'en Po-ta, and K'ang Sheng, also gave unqualified support to pushing through Mao's radical agricultural collectivization programs and ultimately his Great Leap Forward and commune movement.[8]

Mao was not alone in his effort to Sinify Marxism. In 1939, Ch'en Po-ta, Mao's drab political secretary at Yenan, published similar dialectical articles entitled "Some Dialectics Concerning Marxist Docrtines" and "General Comment on the Three People's Principles." It is quite likely that Ch'en Po-ta, known for his theoretical and literary talents, acted as a ghost writer for Mao's writings at this time and later in the history of the movement. During the rectification campaign, Ch'en was an instructor at the Central Party School. In 1938 Mao divorced his second wife and bearer of his five children,

Ho Tzu-chen, and took the comely young revolutionary actress Chiang Ch'ing as his new bride. In the marriage of Mao and Chiang Ch'ing, the dogmatic Vice-President of the Central Party School, K'ang Sheng, acted as matchmaker. Both Chiang Ch'ing and K'ang Sheng were from Chu-chang Hsien, Shantung, and they had known each other as far back as the Shanghai days of the 1920s. K'ang was originally responsible for Chiang's joining the party. Ch'en, Chiang, and K'ang were three members of Mao's Yenan coterie.

In the codification of his politico-military tactics, Mao had another highly respected associate at Yenan in the celebrated warrior Lin Piao. There Lin Piao directed K'ang Ta, the "Anti-Japanese Military-Political University" and commanded a division. Having led the vanguard column on the "Long March" retreat to Yenan in 1934, this hungry little tiger of a man subsequently led his guerrilla forces to victory over the Japanese at P'ing-hsingkuan in 1937, a singular feat subsequently championed as a victory for Mao's strategy. In 1936, Lin had published a series of military articles entitled "Struggle and War and Revolution," which received international acclaim; according to the reporting of Edgar Snow, Lin became Mao's intimate associate. In 1937 Lin also married a young revolutionary, one of his students at K'ang Ta, Liu Hsi-jing.

Lin's curriculum at K'ang Ta was abetted by Mao's personal contributions summarizing his tactics of guerrilla warfare. In March of 1938, Mao delivered a lecture at the K'ang Ta entitled Basic Tactics (Chi-Ch'u Chan-shu) setting forth three time-honored principles.[9] The first advocated "avoiding strength and striking at weakness" (pi-shih kung-hsu), a maxim Mao adapted from ancient China's Clausicwitz, Sun Tzu. The second emphasized the killing of enemy soldiers rather than the conquest of territory or strong points, a corollary of Mao's man-over-weapons military maxim. The third urged concentrating one's own forces to annihilate enemy units one by one, a tactic later adopted for the conduct of political campaigns.[10] At K'ang Ta, Mao and Lin Piao were locked in a politico-military symbiosis, each basking in the other's triumphs.

Lin continued his principalship of K'ang Ta until 1944, with some interruptions for rehabilitation of war wounds in the Soviet Union; over the period, with Lin as principal and Mao as Chairman of the Educational Committee, K'ang Ta produced more than 100,000 indoctrinated politico-military cadres. Lin's curriculum supported Mao's innovations in the "Sinification of Marxism" emphasizing close relations between correct military techniques and correct political thinking, and stressing guerrilla tactics. The Mao-Lin joint politico-military educational effort was further welded together in 1942 with the inauguration of the Yenan rectification (Cheng-feng) campaigns. Upon returning from rehabilitation in the Soviet Union, Lin took the opportunity to support Mao at Yenan in opposition to the Soviet clique led by

Wang Ming. Mao simultaneously reorganized the Central Party School, made himself principal and appointed Lin Deputy Principal. Together they proceeded with the unique "Sinification of Marxism" and its propagation until the war's end.[11]

Thus among the Yenan coterie of Mao, Lin, Ch'en, K'ang, and Chiang Ch'ing, all the men were were involved in the summarization and integration of their hard-won revolutionary experiences and in the promulgation through the Central Party School of a uniquely Chinese variant of Marxist dialectics, the thought of Mao Tse-tung. All developed strong commitments to Mao's revolutionary views developed during this era. While it is true that in addition to Mao and K'ang Sheng, Liu Shao-ch'i and Ch'en Yun also contributed articles to the Yenan *Cheng-feng* campaign, the latter authors' contributions dealt exclusively with the matter of the Bolshevization of the Chinese Communist party organization and had less relevance for the broader problem of the adaption of Marxist-Leninist dialectics to the unique conditions of China.[12] Ensuing upon the *Cheng-feng* campaign of 1942-1944, a budding cult of Mao first grew to prominence in China. The party rules adopted at the seventh party congress in 1945 reflected this ascent of Maoist influence stating that "The CCP takes the theories of Marxism-Leninism and the unified Thought of Mao Tse-tung, as the guideline for all its actions." At the same congress, Mao's comrade in arms education, Lin Piao, was elected to the new CC and ranked sixth. Significantly, the eighth congress of 1956 was to pay tribute to Marxism-Leninism as the party guideline while flagrantly omitting any reference to the thought of Mao Tse-tung; the subsequently exposed perpetrator and later labeled "traitor" was no other than Lin's archrival, P'eng Teh-huai.

Ch'en Po-ta had perhaps the closest affinity to Mao's thought. In 1944, Ch'en had refurbished Mao's own agrarian ideas with his own "Notes on Mao Tse-tung's 'Report of an Investigation Into the Peasant Movement in Hunan'." Following the liberation, Ch'en carried over the Yenan legacy on the thirtieth anniversary of the party by publishing an article in *People's Daily* of July 13, 1951 entitled "Mao Tse-tung's Thought is the Synthesis of Marxism-Leninism and the Chinese Revolution" in preparation for the publication of the first volume of Mao's *Selected Works* in October. Ch'en's early commitment to Mao's radical rural collectivization programs of the 1950s is evidenced by his political positions and speeches during that period. In the mid-1950s, Ch'en was Deputy Director of the Party Rural Work Department, despite the fact that he was not much of an economic specialist. In 1955, Ch'en had helped Mao push through the radical agricultural collectivization movement; and, though he was not yet a politburo member, Ch'en delivered a politburo report explaining the "Decision on the Question of Agricultural Collectivization" to the enlarged sixth plenum of the seventh central com-

mittee in October 1955.[13] In 1956, Ch'en was elevated to alternate membership on the politburo of the new eighth central committee.

In the 1958 surge of the Great Leap Forward, Ch'en publicly committed
himself to wholehearted support of Mao's radical movement. In March of
that year, Ch'en supported Mao's efforts to supplant traditional elitist culture
and Soviet professionalism with Yenan-style proletarian culture in his address
to the fifth conference of the Science Planning Committee entitled "Lay
Much Emphasis on the Present and Less on the Past: Learning While Working."[14] In so doing, Ch'en previewed the radicalized slogan he would advance
during the Great Proletarian Cultural Revolution of 1966 for "destroying the
four olds and constructing the four news," and presaging the vicious attack
he would aim at the party's professional propagandists in the July 1966 issue
of *Hung Ch'i* accusing them "of stubbornly insisting in carrying through their
bourgeois line on literature and art which is against socialism and against Mao
Tse-tung's thought." It was in March 1958 that Mao invited Ch'en to assume
the editorship of *Hung Ch'i,* the new party theoretical journal born in the
midst of the Great Leap fervor. Ch'en's extreme statements in the July 1958
issue of *Hung Ch'i* included the first public mention of the term "people's
commune" and provided proof of his strong commitment to Mao's Great
Leap movement and his radical new collectives:

> In this kind of commune, industry, agriculture and exchange are the
> people's material life; culture and education are the spiritual life of the
> people which affects their material life. The total arming of the people
> is to protect this material and spiritual life. Such arming of the people
> is necessary as long as in the entire world the system of exploitation of
> the people by other people is not decisively destroyed. Mao Tse-tung's
> thoughts on this kind of commune are the conclusions he had derived
> from the experience of real life.

And further,

> If the thought of Mao Tse-tung were not victorious in the struggle a-
> gainst erroneous thought of all kinds, and if the Chinese revolution
> did not march forward under the banner of the thought of Mao Tse-
> tung, then there would be no victory for the present Chinese People's
> revolution.

Ch'en's long-standing commitment to the thought of Mao Tse-tung and his
public commitment of the utopian Great Leap and people's commune movement cannot be doubted.

A less obtrusive member of Mao's Yenan coterie, K'ang Sheng, also stepped
forward from seclusion in intelligence work to voice his public support for

Mao's radical rural collectivization programs during the 1950s. K'ang publicly supported Mao's Yenan-style programs of permanent revolution in direct opposition to the Soviet methods in vogue in China at the time of his statements in 1954; presaging by one year Mao's own endorsement of the "socialist upsurge in the Chinese countryside.":

> Collective farms in the Soviet Union have many machines, but output is low and costs are high. . . . This is the problem that must be solved; how to link the tractor stations to the peasants. . . . If the tractor stations continue to be owned in their present form . . . they will become disguised tax collectors, and will hold the peasants to ransom, as the Soviet tractor stations do.[15]

Later, in March 1958, at the Cheng Tu conference, Mao himself advocated as an integral part of his Great Leap Forward that agricultural mechanization should be carried out through the collectives, themselves, buying the equipment out of their own resources and operating it on their own account.[16] Consequently, later in 1958 when the communes were formed, 78 percent of the existing tractors were given over to them. Thus, we can include K'ang among those who early on committed themselves to Mao's radical rural collectivization in opposition to Soviet bureaucratization methods.

The final male member of Mao's Yenan coterie, Lin Piao, also publicly committed himself to an integral part of Mao's utopian communization program by 1958. At the fifth plenum of the seventh central committee in April 1955, Lin was elected to the politburo after a long period of baffling illness contracted during the guerrilla war era. Lin appeared at the first session of the eighth party congress in September 1956, but he gave no address. It was not until the initiation of Mao's Great Leap that Lin sprang into real public prominence in postliberation China; and then his activities in support of the Leap assumed near manic proportions.

At the second session of the eighth party congress, in May 1958, Lin was elected to the powerful standing committee of the politburo, ascending from twelfth to sixth rank in the party hierarchy with the launching of the Leap and personally leapfrogging his military rival P'eng Teh-huai. In May, the reinvigorated tiger Lin Piao began a round of restless activity in support of Mao's resuscitated Yenan-style programs. On the 23rd, Lin attended a memorial service for Lai Do-yo, former head of the Chinese trade unions; on the 25th he, along with the members of the central committee, performed labor at the Ming Tombs Reservoir construction site, presaging the egalitarian activities of the officers to the ranks campaign of the fall, itself a nostalgic throw back to Yenan mass line practices.

In June, Lin accompanied Mao in receiving youth league members, a national judicial work conference, an educational work conference, a civil affairs conference, and received representatives from industrial plants, agricultural cooperatives and from the People's Liberation Army.[17] He also accompanied Mao in receiving delegates to a national militia conference presaging the gigantic "everyone a soldier" campaign of the fall carried out in close conjunction with the commune movement. In June and July, Lin participated in enlarged meetings of the military affairs committee. Lin was also among those welcoming Khrushchev at Peking airport on the 31st. When Khrushchev departed, after ridiculing Mao's Great Leap and people's communes, Lin Piao was again at the airport after standing by Mao at the signing of his joint communiqué with Khrushchev.[18] How many times in these promotional activities must Lin have publicly committed himself to the radical Great Leap and commune movement derived from the thought of Mao Tse-tung?

One ardent public commitment to the thought of Mao Tse-tung and his military policies had appeared on May 23, 1958 in the form of verbal support on the pages of *Chieh-fang Chün-pao:*

> In the process of the Chinese revolutionary struggle Comrad Mao Tse-tung not only fixed . . . a completely correct political line, but also formulated a completely correct military line. . . . Whenever the Thought of Mao Tse-tung is thoroughly carried out in army organization and warfare, we will have victory; otherwise there will be defeat.

Evidently the People's Liberation Army contained some convinced Maoists among its ranks in the summer of 1958, but the army also contained some soldiers as yet unconvinced.

On June 28, 1958, when Chairman Mao spoke to the group leaders forum at the enlarged conference of the military affairs committee, he received strong support from Lin. In his address, Mao summed up some of the recent successes of the rectification campaign in the military and noted that "from the very beginning, the struggle between two lines of military construction has existed."[19] Mao went on to state that "the purpose of this conference is mainly to destroy slavish ideology, to bury dogmatism, to undertake extensive blooming, through the method of rectification, breaking superstitions, enhancing ideology, and absorbing experiences and lessons." In particular, Mao noted that some "dogmatists advocate copying the Soviet Union, but what is of primary importance is self-help," that the Great Leap Forward "has broken superstitions," and that the PLA must "canvass some of the comrades who have rich working and combat experiences to produce our own book of ordinances."[20] Lin Piao interrupted Mao's talk at least twice in voluntary support of Mao's ideas. After Ch'en-yi interrupted Mao's speech to note that some recently withdrawing Soviet advisors had claimed that they had also learned from their Chinese experience, Mao noted that this showed that "the situation of the Great Leap Forward has not only encouraged the people of China, but in the meantime, it has also heartened our Soviet comrades." Then Lin Piao chimed in to support Mao's ideas even further:

> Politically, our army has a system of its own, such as party leadership, political work, and fine traditions. Our party's level of Marxism-Leninism is a very high one, not to mention the Chairman's. . . . As regards the problem of superstructure and the problem of military science and tactics, we have a system of our own. . . . We don't have to learn from the Soviet Union concerning tactical problems, we may study one half, but not the other half. . . . The half that we need not study includes such things as tactical ideas, because we have Chairman Mao's. We must study technology and sciences and modernized war organization. Nevertheless, we must also use our own mass line methodology to study them.[21]

Mao endorsed Lin's words and went on to mention some Great Leap successes noting that the second five year plan of northeast China might produce tens of thousands of tons of steel. He noted further that with such steel and modernized industry it would be easy to develop a modernized national defense industry and that he (Mao) subscribed to the ideas of producing more light arms to arm the broad masses of militia. To this Lin Piao rejoined, "Militia is very important." Mao, then confidently concluded his speech with a promise of achievements to come: "In the past, others looked down on us mainly because we produced too little grain, steel, and machinery. Now let us do something for them to see."[22]

Thus in the summer of 1958, Lin Piao voluntarily and publicly supported the military thought of Mao Tse-tung, with its mass mobilization techniques, in opposition to imported Soviet professionalism. Whereas, some high ranking officers believed that a soldier's job was solely soldiering, Lin Piao, along with Mao, believed that soldiers should also participate in production work and in mass work and that the masses should participate in the militia. Lin Piao was active in promoting these ideals before the June conference, and in the fall of 1958 he became all the more active in publicly promoting them.[23]

By the summer of 1958, the Chairman of the world's largest Communist party, the 17 million man Chinese Communist party and associated 30 million man Communist Youth League, the editor of the world's largest ideological journal *Red Flag* with its nearly 50 million readers, and the future commander of the world's most populous politico-military apparatus, the 2.5 million man People's Liberation Army and adjunct 220 million man militia were all convinced of the validity of Maoist dialectics and each had made important public commitments to the success of the Maoist Great Leap policies which were predicated upon these dialectics. Behind them stood the shadowy intelligence specialist, K'ang Sheng. Chairman Mao, Ch'en Po-ta, and Lin Piao would form a powerful priesthood in 1959 by controlling part of the party, the prime journal of the propaganda apparatus, and most of the People's Liberation Army.

Mao also had four additional less committed but active supporters of his thought in the 1958 politburo, but two of these were to die in the early sixties and the other two were to equivocate their commitments. The first pair were Lo Jung-huan, a veteran political officer in the PLA, and K'o Ching-shih, Party First Secretary and Mayor of Shanghai. Though both abstained from holding high bureaucratic position during the first five year plan, neither served actively in the Central Party School at Yenan. However, each actively supported Mao's programs in his own realm from the midfifties onward.

On Army Day, August 1, 1955, Lo published an article in *People's Daily* entitled "Continue to Promote the Glorious Tradition of the Chinese PLA," which reasserted the contemporary value of the Yenan tradition concluding that some officers believed "there is now no need for the tradition of unanimity of army men and civilians, and support of government and love of people."[24] This article was a harbinger of the Maoist Great Leap policy of temporarily demoting officers and sending soldiers to production tasks which culminated in the "officers to the ranks" campaign. During the Great Leap in 1958, Lo was an active participant in the important second enlarged conference of the military affairs committee in June and July. There he spoke to the 1,000 assembled cadres and criticized the "backwardness of the army" in political and ideological work, and merged with Lin Piao's views expressed at the conference in criticizing excessive reliance upon "foreign" thought, again stressing the relevance of the PLA's own revolutionary experience.[25] Lo undoubtedly also endorsed the militia concept and Mao's associated "everyone a soldier" campaign of the fall of 1958 which was to induct 220 million persons into the militia. By committing themselves to these Maoist programs in the military, Lin Piao and Lo Jung-huan committed themselves by implication to Mao's proposed "militarization of the peasantry" and to the people's communes of which the militia was an integral part. In Mao's own words,

> the establishment of militia divisions on a large scale is not purely a question of mobilization of manpower, collective action, and fulfillment of production tasks. It is a question of having the masses militarize and collectivize their life.[26]

Indeed, the soldiers were indispensible to Mao's radical collectivization efforts. As Gittings shows, the figures for PLA participation in production work almost exactly paralleled the rise and fall of agricultural collectivization from 1956 through 1961.[27] In many communes, the commune and militia structures were practically indistinguishable and military terms like division, battalion, and company were used by the peasants instead of commune, brigade, and team in their revived "war against nature."[28] With Lo's death Mao was to lose one strong advocate in the military.

K'o Ching-shih gave early support to Mao in another realm of Yenan-style policy, art, and literature. K'o was very active in support of the antirightist campaign of 1957-1958, publishing his views in *People's Daily* on August 27, 1957.[29] The next spring, he made a widely publicized tour of the Yangtse Valley cities, with Mao, himself, inspecting and endorsing the progress of the Great Leap Forward. In June he published an article in the first edition of Ch'en Po-ta's *Red Flag* supporting Mao's Yenan views by asserting that "the laboring people must make themselves master of culture." Despite the fact that K'o was to die in the early sixties, his legacy was that his city of Shanghai became a center of radicalism.

Some politburo members were ambivalent in their commitment to Mao's thought. T'an Chen-lin was ambivalent in his advocacy of Mao's agricultural policies. He had not participated in the Yenan rectification campaign, and he did become Deputy Secretary of the secretariat in September 1956; but the following year he became the top agricultural spokesman for the party, publishing his views in *People's Daily* on May 5. He endorsed Mao's twelve year plan for agriculture of the previous year with its advocacy of mass mobilization over material incentives and its recommendation of decentralized "mass line" control. In May 1958, at the second session of the eight party congress, T'an gave the key address on agriculture, and at a national work conference of advanced agricultural workers in December, he was first listed on the presidium membership. Though he consistently urged the rural masses onto greater agricultural output in true Maoist spirit, he showed some important trepidations of his own.[30] Rather than working with the basic-level peasants, he is said to have issued commands blindly and "fanned up the wind of pompous prolixity," lashing the masses to impossible achievement while ignoring the local realities.[31]

There were also those who would go slow to utopia. Despite the myth of being a monolith which the party leadership had been able to maintain during the fifties and early sixties, there have now emerged increasing amounts of evidence regarding policy splits in the monolith dating back to the midfifties. The issue complex dividing the two factions under the facade of unity, centers on the Maoist mobilization model of development with its advocacy of rapid agricultural collectivization and its rejection of the Soviet technical-bureaucratic model of development with its associated professionalism. A number of high-ranking party leaders stood on the other side of this complex. The most prominent along them were Liu Shao-ch'i, Teng Hsiao-p'ing,

P'eng Teh-huai, Chang Wen-t'ien, Ch'en Yun, P'eng Chen, Po Yi-po, and Li Ching-ch'uan. These were all functionaries who evidently harbored reservations against the Maoist Great Leap model *before* it failed and who became increasingly non-Maoist following the failure and during recovery. It is important to note that most of these opponents of Maoist policy were bureaucrats or professionalists. Teng Hsiao-p'ing was head of the party bureaucracy, the secretariat, and P'eng Teh-huai was head of the military bureaucracy prior to 1959; P'eng Chen was Second Secretary of the secretariat, Ch'en Yun served as Minister of Commerce and presided over economic planning during the first five year plan, which followed the Soviet model of technical bureaucratization, and Po Yi-po served as Minister of Finance until late 1953 and as a relatively conservative economic commission head thereafter. In view of Mao's proposal to downgrade the majority of bureaucrats in his decentralization with the Leap, their trepidations are not difficult to understand.

Another characteristic which set off the opponents of the Leap, was their lack of deep positive involvement in Mao's Yenan rectification movement. With the sole exception of P'eng Chen, none of these party stalwarts had served in the Central Party School and involved himself in the creative construction and dissemination of the thought of Mao Tse-tung. Figure 3.1 summarizes the individual politburo members' personal commitments to Mao's Great Leap, by summating four ideologically related behaviors: spreading Mao's thought at Yenan, abstaining from holding bureaucratic position during the first five year plan, actively supporting Mao's Great Leap, and not opposing it through 1958. The resulting figure yields a fairly accurate picture of the distribution of commitment to Mao's Great Leap in the politburo in 1958 given currently available data (see Appendix A). The figure represents an approximately normal distribution running from Mao and the Maoists on the left to Ch'en Yun and the conservatives on the right, with the bulk of the membership bunched in the middle.[3 2]

The middle is largely filled with the eleven politburo members who were not very active in the early stages of radical agricultural collectivization, neither supporting the Leap wholeheartedly nor opposing it with vigor. For the most part they fell in line with the more radical forces led by Mao, but the fact that three-fourths of them were bureaucrats set definite limits to the committing nature of this compliance in Mao's mass mobilization.

Most prominent of those who offered some opposition to Mao's Leap was his informally designated successor Liu Shao-ch'i. Despite the fact that at the second session of the national party congress in May 1958, Liu Shao-ch'i delivered a speech which had been taken by some Western observers as a kick off speech for the Great Leap Forward, the speech is more accurately described as an effort to curtail and normalize the Great Leap extravagancies

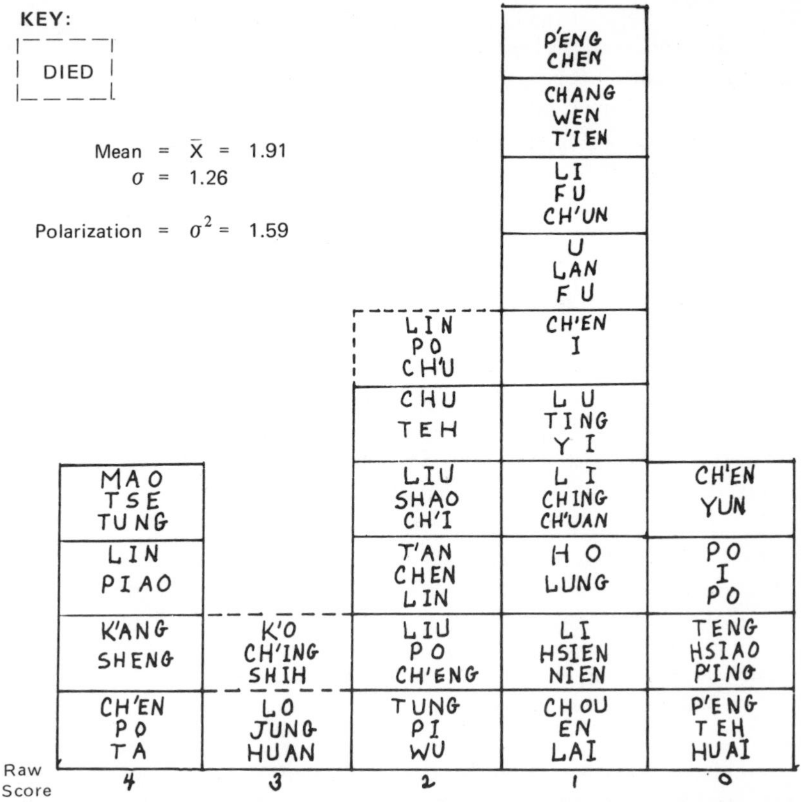

KEY:

```
┌ ─ ─ ─ ┐
│ DIED  │
└ ─ ─ ─ ┘
```

Mean $= \bar{X} =$ 1.91

$\sigma =$ 1.26

Polarization $= \sigma^2 =$ 1.59

Raw Score 4	3	2	1	0
				P'ENG CHEN
				CHANG WEN T'IEN
				LI FU CH'UN
				U LAN FU
		LIN PO CHU	CH'EN I	
		CHU TEH	LU TING YI	
MAO TSE TUNG		LIU SHAO CH'I	LI CHING CH'UAN	CH'EN YUN
LIN PIAO		T'AN CHEN LIN	HO LUNG	PO I PO
K'ANG SHENG	K'O CH'ING SHIH	LIU PO CH'ENG	LI HSIEN NIEN	TENG HSIAO P'ING
CH'EN PO TA	LO JUNG HUAN	TUNG PI WU	CHOU EN LAI	P'ENG TEH HUAI

Figure 3.1: DISTRIBUTION OF COMMITMENT TO MAO'S THOUGHT IN THE POLITBURO, 1958

of May and the preceding four months. In speaking of the leadership for the Great Leap Forward, Liu cautioned as follows:

> Leaders must combine revolutionary enthusiasm with businesslike sense. They must be able not only to put forward advanced targets but also to adopt effective measures in time to ensure the realization of the targets. *They must not indulge in empty talk and bluff.* The targets we put forward should be those which can be reached by hard work. Do not lightly publicize that which is not really obtainable lest failure dampen the enthusiasm of the masses and delight the conservatives.[33]

Three years earlier, Liu had also displayed a desire to go slow with collectivization.[34] Early in 1956, the Chinese leadership was jubilant regarding the

successes for their first five year plan and were calling for its fulfillment one
year ahead of schedule. In this atmosphere, Mao held a conference, in July
of 1955, of secretaries of provincial and municipal party committees. At this
conference Mao criticized certain comrades "who were tottering along like
a woman with bound feet," always complaining that "others are going too
fast." Mao urged a stepping up of the agricultural collectivization movement
in the countryside.[35] Evidently this "woman with bound feet" was none
other than Liu Shao-ch'i. If Liu was opposed to radical agricultural collectivization and took public stands on this matter, then certainly Liu must have
been predisposed to be very skeptical of the ultimate in agricultural collectivization, the establishment of people's communes in the Great Leap Forward
of 1958. Additional evidence of Liu's early opposition to collectivization is
provided by "The Confession of Liu Shao Ch'i."[36] Therein Liu is quoted
as follows:

> In July 1951, I wrongly criticized the decision of the Shansi Party
> Provincial Committee to develop the mutual aid teams in a higher
> stage in the old bases by forming agricultural producers cooperatives.

> In 1955, Comrade Teng Tzu-hui [Director of the Rural Work Depart-
> ment at the time] proposed the retrenchment and dissolution of
> 200,000 agricultural producers' cooperatives. The central conferences,
> over which I presided, made no refutation of this proposal, and virtu-
> ally approved his plan. Later, Teng Tzu-hui retrenched and dissolved
> 200,000 cooperatives at a central rural work conference.

As another instance of pre-Great Leap opposition to the thought of Mao
Tse-tung, Liu is reported to have made the following statement to a group
of foreign visitors on July 13, 1956:

> In our country the big-scale class struggle is over now. Capitalists, land-
> lords, and rich peasants are stepping into socialism. It is very difficult
> for them to do anything destructive because people are watching them
> everywhere.[37]

Clearly, this statement is a direct contradiction of the Maoist proposition of
continuation of class struggle under socialism.

Liu also fell out of line with Mao's "One Hundred Flowers" policy when
"tens of thousands of persons went out on the street to oppose the people's
government."[38] From later Red Guard newspapers we also have claims that
Liu Shao-ch'i's performance during this period was somewhat lax and something less than admirable when viewed from the Maoist perspective.[39] Quoting Liu's speeches to local party organizations between March and May of

1957, the Red Guard newspaper accused Liu of having, (1) denied the existence of antagonistic contradictions in socialist society; (2) favored material incentives instead of "politics takes command"; (3) preferred flexible to inflexible economic planning; (4) advocated a limited free market in order to compete with state enterprise; (5) supported urban workers' livelihood at a higher level than that of rural peasants; (6) defended the constitutional rights of peasants to withdraw from agricultural cooperatives, of the workers to strike, and of the students to stage demonstrations. All of these charges may be seen as attacks upon the "capitalist" road. Clearly, Liu Shao-ch'i was not a strongly committed Maoist prior to the Great Leap failure.

Seven months after his second session speech, at the sixth plenum held at Wuhan between November 28 and December 10, 1958, Liu advocated a number of measures to curtail the Great Leap extravagances of the preceding summer, all of which were opposed by Mao.[40] The first of these measures was the "Tidying up the Communes" campaign. This campaign cautioned cadres and workers to be humble, prudent, careful, truthful and avoid boastful practices. It entreated them to concentrate on production and realism. The people's commune was not to be taken as a communistic enterprise, but a socialistic one, with individual rewards proportionate to individual labor; some vestiges of private property were to remain with the individual workers; mess halls were to be decentralized to production team management; and all workers were to be guaranteed eight hours for sleep and four hours for meals. The campaign was immediately implemented and served to renormalize life in the countryside. The second of these regressive measures, decided upon at Wuhan, went under the slogan announced in the *People's Daily* editorial of February 24, 1959, to "Take the Whole Country as a Coordinated Chess Game." It applied mostly to industry, and initiated a trend toward recentralized national administrative control of manufacturing and trade. Mao's guerrilla notion of making each locality economically autonomous, had caused many crucial supply shortages in an economy in which locales were growing increasingly interdependent as the industrial division of labor and commerce grew. The supply network needed higher level coordination, and this was not supplied by Mao's grandiose general design. Whereas the commune decision had come down under Mao's name; the Wuhan revisions came under Liu's—the man who gave the major address on agricultural policy at that time. Indeed, on October 24, 1966 Mao announced publicly that he had been opposed to the decisions at the Wuhan Plenum; and it was also revealed that in April 1959, Mao had sent a "letter of instructions" to party committees in an attempt to counter the Wuhan resolutions. So stood the rift between Mao and Liu at the peak of the Great Leap Forward.

Liu was not alone in his lack of commitment to Mao's thoughts leading to the Leap. In October of 1967, Wen Hui Pao of Shanghai revealed the name

and deeds of "the other top person" in authority taking the capitalist road.[41]
The article asserts that in 1956, Teng Hsiao-p'ing approved of Krushchev's
denunciation of Stalin and the personality cult and emphasized the importance of collective leadership in a socialist country. Teng was accused of
collusion with Liu to detract from Mao's personal leadership and both men
were castigated for their joint attempt in the wake of the Great Leap fiasco
to dismantle the communes and rebuild China's agricultural economy along
nonsocialist lines. Teng's Deputy Secretary in the Secretariat, P'eng Chen,
also afforded some opposition to Mao's leap. In particular, in 1957 he opposed the use of certain agricultural techniques endorsed by Mao as condu-
cive to the socialist upsurge in the countryside.[42]

To this pair of leading opponents of Mao's policies we may add the name
of Ch'en Yun, the former Minister of Commerce, who opposed the new line
of Mao Tse-tung emerging in 1957 and leading to the Great Leap. In 1958,
Ch'en Yun was dropped from effective power in the politburo after a long
career as a major economic planner. In his concluding remarks to the eighth
party congress in 1956, Ch'en had said, "We must be prudent and practical,
go forward slowly, gather experience, push ahead gradually."[43] It is clear
that Ch'en advocated an economic strategy opposed to the grandiose Great
Leap of Mao Tse-tung. Yet another economist, Po Yi-po, offered opposition
to the leap. Former Minister of Finance and head of the State Economic
Commission since 1956, the conservative Po stressed the necessity of China's
accumulating capital resources but bridled at some of Mao's ambitious agricultural designs.[44] Away from the center of economic power in luxuriant
Szechuan, the provincial party chief Li Ching-ch'uan, also remained conservative.[45]

The final leading pair of opponents of Mao's leap came from the military,
P'eng Teh-huai, former defense minister and his associate Chang Wen-t'ien. At
the Lushan plenum on July 14, 1959, P'eng publicly stated his position on
the Great Leap in the form of a letter to Chairman Mao:

> The letter vehemently attacked and smeared the Party's general line,
> the Great Leap Forward, and the People's Communes. He slandered
> as an "exaggerated trend" the vigorous campaign launched by hundreds
> of millions of people to build socialism under the guidance of Mao Tse-
> tung's thought, claiming that "the gains could not compensate for the
> losses." He flung mud at the people's communes, saying that they were
> "set up too early" and were a "mess."

> He vilified as "petty bourgeoise fanaticism" the mass movement and
> the revolutionary energy and zeal of the people, and viciously attacked
> our great leader, Chairman Mao. His purpose in making such a hue and
> cry was to do away with all revolutionary mass movements, sap the

revolutionary enthusiasm of the masses and obstruct the advance of the socialist revolution and socialist construction. . . .

As far back as the 7th congress of the Party [Yenan, April-June 1945] P'eng Teh-huai openly opposed the laying down in the Party constitution of Mao Tse-tung's thought as the guiding thought of the Party. At and after the 12th Congress of the Communist Party of the Soviet Union, Krushchev stirred up an adverse current to oppose Stalin's so-called "cult of the individual." Trailing closely behind Krushchev, P'eng Teh-huai strove to impair Chairman Mao's immensely high prestige.[46]

The Regulations of Committees of the Chinese Communist Party in the Army [draft], prepared in 1953, originally included the following article: "The Party Committees take Mao Tse-tung's Thought—which combines Marxist-Leninist theory with the practice of the Chinese revolution—as the guiding principle of their entire work. This article constitutes the core of the entire draft regulations but P'eng Teh-huai had it cut out when he revised the draft. This clearly exposed his opposition to Mao Tse-tung's thought and the Party's absolute leadership in the Army."

Using the pretext of regularization and modernization P'eng ferociously opposed giving prominence to proletarian politics. He negated the historical experience and fine tradition of our Army, concentrated on regularizing it according to the bourgeois pattern, and rejected proletarian revolutionization. He placed military technique in the first place, and denied that political ideological work is the primary factor in building up our army's combat strength. He attempted to abrogate the absolute leadership of the Party in the army and the system of collective leadership in the party committee, and to push through the "system of one-man leadership," clamoring that this should be the "orientation in army building." He tried to abrogate political work in the army, the democratic system and the mass line and damage the principle of unity between officers and men, between superiors and subordinates. . . .

But under the pretext that the situation had changed (since the liberation) and the militia system was now out of date, P'eng tried to abolish the nation-wide militia system and negate the principle of people's war.[47]

P'eng was purged at the Plenum.

Commitment Among the Middle-Level Cadres

The middle levels of leadership in Communist China consist of those cadres who staff the party, government, and military hierarchies between the upper reaches of the politburo and central committee of the party and the basic economic production units of the society, such as agricultural collectives, industrial factories, and financial enterprises. In any bureaucratic hierarchy there exists a large number of persons who are seeking to advance their positions in the hierarchy. In all such hierarchies there are two basic avenues to mobility. First of all, one can advance one's position by demonstrations of skill or expertise in one's areas of competence, thereby contributing more to the overall productivity or manpower efficiency of the unit. Second, one can advance one's position by demonstrations of loyalty to one's superiors, thereby contributing to the maintenance of the integrity or solidarity of the unit. Chinese bureaucracies are no exceptions to these rules. These bureaucracies are staffed with personnel some of whom owe their positions mainly to their expertise and some of whom owe their positions mainly to their demonstrations of loyalty. The latter virtue is broadly termed "progressiveness" or "redness" in contemporary China. Progressiveness is demonstrated by active participation in political campaigns, by high knowledgeability in the ideology of Marxism-Leninism and the thought of Mao Tse-tung, by being ready to criticize the backwardness of one's colleagues in struggle meetings, and in general by being spontaneously and actively political—it consists, then, of the demonstration of loyalty to the political center.

Expertise is demonstrated by the display of good performance in schooling, the exhibition of competence and skill at one's work, and in general by technical knowledgeability in some special field. The fact that there is a trade-off between these virtues among Chinese bureaucrats is demonstrated by the constant allusion to the "red/expert" controversy in the Chinese press.[48] The convinced and committed Maoists are more likely to be found among those middle-level cadres, such as retired military officers in government positions, who owe their positions to their progressiveness.[49] They are the least likely to be found among those middle-level cadres who owe their positions primarily to their technical expertise, such as financial affairs personnel, industrial engineering personnel, etc. The two types of bureaucrats are in competition for the same set of offices; and each of the two types is committed by training or past experience to one of the two virtues. What appears to be a just promotion for one set will undoubtedly be seen as unjust by the other set. Thus among the middle-level cadres, the Maoists are most likely to be found among the unskilled progressives, such as political commissars, and least likely to be found among the technical experts, such as financial administrators. Furthermore, there is likely to be animosity stemming from the experts and directed toward the progressives and their Maoist ideology.

This red/expert bifurcation in the bureaucracy is further buttressed by the fact that the experts, those with extensive education and skills are far more likely to have come from families of considerable economic means which could support the expenses of their education. Hence the experts are least likely to have come from a "proletarian" background and to have economically benefited, relatively speaking, from the revolution.

The nonred experts have further reasons for animosity toward the Maoists and Maoism. During his Great Leap Forward campaign, between 1957 and February of 1958, 1.3 million urban cadres were sent down to engage in labor in the villages. This move was in keeping with the general Maoist maxim of government decentralization and the sending of cadres down to lower levels *(kan-pu hsia fang)* to establish close contact with the masses. To a true progressive, such an assignment might be acceptable; to a careerist bureaucrat, it is the nadir of humiliation.

Commitment Among the Masses

Those persons who are not cadres in China are masses. Two descriptors are particularly relevant when examining the question of conviction among the masses, age and social class. In any nation and in any ideology the young are more likely to become converts and zealots. This is especially true during the period of adolescence. There are many reasons for this phenomenon. The youths are less likely to be shackled by lifetime commitments, such as occupational choice and property possession. Indeed, an ideology which provides a basic statement of relatively consistent values is likely to be useful to the young in the period of uncertainty when they must be able to predict the long course of their society to select a suitable role for themselves within it for the succeeding decades. Furthermore, youth is less likely to have gained the life experiences which provide contradictions to ideology. The utility of ideology for youth is even greater in a nation like China, whose people by 1958 had undergone half a century of civil war, strife, and massive social change. For the Chinese youth of 1958, the council of the elders had lost its relevance to the era; the blueprint of red ideology was more appealing.

Furthermore, a Chinese youth of sixteen or younger at the onset of the Great Leap had received his entire schooling under the Communist regime and was therefore well indoctrinated with the ideology of the newborn Communist nation and the glories of the Maoist-led revolution. Thus, for a number of reasons those persons who were sixteen or under at the time of the Great Leap Forward were more likely to be convinced Maoists.

A second major determinant of ideological conviction among the masses is social class. Certainly, China's "proletarians" are more likely to be convinced Maoists than China's bourgeoisie. The revolution was waged for the sake of the proletariat. Relative to the bourgeoisie, the proletariat gained more materially from the revolution; and in terms of ideological pronouncements, the proletariat is the wave of the future. In accord with Chinese, if not Marxist, practice, we term the workers and peasants the *"proletarians."* The residual occupations of clerks, merchants, officials, housewives, professionals, students in higher education, unemployed, and others, we shall term *"bourgeois."* Within the proletariat, the poor peasants stood to gain more in terms of shared producer's goods and products from the formation of communes than the rich peasants; the manual workers stood to gain more from the equalization of wages than the skilled workers. In general, the unskilled had more to gain than the skilled, the lowly rewarded more to gain than the highly rewarded, the discontented more than the secure.

By way of summary then, the convinced and committed Maoists at the time of 1958 are most likely to be found among the following sets: In the top political leadership among the set whose members had publicly and unequivocally committed themselves to the Maoist Great Leap doctrine; at the middle levels of leadership among those who held their positions by virtue of their progressiveness rather than for their technical skill; at the lower levels, among the youth and among the proletarians. From these sets of relatively committed individuals to extract those who were both convinced of the truth of Maoism and aware of the dependency between it and the Great Leap Forward and the commune prophecy, we must adduce an additional criterion. The individual requires a certain degree of intellectual if not ideological sophistication to be an ideologue. It is unlikely that a poor peasant's profession of Maoism stems from anything more than loyalty to a charismatic leader; it is quite unlikely that all middle-range officials are adept in Maoist dialectics. These are not Maoist ideologues, but possible Maoist sympathizers. Certainly, there were truly convinced and committed Maoists to be found in the politburo, at middle ranges of the government and military hierarchies among the progressive cadres and commissars, and within the masses among the relatively sophisticated and schooled youth at the time. Herein lies the intersection of conviction and commitment at the time of the Great Leap Forward; and these are the persons who should have experienced a sharp dissonance when faced with the disconfirmations wrought by the Great Leap debacles. The most conspicuous reactions were to come from Mao himself and the highly committed members of his politburo.

NOTES

1. Quoted in Stuart Schram, *The Political Thought of Mao Tse-tung.* New York: Praeger, 1969, revised edition, p. 349.

2. Mao Tse-tung, "Sixty work methods" (draft, 2/19/58), *CB,* No. 892, p. 11. These papers represent Mao's own summary of work on the Great Leap over the years and

especially the work of the central committee conferences in January 1958 at Hangchow and Nanning.

3. Ibid., p. 13.

4. *JMJP,* August 13, 1958, as cited in Schram, op. cit., p. 350.

5. *Miscellany of Mao Tse-tung Thought (1949-1968).* Washington, D.C.: Joint Publications Research Service, No. 61269, February 20, 1974, p. 132. (Hereafter *MISC.*)

6. Ibid., p. 134.

7. Wu Chih-pu, "From agricultural producers' cooperatives to people's communes," *HC,* No. 8, September 16, 1958, as cited in Jan S. Prybyla, *The Political Economy of Communist China.* Scranton: International Textbook Co., 1970, p. 285.

8. See Appendix for a complete analysis of the positions of each member of the 1956-1958 politburo on these and subsequent issues related to Mao's thought.

9. Stuart Schram, *Mao Tse-tung.* New York: Simon & Schuster, 1966, pp. 194-195; see also Mao Tse-tung, *Tactics.* New York: Praeger, 1966.

10. For a broad treatment of Maoist guerrilla tactics as employed in political campaigns, see Paul J. Hiniker, "Political communications in Communist China: The mobilization of social support, 1966-1970," paper delivered at the Joint Social Science Research Council, American Council of Learned Societies, *Conference on Government in China: The Management of a Revolutionary Society,* Cuernavaca, Mexico, August 18-23, 1969. For a specific instance of the application of the third tactic to the Socialist Education Campaign in 1965, see the analysis of the twenty-three articles in Chapter 9.

11. Thomas W. Robinson, *Lin Piao, Part I, 1907-1949,* Rand Monograph. Santa Monica: Rand R-526-PR, August 1970, pp. 32-47.

12. For additional background on the Yenan era, see Boyd Compton, *Mao's China: Party Reform Documents, 1942-1944.* Seattle: University of Washington Press, 1952, esp. Introduction, and pp. 1-8. See also "K'ang Sheng," *Issues and Studies.* Taipei: Institute of International Relations. (Hereafter *IAS.*) March 1970, pp. 99-103; and "Lin Piao," *Current Scene,* Hong Kong: American Consulate, Vol. VII, No. 5, March 18, 1965. See especially John W. Lewis, "Leader, commissar, and bureaucrat: The Chinese political system in the last days of the revolution," in Ping-ti Ho and Tang Tsou, eds., *China in Crisis.* Chicago: University of Chicago Press, 1968, for a provocative analysis of the differential roles of Mao and Lin at Yenan as mass leader and elitist bureaucrat respectively. (Hereafter *Current Scene* is *CS.*)

13. See Richard K. Diao, "The impact of the Cultural Revolution on China's economic elite," *China Quarterly,* No. 42, April-June 1970, p. 91. (Hereafter *CQ.*) Mao Tse-tung, "Speech at the supreme state conference" (January 28, 1958), *CLG,* Vol. I, No. 4, Winter 1968-1969, pp. 10-14.

14. *IAS,* April 1970, p. 51.

15. Jack Gray, "The economics of Maoism," *Bulletin of the Atomic Scientist,* Vol. XXV, No. 2, February 1969, p. 45.

16. Ibid.

17. See *New China News Agency,* Peking, May 23, 25, June 6, 11, 17, 1958, as cited in Thomas Robinson, *Lin Piao: A Political Biography,* forthcoming, p. 26. I am grateful to Professor Robinson for supplying me with these materials. (Hereafter *NCNA.*)

18. Ibid.

19. See "Speech at the group leaders forum of the enlarged conference of the military affairs commission" (Excerpts, June 28, 1958), *CLG,* Vol. I, No. 4, Winter 1968-1969, pp. 15-21.

20. Ibid., p. 80.

21. Ibid., p. 80.

22. Ibid., p. 80.

23. For more detailed discussion of Lin Piao's military activities prior to 1959, see John Gittings, *The Role of the Chinese Army*. London: Oxford University Press, 1967, pp. 287-288. Gittings points out that

> It used to be believed that after 1954 Ho Lung, Lin Piao, and Nieh Jung-chen had been quietly pensioned upstairs, and that Lo Jung-huan, who resigned as political director in December 1956, and Liu Po-ch'eng, who also resigned as training director in November 1957, followed the same path. This was seen as the culmination of a consistent effort by Mao to strip his military hierarchy of actual power. It is still arguable that they only resumed control of military affairs after P'eng's dismissal and the collapse of army morale in 1959, and that Lin Piao himself was in retirement until he replaced P'eng. However, all of these leaders except Hsu Hsiang-chien addressed the second Enlarged Conference of the Military Affairs Committee attended by more than 1,000 cadres in summer 1958, which suggests at least that they were still directly concerned with military matters, and probably Military Affairs Committee members. In view of their continuity of control since the early 1930s it seems improbable that it was allowed to lapse to any significant extent during the years 1954-58.

24. Ibid., p. 189.

25. Ibid., p. 285.

26. Quoted in "Report by Teng K'o-ning to Kiangsi's militia work conference" (December 1959), *SCMP*, 2196, as cited in John Gittings, op. cit., p. 212.

27. Gittings, op. cit., p. 182.

28. Ezra Vogel, *Canton Under Communism*. Cambridge, Mass.: Harvard University Press, 1969, p. 247.

29. Donald W. Klein and Ann B. Clark, *Biographic Dictionary of Chinese Communism*. Cambridge, Mass.: Harvard University Press, 1971.

30. Chinese Institute of Agricultural Mechanization, "An outline of the struggle between the two lines on the front of agricultural mechanization," *Agricultural Machinery & Technique*, (Peking), No. 9, 9/8/68, in *Union Research Service*, Vol. 53, Nos. 5-6, 10/15-18, 1968, pp. 50-76, and Nos. 7-8, 10/22-25, 1968, pp. 77-99, esp. pp. 70-71. (Hereafter *URS.*)

31. Ibid., pp. 70-71.

32. In his speech before the Cheng-tu conference on March 22, 1958, Mao himself noted that there was longstanding opposition to his radical collectivization plans and that the distribution of opinion in the party leadership over this issue was approximately normal with most members in the middle:

> In 1956 some things got blown away—the movement to achieve greater, faster, better, and more economical results, the promoters progress, and the 40 articles. There were those three different reactions: regret, indifference, and joy.... Those showing the middle reaction were in the majority while those showing the first and third extremes were in minority. These three reactions applied to many things in 1956. The views concerning resisting Japan and Chiang and the land reform were relatively unanimous, but they varied on the cooperativization issue. Is this assessment accurate? The meeting this time has solved a host of problems. attained agreement, and resulted in documents for the politburo; but there was lack of ideological discussion. Should two or three more days be devoted to the ideological discussion and to expression of what is on our minds?

> See *Joint Publication Research Service*, Washington, D.C., No. 90, pp. 51-52. (Hereafter *JPRS.*)

The powerful subgroup of the politburo, the standing committee was also divided over this issue. In late 1958, the politburo of the 190-man central committee contained

19 full members and 6 alternate members. The powerful standing committee of the politburo contained 7 members. Of these the evidence indicates that Mao Tse-tung and Lin Piao were staunch ideologues favoring the Great Leap Forward. Liu Shao-ch'i, Teng Hsiao-p'ing, and Ch'en Yun evidently harbored reservations against the radical Great Leap policy. Chu Teh was relatively inactive in politics and Chou En-lai, premier of the state council, remained true to character by maintaining the ambiguity of his position.

33. From *Communist China 1955-1959: Policy Documents with Analysis.* Cambridge, Mass.: Harvard University Press, 1962, p. 436, as quoted in Vogel, op. cit., p. 242.

34. See Chin Szu-k'ai, *The Party in Communist China: 1956.* Hong Kong: Union Research Institute, 1957.

35. See Hsiao Tu, "Contention for power inside the CCP," (Supplement), Union Research Service, Vol. 5, No. 3, October-December 1956. See also Stuart Schram, *The Political Thought of Mao Tse-tung.* New York: Praeger, 1969, revised edition, pp. 343-344.

36. *Atlas,* April 1967, pp. 12-17, as translated from the *Mainichi Shimbuh,* Tokyo.

37. See the Shanghai Red Guard periodical, *The Rural Youth,* No. 9, May 10, 1967. See also *CB,* No. 412, September 1956, pp. 9-15, for Liu's advocation of gradual or "step by step" collectivization of agriculture.

38. A good summary of these activities is to be found in Gene T. Hsiao, "The background and development of the Proletarian Cultural Revolution," *Asian Survey,* Vol. VII, No. 6, June 1967, pp. 389-404.

39. See "The real rightist face of China's no. 1 counter-revolutionary revisionist Liu Shao-chi in the 1957 anti-rightist struggle," *Tung-fang-hung* (The East is Red), Peking, January 4, 1967, pp. 2, 4.

40. See Ezra Vogel, op. cit., pp 257-260.

41. New York *Times,* October 31, 1967. (Hereafter *NYT.*)

42. Chinese Institute of Agricultural Mechanization, in *URS,* op. cit., p. 57.

43. Franz Schurmann, *Ideology and Organization in Communist China.* Berkeley: University of California Press, 1968, pp. 144, 196-210. Also, see *Jen Min Shou T'se,* 1957, p. 88.

44. *URS,* op. cit., p. 57.

45. Ibid., p. 73.

46. See *NCNA,* Peking, August 19, 20, 1967. For the text of this letter, see P'eng Teh-huai's so-called "Letter of Opinion" to Chairman Mao, at the 1959 Lushan conference in "Exchange of revolutionary experience" (August 24, 1967), in *SCMP,* No. 4032, pp. 1-5.

47. Ibid. See also "The origin of machine guns and mortars, etc." (August 15, 1959), *CLG,* Vol. I, No. 4, Winter 1968-1969, p. 73 and pp. 45-46.

48. A similar "red/expert" dilemma was notable in studies of the Soviet military bureaucracy in the thirties and forties. See Ithiel de Sola Pool, et al., *Satelite Generals: A Study of Military Elites in the Soviet Sphere.* Hoover Institute Studies: Series B, Elites, No. 5, April 1955, pp. 1-27. See also Schurmann, op. cit., passim.

49. See John P. Emerson, "Employment in Mainland China," in Joint Economic Commission of the U.S. Congress, *An Economic Profile of Mainland China.* New York: Praeger, 1968, p. 432. Emerson notes that the retired military is an important factor in the Chinese countryside. Of the seven million PLA soldiers demobilized by 1957, fully five million were dispatched to agriculture. Many of these served as basic-level cadres during collectivization. (Hereafter *JEC.*) See also *JMJP,* February 24, 1958.

Chapter 4

GREAT LEAPS BACKWARD

We have noted in a preceding chapter how the Great Leap Forward movement provided an empirical test of the validity of the thought of Mao Tse-tung for the achievement of socialism and eventual communism in China. At that point we noted a number of objective indices that would denote progress or retrogression regarding the target of a Communist society and bear directly on Mao's prophecy. These were symbolized by the Maoist Three Red Banners of (1) the people's communes; (2) the Great Leap Forward in steel production; and (3) the general line of socialist construction, especially with regard to overtaking England in industrial production. Judged by each of these objective indicators, the movement failed abysmally.

Great Leap Debacles

The first signs of disconfirmation of the Great Leap towards communism came in the form of a vehement attack on Mao and his Three Red Banners from top party leader, P'eng Teh-huai at the Lushan plenum in August of 1959. P'eng's was an all out onslaught on the Great Leap movement and the thought of Mao Tse-tung. P'eng's onslaught was more than a criticism of the thought of Mao; it was a prophecy of failure. Clearly, when a political head of state is openly attacked by one of his long-standing chief lieutenants, there is cause for a reexamination of policies. However, the reaction of the ideologue Mao was not to moderate his policies. Mao's immediate reaction was to transcend the criticism and raise the disagreement from the level of particular policy planning for the immediate future to the level of "the life and death struggle between the two major antagonistic classes—the bourgeoisie and the proletariat. . . ." P'eng was branded a bourgeois, and criticizing the proletarian line was seen to confirm rather than disconfirm the Maoist ideology. In particular P'eng's action confirmed the Maoist precept on the continuation of the class struggle beyond the socialization of the modes of production. The next step Mao took was to begin proselyting in the army, P'eng's original fiefdom. Lin Piao assumed leadership of P'eng's ministry and immediately reorganized the apparatus to proselyte for Maoist precepts. Attacked by the leader of the army, Mao sought social support from the rank and file of the troops.

Material signs of disconfirmation came upon the heels of P'eng's onslaught. The first Red Banner to bite the dust was the agricultural people's communes; the next banners to be defiled were the Great Leap and the general line in the industrial struggle. The people's communes which were to bring about a great increase in agricultural productivity by unleashing the energy of the masses in more communistic modes of production, resulted in near famine conditions in China by 1961. As shown in Figure 4.1 grain production, which was at 185 million metric tons in 1957 before the establishment of communes, fell steadily to 168 million metric tons in 1959 after a high of 190 million metric tons in 1958, to a postliberation low of 160 million metric tons in 1960. The post-1958 decline in grain production was directly contrary to Mao's explicit personal predictions of great increases for 1959, 1960, and the following years. Famine edema and other signs of malnutrition were rampant in China in this year—and poor weather did not offer a sufficient explanation to famished peasants or squeezed cadres for successive years of poor harvests. Caloric intake was estimated to average 560 calories below the minimum requirement of 2,300.[1] In 1961, for the first time since the liberation, China became a net importer of foodstuffs.[2]

By 1960, the pride of socialist agriculture, the people's communes were in the process of being dismantled. The level of accounting and control in the commune dropped from the 5,000 family commune in 1958 to the 150 family production brigade in the autumn of 1959 to the 30 family production team in the autumn of 1960 and has remained there since. Agricultural collectivization, which had taken place gradually and successfully through the 300 family agricultural producers cooperatives by 1957, first zoomed in 1958 and then rapidly nosedived. By 1963, the remnants of what in December of 1958 were 26,000 robust people's communes, now existed in the skeletal form of 74,000 "people's communes" diminished in size, emasculated in control.[3] In 1961 and 1962, the slogan on the tongues of the cadres

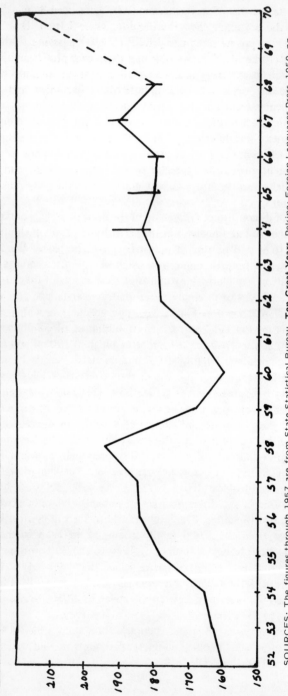

SOURCES: The figures through 1957 are from State Statistical Bureau, **Ten Great Years.** Peking: Foreign Languages Press, 1959, pp. 119-120. Figures for 1957-1965 are from Joint Economic Commission of the U.S. Congress, **An Economic Profile of Mainland China.** New York: Praeger Special Studies, 1968, p. 70 in chapter by T. C. Liu. Figures for 1966-1968 adapted from Werner Klatt in **China Quarterly,** No. 35, (Summer 1968), p. 47. The figure for 1970 is from Arthur Ashbrook in J.E.C. **People's Republic of China: An Economic Assessment.** Washington, D.C.: Government Printing Office, 1972, p. 5. Verticle bars represent a range of estimates. Premier Chou En-lai has reported the 1970 and 1971 figures at 240 and 246 million metric tons respectively. See **China Quarterly,** No. 50, (Spring 1972), pp. 375-376.

Figure 4.1: GRAIN PRODUCTION IN MILLIONS OF METRIC TONS, 1952-1970

was on one side the socialist *(San Mien Hung Chi)* "Three Red Banners" and on the other side the pragmatic *(San Tzu Yi Pao)* "Three Self and One Guarantee." That is to say, private plots and private pork for peasants, free markets for trade, enterprises held responsible for their own profits and losses and the practice of contracting production to private households which guaranteed to produce a specified amount for the government and were allowed to keep whatever surplus they could accumulate. Clearly these practices are a retrogression from the socialist to the capitalist style of economy. It is just these practices which were labeled as instances of "capitalism" in China's countryside. Peasants I have interviewed attributed them to none other than the leading person in authority taking the capitalist road, Liu Shao-ch'i. However, it was with precisely these "capitalistic" practices that the Chinese economy was rebuilt from the ashes of the Great Leap fiasco.

The fate of industry was not far behind. The practice of "politics takes command," of party in leadership over managers in industry, resulted in great confusion, dislocation, and decline of industrial productivity. As shown in Figure 4.2, industrial production which was up 80 percent over 1956 by 1960, dropped to its 1957 level of 20 percent over the 1956 base in the succeeding two years. Steel production from backyard blast furnaces went the way of the communes. Reaching a high of 15 million metric tons in 1960, production declined by almost half to 8 million metric tons over the succeeding two years.[4] In 1962 the managers were reinstalled over the party in industry.

Some specifics of the failure of Maoist economic predictions in grain, steel, coal, and electricity production can be gotten by a comparison of their production targets with their actual achievement during the second five year plan, 1958-1962.[5] The 1962 targets were set first by the moderates in September 1956, then by the Maoists in December of 1957, and finally reset by the Maoists in reaction to the initial discontinuations at the Lushan plenum in August of 1959. The grain production target was set at 250 million metric tons in 1956, changed to 240 in 1957, and raised to 275 in 1959. The actual grain achievement was 167. The steel production target was set at 10.5–12.0 million metric tons in 1956, raised to 12 in 1957, and maintained at 12 in 1959. The actual 1962 steel achievement was 7–10, and probably 8. The coal production target was set at 190–210 million metric tons in 1956, raised to 230 in 1957, and raised again to 335 in 1959. The actual 1962 coal achievement was 180–250. The electricity production target, which was set at 40–43 billion kilowatt hours in 1956, went unfulfilled, as did those subsequently raised by the Maoist advocates of the Great Leap.

Indeed, if one compares the average annual rates of growth achieved under the first five year plan with those achieved under Mao's second, one finds the former significantly superior. Grain production had grown at 3–4 percent

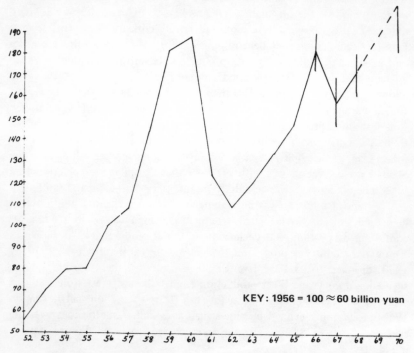

KEY: 1956 = 100 ≈ 60 billion yuan

SOURCE: The figures through 1965 are from the chapter by Robert Michael Field in J.E.C., **An Economic Profile of Mainland China,** op. cit., p. 273. Figures for 1966-1968 are adapted from Robert Michael Field, "Industrial Production in China, 1957-1968." **China Quarterly,** No. 42, (Spring 1970), p. 47. The figure for 1970 is adapted from Arthur Ashbrook in J.E.C., **People's Republic of China: An Economic Assessment,** op. cit., p. 5. Verticle bars represent a range of estimates. Premier Chou En-lai has reported the 1970 figure at 225 billion yuan. See **China Quarterly,** No. 50, (Spring 1972), pp. 375-376.

Figure 4.2: INDUSTRIAL PRODUCTION, 1952-1970

compared with a 0.5 percent average annual *decline;* steel production had grown at 20 percent compared with 10. Although coal production had grown at 15 percent compared with 21 percent, electricity production had grown at 22 percent compared with only 14.[6] Thus Mao's much vaunted goal of over-taking Britain in the output of steel in 15 years became even more remote than before, for Britain was producing over four times as much steel as China back in 1957.[7]

For many years, beginning in 1959, a statistical blackout was imposed on the mainland, but recently Western economists have obtained sufficient information to make overall assessments of the economic accomplishments of Mao's Great Leap.

In spite of the enormous five-year effort expended on industrial construction, Field shows that the 1962 level did not exceed the preleap 1957 high, which had been preceded by five successive years of 14 percent annual growth.[8] He estimates that the leap cost China a full decade of industrial growth.[9] Eckstein gives the same estimate.[10] In surveying the overall economy to 1965, Ta-Chung Liu states that a total of seven years, from 1958 to 1965, was lost without any economic growth in China while other nations experienced a significant measure of growth and development.[11]

So it happened that the Three Red Banners springing from the thought of Mao Tse-tung met with disaster. In 1962, the economy began to pick up again, but now under relatively capitalist practices in agriculture and with professional managers rather than all-purpose party cadres holding the reigns in industry. Roughly speaking, by 1964 or 1965, the economy had recovered preleap, 1957 levels of production. But communism, as measured by our and Mao's yardsticks, was at least as far away as had been perceived eight suffering years before. Reports on Mao's communes, on agricultural production, and on industrial production provided undeniable evidence of Great Leap failure. This evidence became increasingly apparent from the Lushan plenum through the following "three hard years."

Messianism and the Mind of Mao

P'eng's prophecy of failure had come true while Mao's prophecy of progress towards communism had failed. The Great Leap debacle resulted, in the early sixties, in famine and fatalistic folk songs among the peasantry and the people; in disillusionment and corruption among middle-level cadres, including dissension in the ranks of the army; in back-biting and literary barbs from the intellectuals; and in recrimination and faction formation among the politburo leadership.

The reactions of China's peasantry to the Great Leap Forward and its failure are expressed in two popular folk songs of the period. The first folk song captures the naive utopianism displayed by peasants in Hunan province during the summer of 1958:

> Setting up a people's commune is like going to heaven,
> The achievements of a single night surpass those of
>   several millennia
> The sharp knife severs the roots of private property
> Opening a new historical era.[12]

That song composed during the peak of Great Leap enthusiasm contrasts sharply with those composed and sung by peasants of south China during the three hard years of 1959-1961 in the wake of the Great Leap. The following verses, extracted from a collection of such songs, display the disillusionment of the peasantry:

> Comrades have their new shoes on and kick about,
> Cadres have their tummies filled, and shout and shout,
> For the farmer, his arms are skinny,
> And face and legs all swollen up,
> And every bone of his water buffalo sticks out.

> I toil day and night, year in and year out,
> But my rice bowl is empty and the fire of the cooking
>   stove is out;
> No shoes to wear and my buttocks uncovered.
> I still have to walk about;
> Flesh has left my arms and legs.
> And if I have one marrowy bone,
> I certainly doubt.

> I have looked and looked,
> For a few grains of rice in the bowls.
> I found nothing but water,
> I'm furious and bitter,
> Beat me to death, if you wish, comrades,
> But toil for you again? Never!

> They say we have a bumper crop,
> And other farm products are all up,
> But for the whole year I have not had enough rice
>   to fill a cup,
> Today I harvest the paddy,
> Tomorrow my rice bowl is empty.[13]

Mao Tse-tung historically had a high degree of empathy with China'a peasantry. During the period of reported Great Leap success in June 1959, just before the eventful Lushan plenum, Mao himself, during his first visit to his native village of Shaoshan since 1927, penned the following poem:

> My memories of the past are unchanging, and I curse
>   the inexorable flux of time.
> I am in my native place of thirty-two years ago.
> Red flags fly from the spears of enslaved peasants,
> Black hands raise high the lash of the tyrannical landowner.
> Only because so many sacrificed themselves did our
>   wills become strong,

So that we dared command the sun and moon to bring
   a new day.
I love to look at the multiple waves of rice and beans,
While on every side the heroes return through the
   evening haze.[14]

An abrupt change in perspective must have troubled Mao as he became aware of the Great Leap failures. At the eighth plenum of the eighth central committee held in August of 1959 at Lushan, the failures of the Great Leap Forward were reported. The official communique recognized that the economic achievements of 1958 had been exaggerated almost 50 percent. Grain production, the bulwark of the Chinese economy and the indicator of the efficacy of the people's communes, was not reported to be 375 million metric tons as previously claimed, but 250 million metric tons. In fact more recent Western estimates place the figure at about 190 million metric tons. Decentralization of Mao's communes was planned; and Mao's old comrade from revolutionary days, P'eng Teh-huai, delivered his attack on Mao and Mao's Three Red Banners.

Let us imagine for a moment the set of cognitions that must have existed in the mind of Mao at the time of his appraisal of the Great Leap failures. On the one hand there was the evidence that the Great Leap had failed—failed in agricultural production, general industrial production; failed politically in terms of increasing opposition to the leap by some of Mao's lieutenants, by most of the intellectuals, by many of the soldiers and cadres, and even by the peasants; failed in terms of progress towards communist society in terms of decollectivization of agriculture and substitution of professional for party leadership in industry.

On the other hand, the beliefs that supported his initial decision to engage in the Great Leap loomed as large as before—most importantly the ideology of Marxism-Leninism and the thought of Mao Tse-tung. From this ideology, from this intricate interrelated set of hard-won beliefs about the nature of society and the progress of history, it followed that the Great Leap would lead China closer to communism. If the opposite were true, then it must be the case that some of the propositions in the ideology, in Marxism-Leninism and in the thought of Mao, were false. But to accept this, to admit the validity of the words of one's critics, to reject beliefs for which one had suffered for decades, to give up hopes of world Communist leadership for China, indeed to give up hopes of true communism for China was a very bitter pill to swallow for the man who thought he had led China's three-fourths billion people from turmoil and chaos to order, economic development, and a socialist way of life.

Thus we find Mao's mind in an extreme state of dissonance. To reduce such dissonance resulting from the maintenance of incompatible cognitions he could admit his error and moderate his Great Leap policy. He could psychologically diminish the importance of the achievement of communism in China. But that would have horrendous implications for Mao's ideological commitments. On the other hand, Mao could distort the evidence of failure. But the increasing weight of evidence was undeniable. He could promote the exculpating rationalization of sabotage by class enemies. He could diminish the importance of economic achievements, concentrate on specific points of failure in his Great Leap plan, and continue the policy on noneconomic fronts. He could increase the importance of ideological achievements and seek evidence that his ideology was in fact correct. He could obtain such corroborative evidence by attempting additional ideological experiments—such as peoples' wars in the developing nations, such as attempting new Maoist policy implementation in China itself, especially recommunization of the peasantry. In addition, Mao could search for corroborative evidence from other persons that his ideology was correct by converting other people to his ideological fold. He could proselyte for his shaken beliefs and attempt to silence his critics by persuasion. If they persisted in disagreement, they would become "class enemies."

Mao's conviction and commitment to his ideology were too great to allow the option of ideological moderation. In fact he increased his ideological fervor. His general interpretation of the Great Leap failures was that his Great Leap had been sabotaged by demons who had not correctly implemented his ideology because of unmitigated malevolence or unwilling ignorance. His task now was to separate the wheat from the chaff. The masses must be made aware of the continuity of the basic class struggle through "socialist education"; the cadres must be "rectified" and taught correctly to apply the mass line, become aware of the wishes of the masses through extended democracy; avoid the sin of commandism even if it was out of revolutionary enthusiasm. Art and literature must be purified of all bourgeois taints. Finally, the top figures in authority taking the capitalist road, the representatives of the bourgeoisie, and intellectuals who had sabotaged his efforts to bring communism to the fore must be remolded or removed from their high places. No, the ideology had not failed; indeed dialectics were proven correct by the evidence of verbal and material sabotage of communism by class enemies; by the dreadful results of unschooled cadres' neglect of the mass line; by the apparent ease with which the masses had been duped into adopting capitalist practices which would inevitably lead to their exploitation. What was needed was to educate the masses in the ideology; to remove the representatives of the bourgeoisie. In short, what was needed was to proselyte for the ideology and reinstitute Maoist policy. Then, and only then, would the task of an economic upsurge become important again. This time it would succeed.

So it was ensuing upon the Great Leap debacles that ideologist Mao's reaction of increased utopian fervor fell out of step with the emotions of China's disillusioned peasantry. In contrast to the peasantry, Mao's reactions in the wake of the Great Leap debacle are revealed in a poem he wrote about the time of the Lushan plenum, counterattacking the "handful of opportunists in China who hang out the sign board of 'communism' " but who are really "merely dragging up a few chicken feathers and onion peels to serve as their banner against the party's general line, Great Leap Forward, and people's commune. This is really like 'ants trying to shake a large tree.' "

On our tiny globe
a few flies smash into the walls,
They buzz,
Some loudly complaining,
Others weeping.
The ants climb the flowering locust, boasting of
    their great country
But for ants to shake a tree is easier said than done.
Just now the west wind drops leaves on Ch'angan,
Whistling arrows fly through the air.
How many urgent tasks have arisen one after another.
Heaven and earth revolve.
Time presses,
Ten thousand years is too long,
We must seize the day.
The four seas rise high, the clouds and waters rage.
The five continents tremble, wind and thunder are
    unleashed,
We must sweep away all the harmful insects
Until not a single enemy remains.[15]

NOTES

1. Marion R. Larsen, "China's agriculture under Communism," in Joint Economic Commission of U.S. Congress, *An Economic Profile of Mainland China.* New York: Praeger, 1968, p. 265. (Hereafter *JEC.*)

2. Alexander Eckstein, *Communist China's Economic Growth and Foreign Trade.* New York: McGraw-Hill, 1966, p. 265.

3. See Liao Lu-yen's article in *PR*, No. 44, November 1, 1963.

4. *NYT*, March 12, 1967.

5. The raw data for the following comparison of the first and second five year plans were extracted from two courses: Eckstein, op. cit.; and Jan S. Prybylla, *The Political Economy of Communist China.* Scranton: International Textbook Co., 1970. Prybylla provides more information on the struggle between moderates and radicals

preceding the decision to launch the leap. Where there is ambiguity regarding a production target or achievement a range of numbers is provided rather than a single number.

6. See Eckstein, op. cit. We have calculated these comparative growth rates from the data provided in the sources above and are confident of the general thrust of the comparison.

7. Mao's explicit prediction of overtaking Great Britain is to be found in his "Sixty work methods" (February 1958), as translated in *CLG,* Vol. I, No. 4, winter 1968-69.

8. Robert M. Field, "Chinese Communist industrial production," in *JEC,* p. 273.

9. Ibid., p. 285.

10. Eckstein, op. cit., p. 85.

11. Liu Ta-chung, "The tempr of economic development of the Chinese mainland, 1949-65" in *JEC,* p. 53.

12. From Stuart Schram, *Mao Tse-tung.* New York: Simon and Schuster, 1966, p. 273, as translated from the article by Kuan Feng in *Che-hsueh yen-chiu,* No. 5, 1958, pp. 1-8.

13. The foregoing verses were parts of a collection of folk songs popularly sung by peasants and children in South China between 1960 and 1962. This collection was compiled and translated by Professor Zing Yang Kuo in Hong Kong and graciously donated to the author.

14. See Stuart Schram, op. cit., p. 276. Schram's original translation of this poem is to be found in *Problems of Communism,* September-October 1964, p. 39.

15. See Stuart Schram, op. cit., pp. 284-285. Schram's translation of this poem is to be found in *Problems of Communism,* September-October 1964, pp. 42-43. Mao's own interpretation of this poem's imagery is revealed in his second letter to the editorial department of the *Poetry Journal* on September 1, 1959:

> Your letter has been received. I have recently written two poems of seven-character lines, which, if you approve, may be published in *Shih k'an* (Poetry Journal). Rightist opportunists have recently attacked frantically, denouncing the people's enterprises. Anti-Chinese and anticommunist elements the world over, as well as bourgeois and pettybourgeois opportunists who infiltrated into the proletariat and the party, have connived to launch a frantic attack. They seem to be pushing down the K'un-lun mountain range. Comrades, wait! A handful of opportunists in China who hang out the signboard of "communism" are merely dragging up a few chicken feathers and onion peels to serve as their banner against the party's general line, great leap forward, and people's commune. This is really like "ants trying to shake a large tree, so ridiculous that they do not gauge their capability at all." The reactionaries throughout the world have also cursed and scolded us bitterly since last year. As I see it, this is very good. It would be really inconceivable if the great enterprises of 650 million people were not cursed by the imperialists and by their lackies in various countries. The more severely they curse, the more jubilant I become. Let them scold for half a century! By that time, let us see who has won and who has been routed. This poem of mine is also intended to reply to these eight-forgetful (rotten) eggs.

A note by the compilers of the Chinese pamphlet containing this letter, confirms that the two seven-character line poems are "Shaoshan Revisited" and "Ascent of Lushan." The latter is translated in *CLG,* Vol. I, No. 4, winter 1968-1969, pp. 77-78.

Chapter 5

SOCIAL SUPPORT:

The Initial Surge

In order that Mao retain his belief that the Great Leap Forward and people's commune program were leading China closer to communism, it was necessary that he have some degree of social support to withstand the foregoing disconfirmatory evidence. If Mao were a single isolated believer, it is unlikely that he could maintain his belief. Given that Mao was not an isolate, his desire to go forth and seek social support should depend upon the relative lack of unanimity of social support among his group of close associates and the amount of ridicule he received from sources outside his close associates. There is strong evidence that the most highly committed Maoists on the politburo, as shown in Chapter 3, supported the Maoist belief in the leap and the class struggle rationalization for its failings (see Figure 3.1 p. 94). A group of Mao's close associates, including his wife, Chiang Ch'ing, rallied around him during this crisis. In the early 1960s Chiang Ch'ing became active in radicalizing art and literature along Maoist lines. Mao's close associates certainly included many of the members of the politburo and certainly many members of the standing committee of the politburo; some were definitely convinced and committed Maoists. First among these was the guerrilla warrier Lin Piao, and second was the Maoist theoretician, Ch'en Po-ta and third was K'ang Sheng. At this crucial time, the unflagging support of Lin Piao for

Maoist policies was displayed in Lin's first published article as the newly appointed Minister of Defense in the month following the Lushan plenum. In this *People's Daily* article entitled "March Ahead Under the Red Flag of the General Line and Mso Tse-tung's Military Thinking," Lin declared his unconditional loyalty to the People's Liberation Army, the party and Mso Tse-tung:

> We have continued to develop our army's long-standing glorious tradition of simultaneously carrying out the three great tasks of fighting, mass work, and production, and we have launched various activities in support of the mass movements in line with the stages of socialist transformation and socialist construction. . . .
>
> Participating directly in the mass movement, the officers and men of the People's Liberation Army see, above all, the tremendous endeavours and magnificent successes of hundreds of millions of people. This is the main current, the essence of the mass movement. In the people's communes, for example, we see not only the powerful vitality and unparalleled superiority of this new-born social organization and the important role it plays in developing the national economy and culture and in raising the living standards of the people, we also came to realize that in the event of a war of aggression launched by imperialism against our country, the people's communes, in which township administration and commune management are merged into one and industry, agriculture, trade, education and military affairs are integrated into one, are the mighty prop for the task of turning the whole population into fighting men, of supporting the front, of defending the country and overwhelming the aggressors. Seeing this revolutionary creation of the masses of people which can accelerate the advance of the socialist cause and at the same time promote the building of national defense, what else can anyone who genuinely desires a prosperous and powerful motherland do but support it wholeheartedly and praise it with deep emotion?[2]
>
> As two opposing classes, the bourgeoisie and the working class do not exist within our army, but the struggle between bourgeois and working-class ideology does exist. The ideological struggle is a reflection of the struggle between the two roads, socialist and capitalist, in the transition period. . . . Either socialist or capitalist ideology must dominate the minds of people. Therefore, in the transition period, the struggle to enhance proletarian ideology and liquidate bourgeois ideology remains vital at all times in building up the army. None of the work of our army, including its modernization, can be divorced from this ideological struggle. The political and ideological struggle between the working class and the bourgeoisie . . . is far from over to this day and will not end until classes are finally and completely liquidated. Consequently, our work of socialist ideological education cannot be completed all at once.[3]

The officers and men of our army ardently love socialism, fight for it resolutely and can withstand tests of great stress. Those who insist on taking the road of capitalism and are deliberately against socialism are merely a handful of individuals from alien classes who have sneaked into the army.[4]

Lin Piao in the same article also pointed to Mao's thought as establishing the necessity of providing the means of conquering the forces of reaction in China:

We officers and Communists working in the army must be alert at all times against the intrigues of the enemy—both against invasion by the enemy with arms and against "sugar coated shells" of all kinds of sabotage from within. . . .

To study Marxist-Leninist theory and the writings of Comrade Mao Tse-tung conscientiously and to establish proletarian world outlook firmly are the incumbent duty of every officer and Communist in our army.[5]

Lin Piao's article praising the thought of Mao Tse-tung was immediately reprinted in the next edition of *Red Flag* by its editor, Ch'en Po-ta. One month later, Ch'en Po-ta again demonstrated his undiminished support for Mao and Mao's thought by reprinting the following "folk song" on the pages of his theoretical journal:

> Chairman Mao is infinitely kind
> Ten thousand songs are not enough to praise him.
> With trees as pens, the sky as paper
> And an ocean of ink,
> Much would still be left unwritten.[6]

Ch'en also vociferously opposed Mao's class enemy in his timely article in *Hung Ch'i* entitled "The Struggle Between the Proletarian World Outlook and the Bourgeois World Outlook."[7]

Finally, K'ang Sheng, an infrequent publicist, wholeheartedly supported Mao in his article of October 1, 1959, "A Communist Should Be a Marxist-Leninist, Not a Fellow Traveller of the Party." Here he echoes Mao's own view:

This [the Great Leap achievements] is a powerful reply to, and retaliation of the various attacks and slanders of the right opportunists against the general lines the Great Leap forward and the people's communes. This battle is a combination of the sharp struggles between the bourgeoisie and the proletariat in China in the past ten years.[8]

In this struggle against right opportunism, every member of the Communist Party should become more cognizant of the law of class struggle in the transitional period in our country. . . . He should take a resolute part in the struggle against right opportunism, study Marxism-Leninism and the Thought of Mao Tse-tung more deeply and be determined to be a thorough Marxist-Leninist, not a fellow traveller of the Party.[9]

Thus, in the fall of 1959 a trusted coterie from the cult of Yenan, Chiang Ch'ing, Lin Piao, Ch'en Po-ta and K'ang Sheng unflinchingly praised the besieged chairman, and denigrated the onslaughts of his class enemy.

Despite the fact that fully thirteen members of the politburo contributed articles to the volume *Ten Glorious Years* in the fall of 1959, only two, Lin Piao and K'ang Sheng, publicly echoed Mao's rationalization at the Lushan plenum by labeling P'eng Teh-huai's onslaught as an example of the severe class struggle between the ideologies of the proletariat and the bourgeoisie. And only these two also recommend in their articles the intensive study of and proselyting for the thought of Mao Tse-tung. The remainder indulged in more superficial rhetoric, some ignoring and even contradicting Mao's thought. Whether other politburo members besides Lin, Ch'en, and K'ang have publicly supported Mao elsewhere in the fall of 1959 is difficult to discern.

That Mao's social support within the politburo was divided is clearly demonstrated by the onslaught of P'eng Teh-huai at the Lushan plenum of August 1959, the positions of Liu Shao-ch'i and Teng Hsiao-p'ing on radical Maoist collectivization schemes, and the position of Ch'en Yun on the economics of the Great Leap Forward. Although one cannot determine with certainty the positions of all the members of the politburo on Maoist policy and the Great Leap Forward movement, it is clear that Mao did have some strong social support for his policies and class struggle rationalization in the politburo from his most highly committed supporters and also some strong social disparagement for his policy within it. The politburo, as a reference group for Mao, was split. Liu Shao-ch'i, for example, was conspicuously restrained in his mention of Mao's thought in the article he prepared to honor the tenth anniversary of the Chinese People's Republic,[10] while being profuse in his praise of Marxism-Leninism.

Among important political personages below the level of the politburo, there is evidence that support for Mao and his policies was also split in late 1959. In the fall of 1959, a nationwide "cult of Mao Tse-tung" made its appearance. For the first time, Mao Tse-tung was publicly acclaimed by a high-level party personage as "the outstanding contemporary revolutionary statesman and theoretician of Marxism-Leninism." Liu Lan-t'ao, a member of the CAP Central Committee, penned the following panegyric on the occasion of the tenth anniversary of the CCP, one month after the Lushan plenum:

Comrade Mao Tse-tung is the most outstanding exponent of the heroic proletariat of our country, the most distinguished representative of our superior traditions in the entire history of our great nation, a beacon on our country's road to Communism, and the most outstanding contemporary revolutionist, statesman, and theoretician of Marxism-Leninism. He has creatively enriched the treasures of Marxism-Leninism on a series of important questions. The 600 million or more people of our country have placed in him their hopes for their own happiness and future, and consider him the incarnation of Communism and truth and the system of invincibility.[11]

In addition, the method of testing the loyalty of party leaders on the basis of their appreciation of and commitment to the thought of Mao Tse-tung made its appearance at this time. The loyalty criterion was phrased as follows: "The yardstick to judge whether any individual is a genuine Marxist is his comprehension of Mao Tse-tung's ideology."[12] The extremity of ideological fervor displayed by members of the "cult of Mao Tse-tung" in late 1959 is well illustrated in the following passage by Liu Tze-chiu extracted from an esoteric political journal:

What I call "belief" means believing in Mao Tse-tung's thought; moreover, this belief must be steadfast and immovable. In the course of China's revolutionary struggles and socialist construction, vast practical experience has demonstrated that Mao Tse-tung's thought is the only correct thought. It is the incarnation of Marxism-Leninism in China; it is the symbol of truth. Therefore, if a person at any time whatever, in any place whatever, regarding any question whatever, manifests wavering in his attitude toward Mao Tse-tung's thought, then, no matter if this wavering is only momentary and slight, it means in reality that the waverer departs from Marxist-Leninist truth and will lose his bearings and commit political errors. So we must follow Chairman Mao steadfastly and eternally forward, following a hundred percent and without the slightest reservation the way of Mao Tse-tung.[13]

On the occasion of the tenth anniversary celebrations of the CCP, in October 1959, in the wake of the commune disorders a chorus sang a song, the strains of which were to haunt party leaders and common folk alike in the years following the Great Leap debacles. The opening lines of this musical ecomium rang clear:

The East is red,
Rises, the sun,
China has brought forth a Mao Tse-tung.
He plans blessings for the people,
He is the great savior of the people.[14]

The following year witnessed with fanfare the publication of Volume IV of Mao's *Selected Works*. This served as the occasion to initiate a nationwide campaign to publicize Mao's thoughts and urge the broad masses of people to study Mao's newest edition of theoretical offerings. As a precursor of the next decade, the spirit of this campaign was quickly picked up within the ranks of the People's Liberation Army. In the words of one militant Maoist writing in October 1960:

> Comrade Mao Tse-tung's military dialectics is broad and profound. . . . Comrade Mao Tse-tung's military dialectics is practical philosophy. It was born in the revolutionary wars and demonstrated infinite fighting power in them. It radiates dazzling rays of victory like the sun and the moon in the sky. It will live forever.[15]

Also auguring the next decade, the PLA's praise of Maoist dialectics was picked up and amplified for the civilian populace one week later:

> Comrade Mao Tse-tung is always able to see the essence of things and the future development, and able to point to the sun that is about to emerge from behind the clouds, to point to the coming dawn in the night, and to point to the correct direction in a maze of complex surroundings, thereby guiding the Chinese people from victory to victory.[16]

Clear indications of outside ridicule of Mao and his policies were also present at the time.[17] The first came from a group of intellectuals. In the summer of 1959, Wu Han, a high intellectual and Deputy Mayor of Peking, published an article entitled "Hai Jui Scolds the Emperor."[18] This article soon formed the basis for a play that was staged in Peking in February 1961, and the author and his writings soon formed the nucleus of opposition within the intellectuals to Mao Tse-tung. The publication of the spring of 1961 of a number of articles by Wu Han and two other recalcitrant intellectuals was officially cited five years later as veiled attacks upon the thought of Mao Tse-tung and the Maoist Great Leap policies. The first article in question was "Hai Jui Dismissed from Office" written by Wu Han and published in *Pei-ching Wen Yi* (Peking Literature and Art) in January 1961. The other articles came in the form of columns in the Peking press during 1961. The press vehicles in question are *Ch'ien Hsien* (Front Line), of which Teng T'o was editor and chief, and *Pei-ching Jih Pao* (Peking Daily). Teng t'o is the author of "Evening Chats at Yenshan," the second series of articles in question. The third series of articles in question is "Notes from a Three Family Village" allegedly authored by the triad of intellectuals, Teng T'o, Liao Mo-sha, and Wu Han.[19]

Wu Han's article, "Hai Jui Dismissed from Office," received the following analysis in the official Chinese press in 1966:

Today the reactionary nature of this drama has become increasingly evident. It directed its spearhead precisely against the Lushan meeting and against the Central Committee of the Party headed by Mao Tse-tung with a view to reversing the decisions of that meeting. The clamorous message of the drama was that the dismissal of the "upright official Hai Jui," in other words, of the right opportunists, was 'unfair' and that the right opportunists should come back to administer 'court affairs,' that is to carry out their revisionist programme.[20]

Teng T'o's articles, "Evening Chats at Yenshan" and "Notes from a Three Family Village," were put in the same general anti-Maoist category as "Hai Jui Dismissed from Office." The following passage from the 1966 critique demonstrates this point:

In all cases the points of departure and theme essays were important points intimately bound up with reality, and were by no means just the "idealizing of the ancients." . . . "Evening Chats at Yenshan" and "Notes from a Three-Family Village" are shot through with the same black anti-Party, anti-popular and anti-Socialist themes as that followed in "Hai Jui Scolds the Emperor" and "Hai Jui Dismissed from Office," namely slanderous attacks on the Central Committee of the Party headed by Comrade Mao Tse-tung; attacks on the General line of the Party; all-out support for the attacks of the Right opportunists who had been "dismissed from Office" in an attempt to reverse earlier correct decisions concerning them; and support for the frenzied attacks of the feudal and capitalist forces.[21]

That Mao's Three Red Banners were a central target of the intellectuals' attack in the spring of 1961 is demonstrated by the following excerpt from the 1966 critique:

In stirring up this evil wind, "Three Family Village" raised a hullabaloo and cleared the way for the release of all kinds of monsters from confinement, collaborating from within with sinister forces from without. In league with the reactionaries in China and abroad and with the modern revisionists, it made dastardly attacks on the Party's general line for socialist construction, the Great Leap Forward and the People's Communes, and painted modern revisionism in glowing colors in a vain attempt to create public opinion favorable to a comeback by the Right opportunists.[22]

The same critique alleged that later in the fall of 1961 Teng T'o made a more basic attack: Teng T'o was alleged to have attacked the great thought of Mao Tse-tung:

> On November 10, 1961, Teng T'o came out with his article "Great Empty Talk" in *Notes from a Three Family Village*. In ostensibly criticizing a child's poem, he indirectly condemned the statement that "The East wind is our benefactor and West wind is our enemy" as "empty talk," "jargon," "cliches," and "pomposity." This was a flagrant denigration of the Marxist-Leninist scientific thesis that "the East wind prevails over the West wind" as "empty talk." . . . What was Teng T'o's purpose? It was to slander the great thought of Mao Tse-gung which leads us forward, as "empty talk" to get us to abandon Mao Tse-tung's thought in our political life and to give up the Marxist-Leninist line.[23]

Thus, in late 1959 and the early 1960s, after Mao's Great Leap failure, there existed in China both passionate social support for the thought of Mao Tse-tung in the politburo and below and simultaneously, significant social disparagement of the thought of Mao Tse-tung from inside and outside his group of close associates. The conditions were ripe for concerted Maoist proselyting.

NOTES

1. *CS,* Vol. 7, No. 5, p. 13.

2. Lin Piao "March Ahead. . . ." in *Ten Glorious Years.* Peking: Foreign Languages Press, 1960, pp. 67-89, as selected from the book, *The Tenth Anniversary of the People's Republic of China.* Peking: People's Publishing House, December 1959, Chinese edition. See also *JMJP,* September 27, 1959, and *HC,* October 1, 1959.

3. Ibid., p. 72.

4. Ibid., p. 73.

5. Ibid., pp. 86-88.

6. *HC,* November 1959.

7. *HC,* No. 22, 1959.

8. K'ang Sheng "A Communist should. . . ." in *Ten Glorious Years,* op. cit., pp. 245-254, esp. p. 245.

9. Ibid., pp. 253-254.

10. Liu Shao-ch'i, "The victory of Marxism-Leninism in China" in *Ten Glorious Years,* op. cit., pp. 1-34, esp. pp. 33-34. See also *JMJP,* October 1, 1959; and James T. Myers, "The Fall of Chairman Mao," *CS,* Vol. VI, No. 10, June 15, 1968, p. 7.

11. See Liu Lan-tao, "The Chinese Communist party is the supreme commander in building socialism," *JMJP,* September 28, 1959 (*CB* No. 598) as cited in Philip Bridgjam, "Mao's Cultural Revolution: Origin and development," *CQ,* No. 29, January-March, 1967, p. 3.

12. See Bridgham, loc. cit.

13. Liu Tzu-chiu, "Mao Tse-tung szu-hsiang shih wom-men shen-li ti ch'i chieh," *Chen-chin Hsueh-hsi,* No. 19, 1959, pp. 3-4, as quoted in Stuart Schram, *The Political Thought of Mao Tse-tung.* New York: Praeger, 1963, p. 302.

14. See James T. Myers, loc. cit.

15. Fu Chung, "Great victory for Mao Tse-tung's military dialectics," *JMJP,* pp. 6-7, October 1960, (*SCMP* 2360) as quoted in John Gittings, *The Role of the Chinese Army.* Oxford: Oxford University Press, 1967, p. 241.

16. See Ouyang Ch'in, *JMJP,* October 12, 1960, as quoted in James T. Myers, op. cit., p. 7.

17. Indirect criticism stemming from outside the Chinese populace was also evident at this time. In the summer of 1960, the Soviets withdrew their technicians. In the same year, indirect social support from outside the Chinese populace came to Mao in the form of hundreds of visitors from the revolutionary underdeveloped areas of the world, Africa, Asia, and Latin America. See also *HC,* No. 10, 1960, as quoted in Stuart Schram, op. cit., pp. 261-263.

18. See *JMJP,* June 16, 1959.

19. See Yao Wen-yuan, "On 'Three-Family Village'—The reactionary nature of evening chats at Yenshan and notes from Three Family Village," *Chinese Literature,* No. 7, 1966, as exerpted and translated in Asia Research Center, *The Great Cultural Revolution in China.* Hong Kong: Green Pagoda Press, 1967, pp. 91-115. (Hereafter *ARC.*)

20. Ibid., p. 95.

21. Ibid., p. 98.

22. Ibid., p. 101.

23. Ibid., pp. 105-106.

PART II

PROSELYTING: SECURING SOCIAL SUPPORT

There is an ancient Chinese fable called "The Foolish Old Man Who Removed the Mountains." It tells of an old man who lived in Northern China long, long ago and was known as the Foolish Old Man of North Mountain. His house faced south and beyond the doorway stood two great peaks, Taihang and Wangwu, obstructing the way. With great determination, he led his sons to digging up these mountains, hoe in hand. Another graybeard, known as the Wise Old Man, saw them and said derisively, "How silly of you to do this! It is quite impossible for you few to dig up these two huge mountains." The Foolish Old Man replied, "When I die, my sons will carry on; when they die, there will be my grandsons, and then their sons and grandsons, and so on to infinity. High as they are, the mountains cannot grow any higher and with every bit we dig, they will be that much lower. Why can't we clear them away?" Having refuted the Wise Old Man's wrong view, he went on digging every day, unshaken in his conviction. God was moved by this, and he sent down two angels, who carried the mountains away on their backs.

Mao Tse-tung,
*speech to seventh party
congress, 1945 at Yenan*

Chapter 6

THE SPAWN OF LUSHAN

Please look at this item, which may be interesting. I have written a few words purporting to refute Khrushchev. Later I will write some articles proselyting in favor of the people's communes. The Khrushchevs oppose or are skeptical about these three things: one hundred flowers blooming, people's communes, and the Great Leap Forward. I can see that they are in a passive position, while we have taken extreme initiative. What do you think? We must use these three things to challenge the entire world, including a large number of opponents and skeptics within the Party.[1]

These fervent words were written by Mao Tse-tung to his close comrade in the central committee, Wang Chia-hsiang, after two and a half weeks of mixed ridicule and praise ensuing upon P'eng Teh-huai's smashing "Letter of Opinion" at the Lushan plenum. This was the explicit call for worldwide proselyting for Mao's Three Red Banners that was to inundate the next decade.

The Great Leap failures pronounced by P'eng at Lushan proved a watershed in the party's history under Mao—a great divide between the politics of consensus and the politics of polarization. After Lushan, Mao and his committed followers increased their proselyting for Mao's thought and its sanctioned policies; the uncommitted members felt no need to proselyte and fell from the fold. Within the politburo the committed Maoists kept Mao's red flags flying and thereby distanced themselves from the majority of their colleagues—uncommitted members of the growing bourgeois schism. As economic failure forced Mao away from domestic policy formation to foreign affairs; the third world roiled with his revolutionary experiments and the Soviets reeled beneath his ideological chastisements. In domestic affairs Mao launched wave after wave of mass campaigns in search of social support from the young and the proletarian; but the party apparatus proved locked from his grasp, and the army remained his main instrumentality.

Mao's immediate psychological reaction to P'eng's "Letter of Opinion" at Lushan was unprecedented in his two decades of rule. In addition to his expression of fervent desire to proselyte for his ideology, Mao displayed all the symptoms of a convinced and committed ideologue suffering an extreme state of cognitive dissonance. Mao delivered his speech at the Lushan conference on July 23 after twenty days of "stiffening his scalp" in silence and forebearance as he listened to the negative information on the Great Leap forthcoming from his comrades. His opening lines indicated the extremity of his felt inner dissonance:

> You have spoken so much; permit me to talk some now, won't you. I have taken sleeping pills thrice. Can't sleep. Let me talk about this kind of opinion.[2]

This kind of opinion about which Mao spoke was represented by P'eng Tehhuai's "Letter of Opinion" of July 14, 1959, criticizing the Great Leap Forward and commune policy. Mao's reaction to this kind of opinion was to increase in inner ideological fervor to the extent of labeling his former comrade-in-arms as a member of the bourgeois class enemy and threatening to fight a guerrilla war to rid the country of the likes of him and to carry on with his commune policy:

> P'eng Teh-huai's letter of opinion constitutes an anti-party outline of rightist opportunism. . . . It is by no means accidental or individual error, but is planned, organized, prepared, and purposeful. . . . P'eng Teh-huai's letter is in the nature of an outline; it is opposed to our general line. Don't you see that though superficially he seemed to support it, he has written very meticulously, stressing that the contradiction was the imbalance of proportion, alleging that massive steelmaking was extravagant and that petty-bourgeois fervor has spread to all places and all sectors, and saying that the people's communes should better be developed one year later, and that America's Dulles has also said that our proportions were not balanced. If the Chinese People's Liberation Army should follow P'eng Teh-huai, I will go to fight guerrilla war.[3]

Mao's perception of the situation was much more sanguine than that of his critical comrades. In his Lushan speech he reasserted the correctness of his Great Leap policies and persisted in his predictions of commune success. Of the people of China, Mao claimed that fully 70 percent followed his policies, of whom 30 percent were active elements, proletarians:

How many people are there to make up this 30 percent? About 150 million people who must develop communes, establish mess halls, and undertake mammoth cooperation. They are extremely active and are willing to do it. You say this is petty-bourgeois fervor? This is no petty bourgeoisie; they are poor peasants, lower-middle peasants, proletariat, and semiproletariat. Those who follow the mainstream (40%) might also be disposed to form communes, and there are some 30 percent who are unwilling.[4]

Mao admitted to some mistakes in the implementation of his Great Leap but claimed these could be, and indeed had been in part, overcome by concerted ideological study:

Who were these who had some petty-bourgeois fervor? "Communist wind" consisted mainly of cadres at the *hsien* and commune levels, especially some commune cadres who squeezed production brigades and teams. This was bad and the masses proved to be unreceptive. It became necessary to rectify and persuade them firmly. One month was spent for this, and by March and April this wind was repressed. . . . This proved our Party was great, wise, and correct. If you won't believe it, there were historical data to prove it. During March, April, as well as May, several million cadres and several hundred millions of peasants were educated. . . . One should read some before one has the right to speak. It is necessary to squeeze out some time for the entire party and nation to launch a study movement.[5]

Mao's call for study at Lushan was indeed followed by a national political campaign of several months' duration to study Marxism-Leninism and the thought of Mao Tse-tung.

Mao discounted both the severity and the accuracy of the reports of Great Leap failures, and although he could not totally deny them, he enjoined his comrades to be as staunch and unwavering as he in their ideological conviction in the validity of the Great Leap Forward, the general line, and the people's communes. In so doing he fell into the ancient trap of blaming the messenger for the message:

If the newspapers you are publishing will print only bad news, and if you have no heart to work, then it won't take a year, but it [the nation] will perish within a week's time. When 700,000 items are published, and they are all bad things, then it is no longer a proletariat. This would be a bourgeois nation. . . . Of course there is no one at the conference who would suggest this. I am merely exaggerating. Suppose we do ten things and nine of these are bad and are published in the newspapers. Then we are bound to perish, and should perish. In that event, I would go to the countryside to lead the peasants to overthrow the government. If the Liberation Army won't follow me, I will then find the Red Army. I think the Liberation Army will follow me. . . . In order to ask others to be firm, one must be firm himself; in order to ask others not to waver, one must not waver himself. . . . It would indeed be a wonder if the rightists don't welcome the thesis held by these [wavering] comrades. Such a peripheral position is quite dangerous, and just wait and see if you don't believe it.[6]

Indeed, the press did close down its reports of Great Leap failures in a statistical blackout that lasted several years. Finally, Mao reasserted in this speech the basic ideological correctness of his commune policy and attributed prevalent belief in the Great Leap failure to exaggerated criticism by rightists and to some real errors of timing committed by himself and his supporters:

Now about the problem of mess halls. A mess hall is a good thing that cannot be unduly denounced. I am in favor of developing them successfully. . . . The mess hall is not our invention; it has been created by the masses. . . . The Ch'ang li investigation group of the Chinese Academy of Sciences alleged that the mess hall had no merit at all, thereb attacking one point without mentioning the rest. . . . Nobody can be without shortcomings; even Confucius had his mistakes. I have seen Lenin's own drafts that had been corrected pell-mell. If there were no errors, why should he correct them? We may set up more mess halls. Let us experiment with them for one or two years, and I figure that they can be completed. The people's communes won't collapse; not a single one has collapsed yet. We are prepared for the collapse of one-half of them, and after 70 percent has collapsed, we would still have 30 percent left.[7]

In admitting to real errors of timing, Mao confessed responsibility for "two crimes, one of which involved calling for 10,700,000 tons of steel, or for massive steel smelting." He noted, "There is also the general line, for which, be it true or false, you also share some responsibility. The general line has been implemented in industry and agriculture." On the topic of communes, Mao was unwavering in principle if not in timing:

As for the people's commune, the entire world has opposed it, including the Soviet Union. . . . I said the commune is a system of collective ownership. I said that the process of transition from a collective ownership system to a communist all-people's ownership system may take more than two five-year plans, and that it might take a twenty-five-year plan! In regard to speed, Marx also committed many errors. He hoped everyday for the advent of the European revolution, but it did not come. . . . It was only by the time of Lenin that it finally came. Wasn't this impetuous? Wasn't this bourgeois fanaticism? Marx also opposed the Paris Commune at the beginning. When the Paris Commune was established, he supported it.

Haven't we failed? . . . No, it is only a partial failure. We have paid a price, blown some "Communist wind," and enabled the people of the entire nation to learn a lesson. . . . What I did was the smelting of 10,700,000 tons of steel and the participation of 90 million people in it, and this was a great disaster for which I must be responsible myself. Comrades, you should analyze your own responsibility and your stomach will feel much more comfortable if you move your bowels and break wind.[8]

Thus we find reflected in Mao's speech at Lushan the signs of inner dissonance between his fervent ideological conviction that the Great Leap Forward and commune movement were moving China closer to a true communist society and the knowledge brought him by his comrades of the Great Leap failures. Mao openly complained of sleeplessness and inner tension. He expressed an increase in inner ideological fervor: He was stronger and more unwavering than ever in upholding his threatened people's commune ideal; he was stricter than ever in upholding the ideology, threatening wavering middle-of-the-roaders with dire consequences; he was more all-encompassing than before in applying the designation of class enemy to his former comrades. He showed signs of distorted perception in his sanguine estimate that the bulk of the population supported his Three Red Flags and in his attempts to discount some reports of Great Leap failures. He displayed a semireligious crusading spirit in threatening to fight a guerrilla war for his Three Red Flags and against the sabotaging bourgeois class enemy and in his call for renewed ideological study of Marxism-Leninism and the thought of Mao Tse-tung to resolve current difficulties. The key to Mao's behavior at Lushan and to the curious politics of China in the decade of the sixties lay not in Mao's profit motive for maximizing his political power but in his prophet motive for securing ideological confirmation. The prudent precepts of a political power seeker would dictate in such a situation the cool acceptance of facts, moderation of failed policies, and coalition formation with correct party critics. The precepts of a pure power seeker would not sanction Mao's tirade that occurred at Lushan nor the twin activities resulting from the conference that marked the next decade: a persistence in the doctrinal prediction of success for the failing people's communes, and fervent proselyting for the thought of Mao Tse-tung which sanctioned the Great Leap—as well as its failure.

After Mao's Lushan speech, after Mao admitted error with backyard blast furnaces and reduced the 1959 steel production figures by one-third, after the official *People's Daily* claims of April 15, 1959 of 375 million metric tons

of grain produced in 1958 had been officially lowered by one-third, and after
the Lushan conference decision to downgrade the people's communes to a
three-level collective ownership system with effective control resting with
the smaller production brigade, Mao still persisted in his doctrinal prediction
of success for the people's communes! At Lushan, during the first week in
August, Mao selected, favorably annotated, printed, and distributed to comrades three articles that dealt with the people's communes. In commenting
on August 5 on the article dealing with the restoration of mess halls in one
commune, Mao displayed his desperate search for confirmation of his ideology, seeking isolated cases of success among the welter of commune failures
to prove his prophecy:

> This piece seems worthy of reading, and is, therefore, printed and dis-
> tributed to comrades. Tens of mess halls of a brigade were suddenly
> dissolved, and after a while they have been reactivated. The moral is
> that one must not capitulate in face of difficulties. Things like people's
> communes and collective mess halls have deep economic roots. They
> should not nor can they be blown away by a gust of wind. Some mess
> halls might be blown away by the wind, but there are bound to be some
> people or a majority of people who will start them again. Perhaps after
> a few days, or a few months, or even a longer time, they will be blown
> back again.[9]

A similar adamancy of ideological conviction and search for confirmation is
displayed in Mao's comments of the next day on the article concerning the
successful Wang Kuo-fan commune:

> These two articles are to be printed and distributed to the comrades.
> The responsible comrades of the various provincial, municipal, and
> district party committees are hereby requested to distribute the article
> on the Wang Kuo-fan commune to all communal party committees
> under their jurisdiction, and also to ask the latter to study what experi-
> ence could be adopted. In my view, they can all be adopted. . . . I think
> it would be possible for each special district to find one or more suc-
> cessful communes like the Wang Kuo-fan commune. Please search care-
> fully, and study them after you have found them. Also, write some
> articles for publication in order to propagate your experiences.[10]

The second of these articles entitled "What Are the People That Have More
Complaints in Rural Villages Now?" was annotated by Mao as "related to
those people who have more complaints at Lushan now," namely rightist
class enemies.[11] As proof of his contention that a nationwide conspiracy of
rightist class enemies was sabotaging his Great Leap, Mao circulated on
August 10 yet another annotated article entitled "Report' Concerning the

Dissolution of Wu-Wei Hsien Mess Halls by Order of Chang K'ai-fan, Secretary of Anhwei Party Committee." This article, Mao contended, demonstrated that not only are there "right opportunists in the Central Committee, that is, those comrades of the Military Club; they are also found at the provincial level."[12]

Simultaneously, this desperate search for confirmation of the doctrinal prediction was reflected in a resurgence of utopian commune construction activities at the provincial level. In Kwangtung province on August 10, *Nam Fang Jih Pao* carried an editorial attacking those "recklessly trying to scandalize our Great Leap Forward" and urging people to "summon the zeal to resist this rightist tendency. . . . If such a phenomenon is not changed, we shall have no way to fulfill our purpose of a continuation of the Leap Forward."[13] By mid-September, this newspaper had begun a series of articles to "systematically refute the false utterances directed against the Great Leap Forward and the people's commune."[14] The resurgence of communes reached its peak in Kwangtung with the October 1 celebration of the tenth anniversary of the founding of the Chinese People's Republic. At this time, a meeting of the Kwangtung provincial people's council was held to mobilize local residents for the new utopian surge.[15] However, inconspicuously, the pragmatic political leadership were folding the structure of communes and silently stealing into the indifferent night of reality. The central committee directive of September 23 had clearly allowed for more private marketing than in the previous year. Private plots grew. The rural people's communes were folding. In the spring of 1960, Mao's Lushan exhortations on communes were temporarily heeded: last-gasp effort in the search for confirmation of the people's commune precept occurred with the nationwide campaign to construct urban communes.[16] Although this new administrative unit for combining agricultural and industrial labor had been introduced in Ch'eng-chow and Ch'eng-tu in 1958 as a further step toward communism, the movement did not spread to the bulk of the nation until the spring of 1960. In Canton, the urban commune movement began in February 1960 and peaked in April with 3,8000 commune workshops and 61,000 workers.[17] However, the urban communes were much more of an ideological formalism than their fading rural prototypes; they were sustained in their short life span by the practical necessity of distributing food from rural to urban areas during the Great Leap debacles. Although several thousands of workers and unemployed were organized into newly established handicraft factories, the greatest change in life ways was brought about by the organization of new plots of land and new mess halls. In May, 1960, the Kwangtung provincial party committee declared:

> In the course of the movement for the establishment of people's communes in the cities, all residents . . . must participate. Each of the

people's communes must have an appropriate amount of land and an appropriate number of peasants. . . . Agricultural production conducted by the urban people's communes must be geared to the needs of the livelihood of the people.[18]

By the summer of 1960, virtually all residents of Canton participated in the urban communes, but the mess halls faded within months after their formation and as the rural communes were downgraded, so the urban communes faded away as the food shortage eased.

Besides the active search for empirical confirmation of the commune precept, the other major activity of the Maoists emanating from the Lushan plenum was fervent fundamentalist proselyting for the thought of Mao Tse-tung, i.e., the attempt to find in the affirmation of other persons confirmation for the validity of the failed dialectics. In fact, there was more proselyting for the Great Leap Forward movement and the principles upon which it was based after the movement had failed than while is was being planned and implemented! Mao persisted in apocalyptic hope. The public rationale for the movement shifted from the economic to the unabashedly ideological; the target audience shifted away from the bourgeois to the more supportive proletarian; and the class struggle rationalization of failure reached ever increasing heights as new critics appeared in the party and the politburo polarized.

Escalating Commitment in the Politburo

Between late 1959 and late 1962, members of the politburo evidenced changes in their commitment to the thought of Mao Tse-tung. In the first year and a half, the radical Maoists were on the rise; in the last year and a half the opposition began to rear its head. These oscillations culminated in Mao's return to the "first line" in September 1962 when he convened the tenth party plenum. He was then to face a more polarized politburo.

Immediately following the ideological disconfirmations with the reports of Great Leap debacles and failures of the people's communes at Lushan, it was Mao himself who initiated extensive proselyting activities for the ideology of Marxism-Leninism and the thought of Mao Tse-tung. In his Lushan plenum speech of July 23, Mao called for the launching of an ideological study movement in the party. Following the speech at the conference he proselyted for the people's commune by annotating and distributing articles favorable to them, while persisting in his doctrinal prediction of their success. Just three days after his speech, Mao clarified to assembled comrades the non-party targets of his proposed proselyting movement:

Nonetheless, both within and without the Party, a new phenomenon has appeared: Rightist sentiments, rightist ideology, and rightist activities have grown and become rampant, as manifested in a number of materials printed and distributed to comrades at this conference. . . . This situation is of a bourgeois nature. Another situation is of the nature of ideology within the proletariat. They like us all want socialism, not capitalism. This is the basic similarity between us and these comrades. However, there is some divergence between their viewpoint and ours in that their sentiment is somewhat abnormal. They have lacked confidence in overcoming prevailing difficulties. They have unconsciously put themselves in the awkward position between the leftists and rightists, thus becoming typical middle-of-the-roaders. . . . We believe that the attitude of these comrades could be changed. Our task is to rally round them and to strive for a change in their attitude.[19]

Having specified the proletariat as the principal target of this proselyting campaign, Mao proceeded to specify some of the study materials to be used by his party comrades during the campaign. On July 29, Mao advocated that they read the Preface to Marx's *Critique of Political Economy* to help them correctly to answer the question of whether the people's communes are in keeping with the demands of history and hence destined to survive.[20] One day before the end of the Lushan conference, Mao called the attention of his comrades to two more fundamental Marxist books, both of which were to be read by cadres and masses alike over the course of the next two years.

Comrades: I suggest that you read two books: One is *The Small Dictionary of Philosophy,* and the other is *Textbook of Political Economy.* Both books should be read within two years . . . with a view to criticize dogmatism in the past from a theoretical point of view, but not empiricism. The principal danger now is revisionism.[21]

Mao's pressing need for social support to bolster his shaken ideological views is well expressed by a few of his words to his comrades on the closing day of the conference regarding the significance of a certain classical essay. Withdrawing into the wellsprings of his belief system, Mao metaphorically resuscitated the pantheon of his teachers with an anachronistic assemblage of supportive living souls:

We should invite such fellows like Engels, Kautsky, Plekhanov, Stalin, Li Ta-chao, Lu Hsun, and Ch'u Ch'iu-pai "to a discourse on the quintessence of the universe and to distinguish the merits of all things," to speak about the necessity of the Great Leap, the causes of communes, and the extreme importance of putting politics in command. Thus, Marx would "survey it" and Lenin "would calculate it meticulously in order to be sure of its utility." When I was young, I used to read this essay. Now after a lapse of forty years, I recently remembered it, and when I turned over the book to read it, I thought I had found an old friend. Thus, I want to offer it to the comrades.[22]

Less passively, on the same final day of the Lushan conference, Mao reaffirmed two of his own basic ideological precepts on the utility of the dialectical analysis of history and on the continuation of class struggle. He then employed these precepts first to analyze the situation at Lushan, and to account for the rightist opinion deviates that had cropped up within the party, and second to specify the means of resolving the "social contradictions" he had uncovered. At this point in time, August 1959, the rightist opinion deviates were to be altered in their ideological views by the democratic method of persuasion:

> The struggle that has arisen at Lushan is a class struggle. It is the continuation of the life-or-death struggle between the two great antagonists of the bourgeoisie and the proletariat in the process of the socialist revolution during the past decade. . . . With the cessation of the old social struggle, new social struggle will arise. In short, in accordance with materialistic dialectics, contradition and struggle are perpetual; otherwise there would be no world. . . .

> This is a class struggle in society, and the intraparty struggle has merely reflected the class struggle in society. This is by no means surprising. . . . They [party rightists] must be handled as a contradiction among the people. It is necessary to adopt the policy of "solidarity-criticism-solidarity," "taking lessons from the past and being alert in the future in healing illness and saving life," "stringent criticism but lenient punishment," and "watching first and helping second." It is not only necessary to keep them in the Party, but also to keep them in the Provincial Committees and in the Central Committee, while certain comrades should even be kept in the Politburo.[23]

About one month after the close of Lushan conference, Mao found a much more receptive audience for his views in an extraordinary meeting of the combined members of the military affairs committee and the foreign affairs conference, the future architects of the revolutionary new socialist man in China and the future engineers of burgeoning Maoist "people's wars" in the developing nations. Addressing the members of what he described as a "very successful" meeting and receiving support from Lin Piao, Mao reasserted his Great Leap ideas and attacked his critics in the party. Mao noted with satisfaction that the "Lushan Conference and this conference, as well as party organizations at all levels throughout the nation, are discussing the resolutions of the Eighth Plenary Conference of the Eighth Congress. They are taking advantage of this event to educate the broad masses so that they may be further enhanced and awakened. This has completely borne out the fact that the overwhelming majority—say, 95 percent—do not support them [party rightists]."[24] Mao again accused his party critics of employing hindsight and of grossly exaggerating trivial shortcomings in the Great Leap movement; he also suggested that they were "betraying their fatherland by conspiring with foreign countries."[25] Relentless in his proselyting for the Great Leap Forward, Mao reasserted his view that, "the current task is that the entire people and party should build China into a great power within a few five-year plans."[26] To this end, Mao renewed his call for "solidarity" and "discipline." In this audience his call impinged upon more receptive ears.

In 1960, Mao, himself, was to pen a revealing and highly critical set of study notes on the Soviet Union's *Textbook of Political Economy*. In his extensive notes, he reaffirmed the correctness of his Great Leap ideology, reasserted the promise of Great Leap success, and pronounced themes of proselyting proletarians that were to be greatly amplified when the Maoists gained control of the propaganda apparatus six years later. Giving extensive reference to China's guerrilla heritage, Mao criticized some of the fundamental viewpoints of the Soviet text. It does not discuss the "mass line" and "politics in command" nor "walking on two legs," while it one-sidedly stresses material incentives; furthermore, it does not "start from contradictions in its study of socialist economy."[27] Mao asserted that China would eventually carry through the organizational transformation from ownership by the production team to ownership by the commune to ownership by all the people; 1960, itself, would be a year of "great development of production."[28] In this specific prediction, Mao was greatly mistaken. Mao then went on to stress the need to proselyte for proletarian ideology stating that it will take ten to twenty years, or half a century, to utterly destroy the remnant forces of bourgeoisie ideology and their influence.[29] Later he emphasized, "The question of the struggle between the two roads of socialism and capitalism and the question of employing socialist ideology to remold man and discipline him are a big problem in our country."[30] Ominously Mao wrote the following critique of the media:

> If [newspapers, periodicals, broadcasting stations, and motion pictures] lie in the hands of a limited number of right opportunists, then the vast majority of people throughout the country who are in urgent need of a Great Leap Forward will have their rights in these sectors taken away from them. . . . In short the people must have the right to take charge of the superstructure.[31]

In the cold of winter 1959, following the brittle Lushan plenum at which Comrade P'eng Teh-huai delivered his shattering attack on Mao's Three Red Banners and bludgeoned the Maoists with irrefutable evidence of Great Leap failures, the clarion call went out from on high to assemble the proletariat for vocal affirmation of the correctness of the Three Red Banners coupled with concerted study of the thought of Mao Tse-tung. This initial broadside of Maoist proselyting took the form of a national Mao study campaign in the winter of 1959 and the spring of 1960, with reports of concerted Mao study activities emanating from the provinces scattered throughout China. Anhui, Fukien, Kirin, Kwangtung, Peking, Shanghai, and Shansi all provided documentation of this initial proletarian "cultural revolution." At this tender stage in the phylogeny of the cultural revolutionaries, proselyting activities were dimly focused upon the proletariat broadly construed to include cadres, youth, peasants and workers. Most attention was concentrated upon assembling professions of social support from proletarian believers, and less attention was given to the disparagement of bourgeoisie disbelievers.

The precursors of Red Guard proselyting activities of 1966-1967 can be seen in the December 17, 1959 issue of *Hupeh Jih Pao* (Hupeh Daily). This issue of the paper carried a lead article entitled "Arm the Youths with the thought of Mao Tse-tung."[32] The text of this article leaves little room for doubt regarding the desire and ability of the ideologically shaken Maoists to assemble social support for their ideals in the face of empirical evidence of ideological failure:

In the past year or more, the general League branch in Shih-yuanho administrative *ch'u* of Ch'engkuan Commune in Lotien *hsien* has been carrying out a political and theoretical study movement centering on the writings of Chairman Mao among the League members and youths. Up to the present, the administrative *ch'u* has established a school devoted to the study of Mao Tse-tung's works and eight evening League schools which are run by the production brigades. Small groups have also been established by the production teams for the study of Chairman Mao's works. Eight volumes of *Selected Works of Mao Tse-tung*, 42 copies of "On the Correct Handling of Contradictions Among the People," and 54 copies of "Be Concerned with Livelihood of the Masses and Pay Attention to the Method of Work" were purchased. Some 800 League members and youths have successively studied "On Contradictions," "On Practice," "Be Concerned with the Livelihood of the Masses and Pay Attention to the Method of Work," "On the Correct Handling of Contradictions Among the People" and other documents.

Through this study campaign, League members and youths in Shih-yuanho administrative *ch'u* have deepened their understanding of the correctness and greatness of the general line, the Great Leap Forward and the People's commune as well as the struggle between the two roads in the countryside, thereby greatly heightening their level of consciousness.

Youth was not the only population segment sought out by the Maoists for social support following the disconcerting events communicated to them at the Lushan plenum. In keeping with Maoist proselyting directives stemming from the events of this conference, cadres, workers, and peasants became active students of the thought of Mao Tse-tung. For example, on February 7, 1960, *Nam Fang Jih Pao* (Southern Daily) carried the following report that "the Movement for Studying the Thought of Mao Tse-tung is in Full Swing in Kwangtung Province":

> While implementing the resolution of the Lushan Plenum Kwangtung province has plunged itself into a movement for studying Mao Tse-tung's Thought with emphasis on the significance of the general line.
>
> In order to speed up the development of the movement, the first secretaries of Party organs at different levels are taking personal command, planning ways and means to solve difficult problems as they proceed, and mobilizing the masses far and wide. Cadres, workers and peasants all pledge that they will seriously study Mao Tse-tung's thought, and apply the theoretical knowledge they have acquired to the actual work they are doing. In Party committees are the *hsien* level and above, small teams or groups for the study of Mao Tse-tung's Thought have been set up, and in all departments, units, people's communes and production brigades, secretaries of the relevant Party committees have been appointed to supervise the theoretical work. Those of the Canton Municipal Public Security Bureau who have made faster progress have already finished the second assignment. Most of them have been studying the *Selected Works of Mao Tse-tung* regularly one hour a day. Workers of factories and enterprises in Canton have generally completed the study of the general line and have started on the second assignment. In some areas, cadres at the basic level are organized into small guiding teams to aid the worker and peasant masses in the study of the Mao Tse-tung's works.[33]

Besides nurturing the movement aimed at assembling social support by the mass study of the thought of Mao Tse-tung, the Maoists issued repeated calls to party cadres and proletarians alike to apply the basic principles of Mao to the solution of practical problems in their search for empirical confirmation of the correctness of the ideology. This secondary aim of the Mao study movement is well illustrated in an article by P'ei Feng-hua, First Secretary of the CCP Yung-t'ai Hsien Committee, in the February 2, 1960 edition of *Fukien Jih Pao* (Fukien Daily). The article entitled "Study Comrade Mao Tse-tung's Method of Work" describes how one can employ dialectic as expressed in his "On Contradictions" to search out the principal and secondary contradictions inherent in production situations to solve economic problems and increase production.

The initial 1960 broadside of mass Maoist proselyting among the proletarians was to be led by the party vanguard. They were to be abetted in their efforts by the support of existing professional, cultural, and educational workers and by recruitment from the ranks of the proletariat of active and talented novices.[34] In June of 1960, Ch'en Po-ta attended an important national conference of 6,000 cultural and educational workers which represented the zenith of this early cultural revolution. Although the Minister of Culture, Lu Ting-yi, delivered a brief and perfunctory inaugural address, the keynote speaker was more impassioned. Lin Feng, a member of the central committee, delivered the keynote address of the conference entitled, "All-Out Effort in Cultural Revolution Among Worker-Peasant Masses and Labor Performance by Intellectuals."[35] This address was replete with references to Mao's thought and especially to his Yenan Line on art and literature and the successes at Yenan. For the present, Lin recommended establishing full-time primary schools under the auspices of the people's communes. Lin Feng shared Mao's persistent prediction of the viability of communes as he proselyted for the application of his thought.

So it was that the early "cultural revolution" was set off by the party apparatus in 1960 with a call for national and regional conferences of cultural and educational workers in Peking, Shanghai, and other major cities. But in this version of the "revolution," the domestic class enemy was played down. These conferences stressed the development of a study movement among workers and peasants with particular emphasis on the works of Mao Tse-tung; the strengthening of the cultural forces of the working class; and the need to oppose foreign imperialistic powers.[36] In line with the decisions of the conferences, the works of Mao, phonetic readers, and "works of the masses" dominated the publishing program of the year. In October of that year, Volume IV of *The Selected Works of Mao Tse-tung* was published with much fanfare. Newspapers, of course, also played an important part in the mass education and propaganda drive.

The slogan adopted during the year with regard to the newspapers was "let newspapers be run by the whole party." To achieve this, writing teams or correspondent groups were established in all communes, schools, factories and enterprises. These teams or groups were under the direct leadership of the first secretaries of party committees at all levels and in all spheres. Workers and peasants were encouraged to make contributions.[37] Writing teams or correspondent groups often accounted for a substantial part of the journalistic output of their area. Although national statistics were lacking since late 1959, in the Pai Ho commune in Meng Chin, Honan, sixty-four reporting teams, comprising 428 correspondents, sent more than 3,600 articles to newspapers and magazines during one year and more than 1,170 of these were published.[38] In the first four months of 1960, 40 percent of the articles sent out from the Anhui suboffice of the *New China News Agency* originated from correspondent groups.[39]

Although the writing teams produced an increased amount of material for the newspapers, the shortage of paper limited their size and circulation. In order to expand the reading public, without increasing circulation, greater efforts were made to organize newspaper-reading groups during the year. For example, the Kashgar special district in Sinkiang, a culturally backward border area of eighty-four peoples' communes, had set up 14,800 such groups by the end of March, 1960.[40] In Yung-chi Hsien, Kirin, a newspaper-reading network was completed in the first half of 1960, including 4,000 newspaper-reading cadres.[41] In these groups, newspapers were shared and literate cadres read out the contents to those who were illiterate.

Mass participation in literary activities was one of the features of the early "cultural revolution." In April, 1960, it was estimated that there were over 3,000,000 participants among the workers.[42] Peasants who were engaged in some form of literary activity were even more numerous, and writers' associations were set up in many people's communes throughout the year. In Hupeh province alone there were reported to be more than 80,000 writing teams.[43] Workers in Shansi province were credited with producing more than 8,000,000 literary works during a two-year period, ending May, 1960, while 267 writing teams in the Su Chi people's commune in Anhui province were said to have written more than 1,030,000 folk songs, 143 dance songs and 270 plays during the same period.[44] These literary "works of the masses" were soon to wane.

The year 1961 was to prove a hard one for Maoist proselyting. In his opening speech before the ninth plenum in January, Mao called mainly for more investigation and study. He noted that comrades of the central committee had concentrated in the past year on international questions and had done it well. He then urged a renewed focus on internal questions "to oppose counter-revolutionary elements and rigid bureaucratic elements, and to organize poor and lower middle peasant committees to replace them."[45] This early call for the formation of peasant committees was to be repeated by Mao through 1965 with very little response from the party. Mao went on to restate his assertion at Lushan that the party, itself, contained elements representing the bourgeoisie and the petty bourgeoisie and insisted they be cleansed from the organization. He also reminded his party audience that he had talked about "light industry, heavy industry, and agriculture," "simultaneous development of agriculture and industry" and "walking on two legs" for five years. In 1961, he hopefully stated, "Now they may possibly be realized."[46] Mao was again mistaken in his prediction.

In diametric opposition to the extreme proselyting for the thought of Mao Tse-tung of 1960, 1961 witnessed another major relaxation of party control

over and rectification of the intellectuals. Merle Goldman has aptly characterized this period as the "unique blooming and contending of 1961-62."[47]
Before the formal launching of the campaign, Liu Shao-ch'i publicly initiated
the spirit of the campaign in his speech at the June meeting to celebrate the
fortieth anniversary of the Chinese Communist Party:

> The intellectuals are an important force, indispensable to the success of
> our socialist construction. . . . They have made valuable contributions
> on all fronts of socialist construction. We should continue to enlarge
> the ranks of intellectuals and continue the policy of "a hundred flowers
> blossom and a hundred schools of thought contend," so that the cause
> of socialist science and culture may flourish still more in our country.[48]

Thus the leader of the party's first line, especially since April 1959, was
first to formally sanction the indirect opposition of the intellectuals to the
thought of Mao Tse-tung, even though Liu had not vigorously supported
Mao's 1956-1957 blooming and contending campaign. The polarization between the fervent advocates of the thought of Mao Tse-tung and the party
pragmatists was growing. The June 1960 activities of Ch'en Po-ta and Liu
Shao-ch'i contrasted sharply. In August 1961, Vice-Premier Ch'en Yi inaugurated the movement in a speech that was reminiscent of the one given by
Chou En-lai in January 1956 to usher in the Hundred Flowers movement.
Similar to Chou's earlier speech, Ch'en Yi's speech sought to invigorate the
intellectual community by encouraging greater respect for the scholar and
higher regard for his contribution to the nation, but by now they had less
regard for Mao.[49]

The inauguration of this formal thaw in the party's relations with the
intellectuals required two and a half years after the punitive antirightists
campaign came to an end with the end of 1958. In the latter half of 1959,
following the Lushan plenum, central party controls were strengthened; and
"most significantly, imitations of themes later to be used in the Cultural
Revolution appeared in September, 1960."[50] Efforts were made to teach
the youth about the revolutionary traditions and ascetic ways of the Yenan
period. In 1962, however, there was a relaxation of party controls over the
intellectuals. The drive to revolutionize China's youth was postponed. The
early "cultural revolution" was aborted. Indeed, some PLA cadres, considered
more disciplined than party cadres, were even chastened for treating intellectuals like parasites rather than assigning them special consideration for
their professional achievement.[51]

When Ch'en Yi inaugurated the second and softer campaign of "blooming
and contending," his rules of the game protected the party organization but
left the thought of Mao Tse-tung vulnerable to the criticism of the intellectuals. In this campaign, contrary to the previous period of blooming and

contending, some officials high in theparty hierarchy conspired with the non-party intellectuals to derogate the thought of Mao Tse-tung. They opposed the glorification of the thought of Mao Tse-tung; they deprecated the Great Leap Forward as unrealistic; and they supported the conscientious opposition of contentious individuals like P'eng Teh-huai.[52] These party critics of Mao were to be found principally in the propaganda department and the Peking party committee, the very organizations instrumental in implementing the thaw. These officials were responsible for convening the critical Darien conference of August 1962 and for permitting the publication of satirical literature such as the column "Notes from a Three Family Village," which openly appeared in newspapers such as *Ch'ien Hsien* (Front Line) during the same year. In December of 1961, P'eng Chen convened a secret conference to investigate the Great Leap failures.[53]

The year 1962 opened with a fitting introduction to the critical literary conferences and satirical plays to appear later that year. In contrast to the conference of 6,000 cultural workers attended by Ch'en Po-ta in June 1960, in January 1962 an extraordinary central committee work conference of 7,000 cadres was convened at which Liu Shao-ch'i criticized Maoist mobilization policies as responsible for the disastrous consequences of the Great Leap Forward and commune program. Liu asserted that "it is necessary to point out at a large conference that for all these defects and mistakes in work over the past several years the Center must primarily take the responsibility." A principal cause of these mistakes was that the "mass movements" mobilized for economic development had gotten out of control, "wasting the energy . . . of the masses" and "seriously undermining . . . the enthusiasm and effort of the masses." Besides policy errors in the economic and social fields, the center had promoted an "excessive" political struggle, with the result that "both the masses and the cadres . . . dared not tell the truth," "there was no exchange of opinion between the top and the bottom," and "democratic centralism in the life of the Party . . . had been gravely impaired."[54] Thus, Liu asserted that there were basic policy errors behind the Great Leap and commune program, and to correct the situation he advocated that the party center freely admit these errors to the rank and file of the cadres and get about the business of repairing the institutional integrity of the party as an instrument for carrying out the revolution from above.

Mao's reply at this working conference of the central committee clearly indicated the widening rift between himself and Liu Shao-ch'i resulting from their discrepant reactions to the Great Leap failure. In contrast to Liu, Mao asserted that the party's general line had been basically correct and that "the shortcomings and mistakes" in work lay with the party cadres who had erred in implementing these policies. Rather than citing "mass movements" and mobilization policies as a cause of the difficulties, Mao stood in 180 degree opposition to Liu and stressed the necessity for leading personnel of the party at *all* levels to go before the masses to engage in "criticism and self-criticism." This was necessary to reunite the party and the masses, to "mobilize the enthusiasm of the masses" without which it was impossible to overcome difficulties.[55] Thus, while Mao reaffirmed the basic correctness of his ideology and his policies and advocated enlisting the support of the masses to reform those party and nonparty cadres who were currently representing the "bourgeoisie" in seeking a "capitalist restoration" in China, Liu saw no taints of the class enemy in the party and felt no need to proselyte for Mao's thought.

In his "Talk on the Question of Democratic Centralism," Mao reasserted the validity of his dialectics. He explicitly reaffirmed his 1957 dialectical analysis on the correct handling of contradictions among the people and its prescription for letting the masses engage in politics to arouse their "enthusiasm."[56] Mao reaffirmed his mass line principle of political leadership saying, "Comrades, we are revolutionaries. If we have truly committed mistakes . . . we should solicit the views of the masses of the people and other comrades, and make self-examination ourselves."[57] Finally, Mao reaffirmed his 1957 thesis on the existence of class struggle in a socialist society stating that "the overthrown classes will attempt to stage a comeback, and new bourgeois elements will emerge in the socialist society. There are classes and class struggle throughout the period of socialist society."[58] Of the four basic tenets of the thought of Mao Tse-tung described in Chapter 1, only the tenet of economic construction was not reaffirmed by Mao in this speech, presumably because economic difficulties were not severe and Mao had agreed to a slower pace of his basically correct programs in this sector of society.

In his call for action to overcome these difficulties, Mao urged the party vanguard to take its case to its proletarian constituents, and in alliance with them to correct the mistaken implementation of Mao's basically correct policies and to reform the bourgeois ideology of his opponents who had sabotaged the movement:

> The exercise of dictatorship over the reactionary classes calls not for the elimination of all reactionaries, but for remolding them with the proper method so that they may become new people. Without extensive people's democracy, the dictatorship of the proletariat cannot be consolidated and political power will be unstable. Without democracy, without arousing the masses and without supervision by the masses, it is impossible to effectively exercise dictatorship over the reactionaries and bad elements or effectively to remold them; they will continue to make trouble, and there is still the possibility of a restoration.[59]

So it was that in his effort to seek social support for his failed ideology, Mao mimicked the reactions of besmirched prophets before him by advocating opening the private and privileged sanctuary of the party's methods and teachings to the scrutiny of the masses at large.

Mao had a few firm supporters for his view in January 1962. At the work conference, itself, Lin Piao openly proposed to the 7,000 assembled cadres the panacea to China's problems—to study "Mao Tse-tung's Thought . . . the soul and very life of all work. When one masters it, one becomes proficient in everything."[60] Chou En-lai also supported Mao at the conference.[61] Simultaneously, a larger audience was informed of the persisting Maoist view: The editorial in the January issue of Ch'en Po-ta's *Red Flag* was entitled "Summon Up Full Vigor, Strive for New Victory in Socialist Construction."[62] Thus, under fire, the Maoist assertion of the essential correctness of the Great Leap and its underlying ideology was spread to the larger party and the attentive among the masses at the beginning of 1962.

Opposition to Mao's Great Leap had begun to crystallize in the politburo in 1962. The party bureaucrats, Liu Shao-ch'i and Teng Hsiao-p'ing, had openly opposed Mao's policy at the January conference.[63] Liu had explicitly called for a reversal of verdicts in the cases of the purged military professionalists, P'eng Teh-huai and Chang Wen-t'ien, who themselves implicitly opposed Mao's leap policies through 1962. And at various economic conferences throughout the year, party economic specialists advocated retreats from the leap. Ch'en Yun persisted in his conservative views. Po Yi-po advocated reliance on material incentives as opposed to ideological ones; T'an Chen-lin took tools and tractors from the dying communes and distributed them to state farms.[64]

Indeed, the most vociferous speakers during the remainder of 1962 were not the aroused proletarian masses from whom Mao sought social support for his ideology, but the critical "bourgeois" intellectuals whom Mao had entreated the proletarians to reform. Mao's politburo opponents had many supporters among the intellectuals. They wrote their biting satires of Mao's Great Leap policies across the pages of Peking papers; they spoke their minds at the Darien conference in August 1962, and they fundamentally contradicted Mao's dialectics in the "two combine into one" heresy.

"Notes from a Three Family Village" was one of many literary pieces and plays which employed the traditional Chinese tactic of using historical analogy with double meaning to make a political point. One of its authors, Teng T'o was the former editor of the *People's Daily* and director of the ideological and cultural activities of the Peking party committee since 1959. Along with Wu Han and Liao Mo-sha, he authored an article in 1961 in the fourteenth edition of *Ch'ien Hsien* entitled "A Special Treatment of Amnesia." This article implied that Mao suffered from a form of insanity that led him to irrational behavior and decisions. In another essay, "An Egg as an Asset," Teng indirectly denounced the Great Leap Forward as a dream unrelated to reality which had no basis in economic principles or practical experience. Party and nonparty intellectuals as well had begun to organize and act in opposition to the thought and policy of Mao Tse-tung.

The Darien conference was held for two weeks in August 1962 and presided over by party literary czar Chou Yang. Ostensibly, the conference was convened to discuss short novels about the countryside; in reality the conference was a platform for writers to describe the misery which had befallen the peasants during the Great Leap. It disparaged the use of mass campaigns, and urged writers to show that the Great Leap was not the utopia it was decreed to be, but an illusion based on a theory that had not shown results.[65] At the conference, K'ang Cho, a prodigy of Chou Yang, advocated a literary policy extolling complex "middle characters," in opposition to the one-dimensional, all red heroes fervently championed by the Maoist zealots.

In the "two combine into one" heresy some party intellectuals reinterpreted Mao's 1937 Yenan essay "On Contradiction" to provide a rationale for the dying out of class struggle through group compromise. This position reinterpreted Mao to flatly contradict Mao's own class struggle rationalization for the Great Leap failures and caused continuing controversy from its inception in 1961 through 1964. The author of this view, Yang Hsien-chen, was a member of the central committee and head of the party's higher school until September 1961.[66] Beginning in 1961, Yang delivered a series of lectures and discussion at the school which were hotly debated and eventually found their way into print in May 1964 in a *Kuang Ming Daily* article by two of Yang's students. After many articles on the subject, including treatment in *Red Flag*, Yang's views were subdued and he himself disappeared from the scene.[67]

The leading member of the opposition to Mao's Great Leap policies during the period from late 1959 until late 1962 was Liu Shao-ch'i. In the wake of Great Leap debacles reported at the Lushan plenum, as polarization grew between the Maoists and other party leaders, Liu Shao-ch'i did little to improve the domestic situation from the Maoist point of view. Liu ignored Maoist proselyting; presided over the retreat from Mao's leap; and publicly supported Mao's opponents. First of all, in stark contrast to the expressed motives and actions of Lin Piao, Liu did not share the motive to proselyte for the thought of Mao Tse-tung. As mentioned in Chapter 5, on October 1, 1959, immediately after Lushan, Liu published an article to celebrate the tenth anniversary of the Chinese People's Republic which praised Marxism-Leninism but gave no particular mention to the thought of Mao Tse-tung. In July of 1961, after Lin Piao had launched the PLA campaign to study the works of Mao, Liu presented his view that the party needed to initiate a new study campaign;

but the content of the materials Liu advocated for study differed significantly from Lin's: Liu included Mao's works as the second topic in a list of four, another of which was the Soviet model of economic development.[68] Furthermore, during the same anniversary celebrations, on June 30, 1961, Liu advocated in a speech to party leaders that the party initiate a renewed Hundred Flowers policy, which spurred the intellectuals on to greater ridicule of Mao's Great Leap. Adding insult to injury, in August 1962, Liu printed a revision of his own *How To Be a Good Communist,* which he originally delivered at Yenan in 1939. In 1967 Mao was to publicly villify Liu's publication. In this revision, Liu advoided mentioning the thought of Mao Tse-tung and instead emphasized that "all party members should learn from the thinking of Marx and Lenin and strive to be their worthy pupil."[69] Thus, instead of proselyting for the thought of Mao Tse-tung in the wake of the Great Leap, Liu was providing opportunity for the criticism of Mao's Great Leap, peddling his own works, and legitimizing them with the words of Marx and Lenin. Liu was not necessarily insincere in these actions, but to Mao, as evidenced by his allusion to critical novels in his tenth plenum speech, they were very dissonance provoking provided he were to continue to believe Liu a good Marxist-Leninist. Second, Liu was suspect in the eyes of the Maoists by virtue of the fact that as leader of the "first line" since 1956 and Chairman of the People's Republic since April 1959, Liu presided over the retreat from the Great Leap. According to reliable accounts, after the debacles reported at Lushan, Liu issued in January 1961, a "twelve-point emergency directive regarding rural work" which returned to the peasants the right to cultivate private plots and to sell produce in "free markets" and further stipulated that labor should be given more rest. In 1961 Liu and Teng Hsiao-p'ing drafted several regulations retreating from the Great Leap. In May, the Sixty Articles provided for a drastic decentralization of the communes, restoring production authority to the small production team and the Seventy Articles provided for the normalization of industrial activities.[70] Again at the working conference of the central committee in January and February, 1962, Liu openly supported the criticism of the Great Leap and advocated a conservative economic program. Finally, according to reliable accounts, in late 1962, Liu broadened his January conference support of those sharing P'eng's view and supported an attempt to reverse the Lushan decision on P'eng Teh-huai and restore the Marshall's honor.[71] Liu is alleged to have asserted that P'eng's letter of opinion sent to the central committee at Lushan in August 1959, attacking Mao's Great Leap Forward and the people's communes, had been borne out by the facts, and that the subsequent purge of P'eng had been "unfair and had been carried too far."[72] Supported by Liu and other leaders, P'eng had in June 1962, written a new report of 80,000 words to the central committee demanding a reversal of the verdict in his case. Thus the polarization between Maoists and non-Maoists had increased to a critical point by three hard years after the Lushan plenum: Non-Maoists became anti-Maoists in need of reform.

In recalling the period, Mao's wife Chiang Ch'ing had the following to say:

> This revolution [GPCR] should be traced back to the 10th Plenum of the 8th Central Committee in 1962. At that Plenum our great leader spoke on the problems of class, class contradiction, and class struggle. Why did he bring up these problems? It was because there were people opposing Chairman Mao's proletarian revolutionary line.[73]

Chiang recalled how she had suffered a "grave ailment" in 1960 and how, upon doctor's advice, she had sought solace in the arts. What she found to her dismay was "that what appeared on stage and screen was lavish, foreign, and ancient" art which on the whole only "propagated capitalism and feudalism instead of serving the workers, peasants, and soldiers," as Mao had designated the task of art and literature at Yenan. In 1962 she claims she naively approached Liu Shao-ch'i with her problem and was rebuffed. She then contacted four ministers and vice ministers of the party propaganda department and the ministry of culture with her complaint; "but nobody wanted to listen to me." She asked them to at least allow her the right to publish her comments, but they paid her no heed, "All news organs were under their control."[74] Indeed, neither Liu nor the ministers of culture shared Chiang's desire to proselyte for the ideology of the proletariat.

Subsequently, Chiang relates, she went to Shanghai in the winter of 1962 and met with Municipal Party Secretary K'o Ching-shih, who supported her in her desire to spread the proletarian ideology.[75] During the next six months, while the central committee was holding meetings, Chiang pressed her case with them and was again rebuffed. Chiang requested that Yao Wen-yuan, from the Shanghai committee, be present at the meetings; but he was rebuffed by them as a "goon." While K'o Ching-shih staged a proletarian drama festival of his own in Shanghai later in 1963, Chiang decided to become more active in the reform of the arts on her own. She chose some theatrical scripts and organized (the article) "On 'Hai Jui's Dismissal from Office'." The latter was done with the assistance of Mao and K'o Ching-shih. In the meantime, she claims she was put under surveillance and that her opponents had tape recorded the draft of the article. She succeeded with the aid of some high-ranking members of the PLA in reforming the Peking opera in the summer of 1964 and about the same time, Mao approved an article by Yao Wen-yuan and passed it down for all comrades to study. In April 1965, K'o Ching-shih died. After much forced delay of publication in Peking, it was Yao Wen-yuan's article, "A Review of the New Historical Play 'Hai Jui Dismissed from Office'," in the November 10, 1965 edition of

Shanghai's *Wen Hui Pao* that finally touched off the first volley in the Maoist onslaught aimed at the dissident intellectuals, Wu Han, Teng T'o, and Liao Mo-sha, in the early stages of the Cultural Revolution. Thus one train of events leading to the outbreak of the Cultural Revolution can be traced from P'eng's criticism of Mao's Great Leap at Lushan and the intellectuals' criticism of same in the immediate aftermath, through the ensuing reluctance on the part of many intellectuals and high party officials to proselyte for the thought of Mao Tse-tung. Had the Maoists their way, a more extensive and sustained "cultural revolution" would surely have erupted much earlier in the 1960s; instead they were thwarted in their proselyting efforts by recalcitrant power holders in the party.

Besides Mao, Lin, Ch'en, K'ang, and K'o, the sixth most highly committed politburo Maoist, Lo Jung-huan was also active in Maoist proselyting in the early sixties. After Lushan in April 1960, as a part of the effort to revive the leap, Lo participated in the national conference on militia work and voiced his opinion that "all activities of the people's militia should center on the development of production."[76] In February 1961 he supported publication and study of the unabridged version of Mao's Kutien speech which had been used as a basic document for PLA cadres during the rectification campaign at Yenan.[77] In August 1962 Lo insisted before the civilian and world readers of *Peking Review* on the importance of the application of the Maoist line on the primacy of politics. Lo died the following year.

Let us summarize the polarization that occurred in the politburo during the early sixties. In Chapter 3 we noted that the distribution in the politburo of commitment to Mao's thought in 1958 was approximately normal. It ran from Mao, Lin, K'ang and Ch'en on the left to P'eng Teh-huai, Po Yi-po and Ch'en Yun on the right with most of the members in the middle. Following the disconfirmations announced at Lushan and in accord with the discrepant reactions of members to those disconfirmations, the politburo polarized: The highly committed Maoists escalated their commitment taking on new Maoist actions in support of the ideology; the lowly committed did not engage in new committing Maoist actions; consequently, four years later by 1962, the middle of the distribution was being vacated, the attitudinal discrepancy between the group members over Maoist ideology increased, and the shape of the distribution became skewed. In the interim, the committed Maoists publicly supported Mao's class struggle rationalization in late 1959; they publicly supported Mao at the 1962 conference of 7,000 cadres; or they refrained from openly opposing him during this period. The lowly committed did not engage in any of these highly related actions (see Appendix A). Figure 6.1 uses the best available evidence to reconstruct the distribution of commitment to Mao's thought in the politburo at the time of the tenth plenum in late 1962. Compared with 1958, it is clear that the politburo had polarized.

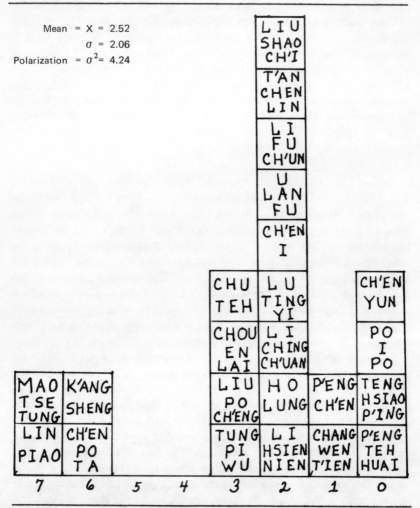

Mean = X = 2.52
σ = 2.06
Polarization = σ² = 4.24

Figure 6.1: DISTRIBUTION OF COMMITMENT TO MAO'S THOUGHT IN THE POLITBURO, 1962

As the politburo polarized over Maoist ideology to 1962, the social disagreement dissonance within it necessarily increased. Mao discovered increasing evidence that the politburo contained representatives of the class enemy within its own ranks. At the tenth plenum in the fall of 1962, Mao temporarily returned to the "first line" to issue his call for increased class struggle involving renewed rectification of cadres, and socialist education of the proletarian masses. Again, in the following four years polarization increased in the politburo. The committed Maoists escalated their commitment by actively supporting Mao's socialist education campaign, publicly endorsing the martyr Lei Feng as the incarnation of Mao's thought in 1963, and by rallying to Mao's call for a true proletarian Cultural Revolution in the spring of 1966. The uncommitted in the politburo found little reason to deepen the class struggle or engage in Mao's campaigns and abstained from action. As shown in Figure 6.2, by the time of the eleventh plenum in the fall of 1966, the politburo was even more polarized over Mao's thought. The social disagreement dissonance was so great and the obduracy of the uncommitted Maoists so intense, that the numerous members of the "class enemy" on the politburo were subsequently purged as formerly "nonantagonistic contradictions" became "antagonistic contraditions."

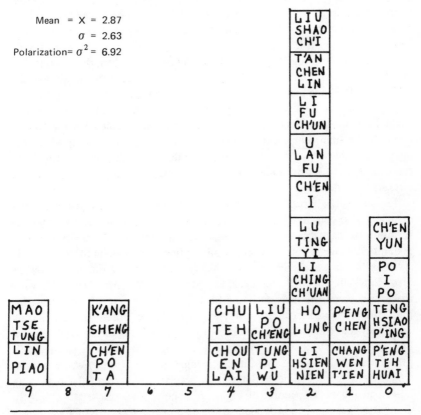

Figure 6.2: DISTRIBUTION OF COMMITMENT TO MAO'S THOUGHT IN THE POLITBURO, 1966

Keeping the Red Flag Flying

In his speech at the Cheng-tu conference in March 1958, Mao had announced the formation of a new set of theoretical party journals to supplement *People's Daily,* the newspaper organ of the central committee. Led by *Red Flag* at the center, these new journals followed the spirit of the Great Leap in that they were to "base their discussions mainly on the situation in their particular province" but also "express their views on the nation, the world and the universe. They may even discuss the sun and the Milky Way."[78] In this speech, Mao had scorned the earlier literary outbursts of bookish bourgeois authorities, encouraged the works of the proletarian masses and "invincible" youth, and asserted that "the future of China's poetry is folk songs first and the classics second."[79] Commending Ch'en Po-ta for his sympathetic speech, "Favoring the Modern and Scorning the Ancient," Mao appointed Ch'en to edit the lead journal, *Red Flag.*[80] In the introductory article to the first issue of *Red Flag* in June, Ch'en himself had accepted the charge for his journal "to hold ever higher the revolutionary *Red Flag* of the proletariat, any remaining flag of the bourgeoisie to be removed and replaced by the flag of the proletariat."[81] Thus, the avowed aim of Ch'en's journal was to proselyte for Mao's proletarian ideology. During 1958 and 1959, the contents of Ch'en's *Red Flag* were dominated by themes of economic promise. Especially prominent were statements extolling the Great Leap and people's communes coupled with endorsements of the Maoist tenet of the omnicompetent worker, claiming effort can accomplish seemingly impossible tasks.[82] Thereafter the contents were to change away from the economic toward the ideological with special emphasis on the deepened class struggle, domestic and foreign.

Following the Great Leap failures announced at Lushan, the politburo members who continued to proselyte for Mao's proletarian ideology by contribution to the pages of *Red Flag* significantly changed in composition: The committed Maoists increased their proselyting; the uncommitted desisted. As described in Chapter 3, the most highly committed Maoists by 1958 were Mao, Lin Piao, Ch'en Po-ta and K'ang Sheng. As shown in Figure 6.3 with the exception of the taciturn K'ang Sheng, they were precisely the ones who most sharply increased their proselyting in *Red Flag,* during the sixties over what they had contributed in the late fifties. Considering the remaining members of the politburo and incorporating data on their activities to the tenth plenum of 1962, we find that Liu Po-ch'eng, Chu Teh, Tung Pi-wu, and Chou En-lai were more highly committed to Mao's thought than the remaining fifteen members. Inspection of Figure 6.3 shows that this relatively highly committed group of eight tended to increase proselyting in *Red Flag* during the sixties while the remaining two-thirds of the politburo tended to decrease

KEY: | Committed | Uncommitted X

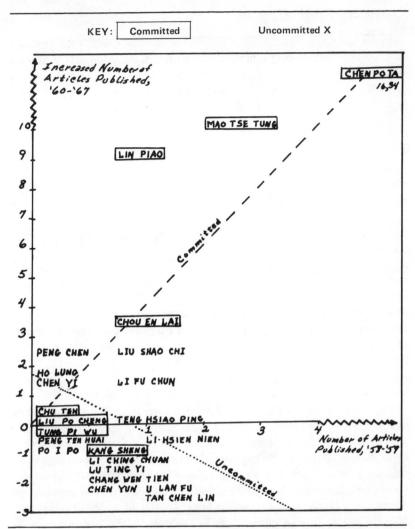

Figure 6.3: ANALYSIS OF COVARIANCE BETWEEN AMOUNT OF PROSELYTING
BY POLITBURO MEMBERS IN *RED FLAG* DURING 1958-1959 AND
INCREASED PROSELYTING DURING 1960-1967, CONTROLLING FOR
DEGREE OF COMMITMENT TO MAO'S THOUGHT.

proselyting. Thus the reactions to the Great Leap failure of the politburo
members further divided the powerful group: The committed Maoists among
them kept the Red Flag flying; the uncommitted did not. Furthermore, as
shown in Figure 6.4, the tendency of the eight relatively committed Maoists
to displace the uncommitted in proselyting in *Red Flag* sharply increased

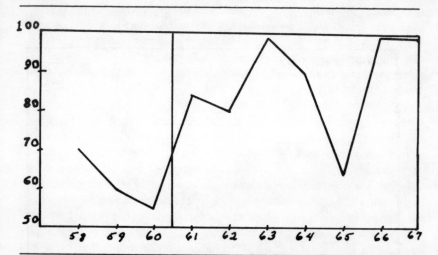

Figure 6.4: PERCENTAGE OF RED FLAG ARTICLES BY POLITBURO MEMBERS
CONTRIBUTED BY COMMITTED MAOISTS, 1958-1967

between 1960 and 1961, shortly after the Lushan plenum, as the worst economic disasters since the liberation bore out P'eng Teh-huai's dismal Lushan predictions.

Dispatching Maoist Missionaries

Not only did the volume, contents and sources of Maoist proselyting change radically following the Lushan plenum, but the target audiences also shifted. The dissonance plagued Maoists sought out those groups expected to be most sympathetic to their ideology while avoiding relations with those who strongly opposed. China's international relations afforded opportunity for Maoist proselyting. In the early 1960s, as domestic economic policy was forced toward more prudence by the Great Leap failures, Mao devoted himself primarily to foreign affairs.[83] As he had stated at the Lushan plenum on August 1, 1959, "we must use these three things [One Hundred Flowers Blooming, the people's communes, and the Great Leap Forward] *to challenge the entire world.*" On April 16, 1960, Ch'en's *Red Flag* published an article commemorating the nintieth anniversary of Lenin's birth, entitled "Long Live Leninism!" Mao probably had a hand in writing it.[84] This article for the first time set forth the basic issues in China's dispute with the Soviet Union. It stressed the worldwide class struggle, opposed revisionism, and asserted that "an awakened people will always find new ways to counteract the reactionaries superiority in arms." Four months *later,* the Soviets withdrew their technicians from China. Opposition to the critical Khrushchev's Soviet Union and appeal to the fertile Third World increased under Mao's guidance in the early sixties. When Mao stepped forward at the tenth plenum in 1962, he echoed his Lushan call for deepened class struggle, a call that was to resonate thereafter in worldwide proselyting as well as Maoist wars of national liberation.

In surveying China's foreign policy for two decades since the liberation, Van Ness notes that "paradoxically" after the failure of the Great Leap in 1959, while China's domestic policy tended toward "moderation," Chinese foreign policy became "increasingly radical, both in the hardening of Peking's anti-imperialist line in relations with countries of the Third World and in the explicitness and bitterness of China's denunciation of the Soviet Union."[85] One might attempt to explain this radical turn in foreign policy as a defensive attempt to gain new allies after being deserted by the Soviets. But the Chinese, led by Mao, initiated the ideological polemics before the Soviets withdrew their advisors and actively pursued them thereafter. Furthermore, Lin's PLA actively engaged the Indians in border battle at the end of 1962, hardly hoping to win friends there, but perhaps hoping to humble the Indian model of development along with the Soviet. A better explanation is provided by Mao's motive to find support for his revolutionary ideology by successful activity in foreign fields while humbling his critics at home and abroad.

Immediately following Lushan, in September 1959 at the extraordinary meeting of the military affairs committee and the foreign affairs conference, Mao became feverishly active in the field of foreign affairs. Subsequently, China's foreign affairs became increasingly revolutionary. Mao's new international activities were characterized by a vigorous upswing in China's contact with the emerging nations. China's relations with the Third World took the form of nourishing new people-to-people relations as well as those between government and government, of assisting wars of national liberation as well as granting economic and technical assistance.[86] In 1959, the Vietnam insurgency began, one knows not the origin. In 1960 alone, new treaties were signed with the Asian nations of Burma and Indonesia; and in Africa the second Afro-Asian People's Solidarity Conference held in Guinea adopted a militant line against imperialism and revisionism; the Sino-African Friendship Association declined. In the five years following the Great Leap failures of 1959, Communist China donated more than six times the 108 million dollars of aid to non-Communist developing nations than she had donated in the four years preceding the failure; in 1961 alone, in the depths of her economic depression, she sacrificed a sum of 163 million dollars to aid Ghana, Mali, Burma, Indonesia, and Nepal—Maoist revolutionary candidates all.[87]

Along the rim of Mao's China, North Korea emulated the middle kingdom. In concert with Mao, Kim Il-sung had initiated a Korean leap on a smaller scale. Employing miniature communes he had increased grain output by 15 to 20 percent in 1958. Significantly, in December of 1961, Kim launched a larger leap with *kun* collectives more analogous to Mao's communes and designed for the "transition to communism." Although one cannot pinpoint the direct influence of Mao, Kim's communes were supported with Maoist assertions of "continuous class struggle, ideology over technology and politics in command." All was done in the "spirit of opposing the old and aspiring after the new."[88]

Considering the Third World as a whole, between 1959 and 1965 China established diplomatic relations with twenty-two new nations. Seventeen of these were African, and among them were the tumultuous Ghana, Algeria, Cameroon, Guinea, Mali, Burundi, and the Congo. Echoing his *Red Flag* article of 1960, in September of 1965 Lin Piao's effort to find support for Maoist dialectics among the oppressed "proletariat" of the world's nations culminated in his famous address, "Long Live the Victory of the People's War." Thus the Maoist's search for ideological confirmation was not restricted to China. Confirmation of Maoist dialectics was indeed sought in "scientific experiments" conducted in the developing nations in the form of dialectically designed wars of national liberation as well as in China's domestic agricultural collectives. Mao's successful revolution in China could be emulated as well as studied by people of such countries through Mao's writings. Khrushchev's Soviet Union which had ridiculed Mao's Great Leap and commune programs in 1958 and after could be dethroned as a model for China and other developing nations.[89] The Maoist tenet of the "continuation of class struggle" so important in his explanation of the Great Leap debacles, could be reaffirmed by successful struggles around the world beyond the middle kingdom as well as within it.

A survey of China's international agreements since the liberation shows that the eight years from the fateful Lushan plenum through the first year of the Cultural Revolution were indeed years of intensified worldwide proselyting by the failed faithful. These years were marked by a steady rise in relations with the developing nations and a steady decline in relations with the Soviet Union. The developing nations were those most likely to afford potential converts to the Maoist ideology; the Soviet Union was that nation whose leaders were most critical of Mao's Three Red Banners. In the eighteen years between the liveration of 1949 and the peak of the Cultural Revolution in 1967, Communist China made nearly 2,300 international treaties and signed agreements with 71 nations.[90] In the eight years prior to the Lushan plenum, 23 percent of China's international agreements were with the as yet unconverted developing nations; in the eight years following the Lushan plenum, fully 43 percent were with these nations and this figure also increased progressively throughout the 1960s. Similarly, agreements with the Soviet Union

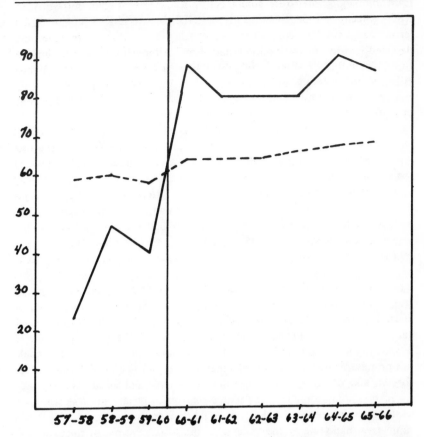

— Adapted from Douglas M. Johnson and Hungdah Chiu, **Agreements of the People's Republic of China, 1949-1967.** Cambridge: Harvard Univ. Press, 1968, pp. 220-222.

- - - Percentage of world's nations that are non-Communist and developing. Adapted from Charles Taylor and Michael Hudson, **World Handbook of Political and Social Indicators.** New Haven: Yale Univ. Press, 1972, pp. 26-29.

Figure 6.5: PERCENTAGE OF COMMUNIST CHINA'S INTERNATIONAL POLITICAL AGREEMENTS NEGOTIATED WITH NON-COMMUNIST DEVELOPING NATIONS, 1957-1966

declined from 15 percent before to 6 percent after the Lushan plenum. Most directly relevant to post-Lushan Maoist proselyting are China's 211 *political* agreements with foreign nations.[91] Figure 6.5 shows the sharp shift in China's political agreements toward Third World countries that occurred after the fall of 1960. After this time, *no* new political agreements were concluded with the Soviet Union. Following the Great Leap debacles, Maoist missionaries were dispatched from the middle kingdom in mounting numbers.

Campaigning and the Domestic Search
for Disciples

The domestic target audience for Maoist proselyting also shifted away from the bourgeois toward the proletarian following the Lushan plenum. After an organizationally hamstrung proselyting drive in the early 1960s, Mao reissued his Lushan call to deepen the class struggle at the tenth plenum in 1962. There Ch'en Po-ta was installed as a vice-chairman of the important state planning commission, K'ang Sheng was posted to the party secretariate, and Lin Piao was thereafter granted an expanded mandate for civilian proselyting. Let us examine the new motives of the committed Maoists following the Lushan plenum.

Under conditions prevailing in China in the latter half of 1959, dissonance theory leads us to expect that the convinced and committed Maoists would become all the more militant in attempts to gain support for their shaken views. Empirical support could be gotten by such methods as successful reimplementations of the commune experiment and other organizational experiments with production brigades and small scale industry such as Tachai and Taching. Political support could be gotten by the Maoists through appeals to powerful figures in the Chinese polity and appeals to the Chinese populace at large. However, the Maoists were greatly constrained in the kinds of political appeals they could make and greatly limited in the types of people to whom they could appeal. In contrast to what their opponents did, they could not promise their audiences the elimination of broad gauge dialectical analysis for the sake of professional rationalized economic and social planning; they could not promise graded economic incentives or greater profits distributed on the basis of specialized skill; nor could they promise more private plots or more free marketing at the expense of the socialist sector of the economy. They could not promise an increase in size and numbers of desirable positions in the government bureaucracy or a curtailment of the long hours spent by the populace in organized political-ideological study. They could not even promise a move toward more regular and tranquil political and social relations within the populace. An attempt to institutionalize any or all of these practices would and did contradict the already shaken ideology of the Maoists and therefore increase their shared dissonance. Even in directing their political appeals to people, the Maoists could not in good conscience admit those of bourgeois class background into their ranks, for this also would add to their dissonance unless these bourgeois persons had undergone thorough ideological remolding.

Social support provides a much more accurate description of the kind of support the Maoist sought from the people of China in their extensive proselyting activities of the 1960s than does political support. This proselyting behavior, this search for social support, is most accurately described as an attempt to find in the affirmation of other persons confirmation for the validity of the failed ideology.

In Communist China every campaign has a specific aim (political objective) and a principal target (set of people) upon whom the campaign is designed to have maximal effects. The aims and targets of campaigns give an indication of the central political problem foci of the leadership in specific time periods. Compared with campaigns launched prior to the Great Leap failure, campaigns launched after the failure had aims of an ideological proselyting nature. And further, of the campaigns launched after the failure, the first were targeted upon those most likely to yield support for the shaken ideology and only later were campaigns targeted upon those judged less likely to support the ideology. Alan Liu has categorized the thirty-two major mass campaigns which occurred on the mainland between 1949 and 1966 in terms of their targets and aims.[92] In this classification each campaign either had a specific enemy target designated for struggle or it did not; and each campaign either aimed at eliciting specific actions from people or it aimed at more diffuse change of thought and value. When one dichotomizes the period at the 1959 Lushan plenum, seventeen campaigns appear before this time. Further analysis supports the prophecy fails-proselyte hypothesis. First of all, of the twelve campaigns that recommended specific change of action as opposed to change of ideology all, except the Great Leap itself, occurred before the Lushan announcements of Great Leap failures. In other words, all post-Great Leap campaigns were essentially devoted to changing ideology rather than enlisting specific actions. Second, of the eleven campaigns in which a specific target group was designated as enemy to be fought, only two occurred following the Great Leap failures, the socialist education campaign and the Cultural Revolution of 1966, and in the former, the target group was initially very ambiguous. In sum, reanalysis of Liu's data supports the contention that a significant shift in the nature of mass campaigns occurred with the Great Leap failure—a shift away from reforming specific enemy groups toward securing proletarian ideological support.

After an initial postrevolutionary clean-up which completed land reform for the peasantry and thought reform of the intellectuals and suppression of counterrevolutionaries, the first campaign of the technical bureaucratization period was launched in the summer of 1952 and targeted against individualism in the bureaucracy. It was entitled the 3-antis *(San Fan)*; anticorruption, antiwaste, antibureaucratism. Shortly thereafter, the 5-antis *(Wu Fan)* campaign was launched, targeted at the bourgeoisie and aimed against the following: bribery, tax evasion, theft of government property, and theft of state secrets. The last major campaign of this period, launched in the summer of 1955 was the 4-antis *(Szu Fan)* targeted against disloyal elements, especially those in the bureaucracy. It dealt in general with methods of political control of the economy.

During the mass mobilization period there were four major campaigns. The aim expanded from simply reforming the bureaucratic behavior patterns to integrating the bureaucrats and rightists with the masses while mobilizing the masses for socialist construction. The targets shifted from bureaucrats to include all rightists, intellectuals in general, middle-level cadres, and most important, China's enormous peasantry. The first of these campaigns was the Hundred Flowers campaign launched in May 1956 which had the aim of letting the intellectuals speak their true minds on the state of leadership and society in China; as a result of what the intellectuals had to say this campaign was quickly converted in June 1957 into an antirightist campaign targeted upon the intellectuals and aimed at converting them to the cause. Shortly thereafter, in August 1957, the first *Hsia Fang* (transfer downward) campaign was launched, sending hundreds of thousands of officials, middle-level cadres and, later, intellectuals down to the villages for contact with the peasantry and manual labor. At the same time the first socialist education campaign was begun with the peasantry which was in the nature of a purge of rightist peasants, i.e., a renewal of attacks on landlord and capitalist elements in the rural areas. Finally, following this series of antirightist campaigns, the Great Leap Forward campaign with its Three Red Banners was launched in 1958 with the aim of bringing communism rapidly to the fore in one fell swoop of "socialist construction." The target most drastically affected in this campaign was the peasantry, although as we have seen it was a total social movement and involved in some degree all segments of the society. Thus, following the revolutionary take-over and prior to the Leap Failure, we find campaigns all generally characterized as rectifications of various "rightist" segments of the society, the two major exceptions were the initial Hundred Flowers campaign and the Great Leap, itself, which was an attempt at rapid ideological realization which permeated the entire society.

The campaigns and subcampaigns that have been carried out during the period following the Great Leap failure are myriad, but they can be classified into three basic movements. After an initial broadside of proselyting for the thought of Mao Tse-tung targeted upon proletarians diffusely construed to include cadres, youth, peasants and workers, the first sharply targeted movement is the ideological indoctrination of military and middle-level cadres began in 1960. Its aim was teaching these cadres Marxism-Leninism and the thought of Mao Tse-tung, the basic principles therein, and what is more important, the correct way of implementing the thought of Mao in everyday practice. The principal targets of this movement were military cadres and military personnel in general. Simultaneously, the movement was targeted on party and youth league cadres and later, especially in 1962-1963, the movement was carried over to the indoctrination of youth using the PLA indoctrination program as a model. Included in this movement were the Army Love the People campaign, the Police Love the People campaign, and the Cadres and People Get Together campaign of 1960. The second of these proselyting movements was the Socialist Education Campaign dating from 1962 whose aim was the increasing of general class consciousness and knowledgeability in the principles of Mao thought on the part of the targets, namely urban and rural proletarian masses and their leaders, the basic-level cadres. This campaign as applied in particular to the basic-level cadres is more appropriately termed the Four Clean-ups. The subcampaigns in this broad movement were the following: Learn from Lei Feng and Send Culture to the Villages in 1963; Learn from the PLA, Learn the Four Gods, Cultivate Revolutionary Successors, and Mass Singing of Red Songs of 1964; and Learn from Tachai Brigade, Learn from Ta Chin Oil Fields, and Learn from Wang Chieh of 1965. The third of these basic movements was the Great Proletarian Cultural Revolution dating from late 1965, whose aim was first the proletarian overthrow and rectification of the target, i.e., leading figures in authority taking the capitalist road, and then the reimposition of a more radical version of the Maoist vision in daily life and study.

NOTES

1. "Letter to Wang Chia-hsiang" (August 1, 1959), in *CLG,* Vol. 1, No. 4, winter 1968-1969, p. 53. Wang Chia-hsiang held high party position as a full member of the central committee and as a member of the secretariat.

2. See "Speech at the Lushan conference" (July 23, 1959), in *CLG,* Vol. 1, No. 4, winter 1968-1969, p. 27.

3. See "Criticism of P'eng Teh-huai's 'letter of opinion' of July 14, 1959" (July 1959), in *CLG,* Vol. 1, No. 4, winter 1968-1969, pp. 25-26.

4. See "Speech at the Lushan conference" (July 23, 1959), in *CLG,* op. cit., p. 30.

5. Ibid., pp. 30-33.

6. Ibid., pp. 35-36.

7. Ibid., pp. 36-38.

8. Ibid., pp. 42-43.

9. *CLG,* Vol. 1, No. 4, winter 1968-1969, p. 64.

10. Ibid., p. 66.

11. Ibid.

12. Ibid., p. 67.

13. Ezra F. Vogel, *Canton Under Communism.* Cambridge, Mass.: Harvard University Press, 1969, pp. 262-264.

14. Ibid.

15. Ibid., p. 265.

16. Ibid., p. 267.

17. Ibid.

18. See *Nan Fang Jih Pao*, May 3, 1960, as cited in Vogel, op. cit., p. 286.

19. See "Chairman Mao's comments on Li Chung-yun's letter of opinion" (July 26), *CLG*, Vol. 1, No. 4, winter 1968-1969, p. 51.

20. See *CLG*, op. cit., p. 52.

21. "Forward to empiricism or Marxism-Leninism" (August 15, 1959), *CLG*, Vol. 1, No. 4, winter 1968-1969, p. 72.

22. The essay referred to is the Ch'i-fa or seven-stanza style essay written by Mei Ch'eng, a Han dynasty poet, and illustrating to Mao that the use of gentle persuasion rather than repression is the best way to "cure" opinion deviates. See "Concerning Mei Ch'eng's *'Ch'i-fa'* " (August 16, 1959), *CLG*, Vol. I, No. 4, winter 1968-1969, p. 131.

23. "The origin of machine guns and mortars, etc." (August 16, 1959), in "In camera statements of Mao Tse-tung," *CLG*, Vol. I, No. 4, winter 1968-1969, pp. 73-74.

24. See "Speech at the enlarged meeting of the Military Affairs Committee of the central committee of the Chinese Communist party and the Foreign Affairs Conference" (September 11, 1959), *CLG*, Vol. I, No. 4, winter 1968-1969, pp. 79-84.

25. Ibid., p. 84.

26. Ibid., p. 83.

27. *MISC*, p. 299.

28. *MISC*, p. 253.

29. *MISC*, p. 253.

30. *MISC*, p. 262.

31. *MISC*, p. 266.

32. *SCMP*, No. 2208.

33. *SCMP*, No. 2208.

34. U.S. Information Service (Hong Kong), "A statistical sketch of the press in Communist China, 1960." *Research Report*, May 1961.

35. *NCNA*, June 1, 1968, and *CB*, No. 622, June 28, 1960. See also Lin Feng, "The tasks of China's Cultural Revolution," *PR*, Vol. 3, No. 25 (June 21, 1960), pp. 14-19; and No. 26 (June 28, 1960), pp. 19-25.

36. *JMJP*, February 29; March 2; May 25 and 27; and June 12 and 23, 1960.

37. *JMJP*, June 11, 1960.

38. Ibid.

39. Ibid.

40. *JMJP*, March 27, 1960.

41. *JMJP*, April 9, 1960.

42. *JMJP*, April 12, 1960.

43. *JMJP*, July 22, 1960.

44. *JMJP*, May 16, and June 10, 1960.

45. *MISC*, p. 244.

46. Ibid.

47. Merle Goldman, "The unique 'Blooming and Contending' of 1961-62," *CQ*, No. 37, (January-March 1969), pp. 54-83. Goldman designated the periods of 1953-1954 and 1956-1957 as the prior two periods of thaw.

48. Liu Shao-ch'i, "Speech at the meeting to celebrate the fortieth anniversary of the Chinese Communist Party," (June 30, 1961), *CB*, No. 655, p. 2.

49. Goldman, op. cit., p. 60.

50. Ibid., p. 59.

51. Ibid.

52. Ibid., p. 68.

53. See Philip Bridgham, "Factionalism in the central committee," in John W. Lewis

Party Leadership and Revolutionary Power in China. Cambridge, Mass.: Cambridge University Press, 1970, p. 222.

54. "Selected edition of Lui Shao-ch'i's counter-revolutionary crimes," pamphlet, April 1967, in *Selections from China Mainland Magazines,* Hong Kong: U.S. Consulate General, No. 652, p. 22 ff., as quoted in Philip L. Bridgham, "The Cultural Revolution and the new political system in China," paper delivered at the sixty-sixth annual meeting of the American Political Science Association, September 1970, p. 5. (Hereafter *SCMM.*)

55. Bridgham, APSA paper, loc. cit.

56. "Talk on the question of democratic centralism" (January 30, 1962), in *CB,* No. 892, October 21, 1969, p. 38.

57. Ibid., p. 37.

58. Ibid., p. 39.

59. Ibid., p. 40.

60. "Expose the great conspiracy behind the three editions of the book 'On self-cultivation by communists'," *JMJP,* April 12, 1967, as quoted in Philip Bridgham, "Factionalism in the central committee," op. cit., p. 224.

61. Ibid.

62. Ibid.

63. Ibid.

64. "An outline of the struggle. . . ," *URS,* Vol. 53, Nos. 7-8, pp. 81-84.

65. Merle Goldman, op. cit., p. 69.

66. Jan S. Prybylla, *The Political Economy of Communist China.* Scranton: International Textbook Co., 1970, pp. 425-427.

67. "While the identity of opposites is relative, their struggle is absolute," *HC,* No. 12, 1964; see also "New polemic on the philosophical front," *HC,* No. 16, 1964.

68. *JMJP,* July 1, 1961, as cited in Cheng Chu-yuan, "The root of China's Cultural Revolution: The feud between Mao Tse-tung and Liu Shao-ch'i," *Orbis,* Vol. XI, No. 4, winter, 1968, pp. 1160-1178.

69. Liu Shao-ch'i, *How To Be a Good Communist.* Peking: Foreign Languages Press, 1962, p. 12, as cited in Cheng, op. cit., p. 1164.

70. See Ting Wang, "The Communist internal party struggle of 1961," *Ming Pao,* Hong Kong, October 23-24, 1966, as cited in Franz Michael, "The struggle for power," *Problems of Communism,* Vol. 16, No. 3, May-June, 1967, pp. 13-16. In a personal interview Prof. Michael corroborated the published account by Ting Wang, a former CCP official with personal knowledge of these events. It is noteworthy that Ting Wang asserts another proposition consistent with our theory, namely that the politburo contained many opponents of Mao's Great Leap before it was launched. He asserts that in three meetings called between December 1957 and March 1958 at Hanchow, Nanning, and Chengtu, Mao informed a group of party leaders of his plan for the Great Leap, adding at the third meeting the proposal to set up the commune system. Mao's plans immediately encountered party opposition led by P'eng Teh-huai, and it was not until the enlarged politburo meeting of August 1957 at Peitaiho that Mao's plan was officially adopted as party policy—after the commune movement was spreading over China. See Michael, op. cit., po. 12-13.

71. Hung Chun, Tso Hing-ping, and Hsin Pei-wen, "Defend Yenan: A vivid example of opposing the party through novels," *JMJP,* November 12, 1967, as cited in Cheng, op. cit., p. 1174.

72. Ibid.

73. "Chiang Ch'ing's speech at the meeting of the central Cultural Revolution group" (September 14, 1968), *IAS,* Vol. VII, No. 8, May 1971, p. 78.

74. Ibid., p. 78. See also "Chiang Ch'ing's speech at the enlarged meeting of the military commission of the CCP central committee on April 12, 1967," *IAS,* Vol. VI, No. 10, July 1970, pp. 82-91.

75. Ko' Ch'ing-shih was a member of the politburo and head of its East China bureau as well as first secretary of the Shanghai municipal party committee. He was quite outspoken in favor of Mao's Yenan policy on art and literature. In December 1963 he spoke before the East China drama festival and attacked traditional art and literature. In August 1964 he published an article of similar views in *Red Flag.* He died in April 1965, but his influence lingered in his staff.

76. See John Gittings, *The Role of the Chinese Army.* Oxford: Oxford University Press, 1967, p. 215.

77. See Gittings, op. cit., p. 104.

78. "Chairman Mao's speech at the Ch'eng-tu conference," (March 22, 1958), *JPRS,* No. 90, p. 46.

79. Ibid., p. 52.

80. Ibid., p. 48.

81. James C.Y. Soong, *The Red Flag (Hung Ch'i), 1958-1968: A Research Guide.* Washington, D.C.: Center for Chinese Research Materials, 1969, p. xi. See also *NCNA,* 6/2/58, as cited in Franklin W. Houn, *To Change a Nation: Propaganda and Indoctrination in Communist China.* Glencoe, Ill.: Free Press, 1961, p. xiv.

82. Soong, op. cit., p. xiv.

83. See Stuart Schram, *Mao Tse-tung.* New York: Simon and Schuster, 1969, p. 276. See also Peter Van Ness, *Revolution and Chinese Foreign Policy: Peking's Support for Wars of National Liberation.* Berkeley: University of California Press, 1970, pp. 16-17.

84. Schram, op. cit., p. 280.

85. Van Ness, op. cit., pp. 16-17.

86. Van Ness, op. cit., passim.

87. Alexander Eckstein, *Communist China's Economic Growth and Foreign Trade.* New York: McGraw-Hill, 1966, p. 307.

88. Robert A. Scalopino and Chonk-Sik Lee, *Communism in Korea: The Society.* Berkeley: University of California Press, 1972, pp. 1099-1113.

89. Khrushchev indulged in deliberate mockery of the people's communes first in private, in his famous declarations of December 1958 to Senator Hubert Humphrey, and then publicly. See Stuart Schram, op. cit., p. 275. Khrushchev also is said to have shown his support of P'eng Teh-huai by "launching an open attack against our people's communes" four days after P'eng delivered his July 14 "Letter of opinion" and by openly praising P'eng after the event as "correct and brave" and as his "best friend." See Bridgham, op. cit., p. 217. From *Survey of China Mainland Press,* Hong Kong: American Consulate General, No. 4047, p. 8 (Hereafter *SCMP.*)

90. See Douglas M. Johnston and Hungdah Chiu, *Agreements of the People's Republic of China, 1949-1967: A Calendar.* Cambridge, Mass.: Harvard University Press, 1968, pp. 220-222. The table is arranged by "revolutionary years," i.e., from October 1 to the following September 30. Our figure was adopted from their individual nation data by classifying any country as a "developing nation" if and only if its 1957 gross national product per capita was less than $450. The latter figures were taken from Bruce M. Russett, et al., *World Handbook of Political and Social Indicators.* New Haven, Conn.: Yale University Press, 1964, pp. 155-157. The resulting classification yielded five developed Communist partners (USSR, Poland, East Germany, Czechoslavakia, and Hungary), eight developing Communist partners (North Vietnam, North Korea, Albania, Mongolia, Rumania, Bulgaria, Yugoslavia, and Cuba), thirteen developed "capitalist"

partners (Finland, France, United Kingdom, Norway, West Germany, Denmark, Sweden, Switzerland, Netherlands, Austria, Italy, Kuwait and USA), and forty-five non-Communist developing nations. The agreements, themselves were economic, political, technological, cultural and legal respectively in order of frequency of occurrence and totaled 2,300. The 211 political agreements included 146 joint announcements or communiques, 22 friendship associations, 39 boundary agreements, and 3 gifts.

91. Ibid.

92. For the classification of 32 mass campaigns between 1949 and 1966 in terms of targets and aims, see Alan P.L. Liu, *Communications and National Integration in Communist China.* Berkeley: University of California Press, 1971, pp. 185-186.

Chapter 7

INDOCTRINATION OF MILITARY

AND MIDDLE-LEVEL CADRES

The next three chapters will demonstrate that ever since the Lushan plenum of 1959 there was continuous proselyting by the dissonance-plagued Maoists for the thought of Mao Tse-tung and the exculpating class struggle rationalization which eventually erupted in the Great Proletarian Cultural Revolution demanding ideological remolding of the polarized opponents of Maoist proselyting. Figures 1.1, 6.1, and 6.2 of the preceding chapters summarized the increasing polarization between non-Maoists and Maoists which occurred on the politburo from the fifth plenum of the eighth central committee in 1958 through the tenth plenum of 1962 to the tumultuous eleventh plenum of 1966. Taken together, these summary data show that the contribution of the highly committed Maoists, Mao, Lin, Ch'en and K'ang to the overall group opinion variance rose steadily from less than half in 1958 through two-thirds by three years after the Lushan plenum in 1962, to three-fourths in 1966 on the eve of the eleventh plenum. Theoretically, with each such escalation in the committed Maoists' social disagreement dissonance, the pressures on them to gain external social support for the thought of Mao and forcibly to reform the thinking of their more highly discrepant politburo colleagues should increase. Indeed, the innerparty "class struggle" theme first raised by Mao at Lushan was renewed by him at the tenth plenum and forcibly acted upon at the eleventh.

The motivation of the committed Maoists to proselyte for Mao's thought took several avenues of release during the early sixties. First of all, proselyting was focused by Lin Piao on the PLA immediately following Lushan. Then it was broadened by Mao and Ch'en Po-ta to include civilian youth and proletarians following the tenth plenum. Upon frustration of this proselyting drive by some leaders at the party center in late 1963, Mao turned more decisively to Lin's PLA as his main instrumentality for proselyting in 1964. In 1965 the inner-party thwarting of Maoist proselyting deepened and the opinion discrepancy between committed Maoists and their politburo comrades widened, finally erupting in the tumultuous eleventh plenum at which attending central committee members were surrounded by Chiang Ch'ing's rampaging Red Guards.

Mao's circle of closs associates changed following Lushan. As Dittmer notes, during the period of economic retrenchment from the Great Leap, Mao's circle of diurnal associates shifted from fellow politburo members to an ad hoc circle of intimates who shared his broad theoretical and polemical concerns, including his former secretary, Ch'en Po-ta, his wife, Chiang Ch'ing, and her old friend, K'ang Sheng.[1] In addition, immediately following Lushan at the extraordinary meeting of the Military Affairs Committee (MAC) and Foreign Affairs Conference in September 1959, Mao received strong ideological support from Lin Piao. Just one year later, Lin supported Mao's thought more publicly:

The publication of the fourth volume of Mao's *Works* is . . . an event of great importance in the political life of the Chinese people. At the same time, it is a great event in the international working class movement because this work is a reflection of the victory of Marxism-Leninism in a big country which has the largest population in the world. Comrade Mao Tse-tung's ideas about daring to win and skill in waging struggle, his ideas about the use of dual revolutionary tactics to counter those of the counter-revolution, his ideas about scorning the enemy strategically and taking full account of him tactically, his ideas about the people's revolutionary forces, inferior numerically, and in equipment, defeating the counter-revolutionary forces which are superior in these respects, and other ideas and theories will retain their great vitality in the long, historical period to come.[2]

This description of Mao's work was written by Lin Piao and entitled "The Victory of the Chinese People's Revolutionary War is the Victory of the Thought of Mao Tse-tung." It was immediately published in the pages of the October 1, 1960 edition of Ch'en Po-ta's *Red Flag*. Simultaneously, it heralded the first major wave of sharply focused and sustained proselyting for the thought of Mao Tse-tung following the Great Leap debacles. This wave of proselyting was targeted upon the ranks of the People's Liberation

Army. It was initiated shortly after the Lushan plenum and directed by Lin Piao. This campaign really had a dual aim. On the one hand, it was aimed at spreading the Maoist rationalization for the Great Leap failures among the troops; on the other hand, it was aimed at spreading the basic principles of the thought of Mao Tse-tung and teaching the correct way of implementing these principles among the soldiers. In his efforts to proselyte for Mao's Great Leap ideology and class struggle rationalization, Lin was actively assisted by the committed Maoist, Lo Jung-huan, who headed the general political department of the PLA until his death in 1963.

The essential rationalization for the Great Leap failures promulgated by the committed Maoists among the troops was three-fold. First of all, economic failings of the Great Leap were attributed to natural disasters, such as floods and poor weather conditions, thereby exempting Maoist principles from castigation, since they do not purport to offer guidelines for weather control—the Commune Resolution notwithstanding. Second, failures of the Great Leap movement were attributed to the deliberate sabotage efforts of class enemies. This "class conflict" explanation is essentially the same as that given by Mao Tse-tung at the Lushan plenum when he raised the level of political conflict at that meeting to a "class struggle, a continuation of the life and death struggle between the two major antagonistic classes—the bourgeoisie and the proletariat—which has gone on through the socialist revolution in the last ten years." The class conflict explanation provided a scapegoat for the failure of the Great Leap by attributing it to ideological rightists rather than ideological leftists. At the same time it confirmed the Maoist precept of the continuation of class conflicts following the liberation, and allowed the Maoists in the unfolding of their proselyting activities, to label those who did not accept the ideology as class enemies, thereby permitting the application of sanctions according to the Maoist code. The third rationalization promulgated by the Maoists for the Great Leap failings was to attribute them to the unwitting failure of the middle-level cadres to correctly implement the directives of the top-level party leadership, in particular, those of Mao Tse-tung. This explanation shifted the blame of failure from the top levels of planning and leadership to the middle levels and thereby kept the authority structure temporarily intact. At this time and viewed in Maoist terms, the failure of the "mass line" during the Great Leap was essentially due to the cadres in the middle, not the leadership at the top nor the masses at the bottom. Hence, to rectify the situation, the cadres in the middle must be taught the basic principles of the ideology to prevent future failures in implementation of the mass line. This rationalization provided the Maoists both with a practical reason for proselyting for their ideology among the troops and a way of testing the middle-level cadres for their loyalty in terms of the way they implemented Maoist principles in the future.

To observe how these rationalizations were proselyted among the cadres, we cite the following passage of November 1960 from the *Bulletin of Activities,* No. 1, January 1961, "Endorsement and Transmission by the General Political Department of Comrade Wang Tung-hsing's Report on Ideological Conditions in the Central Garrison":[3]

For the sake of strengthening the political and ideological work of the primary level, leaders of all levels should watch closely the ideological movements in the Army units and transmit the Central Authorities' urgent directives and letters concerning the policy toward the People's Commune to all cadres and soldiers in order to keep them fully informed of our policy, eliminate their doubts, quiet their feelings and increase their understanding. Three points must be emphasized in their education: (1) While affirming the great victory of the Three Red Flags and making known our promising situation, explain clearly the present difficulties and stimulate the courage of the masses to struggle against difficulties; (2) explain that the series of policies laid down by the Central Authorities, especially Chairman Mao, are always correct as they transmitted the important directives issued by the Central Authorities and Chairman Mao during the past years concerning the People's communes and various policies. Those communes which follow the directives firmly will be well run; others will not be well run. Hereafter, if we can only seriously carry out the policy of the Central Authorities, the problem of food will be solved completely, and all difficulties will be overcome; (3) lead the officers and soldiers to feel that no matter what difficulties are confronting us, we must stand firm and obey the Party. Emphasize solidarity between the armed forces and local authorities and the armed forces and the people.

The following lead passage (from the same *Bulletin of Activities* regarding the "Directive of the Military Affairs Commission and the Central Political Department Regarding Key Points of Political Work in the Whole Army for 1961") underlines the importance given by the PLA leadership to Maoist proselyting in 1960 in the wake of the Great Leap debacles:

The central tasks of political work for 1961 are: on the basis of consolidating achievements of 1960, to continue to carry out thoroughly the resolutions of the Enlarged Meeting of the Military Affairs Commission; to organize energetically the study of Mao Tse-tung's writings and the propagation of Mao Tse-tung's thought; to strengthen the solidarity of the Army units in political, ideological, and organizational matters; to work with ardor to become strong and to win the war against temporary difficulties; and to struggle for making our Army exceedingly proletarian and revolutionary in spirit; equipped with strong fighting power.

Besides seeking support for Mao's rationalizations for the Great Leap failures, the MAC directive reasserts the validity of Mao's class struggle and mass line tenets while insisting upon the continued validity of the Three Red Banners and the necessity of studying and applying Maoist dialectics. The directive stresses the importance of correctly carrying out the "rectification campaign" in the army previously ordered by the MAC. In keeping with Mao's interpretation of the significance of P'eng's onslaught in the preceding year, it stresses the class struggle nature of this rectification campaign, pointing out that "we should especially attend to ideological work, study conditions regularly, and carry out the struggle for strengthening the proletariat and exterminating the capitalists." It goes on to stress the importance of correctly employing the "mass line" principle in the army with middle-level cadres being the transmission belts and again emphasizes the importance of their correctly understanding directives from the top leadership while integrating with the basic levels. The directive goes on to specify how "the study of Chairman Mao's writings" should be organized. Stressing that "we must seriously carry out the directive of Chief Lin [Piao] that 'Mao Tse-tung's thought must be truly and thoroughly studied,' " it states the contents of study for leading propaganda cadres as follows: "Military and political studies of all kinds carried on by cadres and by academies and schools must include Volume IV of *The Selected Works of Mao Tse-tung* as a text for major study." It then cites the coming fortieth anniversary of the party (1961) as a special opportunity for "publicizing Mao Tse-tung's thought." The PLA proselyting was expanded to the international arena by stressing that cadres should combine the study of Chairman Mao's writings with the declaration of the Congress of Communist and Worker's Parties by "insisting on principles and insisting on solidarity, criticize modern revisionism, and remove the influence of P'eng's and Huang's erroneous line." It urges that, "those who are able to study by themselves should study all of Chairman Mao's writings. . . . For ordinary cadres and soldiers the key points in these writings which have close connection with actual life should be selected and emphasized as required reading"; the directive goes on to enumerate the most appropriate methods of Mao study:

> For cadres on duty the primary method of study is self-study, strengthened with guidance given by the organization. Next in importance is group instruction or report meetings. Publications should be prepared to propagate Mao Tse-tung's thought. Soldiers should be well versed in the Two Remembrances and Three Investigations, go deep into the study of the Three Red Banners, and also pay regular attention to the education to be gained by following current events, studying policy, and gaining valuable knowledge of revolutionary traditions. We can learn to know Mao Tse-tung's thought through living education.

The 1960 MAC directive was not composed of empty words. Mao's thought was to become "living ideology" in the literal sense. Important action commitments were elicited from the soldiers. This is evidenced by the newly allotted time budgets for the common soldiers.[4] The MAC directed during 1961 that of all the time the troops spend in training of any kind, 60 percent should be military training and 40 percent should be political and cultural training. Further, "in order to strengthen the political and ideological education within company units," it was considered that of the 40 percent time allotment, 62 percent would be political education and 38 percent would be cultural.

While the common soldiers' life-ways were changed by a radical politicizing shift in his time budget, the soldiers' organizational environment was further politicized. First of all, the directive stressed the need for continued reorganization of party and youth league branches in the armed forces. Second, it emphasized the importance of recruitment of ideologically progressive party and youth league members into the army, so that two-thirds of army youth would be members. In the winter of 1960, the pages of *China Youth News* carried news of Lin's "Five Good" campaign to the prospective recruits. Again, in the organizational sphere as in the ideological sphere of proselyting, the words of the MAC had a strong impact on the everyday lives of the soldiers. During the last two of "the three hard years" (1959-1961), Lin Piao was quite successful in implementing important organizational changes. Eighty-two percent of the party committees in the army were shaken up and 78,000 cadres were assigned to give "concrete assistance" at the company level.[5] By the spring of 1961, all units of company size had associated party committees and 80 percent of all platoons had party cells with 50 percent of all squads having at least one party member.[6] All of these changes entailed increased party recruitment in the army with 229,000 new party members listed there in 1960.[7] In late 1961, the PLA compiled and edited a new book, *Selected Readings from the Works of Mao Tse-tung,* and issued it to all military units for study.

In sum, the years 1960 and 1961 were times of strenuous proselyting for the thought of Mao Tse-tung in the armed forces. In the process, the People's Liberation Army was politicized along Maoist lines involving significant changes in the daily routines of the common soldier as well as severe organizational shake-ups in the party and youth league branches which infiltrate the PLA. Further plans were laid for a reinvigoration of the enormous militia. Youth work was especially emphasized in these early years. By the end of 1961, Lin Piao's PLA was well on the way to becoming a disciplined organizational weapon for Maoist proselyting among the civilian Chinese populace.

Lin's continuous proselyting for Mao's Three Red Flags and his broader thought expanded the scope of its target audience through the 1960s. Beginning with soldiers and militia, Lin's target expanded to include civilian youth and adults following the tenth plenum in the fall of 1962, and by the end of 1963, Lin's civilian proselyting was touted as *the* model for all Chinese to emulate in their own organizations. Lin's continuous campaign to raise the ideological and political standards of the PLA with respect to Maoist tenets dates back to Mao's address at the extraordinary meeting of the Military Affairs Committee (MAC) and the Foreign Affairs Conference of September 1959. It can be traced from there through the important meeting of the enlarged session of the MAC held from September 14 to October 20, 1960. There Lin Piao penned the following portentous statements in the draft resolution of the conference:

> The Thought of Mao Tse-tung developed and improved Marxism-Leninism through concrete practice in the Chinese revolution. . . . The Thought of Mao Tse-tung is the guiding force of the Chinese people's revolution and of socialist construction, a powerful ideological weapon against imperialism, revisionism, and dogmatism.[8]

Lin then called upon the PLA to "Raise high the Red Flag of the Thought of Mao Tse-tung, to become thoroughly acquainted with it, and to insist upon its supremacy in the conduct of all affairs." The resolution then proposed as a principal measure an "intensive, repeated, and widespread" campaign of "propaganda about the great significance of Mao Tse-tung's Thought." At this point, the coincidence of the motives of both Lin Piao and Chairman Mao to proselyte for the shaken thought of Mao Tse-tung cannot be doubted. The important draft resolution of this conference was submitted to Mao himself for approval before publication.[9] In addition, at this second extraordinary session of the MAC, Lin made a number of innovations on Mao's tenets that converted his Yenan ideology of old into the "living ideology" of contemporary China. Here Lin Piao propounded four basic principles—subsequently known as the "four firsts"—which provided the theoretical foundation for the renewed emphasis upon political work. Here Lin Piao initiated the five good movement which calls for good performance in political thinking, military training, style of work, fulfillment of tasks, and physical education.[10] The "five good" soldier should study Chairman Mao's writings, adroitly use and protect his weapons and equipment, obey orders quickly and agilely, acquire good habits of cleanliness and hygiene, etc. In accordance with the precept of Lin Piao that "one who knows nothing about exploitation knows nothing about revolution," young soldiers were invited to recreate in their imaginations the bitter days of preliberation—a process known as the "recollection of past bitterness and appreciation of present sweetness." They sang nostalgic revolutionary songs, interviewed time-honored veterans, visited exhibitions of revolutionary relics, and read the memoirs of war-time heroes.

To Mao's delight in the early sixties, Lin's recreation was the recreation of their spirit of Yenan.

Of great import for the later sixties was the fact that proselyting for the thought of Mao Tse-tung by the military leadership under Lin Piao was not restricted in target to the military rank and file. The original resolution of the enlarged session of the Military Affairs Committee of October 1960 was endorsed by the party central committee in words explicitly pointing out its relevance to political activities in the civilian sphere:

> This resolution is not only the right direction and the basic principle for the reconstruction and political work of army units, but it can also be of use to all levels of party organizations, government organs and schools, enterprises, etc., and should be distributed to all organizations of district committee level and above.[12]

This mandate for Maoist proselyting among civilians continued in force throughout the 1960s and was utilized with increasing vigor. Since the enlarged session of the MAC, political work conferences were held by the general political department of the PLA approximately once a year. Each assessed the progress of the movement, and each called anew for efforts in implementing Maoist programs and proselyting for the thought of Mao Tse-tung. Successive PLA political work conferences were held in March 1961, October-November 1961, February 1963, December-January 1964, and December-January 1966, totaling seven since Lushan. The PLA political work conference of October 18-November 11, 1961, adopted four sets of regulations governing political work, which redefined and reemphasized the importance of the company political instructor, the party branch, the revolutionary servicemen's committee, and the Young Communist League branch.[13] As a result, the main burden of party recruitment in this youthful army fell upon the youth league.

As Lin Piao intensified the indoctrination of the troops during the early 1960s with the thought of Mao Tse-tung, he simultaneously expanded the targets of indoctrination to include the membership of the PLA's auxiliary force, the people's militia. Under Lin's auspices, a number of provincial militia work conferences were called. The provincial militia work conferences of winter 1959-1960, in spite of the Great Leap debacles encountered during the past year, called for a "new high tide in militia building." Four points were emphasized at these conferences: stronger party leadership, training of militia cadres, more political work for the hard core, and strengthening of "tactical" troops. Following these provincial conferences, a national militia work conference was held in Peking in early February 1960, at which it was "unequivocally decided to continue the policy of further intensifying militia construction and the large-scale organization of militia units in the future."[14] However, later in 1960, the call for a large-scale militia build-up was quietly dropped, while military training and production work for the militia were no longer placed upon an equal footing. The new slogan was that "production is the keynote in militia work." As conditions in the countryside grew worse during 1960, the militia structure deteriorated along with the commune structures. In 1962, Mao Tse-tung issued a personal directive calling for militia work to be put on "a solid basis organizationally, politically and militarily." Subsequent expositions of these "three bases" made it clear that development would be firmly grounded upon strong political control and class indoctrination, a well-defined organizational structure, and regular military training under supervision.

> A solid political basis means strengthening the people's militia politically according to the Party's class line, making sure the organizations and the armed forces of the militia are entirely in the hands of the most reliable class brothers who are loyal to the party, the people, the revolution and the cause of socialism.[15]

Now militia organizations also were to have political cadres attached to them, and to carry out political and ideological education.

The vigorous proselyting activities of Lin Piao for the principles of Mao Tse-tung were targeted principally at the soldiers between 1959 and 1962. These contributions of Lin Piao can be summarized as follows: When P'eng Teh-huai was deposed as minister of defense in 1959, the *Liberation Army Daily* published the following editorial on August 8: "Some people have failed to realize the value of Chairman Mao's military writings. . . . In the study of Chairman Mao's military writings, they doubted whether Chairman Mao's military concepts could direct military training and warfare." In direct contrast to this public explanation of P'eng's dismissal, Lin Piao upon his assumption of duties of minister of defense, wrote the article for *People's Daily* on September 29, 1959, entitled, "March Forward Under the Red Banner of the Party's General Line and Mao Tse-tung's Military Thought." In 1960, Lin Piao invented the "four firsts" slogan (human factor over technology, political work over other work, ideology first, and living ideas before ideas in books). In May of 1961, Lin called for the development of the "three-eight style" in the performance of duty (three referring to the three mottos (1) stick to the firm and correct direction of political work, (2) develop a hard-working spirit and modest manner in doing things, (3) apply strategy and tactics in a living way; and eight referring to four pairs of characters denoting virtues of (1) solidarity *(tuan-chieh),* (2) alertness *(chin-chang),* (3) solemnity *(yen-su),* and (4) liveliness *(huo-po)).* In October of 1961, the PLA political work conference resolved to adopt "Ten Principles for Grasping Living Ideas." In January of 1962 the "four good company" campaign was launched in the armed forces at the company level calling for good orientation in political thinking, good development of the three-eight style, good practice in military training, and good management in daily life. In July of 1962, a set of regulations governing ideological education at the company level was issued. From the immediately preceding summary of slogans, resolutions, and directives and from the description of the contents of some of the major directives presented earlier in this section, it is evident that the convinced and committed Maoist Lin Piao conducted an energetic and effective campaign among the troops between 1959 and 1961 aimed at spreading the knowledge of Maoist principles among middle-level military cadres and the rank and file of the troops.

Lin Piao's proselyting activities and successes were not to go unnoticed by Mao Tse-tung in the future unrolling of his proselyting drive. Fifteen months after the tenth plenum of the central committee of the party of September 1962, Lin Piao's proselyting drive in the armed forces was set up as a model for other sectors of the society to emulate in the waging of their efforts, broadly termed the Socialist Education Campaign. The target for Lin Piao with his successfully indoctrinated People's Liberation Army was to be expanded to include other nonmilitary sectors of Chinese society. The expanded mandate granted Lin Piao for Maoist proselyting is well codified in the regulations drawn up at the next conference on political work of the armed forces called by Lo Jung-huan's general political department of the PLA in February 1963, just six months after Mao's call for socialist education at the tenth plenum. The regulations were promulgated by the central committee of the CCP on May 17.[16] The major points of these important "Regulations Governing the Political Work of the Chinese People's Liberation Army" include the following: (1) to value and learn from Mao's thinking; (2) to carry out the mass line and promote the three democracies; (3) to promote the three-eight working mode; (4) to revive the proletariat and destroy the bourgeoisie; (5) to grasp live ideas; (6) to strengthen the organization of party branches; (7) to intensify work among the youths; (8) to do the ideological work well (referring to the political directors); (9) to establish a contingent of cadres who are both red and expert; (10) to intensify the political work in military technical business and scientific research; (11) to do the militia work well and participate in the socialist reconstruction actively; (12) to strengthen the political and ideological leadership of the party commissars among the troops; (13) to improve the methods of work of the political organizations.

One of the most important sets of regulations drawn up at this conference dealing with the PLA's conduct of Mao's Socialist Education Campaign is entitled "General Principles Governing the Political Work of the Chinese People's Liberation Army" and consists of seven articles.[17] The first article explicates the dual protecting and proselyting roles of the PLA as follows:

In the new historical period of socialist revolution and socialist reconstruction in China, our army is both the protector and constructor of
our socialist cause. We must continue to hold up the Great Red Banner
of Mao Tse-tung's thinking and the three Red Banners of the Party's
general line, Great Leap Forward and commune System for socialist
construction.

Thus in 1963 when the people's communes were operating in the downgraded
form of small production teams, the PLA was explicitly entreated to persist
in proselyting for the Three Red Banners!

The second article lists the central tenets of Maoist ideology that are to be
upheld and promulgated by the People's Liberation Army and demonstrates
clearly that Lin Piao was the paragon of Maoist proselyters:

Mao Tse-tung's thinking is the guidepost for the Chinese people's revolution and socialist reconstruction and also for the reconstruction and
political work of the Chinese People's Liberation Army. Comrade Mao
Tse-tung is a great contemporary Marxist-Leninist. Mao Tse-tung's
thinking is a creative advancement of Marxism-Leninism through the
application of the universal truths of Marxism-Leninism in an era when
imperialism is heading for collapse and socialism heading for victory,
and amidst the concrete implementation of China's revolution and the
collective struggle of the Party and the people. Mao Tse-tung's thinking
is a powerful ideological weapon against imperialism, modern revisionism and dogmatism. Comrade Mao Tse-tung has laid down not only the
Party's correct political line but also the correct military line in accordance with that political line. Comrade Mao Tse-tung's theories, principles and writings concerning class, class struggle, proletarian revolution,
proletarian dictatorship, pragmatism, contradictions, ways to handle
the internal contradictions among the people properly, the assertion
that the East wind will prevail over the West wind, the general line for
foreign policy, the assertion that all imperialists and reactionaries are
paper tigers and the enemies should be held in contempt strategically
while they should not be underestimated tactically, war and peace, the
assertion that men, not material, are the deciding factor in war, the
general line of socialist construction, the big leap forward, the people's
communes, the relations between economic reconstruction, the strate-
gies and tactics for the people's revolutionary war, the assertion that
politics holds the command, the relations between Red and expert, the
Party's mass line and its way of working, the purposes and principles of
the people's army, the absolute leadership of the Party over the army,
the Party's committee system, the system of political commissars and
the system of political work, the political work to solidify the soldiers
and the people and to disintegrate the enemy troops, the democratic
system and combat spirit of the troops, the militia system and the idea

of "everyone being soldier," etc., not only have provided the basic assurances for the victories of our army in the past, but also will serve as a guidepost for our actions from now on.

The fifth article of the February 1963 regulations describes the principal contents of political work of the PLA both interior and exterior to the PLA. Within the PLA, the major task is to "regiment all the personnel to study Marxism-Leninism and Comrade Mao Tse-tung's writings." Furthermore, it is a general task of the PLA "to undertake cultural work, to adhere to the Party's policy relating to literature and artistry, to sponsor public cultural recreational and sports activities; and to organize cultural studies." Thus, explicit mention is given here to the PLA's expanded mandate for proselyting among the civilian population.

Yet another set of these regulations outlines the methods by which such political work is to be carried out. It emphasizes the controlling role of the general political department of the PLA in implementing these proselyting activities.[18] This set of regulations notes, first of all, that the general political department of the PLA is under the direction of the central committee of the CCP. Second, the most basic tasks of the general political department are to hold up the red banner of Mao Tse-tung's thinking and to arm the brains of all the military personnel with Marxism-Leninism and Mao Tse-tung's thinking. In carrying out these tasks, the general political department is authorized to regiment the troops to study Marxism-Leninism and the thought of Mao Tse-tung; to direct the organizational work of the Communist youth league among the troops; to direct the troops to carry out public, cultural, recreational and sports activities; to publish newspapers and periodicals; to direct all the troops to conduct public revolutionary contests and to honor heroic personalities and publicize their deeds; and to direct the political work in schools and so cultivate the cadres that they become both red and expert. Adopting this content and utilizing these methods, Lin's PLA was to be confirmed by Mao as his primary proselyting vehicle for all Chinese society at the time of the next PLA political work conference in December 1963.

Previewing Lin Piao's post-tenth plenum proselyting activities, it is noteworthy that in February of 1963, in conjunction with the national Socialist Education Campaign, the conference of political work in the armed forces also produced a resolution on "Twelve Point Fundamental Experience in Rebuilding Company-Level Units" summing up the successful methods and achievements of the Mao study campaigns in the army. Immediately following this conference, the "good eighth company on Nanking Road in Shanghai" and serviceman Lei Feng were set as model unit and model soldier for the People's Liberation Army. At the same time, with the PLA taking an early lead in the proselyting of China's youth, Lei Feng was set up as model for *all* of China's youth in a nationwide emulation and study campaign.

The major targets of proselyting for Mao's thought conducted by Lin Piao and the PLA was expanded from soldiers (1959-1962) to include youth (1963) and on New Year's Day of 1964 to include the whole of Chinese society. In its New Year's Day editorial of 1964 entitled "March Forward in the Wake of Victory," the *People's Daily* for the first time called upon the general public to "Learn from the People's Liberation Army" and its experience in political work. The motivation underlying the expansion in 1964 of the target of PLA proselyting will be dealt with in succeeding sections, but a preview of its phasing and scope seems prudent in the present context. On February 1, 1964, the *People's Daily* editorial, entitled "The Entire Nation Should Learn from the Liberation Army," included the following organizational directive, calling on "all Party and political organizations, mines and plants, enterprises and civic bodies to intensify their political work and establish a permanent systematic setup exclusively responsible for political work." Just as in the proselyting movement in the PLA, the reform of cadres and the rectification of the political commissar apparatus was conjoined with and followed by an extensive campaign to spread the principles and thought of Mao Tse-tung to the basic rank and file of the soldiers; so it was that in 1964 the call for the establishment of systematic network responsible for political work (staffed heavily by members and retired members of the PLA) in the basic institutions of Chinese society was followed by the exhortation to the great masses of Chinese society to study Mao Tse-tung's thought. On March 20, 1964, the *People's Daily* editorial was entitled "Study Mao Tse-tung's Thought Diligently." Its contents urged all persons in all reaches of society to read Mao's writings day and night, at work, during travel, or at home, making it a nationwide mass movement. By June 1964, PLA political departments had been established in more than twenty government ministries.[19]

The diffusion of the Mao study campaign emanating from the organizational apparatus of the PLA in 1959 has been traced continuously through 1964, progressively involving soldiers, youth, and the total population. This movement reached a peak in 1965 and crested in 1966 in the Great Proletarian Cultural Revolution, displaying increasing militancy of aim.

On New Year's Day of 1965, the general political department's editorial in *Liberation Army Daily* called for "raising higher and higher the Red Banner of Mao Tse-tung's Thought." In this year, especially, the PLA publicly championed Mao's Yenan philosophy of national development. The multifunctional Yenan Nanniwan production brigade that was composed during the early 1940s of PLA soldiers from the 359th brigade of the 120th division of the eighth route army who reclaimed and worked the arid area was a prototype of Mao's people's communes organization.[20] In the summer of 1965, the "spirit of Nanniwan" was championed in the nation's press along with its more recent offspring of Tachai brigade and Taching oil industry.[21] In September, Lin Piao himself contributed a second signal article to Ch'en Po-ta's *Red Flag* which, similar to his 1960 article, carried the ominous title, "Long Live the Victory of the People's War."

Seven months later, in its editorial of April 18, 1966, the *Liberation Army Daily* provided the earliest public policy statement of the revolution to come. This was a public policy shift from proselyting to revolution and ideological purge. The editorial was entitled, "Raise Higher the Red Banner of Mao Tse-tung's Thought to Join in the Social and Cultural Revolution" and pointed out that the PLA would play a leading role in the revolution to come. On August 1, 1966, heralding the Great Proletarian Cultural Revolution, the *People's Daily* editorialized as follows: "The Entire Nation Should be Turned into a University of Mao Tse-tung's Thought." Noting the leading role of the PLA in the implementation of such a transformation, the editorial contained the following quotation:

> In recent years, acting on orders received from the Party's Central Committee, the Central Military Commission and Comrade Lin Piao, the Liberation Army played an active role in the Great Proletarian Revolution by raising high the Great Red Banner of Mao Tse-Tung's Thought, studying and applying Chairman Mao's writings, and developing the Three-Eight Style.

This is precisely what Lin Piao and his politicized PLA had been continuously engaged in for the seven years since Lin's ascendance to the post of minister of defense in the face of the Great Leap debacles reported by P'eng Teh-huai at Lushan.

But we have gotten ahead of our study; let us return to the situation in China at the time of the tenth plenum in September 1962 and observe the origin and fate of the second large wave of proselyting activity, the Socialist Education Campaign, that was to be carried out by the organizational apparatus of the party in the nonmilitary sector of society and targeted upon the proletarian masses. An examination of the conduct of this campaign by the party apparatus will reveal why it was that the People's Liberation Army eventually led a radicalized extension of this campaign, the Great Proletarian Cultural Revolution, in the civilian sector of Chinese society.

NOTES

1. Lowel Dittmer, *Liu Shao-ch'i and the Chinese Cultural Revolution: The Politics of Mass Criticism.* Berkeley: University of California Press, 1974, p. 49.

2. See Lin Piao, "The victory of the Chinese people's revolutionary war is the vic-

tory of the thought of Mao Tse-tung," *HC,* October 1, 1960, as quoted in John Gittings, *The Role of the Chinese Army.* New York: Oxford University Press, 1967, pp. 235-236.

3. The translations of these secret military papers of 1961 are in J. Chester Cheng, ed., *The Politics of the Chinese Red Army: A Translation of the Bulletin of Activities of the People's Liberation Army.* Palo Alto, Calif.: Hoover Institution on War, Revolution, and Peace, 1966. The bulletin was irregularly published by the general political department of the PLA and distributed only to party cadres at the regimental level or above. The journal is entitled *Kung-tso T'ung-hsun* translated as *Bulletin of Activities.* (Hereafter *KTTH.*)

4. *KTTH,* p. 116.

5. See Alexander George, *The Chinese Communist Army in Action.* New York: Columbia University Press, 1967, pp. 205-207. See also Ellis Joffe, *Party and Army: Professionalism and Political Control in the Chinese Officer Corps, 1949-1964.* Harvard East Asian Research Center, 1965, p. 53.

6. Ibid.

7. Ibid.

8. *KTTH,* No. 3, 1960, No. 1, 1961 and No. 2, 1961, in J. Chester Cheng, ed., *The Politics of the Chinese Red Army,* op. cit.

9. Ibid.

10. John Gittings, op. cit., p. 245.

11. Ibid., p. 249.

12. Ibid., p. 254.

13. Ibid., p. 247.

14. Ibid., p. 215.

15. See Lin Yun-cheng, "The role of the people's militia," *PR,* No. 5, February 1965, as cited in John Gittings, op. cit., p. 220.

16. Chu Win-lin, "Regulations governing the political work of the Chinese People's Liberation Army," *IAS,* Vol. II, No. 1, October 1965, pp. 29, 35.

17. *IAS,* Vol. II, No. 1, October 1965, pp. 38-42.

18. "Regulations governing the work of the general political department of the Chinese People's Liberation Army," *IAS,* Vol. II, No. 1, pp. 42-46.

19. Gittings, op. cit., pp. 254-258.

20. Chalmers Johnson, "Chinese Communist leadership and mass response: The Yenan period and the Socialist Education Campaign period," in Ping-ti Ho and Tang Tsou, *China in Crisis,* Vol. 1, Book 1. Chicago: University of Chicago Press, 1968, pp. 423-425.

21. *JMJP,* July 11, 1965, as cited in Johnson, op. cit., p. 434.

Chapter 8

SOCIALIST EDUCATION AND

THE PROLETARIAN MASSES

This Socialist Education movement is a great revolutionary movement. . . . This is a struggle that calls for the reeducation of man. This is a struggle for reorganizing the revolutionary class armies for a confrontation with the forces of feudalism and capitalism who are now feverishly attacking us. We must nip their counter-revolution in the bud. We must make it a great movement of reforming the bulk of elements in these counter-revolutionary forces and turn them into new men.[1]

With this renewed call for proselyting and enhanced class struggle, Mao Tse-tung began the Socialist Education Campaign when he returned to the "first line" at the tenth plenum of the eighth central committee of the Chinese Communist Party in September 1962. The major domestic thrusts of this Socialist Education Campaign to be conducted through the conventional party apparatus were two: One was directed at the youth; the other was directed at the peasantry. Both were to be subverted by central members of the party organization. Again, Mao's overall aim in the campaign was proselyting for Marxism-Leninism and the thought of Mao Tse-tung, with special emphasis on the tenet of class struggle, which provided an exculpating rationalization for the Great Leap failures. Such proselyting was to take several forms in this campaign: spreading Mao's ideas to youths and peasants; organizing a vanguard of disciples to the Maoist cause; and putting Mao's ideas into actual practice.

Mao's high hopes for the success of the Socialist Education Campaign are illustrated by the following excerpt from his speech:

Class struggle, production struggle, and scientific experiment are the three great revolutionary movements that build up a powerful socialist nation. They are a guarantee for the Communists to do away with bureaucratism, to avoid revisionism, and dogmatism, to stand eternally invincible. They are an assurance for the proletariat to be able to unite with the massive labor populace in order to realize democratic dictatorship of the proletariat.[2]

That Mao conceived of the Socialist Education movement as a revolutionary movement to reeducate man according to his ideology is attested by the following excerpt from this speech:

This Socialist educational movement is a great revolutionary movement. It not only covers the problem of class struggle, but also includes the question of cadres joining in the production labor. It also embodies the kind of work in which one will learn how to solve a group of problems in enterprises and industries through experiments with a strict scientific attitude. This may seem very difficult. Actually, all that is required is diligence, and the solution will not be difficult to find. This is a struggle that calls for the reeducation of man. . . . They [cadres] will no longer be floating on water, no longer bureaucrats and overlords, no longer divorced from the masses. . . . When this educational movement is completed there will emerge throughout the nation a new climate of progress into "greater prosperity."[3]

In a speech delivered to the tenth plenum on the morning of September 24, Mao reaffirmed his tenet on the continuation of the class struggle following the revolution, with examples drawn from both China and the international scene.[4] The international scene provided most support for Mao's revolutionary ideology, and he devoted considerable time to it:

At Peitaiho [August, 1958] I presented three problems: classes, the current situation, and contradictions. I raised the problem of classes because it has not been resolved yet. We need not mention domestic problems. In the international situation, we have the existence of imperialism, nationalism and revisionism in bourgeois countries where the class problem is still unresolved. Thus, we have the anti-imperialist task, as well as the task of supporting the movement of national liberation. This means that *we must support the broad masses of people in the three continents of Asia, Africa and Latin America, including workers, peasants, the revolutionary national bourgeoisie, and revolutionary intellectuals. We must rally with so many people, but not include the reactionary national bourgeoisie.*[5]

Later in his speech, Mao provided additional support for his tenet of class struggle: "Since World War II, in Asia, Africa or Latin America, determined struggles of national liberation have developed year after year." Mao then cited eleven consonant examples of successful people's struggles to prove his point and concluded that "the international situation is excellent."[6]

Reaffirming his class struggle tenet and buttressing his case with a quotation from Lenin, Mao presented his own dialectical analysis of the situation in the international class struggle and warned of "revisionism" in China.[7] Mao did not perceive the domestic situation as propitious; domestic class enemies existed in the form of critical intellectuals who utilized nove.s "to engage in anti-Party activity."[8]

To reduce these social contradictions, Mao proposed a renewed study movement with special emphasis upon the class education of youth to prevent China from heading in an antisocialist direction.[9] Thus, Mao's tenth plenum kick-off of the Socialist Education Campaign publicly reasserted what he had been more privately concerned about since the Great Leap failures reported at Lushan, proselyting those allies of the proletariat he expected would support his ideology while giving less attention to those who sharply disagreed. Domestically, in addition to party cadres, he focused upon youths and proletarians; in foreign affairs, he focused on other emerging nations. Increasingly, the class enemies, domestic and foreign, were seen in league with other. The implementation of the Socialist Education Campaign was to reveal the personal identities of highly placed domestic class enemies. Later, increased ideological polarization on the politburo would cause Mao's attention to turn to them more forcefully.

The Socialist Education of Protean Youth

As everybody knows, Chairman Mao at all times stands higher and sees farther than anyone else. . . . The way he looks at problems must be like standing on top of a skyscraper, looking out and down at the streets and highways below. Each path, each turn, each curve comes into his view. How is it possible for him to lose direction?

So read the pages of the initial issue of *Chinese Youth* in 1963 signifying a major domestic prong of the Socialist Education Campaign targeted upon China's youth. As a subpart of this campaign, the regime launched a nationwide emulation movement of "Learning from Lei Feng" the following month. The acknowledged aim of this movement was "class education" of youth.[10] The first public notice in the mass media heralding the campaign appeared in *People's Daily* on January 25 and stated that the ministry of national defense had conferred the glorious title of "Lei Feng Squad" on a squad of a certain PLA unit because the unit had a "good fighter" by the name Lei Feng who had lost his life in service.[11] On February 7, *People's Daily* devoted almost two pages to the dreams and deeds of Lei Feng, including the following excerpt:

> Yesterday I had a dream. I dreamt of seeing Chairman Mao. Like a compassionate father, he stroked my head. With a smile he spoke to me: "Do a good job in study; be forever loyal to the Party, loyal to the people!" My joy was overwhelming; I tried to speak, but I could not.

The organizational implementation of the Lei Feng campaign was led *not* by the party but by the People's Liberation Army. On February 9, 1963, the general political department of the PLA issued a "notification of the propaganda and study of Comrade Lei Feng's exemplary deeds in the whole army."[12] On March 2, a resolution was passed by the standing committee of the All-China Federation of Democratic Youth calling upon all members to give a positive answer to the exhortation of "learning from Comrade Lei Feng" as proposed by Chairman Mao.[13] The next day, the All-China Federation of Trade Unions issued a "notification on organizing the masses of employees and workers on an extensive nation-wide scale to learn from Comrade Lei Feng."[14] Pursuant to the resolutions of the top echelons of these mass organizations, the Learn from Lei Feng Campaign moved into full swing through local subunits of these organizations.

The ideological contents to be communicated in the course of the Lei Feng campaign are well codified in the official notifications of the People's Liberation Army, the Communist youth league, and the All-China Federation of Trade Unions as follows:

The first document is the "Notification of the Propaganda and Study of Comrade Lei Feng's Exemplary Deeds in the Whole Army" issued by "general political department, PLA," on February 9, 1963:

> the following points are to be emphasized in propaganda and study: 1) [Lei Feng's] firm class stand, his distinct love and hatred and his revolutionary spirit of being always mindful of his origin and loyal to the Party and Chairman Mao and to the cause of emancipating mankind; 2) his constant attention to the interests of the Party, his invariable consideration for the revolutionary needs, his determination to become an ever rust-free screw and his spirit of serving the people with all his heart; 3) his noble Communist virtues of endurance to hardship, simplicity, diligence, absolute selflessness and readyness for others; 4) his endeavor in studying Chairman Mao's works, his self-consciousness in accepting Party education, his strict demand on himself, and his studious spirit in making improvement by actively training and seriously transforming himself.

A similar document on the "Notification of the Launching of the 'Learnining from Lei Feng' Educational Activities among the Youths on an Extensive Nationwide Scale" was issued by the Communist Youth League committee on February 16, 1963. Finally, on March 6, 1963 the All-China Federation of Trade Unions issued a similar "Notification on Organizing the Masses of Employees and Workers on an Extensive Nationwide Scale to Learn from Comrade Lei Feng." The contents of the Lei Feng campaign were the heightening of class consciousness, the inculcation of Communist virtues, and the dissemination of the thought of Mao Tse-tung.[15]

In contrast to Mao's enthusiasm and PLA activism, some politburo members dragged their feet in the implementation of Mao's campaign. The party organization proper was not united behind it. Evidence of post-Great Leap polarization in the politburo is provided by the Lei Feng campaign inscriptions penned by the members six months after the tenth plenum which launched the Socialist Education campaign. On March 2, 1963, a special "Learn from Lei Feng" issue of the *China Youth* magazine published inscriptions, poems, and essays by Mao Tse-tung, Chou En-lai, Tung Pi-wu, Kuo Mo-yo, Lo Jui-ch'ing, and Hsieh Chueh-tsai. In the March 6, 1963 edition of the *Liberation Army News* inscriptions by Liu Shao-ch'i, Chou En-lai, Chu Teh, Lin Piao and Teng Hsiao-p'ing were published. The inscriptions by Mao, Liu, Chou, Chu, Lin and Teng were reproduced on the front pages of various local magazines and newspapers. It is revealing to note the inscriptions of the various members of the standing committee of the politburo with regard to which do or do not pay tribute to Mao Tse-tung.

Mao Tse-tung's inscription reads: "Learn from Comrade Lei Feng." Lin Piao's inscription reads: "Follow Lei Feng's example and be good fighters of Chairman Mao." Chu Teh's inscription reads: "Learn from Lei Feng and be good fighters of Chairman Mao." Chou En-lai's inscription reads: "Comrade Lei Feng is the worthy son of the laboring people and the good fighter of Chairman Mao; learn from Lei Feng his class stand to distinguish between what to hate and what to love, his revolutionary spirit of acting according to his words; his Communist style of devoting to public affairs and forgetting private interests, and his self-sacrificing proletarian fighting spirit."

It is significant that none of the remaining three members of the standing committee of the politburo pay homage to Chairman Mao with their inscriptions. Liu Shao-ch's's inscription reads: "Learn from Comrade Lei Feng his ordinary but great Communist spirit." Teng Hsiao-p'ing's inscription reads: "Whoever wishes to be a true Communist should learn from Comrade Lei Feng, his qualities and style." Ch'en Yun is the single member of the standing committee of the politburo who did not publish an inscription on Lei Feng.

As the leading member of the politburo after Mao himself, Liu again

proved himself a doubting disciple. On May 15, Liu did indeed try to educate young party members ideologically, but he did not proselyte for Mao's
thought. Speaking before the Nguyen Ai Quoc party school on this day, he
urged the party neophytes to study "Marx, Engels, Lenin and Stalin" while
conspicuously omitting any reference to the thought of Mao Tse-tung.[16]
Below the politburo, other party members displayed views in concert with
Liu's.

Evidence of anti-Maoist polarization further down the party hierarchy
was forthcoming in November 1963. Just fourteen months after Mao's tenth
plenum exhortation for reeducating man according to the socialist ideology
some intellectuals again set forth the traditional heresy. In November, a
formal conference on Confucianism was held in which the sage was praised
as an example to be emulated by modern Chinese.[17] Clearly, Lei Feng and
Confucius provided mutually antithetical emulation models for Chinese
youth; the former was the ideal of the proletarian; the latter was the model
of the traditional scholar *literati* bureaucrat. During 1963 and 1964, attacks
on the Maoist Great Leap Forward policy continued to come forth from the
intellectuals. A leading anti-Great Leap spokesman at this time was K'ang
Cho, a subordinate and prodigy of the recalcitrant party literary czar, Chou
Yang. In December of 1963, Mao acted forcefully and spoke out against
such intellectuals; and in the middle of 1964, the Peking opera was forcefully reformed by Chiang Ch'ing and her associates in eliminating traditional
themes and substituting proletarian themes.[18]

Socialist Education of the Agrarian Masses

In social struggle, however, the forces representing the advanced class
sometimes suffer defeat, not because of incorrectness of ideology, but
because in comparison of struggling strengths the forces representing
the advanced class are temporarily inferior to the reactionary forces.
Hence it is only a temporary defeat. Eventually success will come to the
side of the ideologically advanced class.

A test in actual practice is tantamount to another "leap forward" of
one's cognition. The leap forward at this juncture bears greater significance than the previous one. Because only through this second leap forward can a corroboration be found for the leap forward of the first
time. This is to say that there is no other way to verify the truth other
than this second leap forward in which the correctness of the ideology,
theory, policy, plan, method, etc. obtained during the process of the
objective outside world will be determined. The purpose of the proletariat in acquainting itself with the world is world reformation. There
can be no other purpose.

Among our comrades today, many are still ignorant of this epistemology. . . . Therefore, it is necessary that our comrades receive education and training in order to acquaint them with dialectic materialism.[19]

With this ominous introduction alluding to effecting a "second leap forward" to corroborate the truth of the leap forward of the first time," Mao personally directed the conduct of the Socialist Education Campaign in the countryside in May of 1963. This second major prong of the campaign was targeted broadly on the proletarians and focused particularly upon the peasantry and the basic-level rural cadres. The underlying aim of this subcampaign was to secure empirical and social support for the validity of the tenets of Mao's ideology for achieving the socialist transformation through an educated proletarian reconstruction from below of the retrogressed rural economy. The proletarian movement in the countryside was to be coordinated by party cadres.

The proposed Socialist Education movement in the countryside was in concert with Mao's tenth plenum emphasis of the continuation of class struggle and his reaffirmation of the Great Leap principles for achieving the socialist transformation. In addition to Mao's call for the "reeducation of man," the official communique of the tenth plenary session of the eighth central committee of the CCP had reasserted the Maoist principles on the continued existence of classes and class struggle throughout the period of transition from capitalism to communism and had reaffirmed that the broadest masses and cadres have always "firmly believed in the correctness of the general line for socialist construction, the Big Leap Forward and the People's Communes—The Three Red Banners."[20] Mao had also stressed the need for three great revolutionary movements of "class struggle, production struggle, and scientific experiments" to build the great socialist nation.[21] The Socialist Education Campaign was intended and designed by Mao to be an integrated example of these ideas put into practice.[22]

Mao's May 1963 resolution describes the basic aim of the Socialist Education Campaign as an educational movement designed to promote Maoist dialectics and the collectivist ideology of the proletariat and to dispel the bourgeois ideology of self-interest and private enterprise. The use of three Maoist principles is evident in the proposed movement: the employment of dialectical analysis to design the movement; the advocacy of mass line leadership techniques to unify cadres and masses; and the advocacy of social struggle to unify the proletarians and transform the bourgeoisie. The first portion of the resolution analyzes the situation in terms of class contradictions; the second portion of the resolution proposed methods of resolving the contradictions. First of all, allusion is made to the general Maoist maxim of the continued existence of class struggle in a socialist society progressing towards communism. The maxim is then applied to the situation in rural

China in the early 1960s. The proletarians and their allies form the great majority and are seen to consist of the poor and lower-middle peasants and the bulk of the rural cadres; the bourgeois enemy is composed of the ex-landlords, rich peasants, financial speculators, counterrevolutionaries, and certain of the cadres who have been corrupted by the ideology of the former exploiting classes. The bourgeois sins of the minority of the cadres consist of an attitude of "overlordship" with respect to the masses and certain corrupt economic practices regarding the management of account books, warehouses, properties, and work points. Second, in order to resolve this basic social contradiction, a number of steps are proposed. The proletarians and cadres must be made aware of the continued existence of class enemies and their effort to make a comeback. The poor and lower-middle peasants must be organized from below and within the communes to oversee and reform corrupt cadres, to develop their own class consciousness, and to oppose the exploitation by rich peasants and bourgeois elements. The cadres must regain contact with and understanding of the masses through participation in productive labor with the masses. Through a continuous mass movement of this nature the ideology of the proletariat would triumph over the ideology of the bourgeoisie. The textual exposition of the proposed movement takes the form of ten articles.

Evidence of Mao's attempt to reduce the dissonance he felt between his fervent belief in the Great Leap as a means of realizing true communism for China and his knowledge of the Great Leap debacles and subsequent retreat is apparent in his introduction to the May 1963 resolution. There it is stated that the resolution had been in active preparation for three years "from 1960 when the Central Committee promulgated the 12 items of work for reorganization of the rural society to the present,"[23] i.e., since the enactment under Liu Shao-ch's leadership of the emergency directive retreating from the Leap, reducing the communes to the production brigade level of leadership and restoring to the peasants the rights to cultivate private plots, to sell their grain in "free" markets, and to spend less time working. Subsequently in March 1961, Teng Hsiao-p'ing and P'eng Chen had drafted the Sixty Articles on Agriculture resulting in further reduction of control in the communes to the small production team level. With the twelve articles as trigger, Mao had ordered some investigations into the rural situation in various provinces and, after studying the reports, proposed the May 1963 resolution. The underlying rationale for his recommendations was, as shown earlier, preparation for a "second leap forward" as a corroboration for his ideology.[24]

In May 1963, Mao once again showed his intensified commitment to his Great Leap and commune program by writing his "Instruction on the Commune Education Movement" in which he boldly stated that "this revolutionary movement is the first great struggle since land reform. . . . This kind of struggle involving all, both within the Party and outside the Party, has not been waged for over ten years."[25]

Later in 1963, another set of ten articles on the conduct of the Socialist Education Campaign in the countryside was promulgated in the name of the central committee.[26] However, there the similarity ends. These later ten articles of September 1963 were not drawn up by Mao Tse-tung, but by some other members of the party center. They were concocted under Liu Shao-ch'is leadership, certainly involving P'eng Chen and probably Teng Hsiao-p'ing and some other members of the secretariat. These more concrete later ten articles did not even follow Mao's point by point, but dealt with ten selected aspects of the earlier resolution. Although the brief introduction gave lip service to Mao's tenth plenum address and Mao's earlier ten articles, no serious treatment was given to Maoist dialectics or an attempt to gain empirical support therefor. Absolutely no mention was given of a "leap forward," much less a "second leap forward."

Whereas the earlier ten articles had emphasized raising the class consciousness of poor and lower-middle peasants through ideological study, the organization of these awakened peasants into strong associations at team, brigade, and commune levels, and the unleasing of these awakened peasants to struggle against errant party cadres and class enemies, the later ten articles subverted the essence of the proposed mass movement and attempted to convert it into a gradual bureaucratic reform movement *from above*. The later ten articles even went so far as to state that "experiences in spot testings at various places have proved that to consolidate over 95% of the cadres is a *prerequisite* to the consolidation of over 95% of the masses."[27] Furthermore, they advocated holding party meetings at the basic levels for criticism and self-criticism *among* party members and, at the provincial, regional, and county levels, party members were to form their own work teams. Thus the party was to do its own rectification and its members were not to be exposed to the humiliation of struggle by poor and lower-middle peasants from below. In addition, the main targets in the later resolution were not party cadres, but the disruptive social factors of rich peasants, speculators, profiteers, saboteurs, and common criminals; these were to be the main "targets of our [party] blows." Thus the target of "class" enmity was to be deflected from members of the party apparatus. In sum, the later ten articles were not designed to mobilize the masses of poorer peasants for class struggle, an action recommended by Mao at the ninth plenum in January 1961, rather they were designed to protect the party apparatus and make it more efficient.

One year later, in September 1964, yet another version of the ten articles was drawn up and promulgated by Liu Shao-ch'i himself. These revised later ten articles closely followed the format of the September 1963 prototype and changed only a few words here and there to give the impression of more concern with mobilization of the masses; but the basic design of the later ten articles remained intact. Despite the belated emphasis on forming "staunch" poor and lower-middle peasant associations, and despite the new inclusion of special stages in the movement for "mobilization of the masses to struggle against the enemy,"[28] Liu's revised later ten articles captured neither the spirit nor the intent of Mao's early ten articles of May 1963. The polarization between the proselyting Maoists and the recalcitrant party bureaucrats had already reached a critical point with the promulgation of the later ten articles in the fall of 1963.

Frustration of the Maoist Proselyting Drive

In May, 1963 Chairman Mao personally formulated the "Decision Concerning Some Question in the Current Rural Work (First Ten Point Decision). After that, in September, certain comrades at the Party Central dished out the "second ten point decision" (Some Concrete Policy Decisions on the Rural Socialist Education Movement), which was distributed on November 14. . . . In the summer of 1964, having discovered that some articles in the "second ten point decision" would interfere with the free mobilization of the masses, I made some revision and the revised draft was sent out on September 18.[29]

So stated a contrite, if bewildered, Liu Shao-ch'i in his confession at the work conference of the party central committee in October 1966. His statements provided confirmation of the existence of foot-dragging in the conduct of the Socialist Education Campaign on the part of high-level party bureaucrats in the latter part of 1963. His confession and self-criticism early in the Cultural Revolution also signified the extreme importance the Maoists attached to mobilization of the masses for affirmation of their ideology as far back as 1963.

Evidence from an account of the implementation of the Socialist Education Campaign at the provincial level provides further support for the existence of foot-dragging in the party regarding the implementation of this campaign.[30] In his description of the campaign in Kwangtung, Vogel notes that "for all his support of Chairman Mao, in the months after the Tenth Plenum neither T'ao [T'ao Chu, first secretary of the central south region, including Kwangtung province] nor his party hierarchy in Canton showed any signs of pursuing the class struggle. In previous calls such as this, big cadre meetings and work teams were organized immediately, but in this case nothing happened."[31] The meeting of the Kwangtung provincial people's council of October 18-19, 1962 to implement the call of the September tenth plenum placed its emphasis on technical reform, making virtually no mention of "class struggle," much less a campaign.[32]

In mid-April 1963, the provincial party committee did follow the army's example in launching a "five good campaign" in the countryside; but it was in fact another labor emulation campaign with emphasis on production and in the materials used for the campaign theme was not even a mention of "class struggle."[33] Later in the same month T'ao Chu set forth the idea of establishing poor and lower-middle peasant associations, but in doing so he merely suggested occasional meetings of poorer peasants, a far cry from Mao's intended instrument of class struggle.[34] A few days after the release of the May 1963 Resolution, Kwangtung provincial officials announced the establishment of poor and lower-middle peasants associations and entreated lower cadres that these should not be merely perfunctory associations.[35] However, the same directives made it clear that the poor and lower-middle peasants associations were to be placed under the leadership of the local party organizations; that they were urged to take the lead in promoting economic production; and that they were not just to attack but to "unite with" richer middle peasants.[36] With the publication of the September 1963 resolution, the provincial party bureaucrats were aided in their toning down of the Socialist Education Campaign.

In December of 1963, the two tendencies came to a confrontation. At the 1,000-man provincial agricultural work conference held in Canton from December 21 to 29, 1963, the focus of discussion was still on agricultural technology and production; the report of the conference did not even mention class struggle. At the very end of December, however, the themes introduced earlier by the PLA of recalling the class struggle and praising the triumphs under socialism were picked up by the Canton municipal people's congress and continued to be prominent throughout the Socialist Education Campaign in Kwangtung.[37] The devices employed by the local party bureaucrats to thwart Mao's proselyting efforts, the "waving of red flags to oppose the red flag" by quoting Mao's works to support their own point of view and the ritualization of the study of Mao's works by not taking the content seriously were to pale before the growing presence and vicil power of the PLA in 1964.

Another source of data provides evidence for an actual decline in public participation in political campaigns during the same period. The data come from the sample survey of mainland refugees examined later with regard to changing levels of media exposure. A major index of participation in political campaigns is the amount of time per week that a mainlander spends in meetings, since a large share of this time is spent in political study. As a campaign increases in intensity, this index rises; as a campaign declines, the index declines. Figures 8.1 and 8.2 show that participation in such meetings was greater among both proletarians and nonproletarians in every recorded year following the Great Leap debacle when compared with participation in

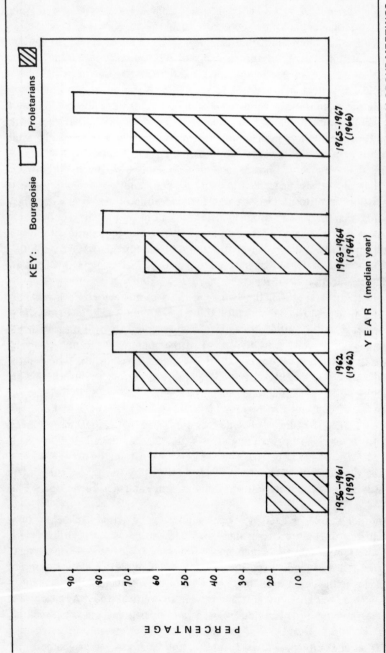

KEY: Bourgeoisie ▢   Proletarians ▨

Figure 8.1: PROPORTION OF PROLETARIANS AND BOURGEOISIE REGULARLY PARTICIPATING IN STUDY GROUP MEETINGS BY YEAR

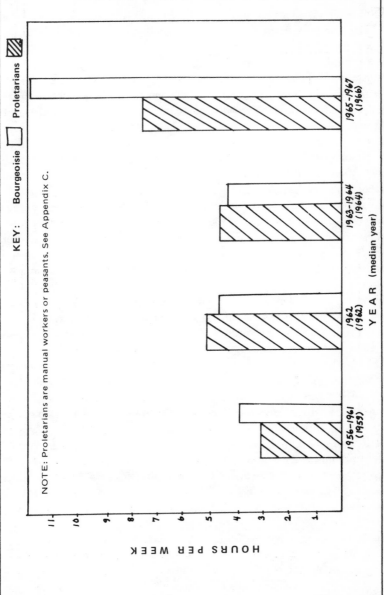

KEY: Bourgeoisie ☐ Proletarians ▨

NOTE: Proletarians are manual workers or peasants. See Appendix C.

Figure 8.2: HOURS OF MEETINGS PER WEEK ATTENDED BY PROLETARIANS AND BOURGEOISIE BY YEAR

meetings preceding the Great Leap of late 1959. Furthermore, immediately following the Great Leap debacle there was a large increase in participation in meetings by proletarians as shown by the average of five hours per week for 1962. Despite the fact that most refugees came to Hong Kong in 1962, the post-1959 low in meeting participation for proletarians and nonproletarians alike was 1963-1964. In other words, based on those refugees who left Communist China between January 1963 and August 1964, we can estimate the amount of time spent in meetings per week in the year preceding their exodus, to be the lowest in the post 1959 sample. This fact can be interpreted as additional evidence for the contention of a slow-down in the pace of Maoist proselyting campaigns in 1963. The phenomenon is most marked when only the proletarian portion of the sample is examined with regard to hours spent in meetings and the proportion of persons regularly attending political study group meetings.

That public participation in political campaigns moved to a higher pitch after early 1964 is evidenced by the figures on meeting participation for our sample that left the mainland in 1966 or 1967, i.e., for those who fled after the onset of the Cultural Revolution. These figures are the highest of all. For 1966, 70 percent of the proletarians regularly participated in study group meetings and they averaged almost eight hours per week participating in meetings of some kind. Fully 90 percent of the nonproletarians in our sample regularly participated in study group meetings at this time and they averaged almost twelve hours per week participating in meetings of some kind. By the end of 1966, the Socialist Education Campaign had deepened into the Great Proletarian Cultural Revolution.

Thus both documentary and survey data show a slowdown in the implementation of the Maoist Socialist Education Campaign in 1963. This slowdown in the implementation of the Maoist campaign, this subversion of Mao's ideological proselyting movement was an index of further polarization on the politburo and an important contributory cause of the Great Proletarian Cultural Revolution. This is quite clear in the "confession of Liu Shao-ch'i" made public during the Cultural Revolution.[38]

Listing the times when he actually "went against the Chairman's thought," Liu cites a number of incidents that occurred following the Great Leap debacle:

> In 1962, I committed the mistake of inclining to the right; in 1964 I once again committed the mistake of inclining to the right, although I appeared to be "leftist" on the surface. The policy line mistakes I committed in the course of the Great Proletarian Cultural Revolution are connected with the above-mentioned mistakes.[39]

In citing his activities while presiding at the central work conference from February 21-26, 1962, Liu admits the following:

> As provincial-level Party leaders in the ministries were asked to discuss this and express differing views some people voiced views in favor of private management while others fundamentally denied the "three red flags" principle, and severely criticized the positive elements. . . . I trusted Chen Yun [known for his conservative economic viewpoint] too much, listened to his views too one-sidedly; and since we shared some views I personally recommended to the Party Central Committee and the Chairman that Chen Yun be appointed to the post of chief of the central financial group. As the Chairman was not in Peking, I went to see him and made my report personally. . . . At the time, leader Teng [Party General Secretary] Hsiao-p'ing spoke at the central work conference on the merits of the "responsibility farm system" in Anhwei, and we did not oppose this view.[40]

Liu admits to another rightist deviation in the summer of 1962 preceding the tenth plenum:

> In the summer of 1962, at the Peitaiho conference, I committed the mistake of a right-wing policy line. After the Chairman returned to Peking, he started drafting the decision for the further strengthening of the collective economy and the decision on commerce. Also at the Peitaiho conference, he brought up the contradictions in class struggle. In September, he held the Tenth Plenum of the Central Committee, adopted the two decisions and a communique, corrected my mistakes for the first time, and fundamentally changed the situation.[41]

More specific references to the three resolutions in question are evident in the following passage from Liu's confession:

> In May 1963 Chairman Mao himself drafted the "early 10 points," concerning "decisions on some current problems in the countryside," then in September some comrades in the Central Committee proposed the "later 10 points" concerning "decisions on some concrete policies regarding the socialist education campaign in the countryside," which was published on November 14. . . . In the summer of 1964 I felt that some regulations in the "later 10 points" were inadequate for all-out mobilization of the masses, and I therefore made some revisions and published the revised draft on September 18.[42]

Summarizing the situation in the politburo at the end of 1963, we see further polarization over Mao's policies. In direct contradiction to Mao's intent to raise class consciousness and mobilize the proletarian masses in his

May 1963 instructions for the Socialist Education Campaign, some "comrades" at the party center had attempted to subvert the spirit of the movement and convert it into a moderated program of bureaucratic and economic reform from above with their own instructions of September 1963. These "comrades" were able to promulgate the September instructions while Mao was "taking a rest" during 1963 following his temporary return to the "first line" during the tenth plenum of late 1962.[4 3] Liu Shao-ch'i and Teng Hsiao-p'ing, the nadir of Maoist proselyting, subsequently moved to the first line. Mao's own instructions of May 1963 and his later ones of January 1965 were both taken as providing guidelines for the conduct of the Cultural Revolution in 1966, but the two sets of instructions of the "comrades" at the party center of September 1963 and September 1964 were to be ignored.[4 4] Thus, some "comrades" at the party center had been insubordinate and by the end of 1964 two competing sets of instructions in the conduct of the campaign were in circulation.

The highly committed Maoists, including Lin Piao, Ch'en Po-ta, and K'ang Sheng, intent on proselyting for the thought of Mao Tse-tung, must have found it difficult to reconcile these two beliefs: Some comrades in the politburo had subverted Mao's personal attempt to mobilize the proletarians; all members of the politburo were revolutionary Marxists. The Maoists could either attempt to reform the thinking of their high-level colleagues or set the stage for purging the politburo of disbelievers. However, these moderate comrades were proving themselves increasingly resistant to reform. In December 1963 Mao counterattacked: He displayed an enhanced desire to proselyte for his ideology and simultaneously raised the level of the targets of reform to include those perceived to have sabotaged his original proselyting movement. In December, Mao simultaneously attacked the "conservatism, arrogance, and complacency" of the foot-dragging party bureaucrats and the intellectual purveyors of bourgeois art and "feudalistic" literature. He turned for support to the increasingly virtuous People's Liberation Army and associated youth as the new vanguard of revolutionary Maoist socialism. It was in December that Mao called upon all political, economic and social organizations in China to "learn from the People's Liberation Army."[4 5]

From December of 1963 through 1964, Mao became increasingly active in proselyting for his Great Leap ideology and the class struggle rationalization for its failure; but now Mao took a firmer foothold in the PLA and directed sharper attacks at party bureaucrats and intellectuals. On December 12, Mao penned a bitter comment on the state of art and literature in China drawn up by his supporter, K'o Ching-shih in Shanghai. Mao complained that "problems abound in all forms of art. . . . The social and economic base has changed, but the arts as part of the superstructure . . . still remain a serious problem.[4 6] The next day Mao produced his instruction of the central committee on overcoming "conservatism, arrogance, and complacency" saying;

> [arrogant people] do not adopt the Marxist-Leninist method of dialectical analysis to deal with work. . . . When one is divided into two (that is there are achievements as well as shortcomings and mistakes), they study only the aspects of achievements. . . . Analyzed according to class origin, arrogance and complacency are fundamentally ideas of the exploiting classes. . . . Another method besides sincerely welcoming criticism of the masses to overcome arrogance . . . is for one to exert oneself in raising one's Communist consciousness. This calls for intensified study of Marxism-Leninism.[47]

In the spring of 1964, Mao supported the virtues of Lin's revolutionized PLA. On February 13, Mao gave a spring festival talk where he stated,

> It is necessary to emulate the PLA and Taching of the Petroleum Ministry. . . . All departments must emulate the PLA and set up political departments to intensify their political work. . . . There are countless numbers of good men and good deeds in our affairs, and there are many good models that should be commended.[48]

Mao also criticized bourgeois art and education saying, "Actors, poets, writers and dramatists must be drawn out of the city and down to the rural areas. . . . I think that educational work should also be reformed."[49]

Later in the spring, Mao made some recommendations for China's third five year plan. In May, Mao complained that there were only "three truly self reliant communes in the whole country."[50] On June 6, Mao gave a long talk criticizing the Soviet model as being inappropriate to the world and Chinese revolution.[51] In industry, Mao said, quality is more important. In agriculture, Mao recommended the spirit of Tachai and self reliance. Planning is not simply calculation, he said, one must put politics in command; in art and literature, the performance of the PLA ranks first, the locals second, and Peking third.

Later in June, Mao championed the twin activities of the PLA in creating successors to the revolution. Speaking on June 16, Mao noted that party provincial first secretaries were also PLA political commissars and should engage in militia work.[52] He then outlined five requirements for cultivating revolutionary successors, led by the requirement that cadres must know Marxism-Leninism not revisionism and including the third requirement that they must unite with the majority of the people while practicing "one divides into two" with respect to those who engage in "intrigues."[53]

In August Mao reasserted his concept of class struggle to attack bourgeois ideas. On August 18, Mao gave a talk on problems of philosophy in which he

by saying, "It is only with class struggle that there is philosophy." Mao went on to endorse *Kuang Ming Jih Pao,* and *Wen Hui Pao* and the PLA newspaper for publishing ideological articles, but asserted he didn't read *People's Daily* because it did not publish such articles until his suggestion to do so.[55] Regarding the May publication of the heresy of "combining two into one," Mao urged *Red Flag* to reprint some better articles and write a report.[56] Again in August, Mao urged proselyting for his dialectics saying,

> With regard to the concept of unity of opposites and with regard to dialectics, it is necessary to carry out extensive propaganda. It is my view that dialectics should be taken out of the realm of the philosophers and placed among the broad masses of people.[57]

The end of 1963 was indeed a watershed in Mao's relationships with the party and the army. Whereas the central party leadership had distorted the intent of Mao's directives on the Socialist Education Campaign, the PLA leadership had fully complied with Mao's directives. Gittings notes that the aim of the political campaigns in the PLA from 1960 to the end of 1963 had much in common with "the nationwide 'socialist education' movement, which is also concerned with bringing politics and the thought of Chairman Mao into every aspect of ordinary life, to raise the revolutionary standards and to find 'revolutionary successors' among the younger generation."[58] The "Learn from the PLA" campaign of 1964 was but an expansion of target of this kind of successful proselyting for the thought of Mao Tse-tung. In so doing, the PLA was justified in its further encroachments into the civilian sector of society by the expanded civilian mandate drawn up at the political work conference of February 1963 which emphasized that

> political work is not only to be carried out by the political cadres, but also by military cadres, administrative cadres, and technical cadres; not only to be carried out by cadres, but also to be carried out by combatants; not only to be carried out by a few advanced elements, but also to be carried out by the masses.[59]

In December 1963, Mao instructed the PLA to make more use of that earlier mandate.

In January 1964, the PLA political work conference heard their achievements of 1963 heralded over Peking Radio when it was announced that 1963 was a "bumper year" for the PLA, in which the class consciousness of officers and men had been greatly elevated, and the army's ideological and organizational work greatly improved.[60] The "Learn from the PLA" campaign was publicly launched by *People's Daily* in an editorial of February 1, 1964, which described the PLA as "an army of extremely high proletarian and combat character" which had gained "valuable . . . experiences in political ideological work" in recent years.[61] Mao called upon all units of the national economy "to study the methods of the PLA, establish and strengthen political work and thus arouse the revolutionary spirit of the millions and tens of millions of cadres and masses on the economic front."[62]

Thus the "Learn from the PLA" campaign sought to publicize throughout the country the successful techniques and activities of political indoctrination and control which had been practiced in the PLA since 1960: the army's "proper handling" for the "four firsts" relationships, its "revolutionary work-style," the emulation campaigns and the five good soldier and four good movements.[63] Although the study of Chairman Mao's writings occupied the prime position in this and every other PLA movement, the lessons learned by the PLA from this study were translated into practical action in every field of army life, however mundane or commonplace.

According to Lin's application of "living ideology" in March 1964, even the PLA "sanitation campaign" including latrine digging was said to have an inner significance for the soldiers taking part, for "when carrying out sanitation work, they also pay attention to doing well in man's ideological work."[64]

The "Learn from the PLA" campaign's distinctive feature was the way in which it inspired the creation of a new political commissar apparatus in industry, commerce and government which was directly modeled on the PLA's own political control system.[65] On the direct analogy of the PLA's company party branch, workshops and departments in industry and commerce were directed to reorganize existing party branches or to set up new ones. "In the PLA," it was explained, "The basic-level combat unit is the company. In the industrial enterprise, the basic-level production unit is the workshop."[66] Meanwhile, all units above the basic level in industrial and communication enterprises were required to organize political departments, with a director and political staff, again on the analogy of the PLA's political department structure, down to regimental level. This extension of the PLA-style control system into civilian institutions was heralded in early April as

a new development of Mao Tse-tung's thinking concerning socialist construction, an innovation relating to the construction and management of modern enterprises, and a fundamental question regarding the orientation of China's socialist construction.[67]

The staffing of this system relied heavily upon political cadres recruited from the PLA. During 1964, Mao attempted to revitalize the propaganda apparatus in party and government with political officers recruited from the People's Liberation Army.[68] In early 1965, it was disclosed that most of the 200,000 ex-PLA officers and personnel at work in the trade and finance sector were staffing this apparatus.[69]

As PLA servicement infiltrated the upper reaches of China's civilian institutions in 1964, PLA recruitment accelerated at the basic levels. In the autumn of 1964, another new stage was reached in militia building at a national militia political work conference in Peking, the first of its kind since 1960.[70] The militia was now defined, for the first time explicitly, as "an important instrument for safeguarding the people's democratic dictatorship" at home, as well as in the more customary terms of its value as a powerful reserve for national defense." The national militia political work conference declared that the Socialist Education movement and the "class struggle" should be the means in the future by which the militia was built up, since "the militia is an instrument used by our country to resist imperialist aggression from abroad and to carry out the people's democratic dictatorship at home."[71] Top priority was now given to militia work in the field of politics. The *People's Daily,* in an editorial on the conference, stressed the importance of continuing "the glorious tradition of exerting firm control of military affairs by the Party." Party committees at all local levels were called upon to strengthen their leadership over militia work, to include such work in their regular schedules for discussion and study, and to consolidate and develop the militia organizations. The new order of priorities had elevated the role of the militia as a "class weapon" over its role in production and even over its military role in national defense.[72]

The year 1964 was a year of vehement Maoist proselyting with the main organizational weapon being the People's Liberation Army and the main source of recruits being China's youth. In May of 1964, the first edition of the little red book, *Quotations from Chairman Mao (Mao Chu-hsi Yu-lu)* was published by the Political Department of the PLA on the eve of the Communist Youth League held in June, the central theme was the problem of revolutionizing young people both at home and abroad in order to make them revolutionaries forever.[73] On July 14, 1964, Mao delivered the polemic "On Khrushchev's Communism and Its Historical Lesson for the World," encompassing a fifteen point program to root out revisionism and prevent the restoration of capitalism in China. Following up the Lei Feng Campaign, Mao called for "cultivating revolutionary successors" who "come forward in mass struggles and are tempered in the great storms of revolution."[74] A major means of cultivating revolutionary successors was to send youths to the countryside. In 1964, some 300,000 youths were sent down. There they emulated the ideals expressed in earlier PLA-initiated campaigns, engaging in discussions with old cadres of the revolution and old peasants who had experienced the sufferings of Chinese rural life when the landlord class held sway. It was hoped that such experiences would dampen the spirit of careerist professionalism in youth and rid them of bourgeois desires for "the good life." In conjunction with this movement, the campaign of "revolutionary storytelling" was heightened. Hundreds of thousands of professional story-tellers in the countryside substituted revolutionary Maoist themes for traditional Chinese stories.[75]

Following the subversion of the Maoist proselyting drive with the promulgation of the "Later Ten Articles" by some comrades at the party center in the fall of 1963, domestically Mao shifted to the more virtuous PLA as the more faithful dispenser of his line in 1964, called upon all organizations to cultivate "revolutionary successors" among youth and angrily renewed this tenth plenum attack upon the critical intellectuals. In foreign affairs also, the committed Maoists simultaneously stepped up their attack. Between late 1963 and mid-1964, Mao in collaboration with K'ang Sheng and Ch'en Po-ta penned nine lengthy commentaries in *Hung Ch'i* and *Jen Min Jih Pao* assailing Khrushchev's revisionist variant of communism, portrayed at the twenty-first and twenty-second congresses of the CPSU in 1959 and 1961 and extolling the Maoist conception.[76] For Mao the foreign and domestic class enemies were portrayed as inextricably intermixed.

In dealing with domestic intellectuals, the committed Maoist Ch'en Po-ta was most active. The deepening of the Socialist Education Campaign can be discerned in the words of Ch'en Po-ta, as editor-in-chief of *Red Flag*. Ch'en's views on the Socialist Education Campaign reached millions of readers, including practically all of the nation's cadres through the issues of *Red Flag* between 1962 and 1966. His treatment of the campaign illustrates the radicalizing of tactics and upward shifting of targets that occurred with Mao's turn to the PLA at the end of 1963. In 1962 and 1963, the treatment of the campaign was relatively defensive in nature and generally portrayed an alliance of the party against the encroaching external forces of revisionism. In 1962, an article entitled "In the Field of Literature and Art, Modern Revisionists Follow in the Footsteps of the Declining Bourgeoisie," emphasized the necessity of taking a firm class stand in art and literature.[77] It asserted that modern revisionists tried to conceal the class nature of their ideology by pretending it was of "the whole people" and based on the principle of "honesty"; but they were really preparing the way "to discard Marxism and publicize revisionism." In mid-1963, an editorial entitled "Cadres' Participation in Collective Production Labor Is a Matter of Fundamental Importance to the Socialist System" emphasized the necessity of taking a firm class stand in leadership.[78] It asserted that only by actually participating in productive labor with the masses could the cadres demonstrate that they were also part of the working people; otherwise they were likely to be perceived as members of the exploiting classes, trying "to undermine the revolutionary proletarian dictatorship and revolutionary party of our country." But the proposed palliatives of adopting a class stand by having intellectuals write from a proletarian class viewpoint and having cadres participating in production paled before the revolutionary themes advanced in *Red Flag* in the period 1964-1966. A new offensive championing the achievements of the revolutionized PLA characterized this later period. For example, in the summer of 1964 an editorial entitled "A Great Revolution on the Cultural Front" referred to the reform of the Peking opera with PLA themes as "a major event. It is not only a cultural revolution but also a social revolution."[79] The new aggressive approach to reforming art and literature harkened back to the abortive "cultural revolution" announced by Lin Feng in 1960, and it pointed forward to "China's socialist revolution in the field of culture and ideology," which was to involve drama, story-telling, literature, music, dancing and other arts in "serving the workers, peasants, and soldiers." At this point, party organizations everywhere were urged to "wipe out bourgeois and feudal forces thoroughly in the ideological sphere in a planned way and step by step." The difference between this attempt at reform and the previous attempts was that the PLA placed muscle behind the would-be reformers. The new radical approach to reforming cadres was illustrated much later in 1966, but the continuity within the Socialist Education Campaign is clear. Looking ahead at an editorial entitled "Put Mao Tse-tung's Thought in the Forefront, Cadres Give the Lead at Every Level," it is apparent that cadre study of the works of Chairman Mao and party emulation of the achievements of Lin Piao in the study and application of Mao's works were the prime techniques advocated. The editorial stated that "Chairman Mao's works are the supreme guide for work in all fields. . . . When Mao Tse-tung's Thought is placed in the forefront our cause advances irresistibly and triumphantly. This was the case during the period of the new domestic revolution at Yenan; it is also the case during the period of the socialist revolution . . . on the fronts of economics, politics, ideology and culture."[80] At this point, it was clear to all that the party contained enemies within itself, "We must rely on Mao Tse-tung's Thought . . . to sweep away all monsters and thoroughly defeat those representatives of the bourgeoisie who have wormed their way into the Party." Thus, between 1962 and 1966, the Socialist Education Campaign was transformed on the pages of *Red Flag* from an attempt to raise class consciousness into an all-out revolution involving the overthrow of some high-placed party leaders.

The underlying continuity of the Cultural Revolution with the Socialist Education Campaign and the dramatic shift that occurred in the movement with Mao's turn to the PLA at the end of 1963 can also be discerned by examination of Vogel's account of the local political-ideological activities of the PLA in the civilian sphere during the Socialist Education Campaign. With the aid of the PLA, Maoist proselyting efforts had received new impetus at the provincial level.[81] Even before the promulgation of the "Later Ten Articles" of September, 1963, the PLA's presence was visible in the civilian sector in

Kwangtung. Traditionally, the army's political department extended contact to civilians on only two annual occasions, at the time of the recruiting campaign and at the New Year; but during the New Year's celebration of 1963, the army in Kwangtung exceeded its traditional greetings to "propagandize the spirit of the Tenth Plenum."[82] In so doing, the army called the attention of civilians to the great successes of their campaigns for the "four good" teams and "five good" soldiers based on the thought of Mao Tse-tung. Further, the soldiers emphasized the importance of relying on poor and lower-middle peasants and of strengthening the collective in their messages to local leaders.[83] Shortly thereafter, PLA propaganda materials replaced party materials as the leading documents in local campaigns. The first major batch of PLA materials stressed the emulation of serviceman Lei Feng, "one of Chairman Mao's good warriors."[84] The "most fundamental article" in all these materials was that of "raising high the three red banners of the General Line, the Great Leap Forward, and the People's Communes and of acting in accordance with the directives of Chairman Mao, and the directives of the Military Affairs Commission and Marshall Lin Piao."[85] In the conduct of this campaign, the people's militia was used as a direct channel from PLA through its military service bureaus in each country and city to the civilian populace. The members of the militia consisted of a "basic" corps of de-mobilized soldiers and virtually all able-bodied young adults. This is precisely the channel used by the PLA to circumvent the party apparatus in their conduct of the Lei Feng campaign.[86]

Shortly after the promulgation of the "Later Ten Articles" of September and Mao's turn to the PLA in December 1963, the role of the PLA in the conduct of the campaign visibly increased in Kwangtung. During the New Year's season of 1964, the "Learn from the PLA" campaign was launched in Kwangtung and civilian institutions were urged to admit how far they lagged behind in comparison to the PLA in such important matters as simplicity of working style, participation in physical labor, participation in mass activities, and thoroughness of studying Chairman Mao's works.[87] Shortly thereafter, the PLA entered the local arena of literature and arts with renewed vigor. In conjunction with the national campaign of May and June 1963 for drama reform, T'ao Chu had set about exhibiting the form of drama reform in the province. In the last half of the year, only 38 or 11 percent of the plays staged in Canton had been modern "proletarian" plays; and only 14 percent of the 1,790 performances given in the province had been modern plays.[88] T'ao's perfunctory show of modern shows was criticized as insufficient; by September 1964, 83 of the plays staged in Canton were modern plays as a result of the replacement of Kwangtung's civilian troups by military troops of the army political department in February, 1964.[89] Even the campaigns for the emulation of heroes were purified in

March with the first civilian announcement that these were not strictly pro-duction-oriented movements, but political and ideological movements.[90] The PLA civilian encroachment of 1964 that was most threatening to the foot-dragging local party bureaucrats was the transfer of demobilized PLA service-ment and militia personnel into the civilian institutions. Although special political study courses for militia members from civilian institutions had been going on since the close of the tenth plenum, the ideological indoctrination of these personnel and the practice of transferring demobilized servicemen to civilian institutions greatly increased in 1964. In April, the Kwangtung provincial military district offered a one-month course for county-level and rural cadres, to teach the experience of the PLA and impart the value of studying the works of Chairman Mao.[91] By late August, 300,000 militia were in training camps in Kwangtung.[92] In the autumn of 1964, the army political department, the militia, and the poor and lower-middle peasants' associations stepped up the pace of the campaign in Kwangtung. Each com-mune headquarters now had at least one cadre supervising militia activities and his primary responsibility was not to the local commune party committee but to the PLA, from whom he could recruit skilled speakers for his local militia recruits.[93]

The growing cadre of militant Maoist disciples cast an increasingly omi-nous shadow across the party structure in China during 1964. In January 1965, Mao was to replace the "Later Ten Points" on the conduct of the Socialist Education Campaign with the "Twenty-Three Articles." Mao's tenth plenum cry for "a struggle that calls for the reeducation of man . . . for reorganizing the revolutionary class armies for a confrontation with the forces of feudalism and capitalism" was finally taking shape under the leadership of the PLA. The campaign was radicalized in 1965. In Kwangtung, new meetings of poor and lower-middle peasants associations culminated in a provincial meeting in June 1965 with heavy participation of military leaders.[94] In August, the intimidated local party leaders finally launched another cam-paign to study the works of Chairman Mao.[95] This time it was in earnest.

NOTES

1. Certain portions of Mao's speech at the tenth plenum are available from later published documents. See "Resolutions adopted by the central committee of the Chi-nese Communist party on problems existing in current rural work" (Draft, May 1963), *IAS*, Vol. 2, No. 8, May 1966, pp. 58-59.

2. Ibid., p. 58.

3. Ibid., p. 59.

4. "Speech at the tenth plenary session of the eighth central committee" (Septem-ber 24, 1962, *CLG*, Vol. I, No. 4, winter 1968-1969, pp. 85-93.

5. Ibid., p. 86.

6. Ibid., p. 90.

7. Ibid., pp. 87, 90.

8. Ibid., p. 93.

9. Ibid., p. 87.

10. For a detailed description of this campaign, see "Learn from Lei Feng movement —A new campaign of class education among young people," *URS,* Vol. 31, No. 24, June 21, 1963.

11. For a comprehensive description of the use of mass media and propaganda in this campaign, see Vincent V.S. King, *Propaganda Campaigns in Communist China. CENIS Monograph,* No. C/66-1. Cambridge, Mass.: MIT Press, January 1966, pp. 16-41.

12. See *JMJP,* February 16, 1963.

13. *China Youth News,* March 5, 1963.

14. *JMJP,* March 8, 1968.

15. See Sung T'ing-chang, Secretary of the CYL Fushun minicipal committee, Liaoning province, "How we launch 'learn from Lei Feng' educational activities," *China Youth News,* Peking, February 28, 1963.

16. *NCNA,* May 16, 1963.

17. See *JMJP,* January 10, 1967, in *SCMP,* No. 3863, p. 1, as quoted in Charles Neuhauser, "The Chinese Communist party in the 1960's: Prelude to the Cultural Revolution," *CQ,* No. 32, October-December 1967, p. 21.

18. See Neuhauser, loc cit. Chou Yang was a leading intellectual, vice-chairman of the All-China Literary and Art Circles and deputy director of the propaganda department of the CCP central committee under Lu Ting-yi until July of 1966 when he was purged as a "counterrevolutionary revisionist, consistently waving a red flag to oppose the red flag." Chou was one of the leaders of the dissidents in the propaganda apparatus accused of obstructing the printing and dissemination of Mao's thought on a large scale. (See *PR,* No. 34, 1966.) In particular, during the Socialist Education Campaign, Chou was said to have resisted Mao Tse-tung's directives to literary and art circles in June of 1964 to reform the Peking opera by promulgating numerous rules and regulations to prevent effective implementation of this attempt at Maoist proselyting. Chou was accused of having maintained that the correctness of the general line had not yet been proved, and that the Great Leap Forward of 1958 had caused a disproportion in the economy.

19. See "Resolutions adopted by the central committee of the CCP on problems existing in current rural work" (Draft, May 20, 1963), *IAS,* Vol. 2, No. 8, May 1966, pp. 46-60.

20. *PR,* No. 39, 1962.

21. *IAS,* May 1966, op. cit., p. 58.

22. For a more comprehensive treatment of the Socialist Education Campaign, see Richard Baum and Frederick Tiewes, *Ssu Ch'ing: The Socialist Education Movement of 1962-1966.* China Research Monographs, Berkeley: University of California, Center of Chinese Studies, 1968.

23. *IAS,* op. cit., p. 46.

24. *IAS,* Vol. II, No. 8, op. cit., p. 47.

25. *MISC,* p. 314.

26. "Some concrete policy decisions on the rural Socialist Education movement" (Draft, September 1963), *IAS,* Vol. II, No. 9, June 1966, pp. 34-44, and No. 10, July 1966, pp. 36-48.

27. Ibid., p. 39.

28. "Some concrete policy decisions on the rural Socialist Education movement" (revised draft, September 1964), *IAS,* Vol. I, No. 10, July 1965, pp. 1-12; and No. 11, August 1965, pp. 27-43, esp. Article 9.

29. See "Liu Shao-ch'i's self-criticism made at the work conference of the CCP central committee," *IAS,* Vol. VI, No. 9, pp. 95-96.

30. For a comprehensive account of the implementation of the Socialist Education Campaign in Kwangtung province we have relied heavily upon Ezra F. Vogel, *Canton Under Communism.* Cambridge, Mass.: Harvard University Press, 1969, pp. 300-320.

31. Ibid., p. 301.

32. Ibid., p. 302.

33. Ibid., p. 306.

34. Ibid., p. 315.

35. Ibid.

36. Ibid.

37. Ibid., p. 307.

38. See "The confession of Liu Shao-ch'i," *Atlas,* April 1967, pp. 12-17, as translated from *Mainichi Shimbun,* Tokyo.

39. Ibid., p. 15.

40. Ibid.

41. Ibid.

42. See Liu Shao-ch'i, "Self-criticism," *Yomiuri,* December 37, 1966, as quoted in Charles Neuhauser, "Comment," *CQ,* No. 34, April-June 1968, p. 142. In this slightly different version of Liu's self-criticism of October 1966, the September 1963 resolution is attributed by Liu to P'eng Chen, and Liu himself assumes the responsibility for revising the resolution in the direction of increased mass mobilization over the summer of 1964 with final publication in September. See also the *Mainichi Shimbun* version.

43. See Ch'en Po-ta's address of October 25, 1966 to the central work conference in *Ko-ming Kung-jen Pao,* Peking, January 12, 1967, p. 3, as quoted in Gene T. Hsiao, "The background of the development of the Proletarian Cultural Revolution," *Asian Survey,* Vol. VII, June 1967, pp. 397-398.

44. See "The official communique of the eleventh plenary session of the CCCCP" (August 12, 1966), *CQ,* No. 28, October-December, 1966, pp. 168-170.

45. For an excellent analysis and chronology of the background of China's Cultural Revolution upon which we have relied heavily, see Philip Bridgham, "Mao's 'Cultural Revolution': Origin and Development," *CQ,* No. 29, January-March 1967, pp. 1-35.

46. *CB,* No. 891, p. 4.

47. *CB,* No. 892, pp. 15-19.

48. *MISC,* pp. 327, 329.

49. *MISC,* p. 333.

50. *MISC,* p. 351.

51. *MISC,* pp. 353-355.

52. *MISC,* p. 356.

53. *MISC,* p. 358.

54. *MISC,* pp. 384-396.

55. *MISC,* p. 386.

56. *MISC,* p. 396.

57. *MISC,* p. 405.

58. John Gittings, *The Role of the Chinese Army.* London: Oxford University Press, 1967, p. 254.

59. Ibid., p. 252.

60. Ibid., p. 255.
61. "The whole country must learn from the PLA," *JMJP,* February 1, 1964, *SCMP,* No. 3164, as cited in Gittings, op. cit., p. 255.
62. Bridgham, op. cit., p. 11.
63. Gittings, op. cit., p. 256.
64. Ibid., p. 253.
65. Ibid., p. 256.
66. Ibid.
67. Ibid., p. 257.
68. Bridgham, op. cit., p. 13.
69. *JMJP,* May 18, 1965, as cited in Bridgham, op. cit., p. 14.
70. Gittings, op. cit., p. 222.
71. *NCNA,* November 10, 1964, report on militia political work conference, as cited in Gittings, op. cit., p. 223.
72. Ibid., p. 224.
73. See *PR,* No. 28, 1964, pp. 6-22, as cited in Schram, op. cit.
74. Joint editorial of *People's Daily* and *Red Flag,* "On Khrushchev's phoney communism and its historical lessons" (July 14, 1964), translated in *CB* No. 737, July 17, 1964, as cited in Bridgham, op. cit., p. 13.
75. See *Chung Kuo Ch'ing Nien Pao* (Chinese Youth News) Peking, March 19, 1964.
76. See Chalmers Johnson, "The two Chinese revolutions," *CQ,* No. 39, July-September 1969, p. 24. See also Lowell Dittmer, *Liu Shao-ch'i and the Chinese Cultural Revolution: The politics of mass criticism.* Berkeley: University of California Press, 1974, pp. 45-46.
77. *HC,* No. 21, 1962.
78. *HC,* No. 13/14, 1963.
79. *HC,* No. 12, 1964.
80. *HC,* No. 8, 1966.
81. Again we have relied upon Vogel's excellent treatment of the conduct of the Socialist Education Campaign in Kwangtung to provide us with an assessment of the campaign's style and pace at the local levels. See Ezra F. Vogel, *Canton Under Communism.* Cambridge, Mass.: Harvard University Press, 1969, pp. 302-318.
82. Ibid., p. 303.
83. Ibid., p. 304.
84. Ibid., p. 305.
85. Ibid.
86. Ibid.
87. Ibid., p. 310.
88. Ibid.
89. Ibid., p. 311.
90. Ibid., p. 312.
91. Ibid., p. 313.
92. Ibid., p. 312.
93. Ibid., p. 316.
94. Ibid., p. 318.
95. Ibid.

Chapter 9

REVOLUTIONARY REFORMATION

OF BOURGEOIS BUREAUCRATS

> *The key point of this movement is to rectify those people in positions of authority within the Party who take the capitalist road, and to progressively consolidate and develop the socialist battle front in the urban and rural areas.*[1]

During the 1965 New Year season, Mao raised the targets of the Socialist Education Campaign; no longer were the military and middle-level cadres, the protean youth or the proletarian masses the main targets of proselyting; the target was now set upon the upper-level (county and above) cadres and eventually upon the "leading figures in authority taking the capitalist road," the most prominent of which were members of the politburo and high-level intellectuals. The aim of the campaign remained proselyting for the thought of Mao Tse-tung, but the proselyting was greatly radicalized. The aim was revolutionary reformation; revolution in the way Chinese conceived of economy, politics, and social organization; revolution in the way politics was actually carried out in China. The proletarian masses and protean youth with the organizational aid of the PLA, armed with the thought of Mao Tse-tung, would rise up and reform the thinking of the bourgeois bureaucrats. Capitalist thinking would fail; socialism would prevail; China would operate according to the thought of Mao Tse-tung.

The first official pronouncement of this raising of level of the targets of the campaign came at a national work conference called by the politburo in January 1965. The product of this conference on January 14 was a document of twenty-three articles entitled "Some Current Problems Raised in the Socialist Education Movement in the Rural Areas" which was drawn up under

Mao's personal guidance. It is significant of the shift in target and aim of the campaign that the document explicitly states that the twenty-three articles were to replace all previous resolutions on the Socialist Education movement.

The first article of this important document deals with the "situation" as follows:

> Since September 1962 when the Tenth Plenary Session of the Eighth Central Committee of the Chinese Communist Party was held, a socialist education movement has been unfolding in rural areas, and the whole Party has unanimously carried out a series of the concerned policies of the Party Central Committee. . . . In recent months over a million cadres have gone deep to the basic units.

The last statement provides further evidence that 1964 had been a year of deepening of the Socialist Education movement.

The current aim of the movement is stated in the following paragraph:

> Practice has proved that as long as the whole Party can more penetratingly and correctly further implement all decisions of the Party Central Committee on the socialist education movement, take firm hold of the keynote of class struggle, take firm hold of the keynote of struggle between the two roads of socialism and capitalism, rely on the poor and lower-middle peasants, revolutionary cadres, revolutionary intellectuals and other revolutionary elements, pay attention to over 95% of the masses, unite with over 95% of the cadres, there will be absolutely no difficulty and it will be entirely not difficult to solve the problems which may be found to exist in the cities and rural areas.

The second article deals with the nature of the movement. After rejecting the ideas that the movement has to do with "contradictions between the 'four clean-ups' and the 'four uncleans' or the difference between contradictions inside and outside the Party," this article states that the fundamental nature of the movement devolves from the basic contradiction between socialism and capitalism—which is clearly a more antagonistic contradiction than either of the former two when viewed from the perspective of a Marxist-Leninist. The article goes on to point out that this latter view

> is in complete conformity with the scientific conclusion which Comrade Mao Tse-tung has made since the Second Plenary Session of the Seventh CCP Central Committee in 1949, that class contradictions have always existed in the whole transitional period, so have existed class struggles between the proletariat and the bourgeoisie and the struggles between the two roads of socialism and capitalism.

This article then delineates the main target of the current movement: "The focus of this movement is to liquidate persons in the Party in authority taking the capitalist road, and to further consolidate the socialist position in the cities and rural areas." Thus the target is set higher and is more sharply delineated.

The third article deals with how "to unify ways of raising problems" as follows:

> From now on, the socialist education movement in the cities and rural areas should be simply called the "Four Cleanups." Cleaning up economy, organization, politics and ideology. In urban areas the socialist education movement has been called sometimes the "five-antis" movement. From now on, it should be called the "Four Cleanups" movement. The name of "five-antis" movement should be abolished.

Thus the scope of the four uncleans had broadened from the earlier particulars such as warehouses and work points to the broad general categories such as economy and ideology. The "uncleans" in socialist China at the mid-sixties were greater than anticipated earlier in the decade.

The fourth article deals with how "to fulfill the criterion of the movement" as follows:

> In June 1964 at the Standing Committee Conference of the Central Political Bureau, which the First Secretaries of all Central Committee's Bureaus attended, Comrade Mao Tse-tung said how to fulfill the criterion of socialist education:
>
> (1) Have the poor and lower-middle peasants stood up?
>
> (2) Has the problem of "four uncleans" concerning cadres been solved?
>
> (3) Have the cadres all taken part in labor?
>
> (4) Has a correct leading core been established?
>
> (5) Are the landlords, rich peasants, counter-revolutionaries, and other bad elements who have been unearthed in their sabotage activities still making use of contradictions to conduct further activities? Or, have we actually mobilized the masses to put them under our strict supervision and definitely transform them?
>
> (6) Has production increased or decreased?

Thus with each successive document on the Socialist Education Campaign since the September 1963 resolution, the importance of mobilizing the masses and the importance of the poor and lower-middle peasants associations has increased. There was increasing insistence that the Maoist message must be carried to the masses and met with the appropriate action.

The fifth article stresses "methods of work" and again reliance on the masses as follows: "(1) In the course of the movement, all Party committees and work teams of all levels in the provinces, districts, and counties must rely on the majority of the masses and the majority of the cadres (including cadres who have cast away their old ideology) to realize gradually a '3-in-1' combination of the masses, the cadres and the work team." Here we note an inchoate form of the "three-way alliance" among representatives of the revolutionary mass organizations, revolutionary cadres, and PLA soldiers that provided the emerging new form of government during the Great Proletarian Cultural Revolution. The shadow of a new government was taking shape.

The sixth section of this seven-section article again deals with mass mobilization and includes a slightly veiled attack on Liu Shao-ch'i:

> (6) In this movement, *it is necessary to boldly mobilize the masses and not allow to act timidly like a woman with bound feet.* At the same time, it is necessary to make careful consideration, act cautiously, pay attention to facts, lay stress on truth, but do not resort to arbitrary or rude methods. It is strictly prohibited to beat people and torture them. Intimidation and compulsion are not permitted.

It seems very likely that our italicized reference is to Liu Shao-ch'i in that the allegation is the same as Mao's 1955 allegation which was also apparently directed at Liu Shao-ch'i for harboring similar reservations against mobilization of the proletarians. However, in 1965 Liu had even less motivation than beforehand to desire such mass mobliization, where as Mao had more. The polarization of opinion between Mao and Liu had increased.

That failure of the party center to mobilize the masses in the Socialist Education movement was a major frustration to the proselyting Maoists leading to the eruption of the GPCR, (Great Proletarian Cultural Revolution) was further demonstrated by Mao's revealing speech in February 1967. Then, in the midst of the GPCR, Mao stated, "In the past we waged struggles in rural areas, in factories, in the cultural field, and we carried out the Socialist Education Movement. *But all this failed* to expose our dark aspect openly, in an all-around way and from below."[2]

That the nonrevolutionary implementation of the Socialist Education Campaign by the party bureaucracy under the leadership of Liu Shao-ch'i was a basic cause for Mao's increased ideological fervor and his consequent promulgation of the twenty-three articles in January 1965 is also supported by the following extract from the confessions of Liu Shao-ch'i:

> Being unable to realize my own mistakes, at the central conference in 1964 I said that contradictions between the "four cleanups" and the "four uncleans" and the contradictions within and outside the Party

were intermingled, while making no explanation about the substantial nature of the movement as was explained in the "twenty-three articles."

This is not Marxism-Leninism. At this point I had forgotten the logic of class struggle, maintained by our party for the past dozen years. That is why I committed the mistake of "actually leaning to the right, though seeming to lean to the left."

My mistake was corrected after Chairman Mao enancted the "twenty-three articles," under his personal chairmanship. The "twenty-three articles" placed the emphasis of this movement on cleaning up the power faction following the path of the bourgeoisie within the Party, and stipulated that the movement be directly strictly and limitedly to a very small number of bad people. I made mistakes in the past. Especially in 1962 and 1964, I made right-inclined mistakes. This time too, I made a grave mistake of right opportunism. However, these mistakes were personally rectified by the great Chairman Mao of our Party and the people, after he returned to Peking.[3]

Due to foot-dragging in the implementation of Mao's proselyting drive in the Socialist Education Campaign by the party bureaucrats under Liu Shao-ch'i's first line leadership, Mao shifted to the PLA for the campaign's leadership in December 1963 and in January 1965 shifted the targets of proselyting to reformation of the ideological heretics high in the party hierarchy. As Mao deepened his proselyting campaign, the tension due to increased polarization of the two camps into ideological fanatics and bureaucratic heretics, became more acute. As such tension increased, Mao and the Maoists had become more committed and hence all the more radical in the search for ideological confirmation. The range of ideological statements and associated speakers that were ideologically acceptable to the Maoists became more restrictive. Acceptable art and literature was now restricted to the purely proletarian. Simultaneously, the latitude of rejection of ideological statements and associated speakers grew. Good Marxist-Leninists of the past were now perceived by radicalized Maoists as representatives of the bourgeoisie who were "taking the capitalist road." Similarly, the set of actions and events that were adjudged relevant to the ideology increased in scope. Formerly trifling human events from the collection of "night soil" in sanitation campaigns to the style of play in ping-pong tournaments and formerly innocuous human activities from the application of cosmetics to the collection of classical art carvings took on new ideological significance.

The renewed search by the Maoists for ideological confirmation transformed the significance of all Chinese activity in 1965. In seeking empirical support for their doctrine, additional "scientific" Marxist experiments were called for, and an army general even publicly attributed the victorious championship play of ping-pong by Chinese to newly aroused "class feelings" and the "living" application of Maoist dialectics. In seeking social support for their doctrine, the Maoists deepened their efforts to promote the study of the thought of Mao Tse-tung by proletarians and political cadres eventuating in Mao's September call for a proletarian cultural revolution. Concomitantly, the Maoists more seriously sought to silence the reports of waxing capitalist practices in economy, bureaucratic practices in politics and elitist-style social organizations. As the Maoists ferreted out the facts of these ideological transgressions in the spirit of inquisition, they fought to dispel the disconcerting disparagement, present and past, forthcoming from the intellectuals and the bourgeoisie. The search for ideological confirmation was more radical than ever before.

In January 17, 1965, *People's Daily* carried an article by Hsu Yin-sheng, a member of the world championship ping-pong team. The article, introduced by the editor and General Ho Long, was entitled "How to Play Table Tennis" and attributed the team's victory to the employment of Maoist dialectics. Although some observers of the China scene have cited this event as an extreme instance of ridicule of Mao Tse-tung in the spirit of "waving red flags to oppose the red flag," Mao himself was delighted by the news report and immediately distributed copies to his comrades:

> Comrade Hsu Yin-sheng's speech and Comrade Ho Long's comment are printed for distribution to comrades of the Central Committee. It is hoped that after you are back at your posts, you will print additional copies of these documents for distribution so as to give them wider publicity. Comrades, this is a challenge to us—a large number of old fighters—from the young fighters. Can it be said that we should not learn anything from them? The whole speech is full of dialectical materialism and opposed to idealism and metaphysics in whatever form. I have not read so good an article for many years. He talks about playing table tennis, but what we must learn from him is theory, politics, economics, culture and military affairs. If we do not learn from the young fighters, then we are finished.[4]

Mao's elation was due to Hsu Yin-sheng's attribution of his victory at table tennis to the living application of the thought of Mao Tse-tung. Hsu's victory was therefore a victory of Maoist dialectics and served to confirm the validity of the ideology. In April, miraculous faith healings were attributed to Mao Tse-tung. In this nationally reported instance of confirmation of Maoist dialectics it was claimed that all the patients in a municipal hospital had recovered due to the hospital staff's utilization of the thought of Mao Tse-tung.[5]

In the radicalized search for social support the fall of 1965 witnessed the unveiling of a new and even more virtuous military emulation model for youth. The new revolutionary hero to supersede Lei Feng was Wang Chieh, whose diary was published and widely publicized in November 1965.[6] Not only was Wang Chieh a young revolutionary fighter of the PLA who loved the people, remembered class struggle, and *read* Mao's works, he was also a dauntless youth who constantly *applied* the thought of Mao Tse-tung to the tasks of daily life. For example, one of Wang Chieh's diary entries describes how his reading of "The Foolish Old Man Who Removed Mountains" prevented him from succumbing to small difficulties and spurred him on to greater struggling strength in his daily activities. The continuity and heightened intensity of Maoist proselyting in the fall of 1965 is further demonstrated by a comparison of the entires in Lei Feng's diary of April 1963 with those of Wang Chieh's diary of November 1965. Twenty-four of the sixty-one entries in Lei Feng's diary mentioned Mao without simultaneous mention of the party; in contrast, fifty-nine of the one hundred and sixteen entrees in Wang Chieh's diary referred to Mao Tse-tung and twenty-five contained direct quotations from his works.[7]

Even the popular songs sung in China in 1965 reflected the great upsurge in Maoist proselyting that had occurred since the initiation of the drive. In this year, "The East is Red" *(Tung Fang Hung),* first introduced in October 1959 during the initial surge of Maoist proselyting, became one of the most widely sung songs in the mainland. Now, more than six years after the Great Leap failure, the words were more meaningful to more people:

> The east is red
> Rises the sun;
> China has brought forth
> A Mao Tse-tung!

The radicalism of the Maoists increased through 1965. In a late May fit of egalitarianism, all ranks and insignia were abolished in the People's Liberation Army by a decision of the state council. The army reverted even further toward the guerrilla paradise lost. As in the civil war period, officers were again known simply as "commanders" and the noncommissioned officers simply as "fighters," but now the contemporary enemy was of a different ilk and had to be fought by innovative methods.

In contrast to the increasingly radical proselyting of the commtited Maoists, the leaders of the party center acted to stifle any upsurge in Maoism. On March 3, 1965 Teng Hsiao-p'ing and Liu Shao-ch'i convened a meeting of the secretariat where they termed the populist criticism of literature inspired by Chiang Ch'ing the preceding year as "excessive" and "hampering" prosperity in creation; henceforth criticism of notables should be carried out according to Liu's "gentle breezes" style.[8]

The fall of 1965 was of great significance for the course of the Socialist Education Campaign and the style of Maoist proselyting. According to official Chinese sources, the Great Cultural Revolution originated at a working conference of the central committee in September 1965 when Mao Tse-tung issued the call "to criticize bourgeoisie reactionary thinking."[9] At this enlarged session of the standing committee of the politburo, which was also attended by "the leading comrades" of all the regional bureaus of the central committee during September and October, Mao issued specific instructions regarding the criticisms of the intellectual Wu Han, and a "group of five in charge of the Cultural Revolution" was formalized. The initial leader of this group was P'eng Chen.

A less publicized, but equally important issue before the central committee at this time, was the question of initiating China's long-delayed third five year plan. Here, too, there was considerable dissention between Mao and the party bureaucrats. Despite the championing of the Yenan "spirit of Nanniwan" in the nations press, one can surmise from the competing ideological positions at the time that the plan set forth by the party bureaucrats recommended centralized control above decentralization and local self-sufficiency, the use of material incentives over ideological exhortation, and reliance upon expertise rather than the "redness" displayed by political activists in mass campaigns. In any case, the result was Mao's "stern criticism and rejection" of the third five year plan drawn up under party auspices.[10] However, this eventuality was not surprising, for Mao still had another plan in mind.

Additional failures of the Maoist line were forthcoming in the fall of 1965. On September 2, 1965, *Red Flag* and *People's Daily* had jointly published Lin Piao's major address, "Long Live the Victory of People's Wars." In this address, Lin extended Mao's guerrilla strategy of employing rural base areas to surround and capture the cities to the international arena, likening the developing areas of Asia, Africa, and Latin America to rural areas surrounding the "cities" of Europe and North America. However, Lin Piao's general prediction of world wide revolutionary Maoist success received a single stunning disconfirmation with a failure of the Communist coup d'etat in Indonesia at the end of the month and the ensuing decimation of the Peking-oriented Indonesian Communist party. Also in October, Peking's proselyting in the developing areas received a setback with the breakdown of the Afro-Asian Conference following the failure of Chinese attempts to excommunicate the Soviet Union from the Communist movement in the developing areas. In the face of failure, Lin Piao increased in ideological fervor. His target audience, however, lay within China's own borders. There were corrupt bourgeois in Peking. In November, Mao dropped from public view for a period of seven months, and Lin Piao stepped forward on the domestic stage.[11]

Amidst all the radical Maoist proselyting of 1965, the strident notes stood out most distinctly. By the fall of 1965, Mao had failed to eliminate the intellectual barbs of bourgeois art and literary men. Even P'eng Teh-huai, the modern "Hai Jui" of Lushan, was appointed to a new party position. In late August, he became third deputy director of the control commission of the CCP southwest bureau in Chengtu.[12] During the September working conference, Mao had failed to secure support for his Great Leap-style program for China's third five year plan. Before the conference began, Lin Piao had predicted success for the "people's wars" in the developing nations; before it ended, the notable failures were reported. At the conference, Mao launched his Cultural Revolution, deepening his search for ideological confirmation.

The attack upon the recalcitrant intellectuals began shortly after the adjournment of the September meeting of the central committee. Yao Wen-yuan's article, "Comment on the Newly Composed Historical Play 'Hai Jui Dismissed from Office,' " did not come from Peking but made a more oblique appearance in the November 10, 1965 issue of the Shanghai *Wen Hui Pao* under Mao's personal direction through the Shanghai municipal party committee.[13] Mao was backed in his attack by Lin Piao and the People's Liberation Army. On November 15, 1965, Lin Piao issued a five-point directive on the work of the People's Liberation Army for 1966.[14] Bridgham's analysis of this directive in the light of later Chinese publications is that it was used to carry out a nationwide rectification-purge campaign of a new type, encompassing both the PLA and the CCP. He points out five unique features of this campaign.[15] First of all, it was directed at leading cadres beginning at the county level and extending up to the regional bureaus of the party. Second, the criterion for testing the loyalty and fitness of all party officials was their attitude toward "The Thought of Mao Tse-tung." Third, admissions were made that large numbers of party officials questioned the value of Mao's work for solving their problems. Complaints were made that some "leadership cadres have erroneous ideas of attaching much importance to professional matters and little to politics"; and complaints were made with reference to putting Mao's thought in command that leading cadres were "outwardly complaisant and inwardly disobedient." Fourth, rectification could be achieved by cadres if they "study Mao Tse-tung's Thought in the spirit of rectification and engage in 'criticism-self-criticism.' " Finally, the campaign was remarkable in that it was carried out under the auspices of Lin Piao's five-point directive with a prominent role for the PLA rather than by the party apparatus. The preparedness of the PLA for actively implementing this campaign is well illustrated by the following passage which appeared on the pages of the army newspaper just eight days after the issue of Lin Piao's directive. The allies were now superhuman heroes of Mao and the enemies were transfigured into supernatural demons:

Only by actually arming ourselves mentally with Mao's thoughts can we be good ceaselessly. The countless model heroes were able to perform heroic deeds of various kinds under dissimilar circumstances because they had attained a revolutionary world outlook devoted to a struggle to the finish for communism. . . . Come ghosts or ghouls, imperialism or revisionists, they have no fear for any enemy and they hold hardship and adversity in contempt. They can weather any kind of political storm and withstand the ravages of a force 12 typhoon.[16]

Another throwback to the Great Leap forward ominously reappeared in 1965. At the end of the year, in his deepened search for social support, Mao circulated the April 1956 text of his previously confidential dialectical plan for socialist construction during the Great Leap Forward, "On the Ten Great Relationships." Mao distributed the document to all party committees at and above the county or regimental level to provide a basis for study and "to solicit opinion" from the lower levels.[17] The move for reimplementation of Maoist practices in China's economy was again underway; this time, more people were privy to Mao's program.

At the end of March 1966, Mao vented his wrath upon the party propagandists who had subverted his proselyting drive. At a central committee work conference he warned: "If P'eng Chen, the Peking Municipal Committee, and the Central Propaganda Department continue to harbor bad people, then [they] . . . should be disbanded."[18] In a talk with K'ang Sheng and others, Mao went so far as to call the propaganda department "the headquarters of the Prince of Hell" which should be "overthrown" because it published satires critical of Mao but impeded publication of leftist critiques of the satirists; he called upon local provinces for a "rebellion and an attack on the Center."[19]

The spring of 1966 saw China's intellectuals inundated by the Maoist onslaught implemented largely by Lin Piao and the People's Liberation Army following their political work conference of January. The main targets in the attack upon the intellectuals were two intellectuals who had satirized Mao's Three Red Flags during the hard years of 1961-1962, Wu Han and Teng T'o.[20] The cultural revolution aimed at the intellectuals was further carried out through the press of Lin Piao's People's Liberation Army. The April 18 editorial of the *Liberation Army Daily* was entitled "Hold Aloft the Great Red Banner of Mao Tse-tung's Thinking and Take an Active Part in the Great Socialist Cultural Revolution"; the May 4 editorial was entitled "Never Forget Class Struggle." Further signs of reorganization of China's intellectuals and educational system came in a series of editorials in *People's Daily* during the ensuing month including the decree of a six-month vacation for all students and the specification of new criteria for selection of students based upon class background and political reliability.[21]

Eruption of the Great Proletarian Cultural Revolution

May 1966 was a pivotal month in the development of the Great Proletarian Cultural Revolution. During this month, Mao reacted to yet another instance of foot-dragging by high party officials in the conduct of his proselyting movement. This time he turned unequivocally to the PLA for the conduct of his radicalized campaign. On May 7, Mao sent a letter to Lin Piao directing him to convert the army into a great school. The curriculum of this school was to be Maoist ideology and Maoist practices. Reasserting the time-honored Maoist tenet of the omnicompetent worker, the following recommendations were made for soldiers, workers, peasants, students, and cadres:

> So long as there is no world war, the armed forces should be a great school. Even under the conditions of a third world war, it is also quite possible to form such a great school, and apart from fighting, the armed forces can also perform various kinds of work. Wasn't this what we did in the various anti-Japanese bases during the eight years of the Second World War?
>
> In this great school, our armymen should learn politics, military affairs and agriculture. They can also engage in agricultural production and side occupations, run some medium and small factories and manufacture a number of products to meet their own needs or exchange with the state at equal values. They can also do mass work and take part in the socialist education movement in the factories and villages. After the socialist education movement, they can always find mass work to do, in order to insure that the army is always as one with the masses. They should also participate in each struggle of the cultural revolution as it occurs to criticize the bourgeoisie. In this way, the army can concurrently study, engage in agriculture, run factories and do mass work. . . .
>
> While the main task of the workers is in industry, they should also study military affairs, politics, and culture. They, too, should take part in the socialist education movement and in the criticizing of the bourgeoisie. Where conditions permit, they should also engage in agricultural production and side occupations, as is done at the Taching oilfield.
>
> While the main task of the peasants in the communes is agriculture (including forestry, animal husbandry, side occupations and fishery), they should at the same time study military affairs, politics and culture. Where conditions permit, they should collectively run small plants. They should also criticize the bourgeoisie.
>
> This holds good for students too. While their main task is to study, they should in addition to their studies learn other things, that is, industrial work, farming and military affairs. They should also criticize the bour-

geoisie. The school term should be shortened, education should be revolutionized, and the domination of our schools by bourgeois intellectuals should not be allowed to continue.

Where conditions permit those working in commerce, in the service trades and Party and government organizations should do the same.

The above is no longer any new idea, creation or invention, since many people have acted in this way for many years, although this has not been popularized. As to the armed forces, they have acted in this way for several decades, but this has now been further developed.[22]

Having delegated a large part of the task of reorganization of the ranks of the proletariat to Lin Piao, Mao set about repudiating the languid party bureaucrats. On May 16, a ten point circular of the central committee was drawn up "under the personal guidance of Mao Tse-tung." As with the twenty-three articles before it, the May 16 circular began by revoking all previous documents on the conduct of this particular campaign because of "feigned compliance" and stubborn resistance on the part of the party leadership of the campaign:

The Central Committee has decided to revoke the "Outline Report on the Current Academic Discussion made by the Group of Five in Charge of the Cultural Revolution" which was approved for distribution on February 12, 1966, to dissolve the "Group of Five in Charge of the Cultural Revolution" and its offices, and to set up a new Cultural Revolution Group directly under the Standing Committee of the Political Bureau. The outline report by the so-called "Group of Five" is fundamentally wrong. It runs counter to the line of the socialist cultural revolution set forth by the Central Committee and Comrade Mao Tse-tung and to the guiding principles formulated at the Tenth Plenary Session of the Eighth Central Committee of the Party in 1962 on the question of classes and class struggle in socialist society. While feigning compliance, the outline actually opposes and stubbornly resists the great cultural revolution initiated and led personally by Comrade Mao Tse-tung, as well as the instructions, regarding the criticism of Wu Han, which he gave at the working conference of the Central Committee held in September and October 1965.[23]

The essence of the Maoist criticism of this report on the conduct of the Cultural Revolution was that instead of advocating deep mobilization of the proletarian masses and stringent enforcement of the dictatorship of the proletariat to quiet the criticism of the bourgeois intellectuals, P'eng had attempted to confuse the party rank and file by reversing Mao's intent by quoting from Mao to oppose Mao, and by diverting the political campaign into an academic debate. The circular proceeds to enumerate ten main errors in the previous outline report drawn up by P'eng Chen.

First of all, rather than boldly encouraging the party to "arouse the broad masses," P'eng used "muddled" language to obscure the class struggle. Rather than encouraging political struggle, P'eng attempted to divert the movement into an academic debate and ignored the "heart of the matter, namely, the dismissal of the Right opportunists at the Lushan Meeting in 1959 and the opposition of Wu Han and others to the Party and socialism." Rather than proposing to "open wide" to let all people express their opinions, P'eng proposed "bourgeois liberalization" only. P'eng denied the "class nature of truth." He proposed a substitution of "academic and professional standards" for class criteria. Whereas Mao says, "There is no construction without destruction," P'eng juggled Mao's words and explicitly asserted the reverse, thereby diminishing the possibility for criticism of "bourgeois ideology." P'eng insinuated that Maoits, rather than the bourgeois scholars, were "scholar tyrants." Whereas Mao called for a "rectification campaign" against the right, P'eng's was targeted upon the "staunch Left." Whereas Mao called for boldly arousing the masses, P'eng shackled the left by urging that the struggle be conducted "under direction," "with prudence," "with caution," and "with the approval of the leading bodies concerned." Finally, P'eng's report obscured Mao's intent by "using the banner of 'under the guidance of Mao Tse-tung's thought' as cover" while it "actually attempts to open up a way opposed to Mao Tse-tung's thought, that is the way of modern revisionism, the way for the restoration of capitalism." Obviously, the kind of cultural revolution Mao had in mind was not codified in P'eng Chen's report.[24]

P'eng's "February Outline," like the "Later Ten Articles" before it, was perceived by Mao as another instance of "waving red flags to oppose the red flag" by high party bureaucrats. Its contents served as a trigger for Mao to unleash a more radical cultural revolution under the direction of Lin Piao and the PLA. As P'eng's preparation of his report neared completion, Chiang Ch'ing, Mao's wife, had convened a forum on the work in literature and art in the armed forces from February 2 to 20 in Shanghai. She had been entrusted with this task by Lin Piao, who forwarded the summary report of the proceedings of the forum to the standing committee of the Military Affairs Commission on March 22 with the appended comment that "the Summary which has been repeatedly gone over by the comrades attending the forum and has been personally examined and revised by the Chairman [Mao], three times, is an excellent document.[25]

The content of Chiang Ch'ing's ten-point summary was diametrically opposed to P'eng's February outline and provided hints of the official codification of the new Cultural Revolution forthcoming in August. The summary stressed throughout the serious study and living application of the thought of Mao Tse-tung. The first two points of the summary on class struggle and proletarian mobilization highlighted the Maoist perspective on the Cultural Revolution:

1. The last 16 years have witnessed sharp class struggles on the cultural front. . . .

2. The last three years have seen a new situation in the great socialist cultural revolution. The most outstanding example is the rise of Peking operas on contemporary revolutionary themes. Led by the Central Committee of the Party, headed by Chairman Mao, and armed with Marxism-Leninism, Mao Tse-tung's thought, literary and art workers engaged in revolutionizing Peking opera have launched an heroic and tenacious offensive against the literature and art of the feudal class, the bourgeoisie and the modern revisionists. . . .

Another outstanding feature of the socialist cultural revolution in the last three years is the widespread mass activity of workers, peasants and soldiers on the fronts of ideology, literature and art. Workers, peasants and soldiers are now producing many fine philosophical articles which splendidly express Mao Tse-tung's thought in terms of their own practice. They are also producing many fine works of literature and art in praise of the triumph of our socialist revolution, the big leap forward on all the fronts of socialist construction, our new heroes, and the brilliant leadership of our great Party and our great leader.[26]

Explicit proselyting for the thought of Mao Tse-tung and the derivative Great Leap Forward through the instrumentality of the revolutionized PLA had now continued unabated for almost seven years since the failure. On May 16, action was taken to establish a new Cultural Revolution group directly under the standing committee of the politburo to replace the discredited "group of five." Significantly, the leadership of this new group was composed of members of Mao's old Yenan coterie. Ch'en Po-ta was appointed director, Chiang Ch'ing, his deputy, and K'ang Sheng, his chief advisor. In late May, the first Red Guard units were formed in a Peking middle school.

Lin Piao immediately assumed the leadership in proselyting before the party politburo. Just two days after the promulgation of the May 16 circular condemning the heretical group of five in charge of the Cultural Revolution, Lin delivered an impassioned speech before the politburo which revealed what Mao's Cultural Revolution was all about.[27] Citing examples from classical Chinese history as well as the contemporary world scene, Lin raised the spectre of a possible coup d'etat by counterrevolutionaries in Communist China. As domestic evidence for his frightening assertion, Lin cited the activities of the recently discredited party leaders: Lo Jui-ch'ing in the military,

P'eng Chen in the party secretariat, Lu Ting-yi in the propaganda department, and Yang Shang-kun in security. To their conspiracy he added the intellectuals, Teng T'o, Wu Han and Liao Mo-sha. What these conspirators had in common, Lin asserted, was that they were "anti-Chairman Mao and anti-Mao Tse-tung's thought." Under P'eng Chen the Peking municipal government had become "a place from which no water could leak and no needle could penetrate." Under Lu Ting-yi the department of propaganda "opposed the study of the Chairman's Work . . . propagated no Mao Tse-tung's Thought but capitalist ideology. . . . When others propagated Mao Tse-tung's Thought, they laughed and sneered, suppressed, attacked and opposed them by all means." The Cultural Revolution was to remove these exponents of capitalist ideology before it was too late, purge the superstructure of opponents of Chairman Mao's thought, and propagate Mao Tse-tung's thought.

Lin Piao asserted that cadres and masses alike must be proselyted with Mao Tse-tung's thought:

> Mao Tse-tung's Thought should be laid before the broad masses; otherwise the appearance of our country could not be changed. We should make Mao Tse-tung's Thought penetrate deeply into the masses. Changes in every respect will occur when Mao Tse-tung's Thought is connected with the masses.

> Mao Tse-tung's Thought is the concentrated expression of the proletarian ideology, fundamentally contrasted with the private ownership system of the exploiting class. We oppose the private ownership system and the idea of self, which are the essential factors in the emergence of revisionism. These factors are quite widespread. In a village there are private plots and collective plots. There is struggle over whether a basket of dung should be sent to a private plot first or to a collective plot first. This is the psychology and ideology of the two roads and the expression of class struggle.[28]

The old cadres must experience a revival in revolutionary ideology: "The old comrades should strictly train and sincerely reform themselves in accordance with the five conditions for the revolutionary successors given by Chairman Mao.[29] Finally, Lin asserted in superlatives that the party leadership must itself strictly adhere to the thought of Mao Tse-tung:

> Whoever is against him [Chairman Mao] shall be punished by the entire Party and the whole country. . . . Every sentence of Chairman Mao's works is truth, one single sentence of his surpasses ten thousand of ours. I have not read Chairman Mao enough and would study harder from now on.

> We should grasp politics and the creative application and study of Mao's works.[30]

To secure such social support for the thought of Mao Tse-tung from the masses, cadres, and party leaders alike was the intention of Mao's Cultural Revolution—an intention that had waxed stronger over almost seven years of dissonant occurrences and frustrated attempts at dissonance reduction through the unresponsive party apparatus.

From June 1 until Mao's return to Peking on July 18, Liu Shao-ch'i presided over the party center. During these "fifty days," Liu was active in the dispatching of work groups from the party center to various universities and middle schools in Peking.[31] Although allegedly complying with Mao's Cultural Revolution directive, Liu admitted in his forced confession of October 23 to the "crime" that he and certain of his colleagues in the party center, government ministries, the new Peking municipal party committee, and local-level organs "took a *de facto* reactionary bourgeois stand, practiced bourgeois dictatorship, suppressed the vigorous cultural revolutionary dictatorship of the proletariat, stood facts on their head, juggled black and white, puffed up the arrogance of the bourgeoisie, and deflated the morale of the proletariat."[32] In particular, many work groups had suppressed the masses from above by usurping the political leadership of the schools. Some even forbade parades, demonstrations, and the posting of *ta-tze-pao*. While the Maoists, through the PLA, were attempting to mobilize the ranks of teachers and students from below, Liu and the party bureaucrats were attempting to stifle the movement and sow confusion. Even the youth league leadership was implicated and disbanded in June. Between Mao and Liu, the polarization grew.

The official codification of Mao's Cultural Revolution came in the form of a sixteen-point document issued by the eleventh plenary session of the eighth central committee on August 8, 1966. It was entitled "Decision of the Central Committee of the Chinese Communist Party Concerning the Great Proletarian Cultural Revolution (adopted on August 8, 1966)."[33] The document is a master plan for proselyting for the basic principles of the thought of Mao Tse-tung and for the implementation thereof—proselyting in radicalized form for the same principles that underlay the Great Leap Forward that failed. Significantly, one hundred members of the central committee were absent from the session which propounded the radical sixteen-point program, and Mao admitted that he received only bare majority support from those present.[34]

The form of proselyting fostered in the Cultural Revolution represented a radicalization of each of the four basic tenets of Maoist ideology that underlay the Great Leap Forward. First of all, the method of dialectical analysis for achieving historical progress was not only employed by Mao to plan the new movement, it was now applied by workers, peasants, and soldiers in their daily life. Even the intellectuals were exhorted to apply the dialectical principle of "one divides into two" and were severely castigated for not doing so.

Second, the mass line principle of political leadership was employed as never before. Now there was not simply the advocation of party leadership over government administration, but new exhortations to the masses to speak their minds, to pen political posters, to engage in nominations of new political leaders, to trample bureaucracy, and to "bombard the headquarters." The radicalized mass line principle was finally formalized in the formation of a new style of government for China based upon "revolutionary three-in-one committees" containing new representatives of the masses. Third, the tenet of continued class struggle was followed not only in the rectification of rightists through political study, but also more fanatically through the unleashing of millions of young Red Guards and Red Rebels to forcefully criticize those displaying the least bit of bourgeois impurity in thought or action. Fourth, the tenet of mass mobilization to heterogeneous production tasks was not yet pushed to the extreme, but the future radicalized forms were being built. Not only were people's communes beginning to be resurrected but Paris communes were explicitly called for and some appeared on the scene. The sixteen-point document, itself, reveals the renewed Maoist radicalism.[35]

The first article deals with "A New Stage in the Socialist Revolution" as follows:

> The great proletarian cultural revolution now unfolding is a great revolution that touches people to their very souls and constitutes a new stage in the development of the socialist revolution in our country, a deeper and more extensive stage. . . . Although the bourgeoisie has been overthrown, it is still trying to use old ideas, culture, customs and habits of the exploiting classes to corrupt the masses, capture their minds and endeavor to stage a comeback. The proletariat must do just the opposite; it must meet head on every challenge of the bourgeoisie in the ideological field and use the new ideas, culture, customs and habits of the proletariat to change the mental outlook of the whole society.

Clearly, the current stage of the movement is designed generally as a proselyting movement for the triumph of proletarian thought and values over those of the bourgeoisie. The particular aim of this stage of the campaign is described in the following paragraph:

> At present, our objective is to struggle against and crush those persons in authority who are taking the capitalist road, to crush and repudiate the reactionary bourgeois academic "authorities" and the ideology of the bourgeoisie and all other exploiting classes and to transform education, literature and art and all other parts of the superstructure that

do not correspond to the socialist economic base, so as to facilitate the consolidation and development of the socialist system.

The main target of the movement is described in article five to "Firmly Apply the Class Line of the Party"as follows: "The main target of the present movement is those within the Party who are in authority and are taking the capitalist road."

The main method of carrying out the current movement among the masses is described in article four to "Let the Masses Educate Themselves in the Movement":

Make the fullest use of big-character posters and great debates to argue matters out, so that the masses can clarify the correct views, criticize the wrong views and expose all the ghosts and monsters. In this way the masses will be able to raise their political consciousness in the course of the struggle, enhance their abilities and talents, distinguish right from wrong and draw a clear line between the enemy and ourselves.

A major difference between the Great Leap Forward movement and the Great Proletarian Cultural Revolution is that the former was aimed primarily at changing the economic base of society whereas the latter was aimed primarily at changing the political, social, and ideological superstructure.

Just how these four Maoist tenets are employed in the design for the Cultural Revolution document may be discerned by an examination of the specific articles. The principle of dialectical historical progress is elaborated in the second artic.e dealing with "The Main Current and the Zigzags":

Since the cultural revolution is a revolution, it inevitably meets with resistance. This resistance comes chiefly from those in authority who have wormed their way into the Party and are taking the capitalist road. It also comes from the force of habit in society. At present this resistance is still fairly strong and stubborn. However, the great proletarian cultural revolution is, after all, an irresistible trend. There is abundant evidence that resistance will crumble fast once the masses become fully aroused. . . . It [the resistance] tempers the proletariat and other working people, and especially the younger generation, teaches them lessons, and gives them experience, and helps them to understand that the revolutionary road is a zigzag one, and not plain sailing.

Just who constitutes the force of the proletariat in this particular historical revolutionary movement is described in the beginning of this article:

The masses of the workers, peasants, soldiers, revolutionary intellectuals and revolutionary cadres form the main force in this great cultural revolution. Large numbers of revolutionary young people, previously unknown, have become courageous and daring pathbreakers. They are vigorous in action and intelligent. Through the media of big character posters and great debates, they argue things out, expose and criticize thoroughly, and launch resolute attacks on the open and hidden representatives of the bourgeoisie.

The principle of correct political leadership emphasizing the mass line is stressed in articles three and nine. The third article, to "Put Daring above Everything Else and Boldly Arouse the Masses," is summarized as follows:

What the Central Committee of the Party demands of the Party committees at all levels is that they persevere in giving correct leadership, put daring above everything else, boldly arouse the masses, change the state of weakness and incompetence where it exists, encourage those comrades who have made mistakes but are willing to correct them to cast off their mental burdens and join in the struggle, and dismiss from their leading posts all those in authority who are taking the capitalist road and so make it possible to recapture the leadership for the proletarian revolutionaries.

The ninth article, on "Cultural Revolutionary Groups, Committees and Congresses," deals with a number of innovations to maintain proper contact between the leadership and masses:

Many new things have begun to emerge in the great proletarian cultural revolution. The cultural revolution groups, committees and other organizational forms created by the masses in many schools and units are something new and of great historic importance. . . . They are an excellent bridge to keep our Party in close contact with the masses. They are organs of power of the proletarian cultural revolution.

Next the article goes on to state that it is necessary to extend committees from colleges, schools, and government to factories, mines, other enterprises, urban districts, and villages and to make them permanent in these organizational locations since the struggle of the proletariat against old ideas, culture, customs, and habits left over from the exploiting classes will be a long one. Finally, the article sets forth a high point of left leaning in the mass line principle with the idea of extended democracy:

In the great proletarian cultural revolution, it is imperative to hold aloft the great red banner of Mao Tse-tung's Thought and put proletarian politics in command. The movement for the creative study and application of Chairman Mao Tse-tung's works should be carried forward among the masses of workers, peasants, and soldiers, the cadres and intellectuals, and Mao Tse-tung's Thought should be taken as the guide for action in the cultural revolution.

In the complex great cultural revolution, party committees at all levels must study and apply Chairman Mao's works all the more conscientiously and in a creative way. In particular, they must study over and over again Chairman Mao's writing on the cultural revolution and on the Party's methods of leadership such, as *On New Democracy, Talks at the Yenan Forum on Literature and Arts, On the Correct Handling of Contradictions among the People, Speech at the Chinese Communist Party's National Conference on Propaganda Work, Some Questions Concerning Methods of Leadership and Methods of Work of Party Committees.*

Just eight days after the promulgation of the sixteen-point central committee decision on the Great Proletarian Cultural Revolution, Mao succinctly summed up his satisfaction with the new movement and revealed his inner drive for mass proselyting, stating that "this is indeed a movement of large scale which has really mobilized the masses." Widespread social support for the thought of Mao Tse-tung sabotaged in the past was materializing at last. Two months of Cultural Revolution later, Mao expressed similar sentiments with regard to Ch'en Po-ta's summary of the achievements of the GPCR:

I have read your revised draft. It is quite good. Please consider where these two phrases—grasp revolution, promote production—should be added. It is necessary to bring a large number of pamphlets and send at least one copy to each Party branch and Red Guard detachment.[36]

Indeed there was much to relieve Mao's long-standing dissonance in Ch'en's "Summing Up the Movement of the Past Two Months." First among these was Ch'en's assessment of the GPCR's achievements:

The Great Cultural Revolution has further pushed the movement of learning Chairman Mao's works to an even greater climax; the Red Guard movement has developed in the country and abroad with glorious results. We can say proudly: The Great Cultural Revolution is even more vigorous and inspiring than the Paris Commune and the October Revolution. It is an even greater and deeper proletarian revolutionary movement which has frightened the imperialists and revisionists; the fools are all dumbfounded.[37]

Second, Ch'en's assessment of the role of the Red Guards carried a ring of nostalgia for the recrudescence of Mao's guerrilla paradise lost:

The exchange of experience can best be conducted in big schools, where marches can be promoted. Let them practice a "Long March," for the

Long March is a declaration, a propaganda team, a sowing machine. These students who walk a lot probably will become useful men.[38]

On October 25 at the same central committee work conference, Marshall Lin Piao left no doubts as to the fact that he conceived of the Cultural Revolution as a radicalized movement to proselyte for the thought of Mao Tse-tung. His opening words were as follows:

I wish mainly to discuss two issues: The necessity of a cultural revolution, and the means of handling it. In other words, do we want a cultural revolution? . . .

The issue is this: What should be the position of the great proletarian cultural revolution? Is it necessary? Is it an extra burden, or is it our obligation? If it is our obligation and we fail to perform it, we are remiss in our duties. A nation under a proletarian dictatorship has three great tasks: political, economic, and ideological construction. In the past, we stressed the former two, but did not fully deploy the third, which is ideological construction, that is, cultural revolution. We must know that if the cultural revolution, revolutionary construction, is not successfully deployed, the results of the other two constructions will be upset. Hence, we must promote the cultural revolution as vigorously as Chairman Mao. The theories of Chairman Mao contained in his written works provide us with the required base for our study. Similarly, we must study the vast amount of his works which are not in written form. Whatever he does, we must do likewise. Whether in practical experience, or in the Marxist-Leninist theory, or in individual talent, Chairman Mao is not only our superior, but also the greatest Marxist-Leninist in the world today. We must closely follow him, imitate him, and emulate him. We must place the great cultural revolution proposed by him in the foremost position and consider it an affair of the state and a political issue. We must treat it as an important part of the class struggle and an important front. This is the only proper thing to do.[39]

Not only was the Great Proletarian Cultural Revolution designed to spread Mao's work to man, but if necessary it would remold the nature of man to make Mao's works work; the new society would not only contain believers in but incarnations of TMTT (the Thought of Mao Tse-tung):

We must create modern men to construct a new society and must also create men with a Communist spirit. What kind of men are communist spirited? According to Chairman Mao, Chang Szute, Pai Chiu-en, Liu Hu-lan, Lei Feng, Ouyang Hai, Chiao Yu-lo, Wang Chieh and Liu Ying-chun are Communist spirited. Our new society needs these people and we have to gradually reform the masses to conform to this new image.

The new society would emphasize a unique form of construction, only glimpses of which were seen in the Yenan and Great Leap eras:

> There are two ways to construct our country. One is the Russian way, giving emphasis to materials, machines, mechanization, and so-called material incentives. The other is our way led by Chairman Mao.
>
> Chairman Mao has led us to create a new type of country. This country . . . puts most emphasis on mechanization. Revolution leads mechanization. In comparison man is more important than machines. Chairman Mao has said that man is the most precious thing in the world.

To reach the new society, the seeds of capitalism must be smashed and the mass line must be implemented:

> During the last two days, everyone has clearly perceived the struggle between the two lines. One is represented by Liu and Teng, which suppresses the masses and is anti-revolutionary. The other is Chairman Mao's path of boldness which has faith in the masses and believes in them. It is also the Party's mass line and the proletarian revolutionary line.

At the working conference on October 26, the day after Lin's speech, Mao openly revealed to the committee the manner in which he had been treated by Liu and Teng during the sixties, stating that "Liu Shao-ch'i and Teng Hsiao-p'ing treated me as if I were their dead parent at a funeral." Indeed they now stood poles apart ideologically. The politburo was irreparably rent, and the Maoists were in the ascendance.

Return of the Red Guards

Having moved aside the personal and organizational barriers to proselyting, the convinced and committed Maoists of Great Leap days, Chairman Mao, Ch'en Po-ta and Lin Piao, were approaching the crest in the waves of radical proselyting for the thought of Mao Tse-tung that they had helped set in motion at Lushan. Close behind them was a disciplined phalanx of revolutionized PLA warriors. Over the country, fanatical youth spread the word:

> Do not say that the strong pass is guarded with iron. This very day in one step we shall pass its summit.
>
> We shall pass its summit! We revolutionary rebels shall pass its summit! We must remold the being of the people. We must defeat the handful of power-holders in the Party organ of the Peking Administrative Bureau who take the capitalist road and the diehards who cling to the

bourgeois reactionary line. We must also criticize and discredit their reactionary line. . . . Our supreme commander is Chairman Mao. Our deputy supreme commander Vice-Chairman Lin Piao.

Our Aim:

1. We vow to defend the Party Central Committee and Chairman Mao, defend the thought of Mao Tse-tung, and propagate the thought of Mao Tse-tung.

2. We smash all set rules and rebel against everything of the old world.[40]

The vanguard in the battle of the cultural revolution unleashed in August of 1966 had been China's youth. The Red Guards were the offspring of one of the five red classes of workers, poor and lower-middle peasants, revolutionary cadres and revolutionary martyrs referred to in the second article of the August 1966 resolution. The first rally of Red Guards in Peking was held on August 18. During the following two months, Mao and the leadership of the Cultural Revolution staged bi-weekly rallies in Peking until a total of eleven million youthful disciples had passed before the reviewing stand waving little red books of quotations from Chairman Mao Tse-tung and shouting slogans in unison.[41] These few months and the series of succeeding months were crammed with disruptive revolutionary antics of the Red Guards, spreading over the Chinese countryside and proselyting for the thought of Mao Tse-tung. Contingents were sent to all provinces, to "exchange revolutionary experiences," and to "link up with other units." Bloody clashes between competing units took place in the streets of China's major cities; criticism sessions were held in which Red Guards attacked both local and central-level officials with shouts of slogans and large-character posters. Turmoil engulfed China during this phase of Mao's Cultural Revolution.

The great upsurge in activity of the Red Guards began immediately after Mao penned and posted his big-character poster on August 5 criticizing "some leading comrades who enforced the bourgeois dictatorship and struck down the surging movement of the cultural revolution of the proletariat." The youth then emulated Mao's example by writing millions of large-character posters and vigorously adopted Ch'en Po-ta's injunction to "destroy the four olds [old customs, old habits, old ideas, and old culture] of all the exploiting classes." However, the Red Guards did not spring from the brow of Mao in the fall of 1966. As we have seen, after an abortive attempt in 1960 to teach youth the ascetic ways of Yenan, activist youth had been successfully cultivated by the Maoists through Lin Piao's PLA in the emulate Lei Feng campaign of 1963, during the cultivate revolutionary successors campaign in 1964, in the emulate Wang Chieh campaign in 1965, and in other minor emulation campaigns. Since the publication on November 10, 1965 of Yao Wen-yuan's article in Shanghai's *Wen Hui Pao* criticizing Wu

Han's play, "Hai Jui Dismissed from Office," youth, particularly students and young teachers, were more actively mobilized by the Maoists in the middle schools and universities. These youths joined in critical choruses of social struggle as the Maoist influenced media criticized their former mentors during the initial Cultural Revolution volley targeted upon the intellectuals. In the year following the publication in Shanghai of the critical article that Chiang Ch'ing had inspired in Yao Wen-yuan, these youths witnessed the Maoist media struggle with more than one hundred of the nation's former intellectual and political leaders.[42] The vigorous Maoist criticism of Wu Han, Teng T'o and Liao Mo-sha was but the forerunner of vituperations levied in newspapers, periodicals, radio, and group struggle at many of the leading members of China's intelligentsia, writers, historians, party secretaries, university professors, film producers, playwrights, musicians, painters, and propagandists alike fell victim to Mao's long-suppressed wrath. Their "crimes" were culled from the seven-year history of criticism of or passive resistance to Maoist proselyting. Individually and in conspiratorial groups they were variously accused of having attacked Mao's Three Red Banners of the Great Leap Forward, the general line, and the people's communes. They had shot "poisoned arrows" at Mao's policies and "used ancient things to satirize the present"; they had sown "poisonous weeds" of ancient heroes and bourgeois values. During the Socialist Education Campaign, they had denied the existence of class struggle and advocated the primacy of production over politics. They had defied Mao's line on art and literature, failing to serve the workers, peasants, and soldiers and maintaining the conciliatory heresy of "two combine into one." They had opposed the propagation of Mao's works and their dissemination to the masses. Instead, they had "waved the red flag to oppose the red flag." In sum, throughout the sixties, many prominent intellectuals and party leaders were perceived by the Maoists of having failed to carry forward proselyting for the thought of Mao Tse-tung and, indeed, of having actively propagated the counterideology. Chinese youths were both the observers and the agents of their ignominious demise.

In the fall of 1966, Mao and the Maoists gave vent to the venom stored and festered by bourgeois barbs and criticism of the thought of Mao Tse-tung since the Great Leap debacles reported at Lushan. After seven years of frustrated attempts at dissonance reduction through the concerted search for unanimous social support for the thought of Mao Tse-tung, the Maoists stormed against the perceived personal sources of their persisting dissonance. At last, the convinced and committed Maoists, Mao, Lin, and Ch'en, abetted by the revolutionized PLA, now a great school of Mao thought for all Chinese society, and revolutionary youth, now a children's crusade of Red Guard contingents, summoned their swollen ranks for one great shuddering cudgeling of the "bourgeois" superstructure. As they smashed the superstructure, they at last grasped monopolistic control of the critical levers of the modern media of mass communication and proceeded unimpeded to spread their radicalized gospel far and wide through print and airwaves. As they leaped into the new era, their media messages galvanized Chinese sociaty and polarized it further into two great camps. At one terminal swirled the forces of Maoism; at the other, diminishing opponents of the study and application of the thought of Mao Tse-tung.

During the next year great waves of Maoist proselyting shook the Chinese scene as Mao's works were diffused far and wide. As the year opened, great hopes were expressed for the application of Mao's ideas to the economy. On New Year's Day 1967, *NCNA* released the following statement referring to 1966, the year of initiation of China's belated third five year plan:

> This year's all-round leap forward on the material front was stimulated by the great leap forward on the ideological front. This great spiritual force that produced the material force is precisely the invincible thought of Mao Tse-tung.

Great hopes were expressed for the spreading of Mao's ideology to the workers and peasants of China in the joint New Year's 1967 editorials of *People's Daily* and *Red Flag*. Speaking to the Albanian military delegation on May 1, 1967, Mao himself stated that ideological change was the goal of his Cultural Revolution:

> What would you say is the goal of the Cultural Revolution? . . . To struggle against powerholders who take the capitalist road is the main task, but it is by no means the goal. The goal is to solve the problem of world outlook; it is a question of eradicating the roots of revisionism.[43]

The incredible vigor of actual Maoist proselyting during 1967 is revealed by Chinese statistics on the publication of Mao's works during that year.[44] Printing presses in China turned out 76,400,000 copies of Mao Tse-tung's *Selected Works,* 350,000,000 copies of the little red book of Mao's quotations, 47,500,000 copies of *Selected Readings from Mao Tse-tung,* and 57,000,000 copies of his poems. The total of all his books and booklets was put at 540,000,000—a figure far in excess of the number of literate Chinese. Millions of these books, translated into twenty-three languages, have been distributed abroad along with hundreds of millions of Mao badges. At long last, the committed Maoists of Lushan days had captured control of a main instrumentality of proselyting, the official mass media of communication.

NOTES

1. For the text of these twenty-three articles see the Japanese journal, *Sekai,* Tokyo, February 1967, pp. 123-129. The author is indebted to Geoffrey Chiang, Editor, Union Research Service, Hong Kong, for assistance with the English translation of these articles. The twenty-three articles, "Some current problems raised in the Socialist Education movement in the rural areas," were sent as a secret document down through the party committees to the level of the hsien (county) and PLA regiments. A published translation of this document is now available in Baum and Tiewes, *Ssu Ch'ing: The Socialist Education Movement of 1962-1966.* China Research Monographs, Berkeley: University of California, Center for Chinese Studies, 1968, pp. 118-126.

2. See *JPRS,* No. 49826, as cited in Lowell Dittmer, *Liu Shao-ch'i and the Chinese Cultural Revolution: The Politics of Mass Criticism.* Berkeley: University of California Press, 1974, p. 63.

3. "The confession of Liu Shao-ch'i," *Atlas,* April 1967, pp. 12-17.

4. See "Comment on Comrade Hsu Yin-sheng's speech 'How to play table tennis' " (January 1965), *CB,* No. 891, p. 49.

5. *Kuang-Ming Jih Pao,* Peking, April 4, 1966; and *China News Analysis,* Hong Kong, No. 610, May 6, 1966, as cited in Richard Baum, "The new revolution: Ideology redivivus," *Problems of Communism,* Vol. XVI, No. 3, May-June 1967, p. 5.

6. Mary Sheridan, "The emulation of heroes," *CQ,* No. 33, January-March 1968, pp. 47-742.

7. Ibid.

8. Lowell Dittmer, *Liu Shao-ch'i and the Chinese Cultural Revolution: The Politics of Mass Criticism.* Berkeley: University of California Press, 1974, p. 61.

9. See *NCNA,* June 6, 1966, as quoted in Bridgham, *CQ,* No. 29, January-March 1967, p. 16. On the basis of his interview with Mao in December 1970, Edgar Snow asserts that a Cultural Revolution group under P'eng Chen had been formed by the politburo in 1964. He also quotes Mao as stating that he had decided to get rid of Liu Shao-ch'i at the politburo meeting of January 1965 at which Mao's twenty-three articles were proposed. See Edgar Snow, "The essence of the Cultural Revolution," in *The Long Revolution.* New York: Vintage, 1972, p. 17.

10. Philip Bridgham, "The Cultural Revolution and the new political system in China," paper delivered at the sixty-sixth annual meeting of the APSA, September 1970, pp. 7-8.

11. For a more contextualized description of the reactions of Lin Piao and Chairman Mao to the series of international failures that occurred in the fall of 1965, see *CS,* Vol. VI, No. 10, pp. 10-11, and Vol. VII, No. 5, p. 5.

12. Chengtu Radio, August 31, 1967, as cited in "Quarterly chronicle and documentation," *CQ,* No. 32, October-December 1967, p. 209.

13. See editorial in *HC,* No. 9, 1966, pp. 31-34, as quoted in Hsiao, op. cit., p. 309.

14. See *NCNA,* November 26, 1965, as quoted in Bridgham, op. cit., p. 18.

15. Bridgham, *CQ,* No. 29, p. 19.

16. *Chieh-fang Chun Pao* (Liberation Army Daily), November 23, 1965, as quoted in Gittings, op. cit., p. 242. (Hereafter *CFCP.*)

17. See "On ten major relationships" (December 27, 1965), *CB,* No. 892, p. 21.

18. Dittmer, op. cit., p. 75.

19. *MISC,* p. 382.

20. See "Teng T'o's 'evening chats at Yenshan' is anti-party and anti-socialist doubletalk," *Kuang Ming Jih Pao,* May 8, 1966.

21. Bridgham, *CQ*, No. 29, pp. 22-23.

22. See "Long live Mao Tse-tung's thought" (A collection of statements by Mao Tse-tung) as translated in *CB*, No. 891, October 8, 1969, pp. 56-57.

23. "Circular of the central committee of the Communist party of China" (May 16, 1966), as translated in *The Great Power Struggle in China, ARC,* Hong Kong: Yee Tong Press, 1969, pp. 429-436.

24. "Outline report concerning the current academic discussion of the group-of-five in charge of the Cultural Revolution," (February 7, 1966), Hsin kang yuan, Peking, No. 18, May 20, 1967, as translated in *ARC, The Great Power Struggle in China,* op. cit., pp. 436-440.

25. See "Summary of the forum on the work in literature and art in the armed forces with which Comrade Lin Piao entrusted Comrade Chiang Ch'ing," *PR*, No. 23, June 2, 1967. See also *ARC, The Great Power Struggle in China,* op. cit., pp. 441-454.

26. Ibid., pp. 443-446.

27. See "Lin Piao's address at the enlarged meeting of the CCP central politburo (May 18, 1966), *IAS*, Vol. VI, No. 5, February 1970, pp. 81-92.

28. Ibid., pp. 90-91.

29. Ibid., p. 91. The five conditions are (1) believe in Marxism-Leninism and the thought of Mao Tse-tung, (2) serve the people, (3) consolidate the majority, (4) practice democratic centralism, (5) struggle against oneself to develop good points, i.e., "liberate ourselves from ourself."

30. Ibid., p. 92.

31. Dittmer, op. cit., p. 111.

32. "Liu Shao-ch'i's self-criticism made at the work conference of the CCP central committee" (October 23, 1966), *IAS*, June 1970, pp. 90-93.

33. *PR*, No. 33, 1966.

34. Dittmer, op. cit., p. 95.

35. See *NCNA*, August 8, 1966 "CCP central committee's decision on the Great Proletarian Cultural Revolution." The remaining seven articles deal with particulars of implementation of the cultural revolution as follows: Article 7 entitled "Be on guard against those who brand the revolutionary masses as 'counter-revolutionaries' "; Article 8 entitled "The question of cadres"; Article 10 entitled "Educational reform"; Article 11 entitled "The question of criticizing by name in the press"; Article 12 entitled "Policy towards scientists, technicians, and ordinary members of working staffs"; Article 13 entitled "The question of arrangements for integration with the Socialist Education movement in city and countryside"; and Article 15 entitled "The armed forces."

36. *CB*, No. 891, p. 74.

37. *IAS*, Vol. VII, No. 2, November 1970, p. 72.

38. Ibid., p. 78.

39. *JPRS*, No. 90, February 12, 1970, pp. 52, 58, and 59.

40. Organizational text (handwritten) of the "passing the summit" revolutionary rebel detachment, August 1, 1967, in *Samples of Red Guard Publications.* Washington, D.C.: U.S. Department of Commerce, *Joint Publications Research Service,* Vol. I, as cited in Richard W. and Amy A. Wilson, "The Red Guards and the world student movement," *CQ*, No. 42, April-June 1970, p. 91.

41. Bridgham, *CQ*, No. 29, pp. 25-34.

42. For capsule descriptions of 117 criticized intellectuals see the useful sourcebook by *ARC, The Great Proletarian Cultural Revolution in China.* Hong Kong: Green Pagoda Press, 1967, pp. 116-193.

43. *MISC*, p. 459.

44. *NYT*, December 27, 1967.

Chapter 10

CATECHIZING THROUGH THE

MASS MEDIA

The Great Leap failures announced at Lushan signaled a watershed in the history of the party under Mao. Reacting to the ideological dissonance brought on by the Great Leap failures, the most committed Maoists on the politburo immediately increased their proselyting for Mao's thought and sought social support for the exculpating class struggle rationalization. Evidence for the above proposition has been presented in the foregoing analysis of party documents and will be further demonstrated by systematic analysis of the party-controlled media of mass communication.

The analysis of successive party documents has demonstrated that before the Lushan plenum, Mao's own speeches were characterized by relative confidence and echoed themes of party unity. After Lushan, Mao's speeches increased their stridency in proselyting for his ideology while earlier themes of party unity gave way to exculpating exhortations to class struggle within the party as well as in the larger Chinese society. Other politburo members reacted differentially to the Great Leap failures. In addition to Mao, the most committed Maoists on the politburo, Lin Piao, Ch'en Po-ta, and K'ang Sheng, further increased their action commitments to Mao's thought, supporting it at Lushan, further supporting it at the critical 7,000 cadres conference, enthusiastically endorsing it again in the Lei Feng campaign, and implementing it further in various ad hoc committee assignments leading to the outbreak of the Cultural Revolution in 1966. The uncommitted on the politburo simultaneously neglected and even opposed the adoption of further Maoist action commitments. The resulting polarization of Maoist commitment on the politburo was to culminate in the unprecedented purge of the uncommitted and the truculent from the politburo during the Cultural Revolution through the extraordinary support of Lin Piao's revolutionized PLA and Chiang Ch'ing's exuberant Red Guards. Following Lushan, the most committed Maoists on the politburo, especially Mao, Lin Piao, and Ch'en Po-ta, increased their proselyting for Mao's thought on the pages of Ch'en Po-ta's ideological journal *Red Flag;* simultaneously, the uncommitted members of the politburo desisted. During the Cultural Revolution, the editorial members and staff of *Red Flag* were to become prime figures in the composition of the leading Cultural Revolution group.

As Mao was restrained by high party figures from intervening strongly in domestic affairs following Lushan, his assumption of foreign policy leadership led to increasing concern with validating his thought through revolutionary experiments in the developing areas of the Third World, and increasing concern with disparaging his critical opponents, personified by Khrushchev, in the Soviet Union. Though somewhat thwarted in his attempts to launch domestic proselyting campaigns through the conventional party propaganda apparatus, myriads of campaigns were launched in civilian Chinese society with the unconventional aid of Lin Piao's PLA aimed at recruiting support for Maoist ideology and themes of class struggle from the ranks of the urban and rural proletarians. The new aim of campaigns to seek ideological support and the new policy of targeting upon the proletarians stood in stark contrast to the bulk of campaigns launched by the party apparatus during the pre-Lushan era. As Mao and the Maoists strove mightily to enlist social support from the masses for their ideology, total control of the mass media of communication took on increased import.

Systematic analysis of the mass media will demonstrate that following Lushan, the contents of some of the media shifted sharply and others more gradually to increased stress upon themes of ideology and class struggle with decreased emphasis upon production. The media that shifted most abruptly to themes of ideology and class struggle were those under firmest control by the committed Maoists. While Ch'en Po-ta's *Red Flag* was the vanguard, the party-controlled *People's Daily* was an obvious and castigated laggard in the great surge of Maoist proselyting that culminated in the Great Proletarian Cultural Revolution. Correspondingly, survey analysis of the media audience shows that new efforts were undertaken to target the media upon proletarian audiences as opposed to the characteristically more bourgeois audiences of the fifties. Let us now examine the structure of the coveted mass communication system in more detail.

Capturing Mass Media

Through skillful use of mass organization and mass media, the Maoists strove to mobilize social support for the ideology that failed. The more extensive the mass communications channels available to them, the greater the degree of social support the convinced and committed Maoists could hope to assemble for their beliefs. On the one hand, the Maoists had partial access to the institutional channels of party and government, and near complete access to the army; on the other hand, they had access, in varying degrees, to the media of mass communications consisting of periodicals, newspapers, radio, film, and special media. Under the system prevailing in Communist China since the Great Leap Forward, the two sets of channels were uniquely interlocked by an array of cadre-led study groups into which various segments of the population were organized for the consumption of the ideological message.

For the average individual living in Communist China during the 1960s, mass meetings and mass media occupied a larger share of the individual's life than ever before. Cadres and masses, proletarians and bourgeoisie, literates and illiterates, men and women, urbanites and country folk were organized in varying degrees for use of these channels. The major themes of the deluge of messages were those of the Socialist Education Campaign: Develop proletarian consciousness, engage in class struggle, appreciate the glories of the revolution, emulate the People's Liberation Army, study the works of Chairman Mao.

Whereas the mass communication system characteristic of most pluralistic Western democracies is like so many webs of privately owned newspapers, magazines, and television stations which directly ensnare the audience in overlapping informational cocoons, the mass communication system in China is more like a single giant web propped up by the party-government apparatus and draped over the entire landscape. High up at its center are the party propagandists who alone are privileged to pull and tug at its top gossamer threads. Far down at its periphery are basic-level party cadres specially tuned to interpret its every shudder and vibration to the ensnared populace. Woven large in the 1950s the vibrant web entangles all, directly and indirectly, the sensitive as well as the dull. Thus, in contrast to pluralistic Western systems, the Chinese system is centrally directed; its messages are mediated and interpreted to the populace by ideologically schooled party cadres; and the reach of these messages is much more pervasive than the mechanical message production facilities would lead one to expect. In the 1960s, the proselyting Maoists rent the web in preparation for controlling all its vibrations.

CENTRAL DIRECTION

First of all, the production of messages in periodicals, newspapers, radio, and film are under the monopoly control of the party. At all levels of the administrative hierarchy the government-owned facilities for the production of mass media messages are heavily infiltrated and supervised by party members. At the central level under the auspices of the state council, one finds the ministry of culture administering the nation's press, the broadcasting administration bureau, the film administration bureau, and the single prominent wire service in Communist China, the *New China News Agency* (NCNA). Supervision and personnel infiltration of the media production facilities at this level are carried out by members of the propaganda department of the central committee of the Chinese Communist party be heavily overlapping personnel. In similar fashion, at provincial, municipal, and county levels of government, the institutions for the production of mass media messages, i.e., newspaper publishers, magazine publishers, radio stations, and film stations, are heavily infiltrated by committees of the Communist party apparatus. By gaining control of the propaganda arm of the party, the Maoists could practically ensure a monopoly on the production of mass media messages.

Although the mass media were centrally directed in China during the first decade of Communist rule, there existed an important policy split within the top-level personnel of the propaganda apparatus during the early 1960s which widened with the passage of time. Control of the central propaganda arm of the party was extremely important to the proselyting Maoists in the wake of the Great Leap failures.

Maoist contention for control of the propaganda apparatus began on the heels of the Great Leap debacle. Under the ultimate leadership of Liu Shao-ch'i and the immediate leadership of Lu Ting-yi, the propaganda department of the central committee circulated a draft directive in July 1961 entitled "Ten Articles on Art and Literature," which essentially reversed the Great Leap application of Mao's Yenan line on art and literature and heretically encouraged the dying out of class struggle. Subsequently, in 1962 the revised draft was approved and transmitted by the secretariat under Teng Hsiao-p'ing to all party units. Contrary to the Great Leap emphasis on contemporary Chinese art and literature the ten articles stressed the importance of classical Chinese literature as well as that of foreign nations, communist and capitalist alike. Contrary to the Maoist tenet of omnicompetence as it applies to the realms of art and politics, the ten articles disparaged the unification of art and political tasks as narrow-minded and one-sided. Contrary to the Maoist mass line tenet, the ten articles revoked the requirement that artists and writers go down to the villages and engage in manual labor. Most importantly, contrary to the Maoist concept of the continuation of class struggle, which provided an exculpating rationalization for the Great Leap failures, the articles stated that

to build the proletarian world outlook requires a period of effort. It cannot be done hastily. In the meantime those who do not have the correct world outlook are not necessarily anti-people and anti-socialism in politics. Therefore, we cannot always treat the problem of world outlook as a political matter.[1]

As Liu asserts under the new policy, Chinese class enemies could not be differentiated out from the "whole people"; however this action may have incensed the proselyting Maoists, they were not stymied. There was another avenue open to proselyting the populace which lay within the party apparatus in the PLA. As early as 1960, Lin Piao and the People's Liberation Army began to encroach upon what was previously the exclusive purview of the party, the field of mass propaganda. One of Lin Piao's first moves in 1960 was to establish an arts institute within the PLA which graduated its first class in 1965.[2] Furthermore, a novel by a member of a PLA drama troupe, *The Song of Ouyang Hai,* the story of a PLA squad leader, was touted as the most literary event of the early 1960s. Not only did the PLA organize special propaganda teams to tour the countryside spreading the Maoist doctrine with oral propaganda and stage shows, but members of the PLA became authoritative critics of the arts, film, theater, and literature. With the opening of the reformed Peking opera festival on June 4, 1964, the struggle of the Maoists for increased control of the party propaganda apparatus reached a higher level. In place of the usual classical themes of Peking opera, the 1964 festival featured thirty-seven plays on "modern," socialist themes. According to *NCNA* reports, twenty-three plays could be classified as dealing with the present socialist revolution and the remaining fourteen with past revolutionary experiences; furthermore, thirteen of the plays dealt directly with the PLA and twelve dealt with the relations between the PLA and the populace. The reaction of the nation's press to the insertion of Maoist revolutionary themes into traditional Peking opera was mixed. On June 11, 1964, party literary czar, Chou Yang editorialized in *Wen Yi Pao* that the insertion of modern revolutionary themes into the Peking opera was desirable, but that the classical art form of the Peking opera and its traditional themes should also be preserved. In opposition to Chou Yang's position, the Maoist Ch'en Po-ta editorialized in the June 30 edition of *Hung Ch'i* that *all* art and literature should serve the interests of the workers, peasants, and soldiers of the nation and not the interests of the exploiting classes. Such was the position advocated by Mao Tse-tung in his "Talks at the Yenan Forum in Literature and Art" in 1942.

The struggle of the Maoists for greater control of the propaganda apparatus reached an even higher level in May of 1966 when the leading newspaper of the central committee of the Chinese Communist party, *Jen Min Jih Pao* (People's Daily), was first attacked by the army newspaper, *Chieh Fang Chun Pao* (Liberation Army Daily), and then reorganized by military personnel. Thus, even though the leading press organ of the party did contain revolutionary themes during the early 1960s these themes and their authors were still judged to be insufficiently revolutionary by the convinced and committed Maoists.

The purge of the party propaganda apparatus began early in the Cultural Revolution with the severe criticism of the director Lu Ting-yi, and two deputy directors, Chou Yang and Lin Mo-han, of the Department of Propaganda of the Central Committee of the Chinese Communist party. All three had had a hand in the drafting and circulation of the obstructive "Ten Articles on Art and Literature" in 1961. In the July 1, 1966 edition of *Hung-Ch'i*, Ch'en Po-ta launched a scathing attack on Chou Yang and Lin Mo-han, accusing them of "usurping the leadership of literary and art circles" and of "stubbornly insisting on carrying through their bourgeois line on literature and art which is against the Party, against socialism and against Mao Tse-tung's thought." Shortly thereafter, on July 10, came the *NCNA* report that Lu Ting-yi had been removed as director of the propaganda department of the party. During the same period, the leadership of the government ministry of culture was castigated. Lu Ting-yi and Lin Mo-han held dual positions in the ministry of culture as minister and vice-minister respectively. In addition to this pair, who constituted examples of the interlocking directorate between the party's department of propaganda and the government's ministry of culture, two other vice-ministers of culture were subjected to attack by the Maoists. The June 9, 1966 edition of *China Youth News* criticized Ch'en Huang-mei and Hsia Yen for supervision of the production of films since 1962 which extolled bourgeois individualism and failed to give sufficient importance to the socialist ideology of workers, peasants and soldiers as advocated by Mao Tse-tung's "Talks at the Yenan Forum on Literature and Art."

In succeeding months, the propaganda departments of eight provincial party committees were purged, such important national newspapers as *China Youth News* and *Chinese Workers Daily* were suspended, and special tabloid newspapers were published by Red Guard and Red Rebel organizations. As public criticism of high-level government functionaries progressed through 1965, 1966, and 1967, the single government ministry whose leadership received the most criticism was the ministry of culture. During this period, 40 percent of the 355 men who led the 49 ministries of the state council as ministers and vice-ministers of the ministry of culture, fully 90 percent were subjected to such criticism, and only one made a public appearance between December 1966 and January 1968.[3]

The degree to which Maoist proselyting efforts were hampered by some high-level party officials and propagandists prior to these purges of 1966 and 1967 is indicated by the following post-GPCR passage on the publication of Chairman Mao's works:[4] "In the past it was quite difficult for the broad masses of workers, peasants and soldiers to get Chairman Mao's works because the renegade, hidden traitor and scab Liu Shao-ch'i and his agents had done their utmost to suppress and sabotage their publication and distribution." Besides alleging early sabotage in the publication of Mao's works, the article goes on to demonstrate the recovery of the purged propaganda apparatus following the Maoist takeover stating that "Peking's Hsinhua Printing Press, with the help of the PLA Mao Tse-tung Thought Propaganda Team staying there, since the beginning of the GPCR has printed more than 13 million copies of the *Selected Works of Mao Tse-tung* in various sizes and languages, surpassing the total number published in the whole country before the GPCR."[5] Clearly, then, the media of mass communication were centrally directed in Communist China, and control of the ideological policy and leadership personnel in the central institutions supervising the mass media became increasingly important to the proselyting Maoists during the 1960s.

CADRE MEDIATION

The consumption of mass media messages by the population is ensured and supervised by ideological party cadres infiltrating the basic production units of the society. Operating between the upper reaches of power in the politburo of the Communist party and the working masses of Chinese society, the basic-level party cadres serve as institutionalized "opinion leaders" to disseminate and interpret the centrally produced media messages to the masses. These basic-level party cadres and their cohorts in the youth league, are much more heavily exposed to the conventional mass media than the rank and file of Communist China. Our survey data indicate that over 90 percent of the cadres (party members, youth leaguers or government officials) are regularly exposed to each of the media of newspapers (94 percent), periodicals (94 percent), radio (92 percent), and film (92 percent). In contrast the total adult population exposure rates are 39 percent, 62 percent, 48 percent, and 69 percent respectively. Clearly, political cadres constitute an informational elite in Communist China. Furthermore, the ideological and interpretative capabilities of the party and youth league cadres are more sophisticated than those of the rank and file, for the former have all participated in rigorous ideological training procedures as a requisite for gaining entrance to their respective organizations. It is one of the basic tasks designated to the party cadre that he organize the masses for exposure to the media. In sum, the cadre represents a formalized "opinion leader," more in tune with the media on the one hand and more influential with the people on the other.

The basic-level cadres constitute a crucial link in mediating the effects of the centrally produced media messages on a face-to-face basis. They lead the masses in discussion of the contents of the media in the small "study groups" that punctuate the society; they organize the "struggle sessions" for the ideological remolding of opinion deviates and designated class enemies. If the Maoists could maintain ideological unanimity among the basic-level cadres who disseminate and interpret the content of the media to the masses, they could go a long way toward obtaining the intended effects of mobilizing the masses for the expression of Maoist beliefs and the implementation of Maoist actions. On the other hand, to the extent that the basic-level cadres were divided in their loyalties, the effects of the Maoist media campaign were impaired.

In fact, there were problems with the cadres following the Great Leap debacle: problems of corruption, divorcement from the masses, and complacency. Thus, one of the major tasks of Mao's Socialist Education Campaign launched in September 1962 was for the basic-level cadres in the rural areas to hold ideological study and struggle sessions to rectify themselves and to be rectified by the poor and lower-middle peasants with whom they were to form a mass-line-style alliance in the course of rural class warfare. As we have seen, Mao's intent was obstructed by central party bureaucrats in the "Later Ten Articles." Furthermore, to rejuvenate the ranks of the nation's political cadres and activists, a nonsuccessful and parallel series of political campaigns was launched simultaneously by the general political department of the PLA and aimed at the youth. In February 1963, the general political department announced the beginning of "learn from Lei Feng" campaign. One month later, the YCL amplified the PLA's call for youths to emulate this virtuous serviceman. In December of the same year, Mao initiated the "learn from the PLA" campaign, in which Lin Piao's reformed army was touted as a great school of revolutionary thought to be emulated by all organizations in China. In May of the following year, the general political department published the first edition of the little red book *(Mao Chu-hsi Yu-lu)* on the eve of the ninth congress of the YCL. The main theme of that congress was Mao's call to "cultivate revolutionary successors," and a major result of this call was the dispatching of hundreds of thousands of youths to the rural areas to share revolutionary tales and experiences with the peasantry. In the fall of 1965, an even more virtuous military hero, Wang Chieh, was set up as an emulation model for the young; in the fall of 1966, millions of youths organized as Red Guards and supervised by the PLA engaged in mass struggle with wayward political cadres, both high and low. Clearly then, there was a number of campaigns launched during the 1960s to revolutionize the ranks of the political cadres and thereby make them more vigorous and more faithful dispensers of the Maoist line. These crucial personal links in the mass communication system were especially important to the proselyting Maoists. In the Cultural Revolution, previously indoctrinated PLA soldiers were to replace them with Mao Tse-tung thought propaganda teams.

PROLETARIAN REACH

Finally, the reach of the media to the large proletarian masses of Chinese society is impressive. While in most developing nations, exposure to the mass media is restricted to an urban elite, which is cut off by a communications gap from the rural masses, such is not the case in Communist China. Our survey projections show that fully 86 percent of the adult population of Communist China is regularly exposed to at least one of the mass media of newspapers, magazines, radio, or film. Only 14 percent are "unreachables." Furthermore, in a developing nation in which 64 percent of the adult population are "proletarian" workers or peasants, we find that fully 60 percent of this mass media audience is proletarian, whereas most developing nations concentrate the media on the educated upper strata. Further examination of the survey data shows that 28 percent of the adult population are regularly exposed to all four mass media. More in keeping with conventional expectations, one discovers that only 46 percent of this media-saturated audience is proletarian. Indeed, as one examines the contents of political campaigns and the social characteristics of the mass media audience in China between the midfifties and the midsixties, one discovers an increasing shift of focus from reform of high-level bureaucrats and bourgeois to attempted mobilization of basic-level proletarians.

These proletarians were the major targets of Maoist proselyting in the Socialist Education Campaign. They formed the basic political constituency of the "dictatorship of the proletariat" to which the Maoists appealed for reform of the "bourgeois" individuals still existing in Communist China in the 1960s. Emulation models such as "Lei Feng," organizational devices such as the establishment of "poor and lower-middle peasants associations" and mass media appeals to the spirit of "class struggle" were all employed to increase the political consciousness of the proletarians in this campaign.

Shifting Production and Consumption of Mass Media Messages

Since the mass media in China are under the monopoly control of the party, the contents of the media reflect party concerns. Given that the party was split following Lushan, the dissonance-plagued Maoist faction strove to secure control of the centrally directed channels of mass communication to proselyte for their proletarian ideology and to silence criticism. Their efforts were only partially successful. From the Lushan plenum until late 1961, some of the media did display an upsurge in ideological themes and an upsurge in references to the exculpating class struggle rationalization coupled with a decline in embarrassing economic reportage. However, following the economic crisis of 1961 and the promulgation under propaganda chief Lu Ting-yi of the reactionary ten articles on art and literature later that year, the Maoist influence on media contents waned. Mao's renewed call for "class struggle" at the tenth plenum in late 1962, was followed by only a temporary surge in references to class struggle and only token attempts to mobilize the proletarians.

Not until the end of 1963, after the promulgation under Liu Shao-ch'i of the reactionary later ten articles on the Socialist Education Campaign and Mao's outcry against party literary heretics and him ominous turn to the PLA, did the party-controlled media such as *People's Daily* respond with content appropriately devoted to ideology and class struggle. And not until 1965, after PLA political departments had become ensconced in several government agencies, did the party apparatus make any appreciable efforts to mobilize the proletarians.

It was a peculiar mix of persuasion and coercion by Lin Piao's revolutionized PLA that induced the lethargic party-controlled civil media to print Maoist themes in 1964. The party within the PLA had a self-contained and parallel propaganda apparatus of its own. Parallel to the civilian *People's Daily* and provincial party press were the *Liberation Army Daily* and regional military newspapers. The PLA even published a popular magazine, *PLA Pictorial.* Parallel to the civilian Peking film studio was the PLA's August First film studio. Parallel to the civilian institutions were the PLA's army of propagandists or commissars organized in the general political department (GPD) of the PLA and present in all military units down to the company level. The military media and commissar system were under the aegis of the GPD. Under the leadership of Lo Jung-huan, the military propagandists increasingly encroached on civilian territory from the "army love the people" campaign of 1960 through the "Lei Feng" campaign of 1963. Upon Lo's untimely death in December of that year, Hsiao Hua, assumed his position and assisted in Lin Piao's larger encroachment with yet more pervasive "learn from the PLA" campaign of 1964. As PLA commissars moved more fully into civilian sectors, the civil party propaganda chiefs under Lu Ting-yi complied with their lead and adopted a posture more similar to the Maoist bastion in the civil field, Ch'en Po-ta's *Red Flag.*

Two surges in Maoist themes in the civil media are evident from a systematic examination of media contents over the period. The first surge following the Lushan plenum was the more spontaneous of the two and was most evident on the pages of *Red Flag.* The second, after Mao's turn to the PLA in late 1963, was relatively more coerced. In both surges the Maoist motive was essentially the same: To proselyte for the ideology and secure social support from the proletarians for it and for the exculpating class struggle rationalization of the Great Leap failure and its carping party critics.

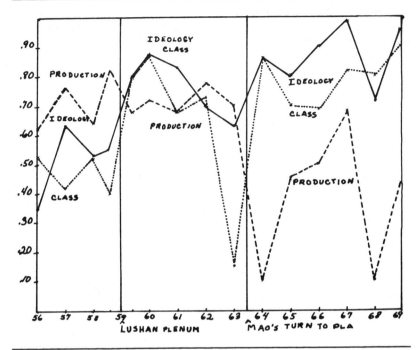

Figure 10.1: PROPORTION OF MAGAZINE ARTICLES MENTIONING IDEOLOGY, PRODUCTION, AND CLASS THEMES, 1956-1969

According to the prophecy fails-proselyte hypothesis, which was supported by the general analysis of political campaigns before and after the Lushan plenum and by the particular analysis of contributions to *Red Flag,* there should be more ideologizing in the national media after the failure of the Great Leap than there was prior to the failure. Figure 10.1 presents a graph of the relative frequency of ideological, class, and production themes in a sample of Communist China's magazines for the years 1956 through 1967.[6] The magazine dominating the sample is Ch'en Po-ta's *Red Flag.*

Dating the point of failure of the Great Leap in July of 1959, the time of the Lushan plenum at which P'eng castigated Mao's Three Red Banners, we find clear support for our hypothesis regarding the contents of magazines: There is a significant steep rise in the proportion of articles devoted to the ideology of Marxism-Leninism and the thought of Mao Tse-tung from the low point in March of 1959 (54 percent) through September of 1959 (80 percent) through 1960 (86 percent) to 1961 (82 percent). Furthermore, the average frequency of mention of ideological themes in the three and a half years leading to the failure of the Great Leap was 53 percent, whereas the average frequency of mention of ideological themes over the eight and one half years following the failure was 79 percent! This is true despite the fact that cadres and workers were constantly exhorted with ideological themes in the years following the Hundred Flowers and during the Great Leap movement. Following the Great Leap failure, the curve of class themes closely follows that of ideological themes, for class struggle provided a rationalization of ideological failure. There is a significant steep rise in the proportion of articles containing class themes from a low in March 1959 (52 percent) to highs in September of 1959 (80 percent) through 1960 (83 percent) and declining in 1961 (58 percent). Again our hypothesis is confirmed: Seventy percent of the articles contained class themes during the eight and a half years following the failure, whereas only 49 percent of the articles contained class themes in the three and a half years prior to it. By way of contrast, we can examine the relative frequency of production themes in China's magazines over the period. Our theoretical assertion was that after the Great Leap, the relative concerns of the Maoist leadership turned from production to ideology as a means of rationalizing away the obvious production failure resulting from their ideological experiment. Here again our assertion is borne out: In the prefailure years 73 percent of the articles in the sample contained production themes; in the years following the failure only 57 percent of the articles contained production themes. Note that it is not our assertion that the decline in mention of production themes is a result of economic failure per se. Such an assertion would maintain that mention of production is a direct function of the level of economic success. But this is not the case: Figures 4.1 and 4.2 demonstrated that production success was curvilinear in both agriculture and industry over the period in question reaching their nadirs in 1961 and 1962 respectively. However, our curve of mentions of production themes declines steadily from the point of failure through 1964, even though the economy had been on the upswing since 1962.

In looking at the frequency of ideologizing over the years, we first turned to an examination of the content of magazines in China since the leading magazine, *Red Flag,* was controlled by the committed Maoist Ch'en Po-ta, since of all the mass media magazines are where one finds the most complex and detailed ideological analysis of events, and since magazines are the most frequently utilized study materials in the daily mass indoctrination practice of "study groups." However, our hypothesis should also be amenable to test in any of the mass media under the control of the Maoist leadership. We also conducted a content analysis of the leading Chinese official party newspaper, *People's Daily,* from which all other newspapers and radio stations in the nation take their lead.[7]

The radical shift to ideological proselyting, did in fact, *not* occur in the recalcitrant party-controlled *People's Daily,* operating under the conservative policies of the 1961 "ten articles on art and literature," until the editors were intimidated by Mao's shift to the PLA in late 1963. As shown in Figure 10.2 another content analysis provides us with data on this point. Examining the proportion of *People's Daily* articles devoted to ideology, we find an average of .20 for the two years preceding the Lushan plenum and an equivalent average of .19 in the three succeeding years; however, in the next five years, beginning with Mao's turn to the PLA in late 1963, we find a sharply increased average of .32 devoted to ideology. Similarly, the proportion of articles devoted to class themes was .12 for the two years preceding Lushan and .13 for the succeeding three years; but again in the next five years after Mao's turn to the PLA it jumped to an average of .26. The reverse holds true for the proportion of articles devoted to production, which averaged .43 for the two years preceding Lushan and .44 for the next three years, but dropped precipitously to .17 for the five years following Mao's turn to the PLA. Thus, systematic analysis of the contents of *People's Daily* reveals that its relatively uncommitted editor was, as alleged by the Maoists, more reluctant to engage in the Maoist proselyting than the committed editor of *Red Flag*. Only under threat of coercion by Lin Piao's PLA in the late 1963 did he comply with the committed Maoists.

In accord with the prophecy fails-proselyte hypothesis, we would expect not only a shift in the proportion of Maoist-controlled media contents devoted to ideologizing, but we would also expect an increase in the organization of audiences for exposure to the increased ideological contents of the mass media. We would expect the Maoist leadership to make increased efforts to organize people for exposure to the increased production of ideological messages. Second, in order to reduce the ideological dissonance due to knowledge of Great Leap failures, through obtaining in the affirmations of other persons confirmation for the validity of the failed ideology, social support would first be sought from those adjudged more likely to be supportive of the shaken ideology, namely the proletariat in preference to the bourgeoisie. Hence the increase in size of the audience for the mass media after the Great Leap failure should be greater among the proletarians than among the bourgeoisie. Figures 10.3 and 10.4 present a tabulation of media exposure over time by social class, resulting from a sample survey of 433 adult mainland refugees interviewed in Hong Kong and Macau in 1964 and 1967.[8]

Consistent with the first proselyting hypothesis, the results show that prior to the leap failure 75 percent of the represented mainlanders were regularly exposed to *either* newspapers, magazines, radio, or film, and 24 percent were regularly exposed to *all* of these mass media; for the three sample points following the leap failure, an average of 96 percent were regularly exposed to at least one of the media, and 52 percent were regularly exposed to all of the media.[9] We are not concerned here with absolute levels of exposure, but

(Text continued on page 245)

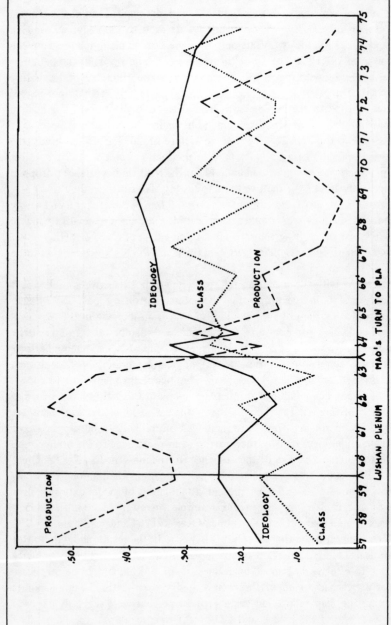

Figure 10.2: PROPORTION OF *PEOPLE'S DAILY* ARTICLES MENTIONING IDEOLOGY, PRODUCTION, AND CLASS THEMES, 1957-1974

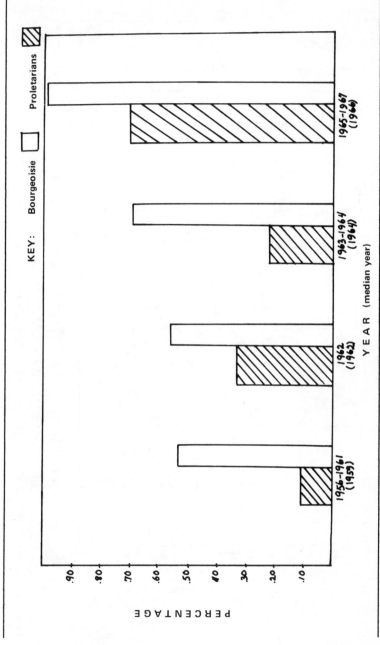

Figure 10.3: PROPORTION OF PROLETARIANS AND BOURGEOISIE EXPOSED TO NEWSPAPERS, MAGAZINES, RADIO AND FILM BY YEAR

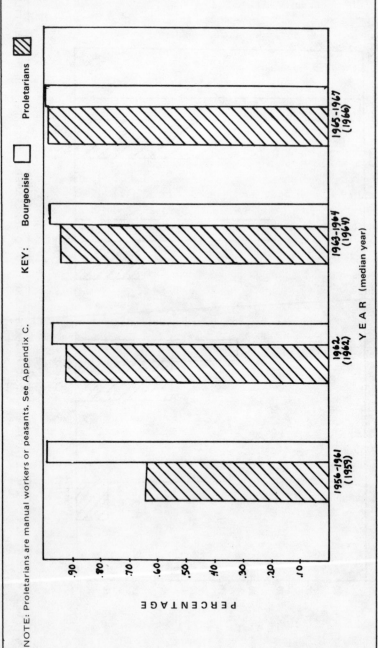

NOTE: Proletarians are manual workers or peasants. See Appendix C.

KEY: □ Bourgeoisie   ▨ Proletarians

Figure 10.4: PROPORTION OF PROLETARIANS AND BOURGEOISIE EXPOSED TO EITHER NEWSPAPERS, MAGAZINES, RADIO OR FILM BY YEAR

PERCENTAGE

.90 .80 .70 .60 .50 .40 .30 .20 .10

1956-1961 (1959)   1962 (1962)   1963-1964 (1964)   1965-1967 (1966)

Y E A R   (median year)

rather with relative levels over time. In terms of exposure to all the conventional media of newspapers, magazines, radio, and film, the adult Chinese audience more than doubled after the Great Leap failure.

Further, when viewed in terms of social class, the first and largest jumps in media exposure following the Lushan plenum were with the proletarians. Of the proletarians 64 percent were regularly exposed to some medium in 1959 before the failure, by 1962—our next sample point—the proletarians' exposure rate was 92 percent. On this measure the bourgeois show no significant difference since practically all of them were exposed to some medium at all times. However, in terms of exposure to all the media, in terms of a media barrage that comes with concerted political campaigns, the proletarians' exposure proportion triples (from 11 percent to 33 percent) between 1959 and 1962, whereas the bourgeois do not show any significant jump over this period (53 percent to 56 percent). Later in 1966, the bourgeois also increase their media exposure (between 1964 and 1966 they move from 68 percent to 100 percent) but over the period, their gains do not compare with those of the proletariat. Thus, consistent with our first proselyting hypothesis, we find increased media exposure of the mainland population following the leap failure; and further, in accord with our second major proselyting hypothesis, we find that these increases are first and foremost among the proletarians, those who were adjudged by the proselyters to be more likely to be sympathetic to and supportive of the shaken ideology.

Finally, examination of these data on the production and consumption of mass media messages during the 1960s, provides additional support for our third hypothesis, which could be termed "proselyters fail-radicalize proselyting." The support for this proposition comes from the observation that there is a second inflection in our time curve of proselyting besides that in the Maoist-controlled media immediately after the Great Leap failure; the year 1963 is the post-Great Leap low in the exposure of proletarians to the combined mass media of newspapers, magazines, radio, and film. Late 1963 was the time at which the recalcitrant editors of *People's Daily* first shifted to Maoist themes of ideology and class struggle. Indeed, all post-Great Leap highs on our indices of ideological proselyting are reached after 1963. There are, then, two inflections in our indices of proselyting through the mass media is explicable in terms of the prophecy fails-proselyte hypothesis for the committed Maoists; the other turning point around 1963, following Mao's tenth plenum speech for socialist education, is explicable in terms of the polarized anti-Maoists' attempt to subvert his proselyting drive and the subsequent radicalized attempt by the Maoists to proselyte for their ideology while adding to their targets of ideological reform those individuals who were perceived as instrumental in subverting the initial proselyting activities.[10] To accomplish this aim, immediately after the publication of the subversive "later ten articles," in late 1963 Mao brought the People's Liberation Army more fully into the business of proselyting and encouraging others to proselyte among the civilian population. The bourgeoisie and its representatives in the party and especially in the party-controlled media became targets of newly radicalized Maoist proselyting. Let us now turn to consideration of the polarization of Chinese society that increased as committed Maoists gained firm control of the mass media and other organs of political power.

NOTES

1. See "Ful text of the 'ten articles on literature and art,' " *Tsukuo,* No. 67, October 1, 1969, as cited in Alan P.L. Liu, *Communications and National Integration in Communist China.* Berkeley: University of California Press, 1971, pp. 56-57.

2. See Merle Goldman, "The fall of Chou Yang," *CQ,* No. 21, July-September 1966, pp. 145-146.

3. See Donald Klein, "The state council and the Cultural Revolution," *CQ,* No. 35, July-September 1968, pp. 83-84.

4. See "Ensuring good quality in publishing Chairman Mao's works," *China Pictorial,* No. 6, 1969, pp. 32-35.

5. Ibid.

6. An article was classified as containing a production theme if it contained any statements regarding economic success or economic failure. Similarly, an article was classified as containing an ideological theme if it contained statements regarding the success or failure of Marxism-Leninism or the thought of Mao Tse-tung. An article was classified as containing a class theme if it contained statements dealing with the success or failure of those individuals or groups distinguished by their proletarian character. (Synonyms for proletarian are "reds" or "progressives," namely those individuals who support the ideology.) The coders were unaware of hypotheses to be tested; the sample of articles was taken from the *Survey of the China Mainland Magazines (SCMM)* with the time points of mid-April and mid-September selected as sample points in which for every year all articles contained in SCMM were content analyzed for themes; this process resulted in the coding of one hundred and fifty-eight articles over the twelve-year period through 1967. In each year, the great majority of articles were taken from the periodical *Hung Ch'i* (Red Flag). The coding for 1968 and 1969 was performed by J. Juszkiewicz.

7. In the contents of *People's Daily* the same categories were used as in the magazine content analysis. This analysis resulted in the coding of 475 articles for the 17 years 1957-1974. The year 1958 was omitted here because that year's issues of *Survey of the China Mainland Press (SCMP)* were missing from the files of the Far East reading room of Regenstein Library at the University of Chicago where the analysis was conducted. For each year, a single month was randomly selected, and all excerpted articles for the chosen month were content analyzed. Three of the years were independently analyzed by another coder at Northwestern University, resulting in intercoder reliability coefficients of .89, .69, and .96 for the ideology, class, and production themes respectively. For further analysis of these data, see Paul J. Hiniker and Jolanta Juszkiewicz, "Cycles of Maoism and pragmatism in the Chinese press, 1957-1974," paper presented at the midwest regional China seminar, University of Chicago, September 1975.

8. The sample survey is broken down by time periods in terms of those whose last year in the mainland (which they are describing) was between 1956 and 1961—averaging 1959, whom we have designated as preleap failure refugees; and postleap refugees, those whose last year was 1962; and those whose last was 1966 or 1967—averaging 1966. In terms of social class "proletarians" are either peasants, fishermen, or manual workers, both skilled and unskilled; "bourgeois" are the residual of housewives, clerks, professionals, government officials, university students, businessmen, unemployed, and others. The time samples are roughly equivalent in educational level, a prime determinant of media exposure in all nations. For a more complete sample description, see Appendix C.

9. Note that the population projections for the total of mainlanders from the proletarian and bourgeois samples is made by weighing the former figure by .70 and the latter figure be .30 consistent with the mainland population distribution. Thus the rough total population estimate of 24 percent exposed to all the mass media prior to the Great Leap failure is computed by reading the proletarian exposure proportion of .11 and multiplying it by the proletarian population weight of .70, yielding .077. This product is then added to .159, the product of the bourgeois exposure proportion of .53 and the bourgeois population weight of .30. The resulting weighted average for the total population is .236. See Appendix C.

10. The time trend data were examined for statistical significance of shifts in trends by using Campbell's method of regression-discontinuity analysis. See Don Campbell, "Reforms as experiments," *American Psychologist,* Vol. 24, pp. 409-429. Examining the content of themes in magazines, both ideological and class themes show statistically significant ($p < .10$) upward shifts in the late 1959 when examined over the years from 1957 to 1961; both also show statistically significant upward shifts again between 1963 and 1964 when examined over the years 1959-1967. Though no statistically significant upward sharp shifts were found for combined mass media exposure, there was a statistically significant upward shift in participation in political study by proletarians between 1959 and 1962 when examined over the few data points available for 1959, 1962, 1964, and 1966.

For a more comprehensive examination of the role of the Chinese press in the early sixties, see Paul J. Hiniker, "Media exposure in China during the Socialist Education Campaign: Some survey results," in Gilbert Chan, ed., *China Under Communism: Domestic Revolution and International Politics, 1949-1975.* New York: New Viewpoint Press, 1977.

PART III

POLARIZATION: UTOPIA REVISITED

... as soon as labor is distributed, each man has a particular, exclusive sphere of activity which is forced upon him and from which he cannot escape. He is a hunter, a fisherman, a shepherd, or a critical critic, and he must remain so if he does not want to lose his means of livelihood; while in communist society, where nobody has one exclusive sphere of activity but each can become accomplished in any branch he wishes, society regulates the general production and thus makes it possible for me to do one thing today and another tomorrow, to hunt in the morning, fish in the afternoon, rear cattle in the evening, criticize after dinner, just as I have a mind, without ever becoming hunter, fisherman, shepherd, or critic.

Karl Marx and Friedrich Engels,
The German Ideology (1846)

Chapter 11

POLARIZATION

With the formal codification and promulgation of Mao's sixteen-point decision concerning the Great Proletarian Cultural Revolution on August 8, 1966 at the eleventh plenum by a rump session of the central committee, the class struggle deepened. The search for confirmation of the thought of Mao Tse-tung finally became unrestrained. By the end of the year with some purging before the eleventh plenum, the Maoists had gained ascendance in the polit-buro, and through the PLA they gained complete control of the propaganda apparatus. 1967 was a year of turmoil in which the deepened class struggle approached the dimensions of full-scale civil war. Meanwhile, the Paris commune was briefly revived in Shanghai. In the struggle the Maoists reinvigorated the purged ranks of middle-level leadership with indoctrinated PLA cadres and youthful activists who continued to struggle the bourgeoisie. By September of 1968, revolutionary committees based on "three-way alliances" had been established as provisional organs of political power in all of China's provinces, and the overt turmoil subsided. The Maoists then began in earnest to reimplement Great Leap-style and Commune programs in the economy, and in October 1968, the twelfth plenum was held; there Liu Shao-ch'i was formally denounced as the "leading figure in authority taking the capitalist road." In April 1969, the Maoists consolidated their power at the ninth party congress; Mao issued a call for unity, and Lin Piao was formally designated as Mao's successor in the new party constitution.

The foregoing capsule summary of the sequence of events in the Cultural Revolution between the eleventh plenum of 1966 and the ninth party congress of 1969 leaves many questions unanswered as to the underlying cause and effects of the Cultural Revolution. Our basic thesis has been that the Great Leap Forward of 1958 was an ideological social movement predicated upon the thought of Mao Tse-tung. When in 1959 the Great Leap failed, it created dissonance in the minds of the Maoists and gave rise to a proselyting urge among the convinced and committed Maoists to assemble social support for their shaken beliefs. Simultaneously, the Great Leap failure had the effect on the unconvinced and uncommitted political leadership of lowering the credibility of Maoist ideology and Maoist policies. The non-Maoists became all the more pragmatic in the face of ideological failure. During the early 1960s, the Maoists engaged increasingly in proselyting activities for their ideology among those segments of society where they could expect to generate social support for their beliefs—among the soldiers, youth, and proletarians. Employing those mass communication facilities at their disposal, the Maoists spread their gospel far and wide. Through the initially restrained use of centrally controlled mass media and cadre-led study groups, the Maoist message eventually penetrated quite deeply into the ranks of the proletarian masses. Clearly, Mao's Socialist Education Campaign and the ensuing Great Proletarian Cultural Revolution had the effect of generating increasing professions of social support for the thought of Mao Tse-tung, especially among PLA soldiers and youth who increasingly became propagandists themselves. However, as Maoist proselyting increased in magnitude and radicalism, opposition to the Maoist ideology solidified among those who were initially predisposed against Maoist policy. Within the Chinese masses, opposition increased among the struggled bourgeois who increasingly differed with the proletarians. Within the middle-level cadres, opposition increased among expert-bureaucrats and intellectuals, who engaged in veiled criticism and feigned compliance with respect to Maoist proselyting and policies; they differed especially with intrusive PLA political warriors. Within the politburo, opposition increased among those initially opposed to the Maoist Great Leap Forward. Some promulgated counterpolicies and protected underlings who tried to sabotage Maoist proselyting; they increasingly differed with the highly committed Maoists including Lin Piao, Ch'en Po-ta, and K'ang Sheng and their Red Guard followers. During the 1960s, increasing Maoist proselyting and increasing opposition to the Maoist ideology mutually reinforced each other to create increasing polarization of Chinese society around the Maoist ideology as an issue: At all levels of society, within the groups, the attitudinal discrepancy increased between Maoists and anti-Maoists. In order to render their social support complete and to gain empirical confirmation of their ideology, the Maoists had to silence the developing opposition and reimplement their radicalized policies. At this point, one may ask what were the effects on Chinese society of this gigantic movement in search of confirmation of Maoist ideology from people and events.

Polarization of the Masses: Proletarians and Bourgeois

In the Great Proletarian Cultural Revolution the proletarians and bourgeois of Chinese society were cleaved as never before since the civil war. One basic Maoist tenet holds to the continuation of the class struggle in socialist society. Assembling social support for this tenet became equivalent to securing support for the exculpating rationalization for the Great Leap failings which allowed them and their ideology to go relatively unscathed with responsibility for the failures. Following Lushan, the theme of class struggle did indeed take on increased salience in the mass media and in ensuing political campaigns. From the point of view of Maoist ideology, the period after the rectification of rightists campaign of 1957 and proceeding through the Great Leap Forward of 1958 was one of class integration. The period following the Great Leap failure was one of intense class struggle and division. During the period of the Great Leap failure those propaganda media under Maoist control were directed toward separating the true proletarians from the true bourgeois enemies. The Great Leap was designed to integrate society; the Socialist Education Campaign and the Cultural Revolution temporarily to cleave society. The ultimate in class integration is a "classless society" of free association and exchange of views between persons independent of social class; the ultimate in class cleavage is complete segregation of people on the basis of class, which, under conditions of competition for scarce resources, leads to social disintegration and civil war.

From the perspective of our theory, the period following the Great Leap failure of 1959 should be one of increasing social polarization as a result of the failure and of subsequent Maoist proselyting efforts. Analysis of the contents of both newspapers and magazines in Chapter 10 showed a general increase in ideological and class themes from the late fifties through the sixties to 1967. Dividing the population into two sets, proletarians and bourgeois as defined in Chapter 3, it seems clear that Maoist propaganda should find less resistance among the proletarians and relatively more resistance among the bourgeois, i.e., there should be a relatively greater proportion of anti-Maoists among the bourgeois as compared with the proletarians. Certainly, Maoist class struggle propaganda, extolling the proletariat and disparaging the bourgeoisie should have more success in recruiting supporters from the lower strata of the proletariat; Maoist propaganda should create relatively more resistance among the threatened bourgeois classes. Now, to the extent that people seek out other people for conversation who are likely to agree with their attitudes on important issues, word-of-mouth communication should become increasingly polarized between the two classes over time, i.e., there should be increasing social cleavage in China throught the sixties.

One way of assessing the amount of cleavage between proletarians and bourgeois is by observing how the two classes of people distribute their informal word-of-mouth communications. The same sample survey of mainland refugees mentioned earlier with regard to media exposure together with another survey of two thousand mainland refugees conducted on Taiwan provide us with information about how Chinese distributed their regular word-of-mouth communication partners between proletarians and bourgeois over the years leading up to and following the Great Leap Forward.[1] The relative concentration of communications within the proletariat and within the bourgeoisie is measured by the phi (ϕ) coefficient. The more equally distributed the communications across the two classes, the lower the phi measure of cleavage; the more proletarians are in contact with other proletarians to the exclusion of bourgeois, the more bourgeois are in contact with other bourgeoisie to the exclusion of proletarians, the higher the phi measure of cleavage. The measure is maximal ($\phi = 1.00$) when there are no cross-class communications and minimal ($\phi = 0.00$) when communications are distributed across classes as would be expected from the population distribution.[2] Thus, the higher the ϕ, the greater the class cleavage.

The effect of the Great Leap failure and subsequent Maoist proselyting was to increase the cleavage between bourgeoisie and proletariat in Chinese society. Examination of Figure 11.1 shows that the average level of class polarization for the four recorded time periods preceding the failure of 1959

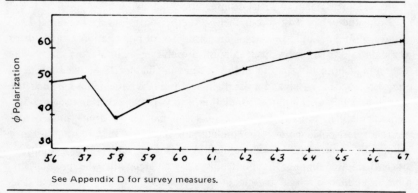

See Appendix D for survey measures.

Figure 11.1: POLARIZATION OF WORD-OF-MOUTH COMMUNICATIONS BE-
TWEEN PROLETARIANS AND BOURGEOISIE (1956-1967)

is ϕ = .48; the average level of polarization for the three recorded time periods following the failure is ϕ = .56. The general trend displayed in Figure 11.1 is one of steadily increasing class polarization stemming from a minimum value of ϕ = .392 in 1958, the year the Great Leap Forward to a maximum of ϕ = .623 in 1966, the year of initial extremes in the Cultural Revolution. In Communist China of the 1960s, increasing class struggles was no chimera; it was day to day reality. The extremes of this class struggle were quite evident during the Cultural Revolution.

INSURRECTION OF YOUTH

By early indoctrination of impressionable youths through the instrumentality of the PLA and Lin Piao's numerous emulation campaigns, the Maoists had created idealistic social support for their ideology and could feel more comfortable with their beliefs. This youthful support found its most zealous representation in the Red Guards, a term taken from Yenan days. The *New China News Agency* dispatch of August 18, 1966, speaks for itself:

On August 18, 1966, at a mass rally to celebrate the Great Proletarian Cultural Revolution, Chairman Mao Tse-tung, our great leader, great supreme commander and great helmsman, joined one million revolutionary people from Peking and other parts of the country in the magnificent Tienanmen Square in Peking, the centre of the proletarian revolution and the capital of our great motherland. . . .

Our Great leader Chairman Mao spent more than six hours with the one million members of the revolutionary masses that morning. He stood side by side with Comrade Lin Piao and reviewed the parade of the one million-strong army of the proletarian cultural revolution. Watching the magnificent march past, he remarked with gratification to Comrade Lin Piao: "This is a movement of a momentous scale. It has indeed mobilized the masses. It is of very great significance to the revolutionization of the thinking of the people throughout the country. . . ."

One thousand and five hundred student representatives mounted the rostrum to attend the rally together with Party and Government leaders. Chairman Mao and Comrades Lin Piao, Chou En-lai and Chiang Ch'ing received them in groups, talked with them and had pictures taken together with them. When Chairman Mao received them, the students excitedly crowded around him and kept shouting "Long live Chairman Mao!"

The rally began at 7:30 in the morning. As the band played "The East is Red," Chairman Mao appeared on the rostrum together with Lin Piao and other comrades. The crowd leapt with joy. A great many hands, holding "Quotations from Chairman Mao Tse-tung" covered with red plastic jackets, stretched toward Tienanmen Gate.

The rally was presided over by Ch'en Po-ta, member of the Political Bureau of the Central Committee of the Chinese Communist Party and leader of the group in charge of the Cultural Revolution under the Party's Central Committee. "Chairman Mao stands among us. This is the happiest and most important moment in our lives. We'll read his works, follow his teachings, act according to his instructions and be his good pupils for the rest of our lives."

The Maoists also combined this channeled idealism of youth with the disciplined force of the PLA to forge a new weapon for remolding bourgeois heretics in mass struggle. An account of this formidable coalition is provided by *Peking Review:*

Comrade Lin Piao has recently given instructions, calling on the Chinese People's Liberation Army to carry forward to a new stage the mass movement for the creative study and application of Chairman Mao's works. This call received resolute and warm support and response from the commanders and fighters of the whole Liberation Army and the broad masses of revolutionary people throughout the country. . . .

Workers, peasants, revolutionary teachers and students, young Red Guard fighters and revoltuionary cadres have held many discussions. They have unanimously expressed their determination to follow closely the Liberation Army, learn from it still better, raise the great red banner of Mao Tse-tung's thought still higher, take a firmer hold of the study of Chairman Mao's works, put it on a still more solid footing and make Mao Tse-tung's thought a programme of their own actions.

Some cadres and group leaders of the Poor Peasant Association of the Youth Brigade of the Ying-menkou People's Commune on the outskirts of Chengtu, an outstanding farm unit of Tachai type in Szechwan Province, held discussions during the work breaks. Brigade leader Chu Hai-ching said: "We should immediately organise all commune members to study Comrade Lin Piao's call, put the study of Chairman Mao's works on a still more solid footing and bring about a new order of things."[4]

As the Red Guards struggled with the "persons in authority taking the capitalist road," the Cultural Revolution proceeded in a whirlwind of turmoil throughout 1967 and 1968, and the dangers of anarchy emerged. The task of maintaining order was made doubly difficult by the fact that the Red Guards split into relatively conservative and ultraleftist factions, which fought each other in the course of struggle, making it difficult for the PLA correctly to identify the more "Maoist" of the multitudinous groups. In the spring of 1967, disruptive Cultural Revolution activities were called off in the countryside. Eventually in 1968, through Mao's own instruction, youth were stilled and less unruly worker and peasant teams took up the task of spreading Mao's gospel under PLA supervision. However, lest one believe that the Red Guard (students) and Red Rebel (workers) organizations were simply annoying gadflies, one should examine the accounts of the pilloried and the purged.

INQUISITION OF BOURGEOISIE

By silencing the sharp criticism of bourgeois dissidents, the Maoists could reduce their ideological dissonance. From the time of the unleashing of Red Guards to struggle bourgeois authorities in August 1966, the inquisition of the bourgeoisie proceeded through violence and turmoil to a rather mechanical dispensing of revolutionary justice three years later. The routinization of the class struggle is well depicted by a Peking scenario exemplary of the long Maoist "reign of terror and virtue" and witnessed forty-one months after the Red Guard rally on Tienanmen Square. The following eyewitness account of the events was provided by a diplomat from a neutral Asian nation.

The observer vividly recounts how about 20,000 members of a "jury" were assembled in January on a sportsground near Peking beneath a huge billboard portrait of Chairman Mao. Three guards handled each of the six prisoners, each of whom wore a placard of crimes on his chest. Five judges marched into the arena, two men in uniform a member of the secret police, and two women, while the band played "The East Is Red." Charges were read and witnesses bawled their evidence through loudspeakers while brandishing copies of the little red book. No defense was allowed and no pleas taken. Following the lead of a group up front, the whole jury rose shouting, "Guilty! Death!" The first prisoner was dragged before the firing squad, tied to a post and machinegunned to death. The whole process had taken 20 minutes. The same procedure was followed with the remaining five prisoners except the procedings were speeded up. The "jury" marched out singing "Sailing the Seas Depends on the Helmsman." Some broke ranks and crossed the arena to spit and even urinate upon the six bodies which were left on the ground all day.[5] What were the men's crimes? The following account was provided by Radio Peking on January 20:

Six prisoners were found guilty this week at a People's Court of political crimes, counter-revolutionary plotting against the masses and the state, and conspiring with the archrenegade, archrevisionist, ugly scab and traitor Liu Shao-ch'i. They were found guilty of corruption, bribery and embezzlement. After a public hearing of evidence, all pleaded guilty and—amid shouts of "Long Live Chairman Mao!"—they were executed on the spot.[6]

Such "public trials" were replicated around China's provinces with the estimate of the numbers executed running into the tens of thousands. Never

since the time of the land reform, when an estimated two million were executed, have so many been summarily executed by civil authorities in China.
However, during the land reform the crimes evolved from possession of
property; in the wake of the Cultural Revolution, the crimes evolved from the
possession of ideas. The new type of trial for thought-crime is illustrated by
a report from Radio Canton of May 12, 1970:

> A young woman was yesterday tried and found guilty at a People's
> Court in Lu Chech of the theft of a bicycle. Her father was also found
> guilty of having failed as head of the family to hold regular family
> classes to study Chairman Mao's "Thoughts." Both admitted their
> guilt. The People's Court shouted approval when the comrade judge
> referred the prisoners to the Public Security Bureau in Namhoi for
> sentence. The trial opened at 7:00 A.M. and closed at 11:30 A.M.[7]

This particular trial was observed by a Hong Kong resident who was visiting
relatives at the Lu Chieh commune. She essentially confirmed the report of
Canton Radio and provided the following additional details of the trial.

> Several neighbors testified against the woman as she sat on a stool with
> her head bowed between two militia men; two of the witnesses hit her
> on the head with copies of the Thoughts of Chairman Mao. The girl's
> father was charged as an accessory to the bicycle theft, but the bicycle
> was never produced and no one was able to suggest what the girl had
> done with it.[8]

Low-level personnel were not the sole victims of Mao's inquisition. The
Red Guards and PLA purge of "bourgeois" shook the hierarchy of party
rule from bottom to top. The bad apples further down the tree from the
"dazzling rays" of Mao's countenance fell the fastest. By 1970, fully 75
percent of the party's 28 provincial secretaries were purged, of them one
committed suicide. Two others were told to meditate on their sins. Of the
67 secretaries and alternate secretaries of the party's six regional bureaus,
55 percent were purged and 17 were suspended to undergo self-criticism
and possible rehabilitation. Of the 172 full or alternate members of the
central committee, 54 percent were purged, 15 were censured and 9 were
suspended.[9] Thus Mao's critics were silenced to a deadly calm.

RESURRECTION OF COMMUNES

The most satisfactory means for the Maoists to reduce the dissonance
between their fervent belief that the Great Leap Forward would rapidly
move China closer to a true Communist society and the reports of the Great
Leap failures was for them to reestablish vigorous people's communes and to

reimplement the other ideological programs of the Great Leap Forward. Besides the ideological proselyting hypothesis and ensuing polarization, our most unequivocal theoretical prediction following the failure of Mao's prophecy is that the Maoists would be strongly motivated to resurrect the people's communes and to reimplement the Great Leap Forward in accord with Maoist tenets for achieving the socialist transformation as part of their search for confirmation of this shaken proletarian ideology.

The first concrete evidence of a serious Maoist attempt to resurrect the people's communes appeared at the provincial level during the initial surge of the Cultural Revolution. On August 13, 1966, the Kwangtung provincial party committee issued a detailed set of instructions specifying how to implement the August 1 decree of the eleventh plenum of the eighth central committee on turning the country into a "great school of Mao Tse-tung's thought." Besides proselyting for the thought of Mao Tse-tung, the most emphatic concrete instruction of the provincial party committee was for the radicalized reestablishment of people's communes as the basic level units of rural work. The Kwangtung provincial party committee's "Ten Great Measures for the Implementation of Chairman Mao's Instruction" proposed nothing less than the radicalized recrudescence of the Communist utopia prophesied by Chairman Mao during the abortive Great Leap in 1958! But now more people were privy to the people's commune rationale by virtue of the GPCR's radical proselyting for the thought of Mao Tse-tung. Once again a Maoist *Gleichschaltung der Gemeinschaft* was blueprinted for the basic levels of Chinese society. The people's communes were to arise phoenix-like from the flaming red tongues of the failed prophecy. The Marxist utopian fervor of the Great Leap Forward of 1958 had been reenkindled in the Cultural Revolution revival of 1966 through the repeated ideological imperative to eradicate the three great differences, between industry and agriculture, between town and countryside, between mental and manual labor. Again, Mao's main means of bridging the gaps and moving to true communism were the resuscitated people's communes, but this time geared by Mao-girded proletarian legions "wielding the sword and the pen" of this Thought.

> Chairman Mao's instruction exhibits to us a magnificent blueprint of communism, points out the concrete road to the elimination of the three great differences and the transition to communism. Previously, we always thought that the scientific prediction of Marx and Engels on the elimination of the three great differences was a matter of the distant future. Having studied this instruction of Chairman Mao, we feel it is already on our agenda, and something quite tangible.

> The most fundamental measure is to turn the whole province into a big school for the study of Mao Tse-tung's thinking. Workers, peasants

and soldiers, students and commercial circles, and all sectors of the economy, must, in their own work posts, take an active part in class struggle, in the Socialist Education Campaign, and in the Great Proletarian Cultural Revolution, and criticize the bourgeoisie. Meanwhile they should also learn politics, military affairs, and culture, becoming truly worker-peasant wielding both pen and sword.

. . . All factories, mines, and enterprises with suitable conditions should engage in farm and sideline production. They should actively integrate the factory with the Communes, having the factory lead the Commune, etc., on a trial basis, thus integrating industry with agriculture.

Commercial points and networks in rural areas should hand over some of their work to the rural Communes, brigades and production teams.

. . . In the future, the development of state-run farming, forestry, and reclamation must follow the line of joint management by the State and the Commune. Existing state-run farms must also at the same time be People's Communes. . . .

In accordance with the characteristics of the Communes which are big and public, the Communes should step by step develop into basic level organizations with agriculture as the main pursuit and at the same time running industry and wielding the pen and the sword. They should, with agriculture as the main pursuit, run one or two major industrial and siedline productions in the light of local conditions, step by step set up small farms, small forestry farms and agricultural machinery stations. Actively and methodically develop Commune industry, handicraft industry and joint management of industry and handicrafts by Commune and brigade. Every year the Communes must spontaneously and methodically send peasants to factories to be rotation workers, seasonal workers, or temporary workers; to join the army; to attend various schools or training courses; to be "political apprentices," to take part in various political campaigns, etc.

The superstructure must serve better the economic basis. Structure should be resolutely streamlined, sweeping away all ideas, viewpoints, regulations and systems that are unfavorable to the diminishing of the three great differences.[10]

This atavistic People's Commune movement contained within the GPCR was an event foreshadowed by the activities of the proselyting Maoists throughout the 1960s.

We have already examined much of the evidence for the protracted search for ideological confirmation of the vaunted thought of Mao Tse-tung. The vehement proselyting for the thought of Mao Tse-tung, both domestic and foreign, spawned by the Great Leap failures of 1959 is chronicled and documented in Part II of this book. Throughout this examination, the persistence of the doctrinal prediction of the success of Mao's Three Red Banners is also evident. In reviewing the evidence for the persistence of this prediction, one finds examples in every year following the failure of 1959. In addition to Mao Tse-tung, the major purveyors of the prediction were among Lin Piao's PLA.

At the Lushan plenum in 1959, Mao himself began the proselyting for the people's communes and the Great Leap Forward. His letter of August 1 to Wang Chia-hsiang provides just one example of his persistent prediction, in his statement that "later I will write some articles proselyting in favor of the people's communes."[11] As a result of the extraordinary enlarged meeting of the Military Affairs Commission of September-October 1960, proselyting for the imminent success of Mao's Three Red Banners was picked up by the PLA and spread through its ranks in 1960 and 1961. In the month following the meeting, it was stated that PLA policy in political education was first of all, "while affirming the great victory of the Three Red Banners and making known our promising situation, explain clearly the present difficulties and stimulate the courage of the masses to struggle against difficulties."[12] The same point was carried over as PLA policy for 1961.[13]

In 1962, as a result of Mao's appearance at the tenth plenum in September, the prediction was promoted, at least perfunctorily, as party policy. In the twelve-article document on strengthening the collective economy of the people's communes adopted by the central committee on September 27, which designated agriculture as the foundation of the national economy, Mao Tse-tung's ideas on the collectivization of agriculture were quoted at length, and the success of his Three Red Banners was reasserted.[14] In this secret party document prepared for distribution to the communes, it was asserted that "the people's communes are on the road to healthy expansion."[15] However, in the same document, the small production team was designated as the basic unit of accounting and control and numerous private sidelines were explicitly permitted for the peasantry. Thus, while the communes were championed as an ideal by the central committee, in practice the emasculation of Mao's great collective was formally acknowledged. Nevertheless, the party architects of the resolution felt compelled to conclude it with the following general endorsement of Mao's Three Red Banners:

> Let all the party comrades, peasants, workers, intellectuals, patriots, and nationalities of the nation unite and under the leadership of Chairman Mao and the Central Committee, raise high the three red banners of the Party's general line of socialist construction, the Great Leap Forward, and the people's communes and, following the Party's line of socialist construction, struggle to fulfill completely these historically significant decisions.[16]

In the regulations drawn up by the conference on political work in the armed forces held in February 1963, Mao's Three Red Banners of the party's general line, the Great Leap Forward, and the commune system for socialist construction were explicitly listed among the central tenets to be upheld in the political work of the PLA.[17] In the epistemological introduction to the early ten articles on the conduct of the socialist education campaign drawn up under Mao's supervision in May 1963, oblique reference is made to a revival of the Great Leap Forward with the statement that

> a test in actual practice is tantamount to another "leap forward of one's cognition. The leap forward at this juncture bears greater significance than the previous one. Because only through this second leap forward can a corroboration be found for the leap forward of the first time.[18]

As shown in Chapter 8, in May and June of 1964 Mao personally complained that there were only three truly self-reliant communes in China and recommend that the spirit of Tachai and self-reliance be adopted in the third five year plan.[19] In the fall of 1965, Mao undoubtedly pressed his Great Leap ideals at the September working conference of the central committee and the PLA began to tout the communistic Tachai production brigade of Shansi province as a unit worthy of full emulation by the peasantry.

In 1966, Chiang Ch'ing's summary of the February Conference on Art and Literature in the PLA reasserted the "Great Leap Forward on all fronts of socialist construction" as an ideal to be upheld in educational work.[20] On May 7, Mao issued his nearly nostalgic directive to Lin Piao urging that:

> Commune peasants, although working primarily on the farms, should study military affairs, politics, and culture. And when conditions permit, they should also operate some small size factories through collective efforts and criticize and repudiate the bourgeoisie.[21]

Following the eleventh plenum in August, promises of a "new Great Leap Forward" on the production front became a major topic of successive New Year's editorials in the nation's leading media.

The actual reimplementation of the Great Leap ideals in the economy was retarded by two factors, both of which were removed by the Cultural Revolution in 1967. The political opposition afforded by the party bureaucrats since the Great Leap failures was removed by the purgings which occurred at the eleventh plenum and during the ensuing inquisition. The economic instability of the nation was more gradually removed. Industrial production steadily improved from the post-Great Leap lows of 1961 and 1962 to a level in 1966 that was some 60-70 percent greater than the 1957 level. During the turmoil of 1967, production dipped to 135-155 percent of the 1957 base, but in 1968 recovered again to 148-166 percent.[22] The more crucial indicator of economic stability for the nation, grain production, fluctuated following the near-famine lows of 1961 and 1962. But bumper harvests of 190 million metric tons were achieved in 1964 and, more importantly, in 1967.[23] By 1968, both political and economic conditions were propitious for a serious attempt to reimplement Great Leap practices in the economy.

By the second half of 1968, the Cultural Revolution was extended into the countryside and with it came a number of Maoist reforms which were strikingly reminiscent of Great Leap days: The introduction of a more egalitarian wage system; the enlargement of the collectives; and the reduction of private plots.[24] The prevalent slogan at the time called for a "new Leap Forward" in production.

Under the accelerated campaign to emulate Tachai, the peasants' share of collective income was no longer to depend solely on work points for performance in production but political participation as acclaimed by other commune members was added as an important criterion. Under this sytem, there was a narrowing of income differentials through simplification of work accounting procedures and greater "mass democracy." At the extreme, steps were taken to eliminate the work-point system entirely and replace it with the "free supply" system that was employed briefly during the Great Leap, which provided for a larger portion of income to be paid in food, clothing, and other necessities, while a smaller portion was paid in cash wages.

In addition to the renewed emphasis placed on political participation and ideological purity as determinants of the peasants' wage, the accelerated campaign to "emulate the Tachai production brigade" also served to refocus attention upon the production brigade as opposed to the smaller production team as the principal unit of the commune. On November 14, 1968, *People's Daily* carried a signal article placing new emphasis on the brigade as a unit which was to "engage in agriculture, forestry, livestock breeding, side-line occupations and fisheries and should also have its own Party organization, government administration, and cultural work."[25] Since 1967, the PLA had assisted with agricultural production and the organization of Mao study in the countryside; now they took the lead in reinvigorating Mao's communes in the move to amalgamate different units to recompose larger teams, brigades, and communes. Under the aegis of Liu Shao-ch'i, the 24,000 robust communes of 1958 had dwindled in size to some 74,000 miniatures of 1964.[26] Now Mao was quoted as saying, "Scattered individual agriculture and handicrafts . . . can and must be led prudently, step by step and yet actively to develop toward modernization and collectivization. The view that they may be left to take their own course is wrong."[27]

The steps actually taken at this time to reinvigorate the communes included the relocation and development under commune control of schools, health centers, stores, and tractor stations.[28] Simultaneously, the Great Leap practice of paring the size of central government bureaucracy was again put into practice. The emulation model for introducing commune-run stores appeared in *People's Daily* in mid-January 1969. It was reported that Anchiapao commune had experienced bad management of scattered shops in which "bad elements" had sneaked into control and engaged in pilfering and corruption. To correct the situation, the poor and lower-middle peasants had set up a supply and marketing center at the commune level and in the production brigades, while the appropriate revolutionary committees set up management groups to run them.[29] Shortly thereafter, the system of commune-run stores spread to other communes. On August 25, 1968, Mao issued instructions that urban education should be put under the supervision of the workers; in the countryside education should be controlled by the poor and lower-middle peasants. Accordingly, it was suggested in *People's Daily* on November 14 that in the countryside, primary education should be the responsibility of the production brigade and the government should reduce its allocation of funds to the schools. The system of production brigade-run schools spread across the countryside in 1969 with teachers now receiving work points like any other commune member instead of salaries, and with students having flexible classroom hours to allow them to participate part time in collective labor. On December 5, *People's Daily* announced that even the "country doctors" were to be transferred to the work-point system in the communes, as health-care clinics were established around the countryside to provide low-cost coverage ($.50 per year in Loyuang commune in Hupeh province) for peasants.[30] The only question was whether the new medical care system was better run by the brigade or the commune. Finally, the communes again took on the task of basic-level industrialization. On September 8, the Peking journal *Agricultural Machinery Technique* published an account of the dispute between Mao and Liu over the timing and extent of agricultural mechanization, with Liu allegedly pressing for concentration on small farm tools and quality in agricultural work. Shortly thereafter, the press reported numerous cases where the state-run tractor stations had handed over their machinery to the communes. The tractor men together with the rest of the commune members were now to receive work points instead of wages. One radio report about a Kiangsu commune stated that the commune industry was turning out more than thirty different products while workers on the commune were rotated between factory labor and farm production.[31]

On February 4, 1969, Shanghai *Wen Hui Pao* commented that communes should turn their members into part-time peasants and part-time workers to accomplish both rural mechanization and eliminate the differences between workers and peasants.[32] The proletarianization of society first attempted in the Great Leap of 1958, and again advocated in radicalized form by Mao's May 7 directive to Lin Piao eight years later, was again being implemented. The era of the omnicompetent workers was at hand again.

Although by 1969, the basic accounting level had not yet been shifted up to the brigade or the commune, the foregoing account of rural recollectivization activities shows clear signs of the intent. Other Great Leap rumblings were also evident at the time, including massive *Hsia Fang* movements of urban dwellers to the countryside, and these continued throughout 1969.[33] However, clear signs of prudence are also evident in the attempt to resurrect the communes, especially with regard to the elimination of private plots and the reestablishment of public mess halls. During 1968 and 1969, scattered reports of a gradual reduction in the acreage of private plots were forthcoming from some of the provinces. One observer has compiled a list of the following seven provinces where such reduction had occurred in some counties by the end of 1968: Hunan, Kiangsu, Heilungkiang, Fukien, Peking, Shanghai, and Kwangtung.[34] A more prevalent phenomenon was the confiscation of formerly barren land earlier reclaimed by private peasants under the promise of private ownership. Relying on the reports of refugees and letters from Kwangtung province, the same observer found evidence for the confiscation of reclaimed land by the collective in the Kwangtung counties of Haifeng, Kaiping, Hsinhsi, and Huiyang, and in the counties of Chiungtung, Chiunghai, Chiungshan, and Lingshui on Hainan Island in addition to Fuching county of Fukien province.[35] Furthermore, this same type of source asserts that public mess halls had been formally restored in Kwangtung in the rural communes of Chiunghai, Chiungtung, and Chiungshan counties of Hainan Island since October 1968. There, as years earlier, individual peasants no longer received any supply of rations and were not permitted to cook in their own kitchens. Later in 1968, similar reports of the appearance of public mess halls came from communes in Wenchang, Huiyang, Taishan, Haifeng, and Kaiping counties.[36] At least in some areas, Mao's Lushan plea in defense of the mess halls was at last being heeded—nine years later.

In 1968, Mao's commune idea introduced a decade earlier was being resurrected following revolutionary tumult and amidst radical shouting of a "new Leap Forward." The new leader of communization was not the party apparatus but the PLA through the instrumentality of the Mao Tse-tung thought propaganda team.[37]

However, the actual reimplementation was proceeding with prudence with poor and lower-middle peasants in charge. In the new commune, agents of the "Archtraitor and renegade" Liu Shao-ch'i, the rich peasants and commandistic cadres, were condemned as "bad factors," sacrificial victims of the accelerated class struggle in the countryside.

Polarization of Cadres: Reds and Experts

In the GPCR the party cadres were cleaved as never before along the lines of commitment to Mao's thought. The non-Maoists were struggled as discernible Maoists ascended to leadership. The basic tenet of political leadership in the thought of Mao Tse-tung is the mass line principle. It is antithetical to bureaucratic rule, asserting that correct political leadership is implemented by cadres who apply general ideological principles to the specific local problems and ideas of the masses. It implies close contact between leaders and followers. During the post-Lushan search for ideological confirmation, Maoist calls to correctly implement the mass line served to allay ideological dissonance in two ways. First of all, by assigning responsibility for Great Leap failures to poor implementation by middle-level cadres, the basic Maoist principles underlying the design of the movement remained sacrosanct. Hence, reassertion of the validity and importance of the mass line principle was crucial to the Maoists in the wake of Great Leap disasters for this tenet, like the tenet on the continuation of the class struggle, provided an ideological rationale for the failures. Second, reassertion of the mass line principle was tantamount to ideological legitimation of ideological proselyting. If the Great Leap failures were partially a result of incorrect implementation of the mass line, then correct implementation of the mass line was called for. But improved implementation of the mass line also implied greater contact between cadres and masses which itself provides greater opportunity to spread the ideology, the thought of Mao Tse-tung, to the masses and to unite it with the ideas of the masses. The latter is equivalent to increased Maoist proselyting. Thus, because of the search for ideological confirmation brought about by the Great Leap failures, one would expect a great upsurge in calls to party cadres to implement the mass line. In the course of the GPCR, the massive party structure was shaken to its foundations in this effort.

As we have recounted in Part II of this book, repeated calls were made by the Maoists for "mobilization of the masses" and correct implementation of the mass line during the 1960s, but Mao's mass line was not necessarily the party line. In their fervent attempts to reduce the dissonance between their knowledge of the Great Leap debacles and their unyielding belief that the Great Leap would move China closer to true communism, the Maoists immediately sought social support for the thought of Mao Tse-tung. In maintaining their faith in the Great Leap promise, the Maoists were increasingly forced to go beyond the conventional conveyors of the mass line, the party cadres, to other more receptive segments of Chinese society in this search for ideological supporters. Beginning with a small nucleus of faithful in the fall of 1959, Mao, Ch'en Po-ta and Lin Piao strove to increase the number of Maoists. The criterion for membership in the Maoist movement remained the same throughout the course of the movement: ardent belief in the thought of Mao Tse-tung as demonstrated by words and deeds. Those social segments predisposed to yield members who would number themselves among the believers came from several sources: from the PLA by virtue of the Yenan tradition still lingering in the military; from China's "proletariat" by virtue of the relative social gains they stood to acquire according to Maoist egalitarianism. Beginning immediately on the heels of the failure in the fall of 1959, the nucleus of convinced and committed Maoists proselyted the PLA and successfully converted many members into believing carriers of TMTT. Following the tenth plenum, during 1963, the converted members of the PLA became themselves proselyters for TMTT among the civilian youth. The emulate Lei Feng campaign was a prime example of this. After the promulgation of the "later ten articles" on the Socialist Education Campaign, Mao turned more decisively to the PLA in 1964 and dubbed it the model for and prime proselyter of the entire Chinese society. The learn from the PLA campaign was a prime example of this. In addition, 1964 saw Mao's dispatch of hundreds of thousands of previously indoctrinated members of the PLA to civilian positions in the lower bureaucracy. After the promulgation of the twenty-three articles, the battle lines hardened in 1965, and two sides regrouped their forces. Arrayed on one side were the augmented ranks of Maoists, Chairman Mao, the PLA, and revolutionary youth; arrayed on the other side the establishment pragmatists, Liu Shao-ch'i, the bulk of the party bureaucracy, and most intellectuals. In their midst stood the uncommitted cadres and masses. After Mao's May 7 directive to the PLA in 1966, the PLA-converted youth became themselves proselyters for TMTT in society and, upon donning Red Guard gear, vigorous fighters of high-level anti-Maoists. With social violence threatening, the PLA stepped more forcefully into the civil fray. As the party establishment quaked, the Maoists secured new access to means of mass communication: Red Guards were permitted to publish freely millions of large character posters and copies of tabloid newspapers; leading Maoists gained unrestricted access to the centralized party media of mass communication. Subsequently, proselyting for TMTT poured forth in incredible volume as the new conveyers of Mao's mass line merged with the masses, and the Maoists assumed the ascendancy. During the Cultural Revolution the ultimate incarnation of Mao's mass line principle made a brief appearance. Together with the resurrection of the people's commune for rural production came the Chinese reincarnation of the Paris Commune for political leadership.

REVIVAL OF THE PARIS COMMUNE

The Shanghai people's commune was established by the forces of Maoism on February 5, 1967. The following day, the Shanghai *Wen Hui Pao* carried the inaugural announcement:

In a voice that broke the silence of the sky, the voice of a giant, the rally solemnly declared to the whole of China and the whole world:

the former Shanghai Municipal Party Committee and former Municipal People's Council have been smashed by the proletarian revolutionaries!

The rally solemnly announced: All power belongs to the Shanghai People's Commune!

The Shanghai People's Commune is a local state organ established under the guidance of the thought of Mao Tse-tung, under the condition of proletarian dictatorship, and after power has been seized from bottom upward from the power holders within the Party who took the capitalist road. It is a new organizational form of the proletarian dictatorship.

The Shanghai People's Commune was formed under the joint sponsorship of the Shanghai Worker's Revolutionary Rebel General Headquarters, the Preparatory Committee for the Shanghai Peasants' Revolutionary Rebel Headquarters, the PLA units stationed in Shanghai, and other rebel groups of revolutionary workers, revolutionary students, and revolutionary cadres.

Thus the new Shanghai commune was established by revolutionary mass organizations and the revolutionized PLA. It was to supplant the traditional party and government organs of political leadership. "Under the guidance of the thought of Mao Tse-tung," it was to practice "the most extensive democracy over the proletariat" and to impose "the most ruthless proletarian dictatorship on the class enemies." Its leading members were "elected by the revolutionary masses according to the principles of the Paris Commune." It was the ultimate institutionalized expression of the mass line principle. To the initially enthralled Mao Tse-tung the newly established commune permitted a glimpse of a utopian communist China in which the Communist party had withered away:

With the Commune inaugurated, do we still need the Party? I think we need it because we must have a hard core, whether it is called the Communist Party or a social democratic party.[38]

ESTABLISHMENT OF REVOLUTIONARY COMMITTEES

Much to Mao's chagrin, the hastily constructed ultrademocratic form of the Paris Commune tended toward anarchism in the revolutionary takeover and the political commune ideal was aborted shortly after the establishment of the Shanghai people's commune. The new form that was substituted was the revolutionary committee. This provisional organ of power was based upon a "revolutionary three-in-one combination" of representatives of the People's Liberation Army, of "revolutionary party cadres," (those adjudged loyal to Mao) and of the "revolutionary masses" (new leaders from the ranks of the Red Guards and Red Rebels).[39] The formation of such revolutionary committees was a complex and drawn-out process encompassing some twenty months of turmoil beginning with the formation of the first revolutionary committee in January 1967.

The organizational implementation of this weeding out of nonrevolutionaries from the party-government was not to be conducted by appointment and dismissal from higher levels in the bureaucracies as is the normal case. Such appointment and dismissal was conducted by mass organizations from below. It was to be conducted by youth organized as Red Guards and Red Rebels.[40] Perhaps it was also intended to be conducted by peasants organized into poor and lower-middle peasants associations. The generic term for these revolutionary mass organizations established for the reform or replacement of bourgeois authorities by Maoist progressives was "Cultural Revolution group." Such groups were first established in schools and universities and then in government institutions at the various territorial levels. Finally, the groups were established in the basic production units of society: factories, mines, business enterprises, urban districts, and villages.[41] Thus, the network of Cultural Revolution groups, committees, and the congresses constituted a parallel organization which infiltrated the conventional party-government hierarchy of regimentation of Chinese society. As such, the network was used by the top-level Maoist leadership to reform and replace the incumbents of the conventional hierarchy. The representatives of the bourgeoisie were replaced by the representatives of the proletariat through the instrumentality of the Cultural Revolution groups. Thus the middle-level cadres were polarized into two sets: those who supported the thought of Mao Tsetung, were active in the Cultural Revolution, and represented the proletariat, and those who did not. Technical expertise carried little weight as legitimization for holding government authority.[42]

The Cultural Revolution groups were backed up in their reform and replacement efforts by a previously reformed organization occupying a parallel position to the party-government hierarchies, namely Lin Piao's People's Liberation Army and the reinvigorated people's militia.[43] The top-level guidance for the People's Liberation Army and the newly formed revolutionary mass organizations was the top Cultural Revolution group of the CCP central committee.[44] The leading nucleus of the seventeen members of this group were all convinced and committed Maoists.[45] The head of the group was Ch'en Po-ta and the first deputy head was Chiang Ch'ing. T'ao Chu and K'ang Sheng were third and fourth as advisers.[46] The remaining thirteen members were most of the editors of *Red Flag*, people related to the People's Liberation Army, and secretaries of various regional bureaus of the CCP central committee. By late 1968, only Ch'en Po-ta, Chiang Ch'ing, K'ang Sheng, Chang Ch'un-ch'iao and Yao Wen-yuan survived in the group.

The timetable for the formation of Revolutionary Committees covered a period of twenty months, from January 1967 to September 1968.[47] In the tumultuous interim, the PLA gained predominance in the new provincial governments. When the process was completed, new revolutionary committees had been established in all twenty-one provinces, three municipalities (under direct control of the central authorities), and five autonomous regions supplating the power of the former party and government organizations. Seventy-six percent of the chairmen of the twenty-nine new revolutionary committees were military commanders or military commissars. Only seven civilian party secretaries remained as chairmen of revolutionary committees.

Once the revolutionized PLA had gained predominance in the provincial organs of power, they set about the tasks of consolidating their positions and implementing the Maoist program. With more faithful dispensers of Mao's mass line in positions of middle-level leadership, three tasks devolved to the new incumbents: carry through the class struggle; consolidate the new organizational forms; spread the thought of Mao Tse-tung. These tasks were summed up by the phrase "struggle-criticisms-transformation" which was to transpire at the level of government and in the basic working units of society. According to the instructions of Chairman Mao,

> The struggle-criticism-transformation in a factory, on the whole, goes through the following stages: establishing a revolutionary committee of the three-in-one combination, mass criticism and repudiation, purifying the class ranks, rectifying the Party organization, simplifying organizational structure, changing unreasonable rules and regulations and sending people who work in offices to grass-roots levels.[48]

Under the aegis of the new revolutionary committees, mass study of the thought of Mao Tse-tung took on new impetus. An intensive investigation of one province, Kwangtung, showed that basic-level groups formed for the study of Mao's works provided the embryonic structures of the new style political organization for the provinces.[49] In Kwangtung as elsewhere the leading positions in the revolutionary committees were occupied by the PLA. The provincial revolutionary committee was responsible for guiding all political, economic, and cultural activities in the province. Over time, the new provincial preparatory revolutionary committee selected municipal, special district, and county revolutionary committees to govern at the local levels. Within Canton, the municipal revolutionary committee in turn selected leading personnel from various schools, factories, commercial enterprises, and government units to constitute the revolutionary committees within their special sectors. Each of these committees reviewed their personnel, retaining thosecadres judged loyal to the Maoist leadership and adding the most promising young revolutionaries from the former Red Guards and other revolutionary mass organizations. Once the personnel were screened for loyalty, they were organized into study groups at all levels. One of the major topics of study was, of course, the thought of Mao Tse-tung.

According to correct mass line practice, the new middle-level leadership kept in contact with the revolutionary vanguard leadership at the top, in addition to the masses at the bottom. In October 1967, after 80 top cadres returned from study in Peking, several hundred leading cadres were organized locally for study in preparation for assuming their new provincial and municipal positions.[50] In December, several hundred more cadres were selected to go to Peking for special study. For those working at the basic levels, study classes were organized under responsible persons in the PLA. Finally, on February 21, 1968, the preparatory committees were replaced by the provisional but more permanent Kwangtung provincial revolutionary committee and the Canton Municipal revolutionary committee. With the revolutionary Maoist leadership ensconced at the middle levels, the mass line dictated reestablishment of close contact with the masses. In a parallel effort, the masses were organized by the developing revolutionary leadership into Mao Tse-tung thought study classes. By the beginning of February 1968, 3,300,000 people in Kwangtung were organized into 23,000 Mao Tse-tung thought study classes.[51] The classes were larger than the conventional "study groups," averaging some 140 persons, but at this early data they included 8 percent of the total Kwangtung population, adults and children alike.

Despite the importance of the revolutionary committees, at all times during the Cultural Revolution, the ever-deepening proselyting for the thought of Mao Tse-tung was orchestrated by Lin Piao and the PLA.[52] Shortly after in the eleventh plenum, on December 17, 1966, all Peking newspapers had carried on their front pages the foreword by Lin Piao to the second edition of *Quotations from Chairman Mao*. Early in the Cultural Revolution, Lin Piao's PLA led youth as the vanguard in Maoist proselyting. On December 19, for example, Lin's right-hand man in the PLA political department Hsiao Hua spoke at the Peking worker's stadium on behalf of Lin, Chiang Ch'ing, Ch'en Po-ta, and Chou En-lai to representatives of 100,000 PLA officers and men who were mainly responsible for receiving 11 million revolutionary students and teachers attending Red Guard rallies in the previous few months in Peking. Almost one year later, when Maoist proselyting was institutionalized in the nationwide campaign to form Mao Tse-tung thought study classes, it was Lin Piao and the PLA who kicked off the campaign in November 1967. On November 6, at a Peking rally commemorating the fiftieth anniversary of the October revolution, Lin Piao heralded Mao's ideological achievements in his speech. Just one week later, Mao. Lin Piao and other party leaders received delegates attending the meeting of representatives of "activists in the study of Mao Tse-tung's works" in the PLA air force units stationed in Peking and other Maoist military men.

The following day, Mao and Lin Piao received PLA cadres, representatives of mass organizations who were attending Mao Tse-tune thought study classes in Peking, local cadres from other provinces and municipalities attending the study classes in Peking, and returned Chinese diplomatic personnel from Indonesia and Burma. At the end of the month, November 29, Lin Piao wrote an inscription for the first congress of activists in the study of Mao Tse-tung's works in the naval forces: "Sailing the seas depends on the helmsman, making revolution depends on Mao Tse-tung's Thoughts." The nationwide campaign for organizing Mao Tse-tung thought study classes was under way.

During 1968, Mao Tse-tung thought study classes sprouted in provinces aroung the mainland as new PLA-dominated revolutionary committees took charge and their task of Maoist proselyting became institutionalized.[53] Nearly 100 percent of the population in Kansu and Ninghsia were reported as enrolled in such classes by October of 1968. At the end of November, 96 percent of the population of the Kiangsi population was enrolled. By July, 34 percent of those in Anhwei were enrolled into classes averaging 40 persons each. By May, 30 percent of Szechuan and by April, 28 percent of Liaoning had enrolled in the classes. By February in Honan and by December in Hunan, 8 percent of the population was enrolled. In addition, several million were reported to have enrolled in the provinces of Hupei and Shensi during the year. Increasingly during 1968, the new middle-level leadership made the mass line Mao's Line. By April, the Maoist leadership in Kwangsi province had distributed one copy of the little red book and one copy of the *Three Good Old Articles* to every poor and lower-middle peasant family, totaling some 6,300,000 copies of each.[54] In addition, every production team in the province had a copy of *The Selected Works of Mao Tse-tung*. Similarly, Anhwei, Heilungkiang, and Yunnan also reported distribution of one copy of the little red book and one copy of the *Three Good Old Articles* for every poor and lower-middle peasant family in each province. Chinghai reported distributing 6,000,000 copies of Mao's writings including Mao's quotations, three articles, and selected works. Honan distributed one copy of the little red book for every poor and lower-middle peasant family, totaling some 8,000,000 copies in all; and Hupei distributed 23,000,000 copies of the little red book. By 1968, provincial competition had developed under the new leadership over the extensive distribution of Mao's writings.

On August 5, 1968, the task of proselyting for the thought of Mao Tse-tung took a new twist as the proletariat, previously proselyted by the PLA, became themselves proselyters just as had happened to youth before them. On this day, PLA members and workers from all over China hailed Mao Tse-tung's gift of mangoes to the worker-peasant Mao Tse-tung's thought propaganda team in the capital. As usual, predominant in the leadership of these new teams of Mao proselyters were PLA political soldiers. This phase of "struggle-criticism-transformation" in the Cultural Revolution was at least partially led by the proletariat.

At the national level, there was no shortage in the publication of Mao's writings for the newly organized distribution and study in the provinces. On January 3, 1969, *People's Daily* summarized the achievements of the new leadership in publishing Mao's writings during the Cultural Revolution from 1966 through 1968. During this period, 150 million copies of *Selected Works of Mao Tse-tung* were printed. This was more than thirteen and a half times the total production of this work in the fifteen years before the Cultural Revolution. In the same period, China printed 140 million copies of *Selected Readings of Mao Tse-tung's Works,* 740 million copies of *Quotations from Chairman Mao,* 96 million copies of Poems by Mao Tse-tung and nearly 2 billion copies of other writings of Mao. Furthermore, it was reported that before the Cultural Revolution, only thirteen printing plants in seven provinces and municipalities printed Mao's works. After the Cultural Revolution, more than 300 printing plants in all provinces, municipalities and autonomous regions except Tibet were printing Mao's works. Besides materials for newly regimented Maoist proselyting, the captive press of China printed little else during the Great Proletarian Cultural Revolution.

Polarization of the Politburo: Maoists and Anti-Maoists

During the GPCR, the politburo was split along lines of commitment to Mao's thought. The committed ascended, and the uncommitted were purged in the greatest political reshuffling since Mao came to power at Yenan. In the wake of the Great Leap debacles and pursuant upon the liberal recovery policies instituted by the stand-in party leadership, it became increasingly important to the Maoists that China be put back on the proletarian road to progress. While it was important in the Maoist proselyting effort that the cadres and the masses know, apply, and support Maoist dialectics, it was particularly important that the top-level political leadership be facile with these dialectics to ensure that China did not move in directions inconsistent with those specified by Maoist ideology.

Thus, a major task of the Great Proletarian Cultural Revolution was to remove "the leading figures in authority who are taking the capitalist road" and to replace them with convinced Maoists. Just as the bourgeoisie was seen to have its representatives in the bureaucracy among the intellectuals and middle-level cadres, the bourgeoisie and its cadre representatives were seen as having leaders in the top echelon of political power in Communist China, the politburo. Essentially, the representatives of the bourgeoisie within the politburo were those members who became increasingly alienated by persistent Maoist proselyting efforts initiated in the wake of the Great Leap failure. In Part I, we presented evidence of early Great Leap opposition in the politburo stemming from Liu Shao-ch'i, Teng Hsiao-p'ing, P'eng Teh-huai, Ch'en Yun, and P'eng Chen.

In Part II of this book we presented documentary evidence of the activities of some politburo members which served to increase Mao's dissonance over the Great Leap debacles. Following P'eng Teh-huai's criticism of Mao's Great Leap program at Lushan in the fall of 1959, a number of politburo members fell out of step with Mao. They did *not* believe as he that the Great Leap Forward would bring true communism to China; and consequently, they did *not* share with him a desire to proselyte for the thought of Mao Tse-tung or the exculpating class struggle rationalization in the face of the Great Leap debacles. As a result they increasingly through the sixties engaged in activities that served to increase Mao's dissonance, and refrained from activities that would reduce it, making it more difficult for Mao to continue to believe that they were still his close comrades in communism. Those comrades who openly or obliquely disparaged Mao's belief in the Great Leap certainly fell into this category. Moreover, under the extreme pressures of the time, those comrades who failed to give positive support to Mao's belief or to TMTT or who failed to criticize the critics of same, were also perceived by Mao as unbelievers. Since Mao so badly needed social support, they were perceived as witting or unwitting enemies of his thought and true communism. By the fall of 1966, politburo polarization had risen to such an extent that excommunication was inevitable.

ELEVENTH PLENUN TOPSY-TURVY

An important event occurred at the meeting of the eleventh plenum of the eight central committee in August of 1966. At this plenum there occurred the greatest shake-up in the politburo since the liberation. Those members of the politburo who had initially been for the Great Leap movement were advanced in position; whereas those members who had initially been against the movement were demoted in position! If we consider the top fourteen members the politburo elected at the eight party congress, this phenomenon is apparent.[55] An important subset of the politburo elite are those eleven members who were elected to the standing committee of the politburo at the eleventh plenum. Of these top eleven members of the reconstituted politburo, all except two held positions on the Great Leap movement that are well known.[56] Of the nine remaining members of the politburo standing committee, two received demotions in rank in the politburo, namely Liu Shao-ch'i and Ch'en Yun. Both of these political figures have been shown to have opposed Mao's Great Leap policy. Of the seven remaining members who received promotions or retained their post-1958 ranking, only one, Teng Hsiao-p'ing, secretary general of the central committee, was opposed to the Great Leap policy; and one, T'ao Chu, was ambiguous in his position. The evidence for the residual five indicates that four were active proponents of Mao's Great Leap. These five rising proponents of Maoist Great Leap policies in order of their ranking in the politburo after the eleventh plenum were as follows: Mao Tse-tung, who retained his number one ranking; Lin Piao, who moved from sixth rank at the 1958 party congress to second; Ch'en Po-ta, who moved from twenty-fourth to fifth; K'ang Sheng, who moved from twenty-fifth to seventh. Li Fu-ch'un, who was not so strongly committed, only moved from thirteenth to tenth. In addition, there are two high-ranking members of the politburo of 1958 who were purged before the eleventh plenum, and both were opponents of Mao's Great Leap: P'eng Teh-huai was purged in 1959; P'eng Chen was purged in 1966. The anomalous rise of the bureaucrat, Teng Hsiao-p'ing, and the soaring ascent of the Mao syncophant, T'ao Chu, were corrected with the Red Guard purge of both: After the November 25, 1966 Red Guard rally, neither was seen at a rally or reception during the rest of the Cultural Revolution. Clearly, the foregoing analysis of changes in the politburo elite between 1958 and 1966 constitutes strong evidence for the assertion that a member's early attitude toward Mao's Great Leap Forward was the major factor in determining changes in rank in the great shake-up in the politburo at the eleventh plenum of 1966. The purges of P'eng Chen and Lu Ting-yi earlier in 1966 support this assertion. Between 1958 and 1966, the politburo was increasingly polarized around Mao's Great Leap policy and its consequences.

NINTH PARTY CONGRESS GAINS

Some twenty-eight months of Cultural Revolution later, at the ninth party congress, polarization of the politburo was completed as the resurgent cult of Yenan completely displaced the clique of pragmatic party bureaucrats. On April 28, 1969, Mao Tse-tung was reelected chairman of the central committee and Lin Piao was elected as the sole vice-chairman and designated in the new party constitution as "Comrade Mao Tse-tungs' close comrade in arms and successor."[5][7] The important standing committee of the politburo was reduced to five men and the unegalitarian practice of rank-ordering members according to standing within the bodies was eliminated by listing members' names according to the number of strokes in their surnames. The new members were Mao Tse-tung and Lin Piao, Ch'en Po-ta, Chou En-lai, and K'ang Sheng. With the sole exception of Chou En-lai, all the members of the new standing committee were members of Mao's Yenan coterie of the early 1940s when he originally codified his dialectics in the guerrilla base area. Furthermore, as shown in Figure 11.2 the new twenty-five member

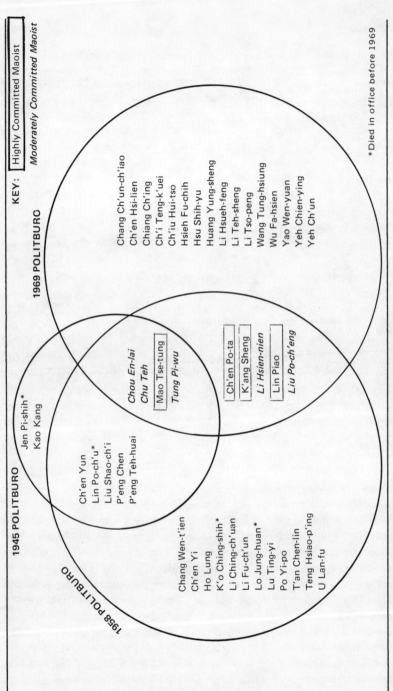

KEY: Highly Committed Maoist

Moderately Committed Maoist

* Died in office before 1969

1969 POLITBURO

Chang Ch'un-ch'iao
Ch'en Hsi-lien
Chiang Ch'ing
Ch'i Teng-k'uei
Ch'iu Hui-tso
Hsieh Fu-chih
Hsu Shih-yu
Huang Yung-sheng
Li Hsueh-feng
Li Teh-sheng
Li Tso-peng
Wang Tung-hsiung
Wu Fa-hsien
Yao Wen-yuan
Yeh Chien-ying
Yeh Ch'un

1945 POLITBURO

Jen Pi-shih*
Kao Kang

Ch'en Yun
Lin Po-ch'u*
Liu Shao-ch'i
P'eng Chen
P'eng Teh-huai

Chou En-lai
Chu Teh
Mao Tse-tung
Tung Pi-wu

Ch'en Po-ta
K'ang Sheng
Li Hsien-nien
Lin Piao
Liu Po-ch'eng

1958 POLITBURO

Chang Wen-t'ien
Ch'en Yi
Ho Lung
K'o Ching-shih*
Li Ching-ch'uan
Li Fu-ch'un
Lo Jung-huan*
Lu Ting-yi
Po Yi-po
T'an Chen-lin
Teng Hsiao-p'ing
U Lan-fu

Figure 11.2: SURVIVAL OF COMMITTED MAOISTS IN POLITBURO, 1945-1969

politburo included both Mao's wife and Lin Piao's wife. Added to the club of guerrilla warriors were members of the revolutionized PLA: twelve of the twenty-five held their primary roles in the PLA. Never since the liberation had the politburo been so dominated by guerrilla warriors. Many of these had been closely associated with Lin Piao and his fourth field army over the years; some survived Red Guard attack by bowing to Mao's call for "self-criticism" and undergoing protracted sessions of "Mao study"; all played key political roles in the Cultural Revolution.[58] Never since the seventh party congress at Yenan had so many politburo members been purged: Only 10 percent between 1945 and 1958 compared to 60 percent between 1958 and 1969.

Indeed, as shown in Appendix A1 and illustrated in Figure 11.2, nearly all the members of the politburo elected or reelected by the eighth party congress in 1956 or 1958 who were not above the group median in action commitments to Mao's thought were purged from the politburo elected at the ninth party congress in 1969. The sole surviving exception was the administrator Li Hsien-nien who stood right at the group median. Purged were the number one and two "capitalist roaders," Liu Shao-ch'i and Teng Hsiao-p'ing. Gone were Mao's vociferous assailants at the Lushan plenum, P'eng Teh-huai and Chang Wen-t'ien. Gone were the conservative economic advisor, Ch'en Yun, and his cohorts in industry and agriculture, Po Yi-po and T'an Chen-lin. Gone were the recalcitrant mayor of Peking, P'eng Chen and the reluctant propaganda chief, Lu Ting-yi. Purged also were the middle roaders, Ch'en Yi, Ho Lung, Li Ching-ch'uan, Li Fu-ch'un, and U Lan-fu. In sum, every member of the former politburo who had not been extraordinarily active in prose-lyting for Mao's thought in the wake of the Great Leap failures was purged.

The enlarged central committee elected at the congress showed signs of a conscious effort to apply the "three-way alliance" principle underlying the revolutionary committee structure at the lower levels. Employing a criterion of primary association, the 279 full and alternate members of the new central committee was composed of: representative of the PLA, about 40 percent; representatives of "revolutionary cadres," about 30 percent; and representatives of the "revolutionary masses," about 30 percent.[59] In addition to PLA predominance, well over half of the members were regional representatives from the civilian provinces or military regions. In terms of personnel, China's new leadership was unquestionably more Maoist than ever. Whereas Stalin's great purges of the 1930s following the failures of collectivization had elevated the technical intelligentsia and banished the old revolutionary ideologues, Mao's Cultural Revolution of the 1960s had reasserted class struggle, elevated the revolutionary ideologues and demoted those supporting the technical intelligentsia! But then, the Soviet Union had neither a Mao Tsetung, a cult of Yenan, nor a dialectically reasoned Great Leap Forward. In Communist China, dialectics were on the rise—again.

The Great Proletarian Cultural Revolution did, indeed, result in the greatest purge of party leadership in the history of the CCP: 63 percent of the members of the pre-Great Leap eighth central committee were not reelected to the ninth.[60] However, this purge bore little resemblance in either style or content to Stalin's purges of the 1930s, for its most fundamental characteristic was the radicalized reimposition of revolutionary Maoist dialectics upon the Chinese party leadership and society. Stalin's purges had decimated the old revoluitonary Bolsheviks through physical assassination. Khruschev's secret speech at the twentieth party congress revealed that 70 percent of the 139 members and candidates of the party's central committee who were elected at the seventeenth congress of 1934 were arrested and shot before the eighteenth congress in 1939.[61] There is no solid evidence of any physical liquidation of high-level political opponents in Mao's reconstitution of the central committee in 1969; constrained by the Maoist tenet of "curing the illness in order to save the man," Mao's witting and unwitting political opponents of the sixties were put through Yenan-style rectification and struggle for ideological remolding. Two-thirds of the full and alternate members of the eighth central committee were publicly struggled between the spring of 1966 and the onset of the ninth party congress. What is more, in terms of content, the old revolutionaries were the most favored in Mao's "purge." The single most favored generational group in the ninth CC were the "hard core" revolutionaries elected to full membership on the CC at the seventh party congress in 1945. This "hard core" was basically composed of those who had participated in the Long March to Yenan in the thirties. The attrition rate among this group was less than half that of the 70 percent rate for those elected to CC membership at subsequent congresses.[62] Thus, while Stalin's purges were conducted by means of assassination, terror, and appeals to transcendent patriotism, Mao's revolution was conducted by means of Yenan-style thought rectification with appeals to revolutionary recrudescence and sharpened class struggle.

While Stalin filled the vacated positions in the party leadership with a younger, technical intelligentsia schooled under the Soviet regime after the revolution, Mao filled the vacated posts in the party leadership mainly with guerrilla-style PLA members differing little in age or educational level from the members of the previous central committee. In the 1930s, Stalin professionalized his army and differentiated it out of domestic politics; in the 1960s Mao and Lin Piao deprofessionalized the army and increasingly brought it into the political mainstream, first as agitators and then as administrators.[63] While Stalin centralized the party-government bureaucracy in the wake of his purge to make room for the new technical intelligentsia staffing the bureaucracy, Mao decentralized national administration in China. While Stalin downgraded the party roles of workers, peasants, and women,

Mao upgraded the roles of the latter and downgraded the bureaucrats. Thus Mao's Great Proletarian Cultural Revolution cannot reasonably be equated with a Stalinist purge, for while Stalin succumbed to the pressures of modernization in his purge, the Great Proletarian Cultural Revolution was a uniquely Maoist revivalism caused by the Great Leap debacles. Teacher Mao, tiger Lin Piao, and humble commoner Ch'en Po-ta, were three dissonance-plagued comrades who reenacted their unique Chinese revolution to preserve their own hard-won ideals by remolding those of their compatriots.

To gain an appreciation of the tangible trends in the radicalized reimposition of Maoist dialectics upon China's party leadership, one need only compare the relative composition of the eighth CC of 1956-1958 with that of the post-Great Leap ninth CC elected under Maoist leadership in 1969.[64] Figure 11.3 summarizes this comparison. As previously noted, of the 195 members of the eighth CC, the generational subgroup which best survived entrance into the 279 member ninth CC was composed of Mao's old hard core of long marchers. Flanking these old revolutionary heroes were 110 men (40 percent) who held their primary positions in Lin Piao's revolutionized PLA. In the best tradition of Maoist omnicompetence, the remolded military was to take on new tasks of civilian agitation and administration. The pre-Great Leap CC contained no more than a third of its membership who held any position in the PLA and only 25 percent had held primary positions in the PLA. Seventy-five percent of these ninth CC military men now practiced the mass line in the provinces. In keeping with the Maoist antipathy for bureaucracy, only 10 percent of the membership of the ninth CC were ministers or vice-ministers in the government bureaucracy and they represented only one-third of the simplified ministries of the state council. Prior to the Great Leap, 25 percent of the membership of the eighth CC were ministers or vice-ministers and they represented two-thirds of the 50 ministries. Other bastions of establishment resistance to revolutionary Maoist practices, the mass organizations, also suffered. The eighth CC contained eight leaders of the Communist Youth League; the ninth CC contained none. The All-China Federation of Trade Unions, Liu Shao-ch'i's fiefdom of old, contributed 12 leaders to the eighth CC; only four of these survived into the ninth CC and each of these had been inactive in union politics since the 1950s. The Maoist ideal of decentralization for mass line leadership was also strongly reimposed. Whereas 66 percent of the members of the eighth CC worked in the capital of Peking, only 36 percent of the members of the ninth CC resided in the capital. This degree of decentralization was even more extreme than the immediate postliberation phase of the early 1950s when 45 percent of the members of the seventh CC worked in Peking, not to mention their 90 percent capital city residence at the peak of the Soviet-modeled five year plan in 1956. The Maoist ideal of class struggle with reliance on the

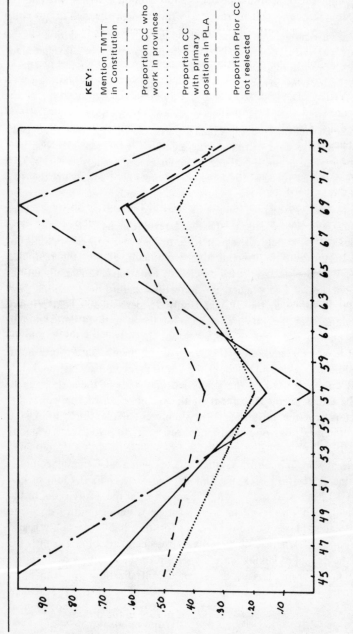

KEY:

Mention TMTT
in Constitution —·—·—

Proportion CC who
work in provinces
·············

Proportion CC
with primary
positions in PLA ————

Proportion Prior CC
not reelected ————

SOURCES: Klein and Clark, **A Biographic Dictionary of Chinese Communism**, op. cit., pp. 1063-1064, 1081-1089, for 1945; **CQ**, No. 56, fall 1973, pp. 804-810 and **PR**, Nos. 35 and 36, September 7, 1973, for 1973. For PLA figures, see William W. Whitson, **The Chinese High Command**, New York: Praeger, 1973, p. 521.

Figure 11.3: TRENDS IN MAOIST LEADERSHIP PRACTICES ON THE CENTRAL COMMITTEE, 1945-1973

proletariat was enforced as never before. Twenty-five percent of the ninth CC were composed of working peasants and common workers, whereas the eighth CC contained no such representatives. Although the eighth and ninth CCs displayed no substantial differences in representation by ethnic group, age (both averaging in the midfifties), or educational level, egalitarianism was enforced by doubling the proportion of women to 8 percent in the ninth CC. K'ang Sheng's wife was one of those incrementing their numbers along with the other Yenan brides in the politburo. In sum, the composition of the ninth CC compared with that of the pre-Great Leap eighth CC demonstrates an increased application of the ideals of the omnicompetent worker-warrior, the mass line, and class struggle. The Great Leap failures had served to exaggerate the Great Leap ideals. In the process, the Great Proletarian Cultural Revolution served to displace the party bureaucrats with the Yenan guerrilla warriors and their heirs.

While the composition of the ninth Central Committee showed an apparent victory for Maoists and Maoist dialectics, other activities of the ninth party congress further institutionalized Maoism in China's social fabric. Auguring the future, Lin Piao laid down the following stringent commandment in his long address to the ninth party congress: "Whoever opposes Chairman Mao Tse-tung Thought at any time or under any circumstances will be condemned and punished by the whole country."[65] Fittingly, Lin Piao also promised "new leaps forward" in economic and socialist construction. The new party constitution adopted by the congress contained another indirect allusion to the Great Leap Forward. A significant new passage summarized the basic ideas of "permanent revolution" as they were first expounded by Mao Tse-tung as a theoretical underpinning of the Great Leap in 1958:

> These [persisting class] contradictions can only be resolved by relying on the theory and practice of Marxist permanent revolution. The Great Proletarian Cultural Revolution in our country is precisely a great political revolution under conditions of socialism, in which the proletariat opposed the bourgeoisie and all exploiting classes.[66]

Furthermore, since proletarian status in Communist China is either ascribed by working-class background or achieved by espousal of the living ideology of the proletariat, Mao Tse-tung thought, the permanent revolution in China is effectively a revolution of the believers in TMTT and their naive constituency against the nonbelievers. Indeed, in Lin Piao's words at the congress, the latter is the key question in the continuing Cultural Revolution:

> Whether the proletariat is able to take firm root in the positions of culture and education and transform them with Mao Tse-tung's Thought

is the key question in carrying the Great Proletarian Cultural Revolution through to tne end.[67]

Mao Tse-tung thought, itself, was enshrined in the new party constitution, as the theoretical basis for the vanguard of China's proletariat:

> The Communist Party of China takes Marxism-Leninism-Mao Tse-tung Thought as the theoretical basis guiding its thinking. Mao Tse-tung Thought is Marxism-Leninism of the era in which imperialism is heading for total collapse and socialism is advancing to world-wide victory.[68]

Mao Tse-tung thought was further sanctified by the rules for the newly enforced dictatorship of the proletariat in the draft of the new constitution of the People's Republic of China. The simplified state constitution proclaimed Chairman Mao as the "great leader of all the people," recorded Vice-Chairman Lin Piao as Mao's designated "successor," and also stated that "Mao Tse-tung Thought is the guiding principle of all work of the people and the whole country."[69] Mso Tse-tung thought, the failed guide to economic development ten years before, had become through a decade of Maoist proselyting the new secular religion of Communist China—preserved and preached by the PLA reconstituted party priesthood, sanctified by the simplified state, and suffused by the "proletariat" into the rest of the "people."

To consolidate the institutionalization of Mao Tse-tung thought achieved by the ninth party congress and to implement Mao's renewed call at the congress for correct implementation of the proletarian mass line across the nation, a new "Mao Philosophy" campaign was launched in 1970 and targeted upon the reconstituted cadres. To correct the thinking of the less progressive cadres, a set of "May 7th" cadre schools were established throughout China for the rectification through work and study, of hundreds of thousands of party and government cadres. The first such school was established on an experimental basis on the farm of Liu Ho township, Chiangan County, Heilungkiang province on May 7, 1968. Neither now nor in 1966 was Mao's dissonance over the Great Leap debacles rendered inoperative. The permanent revolution witnessed in China results from a permanent dissonance inflicted in the mind of Mao at Lushan. At least now the degree of contradiction between TMTT and conditions currently prevailing in China was made the more bearable by the degree of social and empirical support Mao and his Yenan coterie were able to amass for TMTT through the Great Proletarian Cultural Revolution.

NOTES

1. See Appendix C for description of the sample surveys employed.

2. See Appendix D for examples of communications matrices displaying varying levels of class cleavage. For another analysis of occupational groups in the 1960s, see Michael Oksenberg, "Occupational groups in Chinese society and the Cultural Revolution," in *The Cultural Revolution: 1967 in Review*. Ann Arbor: University of Michigan, Center for Chinese Studies, 1968, pp. 1-44. While Oksenberg focusses upon the articulation of interests by particular occupational groups, consistent with our previous analysis of differential media exposure, we have divided the Chinese population into two gross segments: proletarians (64%), including manual workers, skilled workers, peasants, fishermen, and soldiers; and a residual category of bourgeois (36%), including professionals, officials, white-collar workers, students, housewives, unemployed, businessmen or industrial managers. Oksenberg has examined the activities of these groups (excluding separate treatment of housewives, skilled workers, white-collar workers, and fishermen) through published sources. Although there is nothing inconsistent with our broad survey findings on class polarization over the 1960s in Oksenberg's detailed analysis of interest articulation by seven basic occupational groups over the 1960s, he has explicated an additional criterion that forms a basis for polarization and which is invisible in our class dichotomy of the occupational groups. There is reason to believe that conflict also existed *within* occupational groups which "was often based on class and status groups" (p. 38). Thus, among students there was conflict between children of cadres and children from less favored background; among workers there was conflict between permanent and less favored temporary workers; among officials, there was conflict between high-ranking and low-ranking. The Maoists sought to draw support from the lower class *and* status groups during the GPCR. The struggle between the proletarians and the bourgeois thus also involved struggles within the proletariat and the bourgeoisie, but the practical criterion employed by the Maoists in both cases was to pit the "have nots" against the "haves." Nevertheless, our broad analysis of the two class groupings is sufficiently sensitive to show effective Maoist caused class polarization over the period.

3. See Appendix D.

4. See "The army and people throughout the country are determined to master Mao Tse-tung's thought," *PR*, No. 42, 1966.

5. See Richard Hughes, "Mao makes the trials run on time," *New York Times Magazine*, August 23, 1970, p. 22. The following reports of trials by the Chinese media and personal observers were compiled by Hughes.

6. Ibid.

7. Ibid.

8. Ibid.

9. Ibid., p. 67.

10. See Jack Gray, "The economics of Maoism," *Bulletin of the Atomic Scientist*, Vol. 25, No. 2, February 1969, pp. 50-51. See also Kwangtung provincial party committee, "The ten great measures for the implementation of Chairman Mao's instruction" (August 13, 1955, excerpted in "Quarterly chronicle and documentation," *CQ*, No. 28, October-December 1966, pp. 174-177.

11. *CLG*, Vol. I, No. 4, winter 1968-1969, p. 53.

12. See "Comrade Wang Tung-hsiung's report. . . ." *KTTH*, January 1961, as translated in J. Chester Cheng, ed., *The Politics of the Chinese Red Army*. Palo Alto, Calif.: Hoover Institute, 1966.

13. Loc. cit.

14. See "Resolutions on the further strengthening of the collective economy of the people's communes and expanding agricultural production" (Secret document adopted by the tenth plenum of the eighth central committee of the Chinese Communist party, September 27, 1962), as translated in C. S. Chen and C. P. Ridley, *Rural People's Communes in Lien-Chiang.* Palo Alto, Calif.: Hoover Institute, 1969, pp. 81-89.

15. Ibid., p. 81.

16. Ibid., p. 89.

17. See Chu Win-lin, "Regulations governing the political work of the Chinese People's Liberation Army," *IAS*, Vol. II, No. 1, October 1965, pp. 38-42.

18. See *IAS*, Vol. II, No. 8, May 1966, p. 47.

19. See *MISC*, pp. 351, 353-355.

20. See *ARC, The Great Power Struggle in China.* Hong Kong: Yee Yin Tong Press, 1969, p. 446.

21. See *CB*, No. 891, pp. 56-57.

22. See Robert M. Field, "Industrial production in Communist China: 1957-1968," *CQ*, No. 42, April-June 1970, p. 47.

23. See Werner Klatt, "Grain production: Comment," *CQ*, No. 35, July-September 1968. Also see *CS*, Vol. VII, No. 6, p. 8, which provides the following production figures for 1965-1968: 185, 178, 190, and 182 million metric tons respectively.

24. See Steve Washenko, "Agriculture in mainland China–1968," *CS*, Vol. VII, No. 6, March 31, 1969, p. 3.

25. See Colina MacDougall, "The Cultural Revolution in the communes: Back to 1958?" *CS*, Vol. VII, No. 7, April 11, 1969, p. 4.

26. Ibid., p. 5.

27. See *NCNA*, February 12, 1969, as quoted in MacDougall, op. cit., p. 6.

28. Ibid., pp. 6-10.

29. Ibid., pp. 6-7.

30. Ibid., p. 9.

31. Ibid.

32. Ibid., p. 10.

33. See "China's economy in 1969: Policy, agriculture, industry, foreign trade," *CS*, Vol. VIII, No. 11, June 1, 1970, pp. 1-17.

34. See Han Ke-chuan, "Recent developments in rural communes on the Chinese mainland," *IAS*, May 1969, p. 6.

35. Ibid., p. 7.

36. Ibid., p. 9.

37. See Li Tieh-min, "The people's commune: Focal point of resistance to the Cultural Revolution," *IAS*, Vol. VI, No. 1, October 1969, pp. 43-52.

38. See Mao Tse-tung, quoted in a speech by Chang Ch'iao, February 24, 1967, *Tse-Liao chuan-chi* (special issue of reference materials), February 10, 1968, *SCMP*, No. 4147, p. 7, as cited in Philip Bridgham, "The Cultural Revolution and the new political system in China," paper presented to American Political Science Association, September 8-12, 1970, p. 10.

39. "On the revolutionary 'three-in-one' combination," *HC*, No. 5, 1967.

40. See article 2 of August 1966 resolution, *NCNA*, August 8, 1966.

41. See article 9 of the August 1966 resolution, op. cit.

42. *NYT*, November 30, 1968.

43. For a discussion of the important role assigned the militia in the revolutionary takeover, see "Let the militia play its full role in the Great Proletarian Cultural Revolution," *CFCP*, March 16, 1967; *JMJP*, August 6, 1967; and *HC*, No. 5.

44. For a discussion of the role of various Cultural Revolution groups, see article 9 of the August 1966 resolution, op. cit.

45. The listing of the seventeen members of the Cultural Revolution group is taken from wall posters put up in Peking on November 22, 1966, and reported in *Asahi Shimbum* on November 23, 1966. See Asia Research Center, *The Great Cultural Revolution in China*. Hong Kong: Green Pagoda Press, 1967, pp. 419-425.

46. T'ao Chu had long been a supporter of Maoist policies. Through the years back to 1958, he supported Mao's commune policies. Even with the retreat from the communes in 1960, he criticized those commune cadres who were not following the party's mass line. In February 1964, an article by T'ao appeared in *Red Flag* praising the peoples communes and later that year he wrote a pamphlet on the communes in Kwangtung province. In August 1965, T'ao made a speech at the drama festival in Canton advocating that traditional opera should give way to operas with proletarian, revolutionary themes. With the reestablishment of the regions bureaus of the CCP central committee in the early 1960s, T'ao was made first secretary of the Central-South bureau. On July 9, 1966, the *New China News Agency* referred to T'ao Chu as a member of the secretariat of the CCP central committee and as the replacement for the purged Lu Ting-yi as director of its propaganda department. See *ARC*, op. cit., pp. 422-423.

47. *ARC*, 1969, pp. 138-159.

48. See "Long live all-round victory of the Great Proletarian Cultural Revolution," joint editorial of *JMJP* and *CFCP*, September 7, 1968, released in English by *NCNA*, Peking, September 6.

49. See Ezra F. Vogel, *Canton Under Communism*. Cambridge, Mass.: Harvard University Press, 1969, pp. 336-337.

50. Ibid., p. 337.

51. *JMJP*, February 3, 1968.

52. For a useful chronology of important events in the Cultural Revolution between December 1966 and September 1968, see *ARC*, pp. 487-500.

53. See George P. Jan, "Communications and political development: The case of Communist China," paper delivered at the annual meeting of the American Political Science Association, Los Angeles, September 8-12, 1970, pp. 31-36. All the basic data were compiled by George P. Jan and taken from *Jen Min Jih Pao* (People's Daily), Peking. The dates on which the data for a particular province or autonomous region appeared in this newspaper are as follows: Anhwei, July 13, 1968; Honan, January 26, 1968; Hunan, February 21, 1968; Hupei, December 6, 1968; Kansu, October 10, 1968; Kiangsi, May 18, 1968; Kwangsi, November 25, 1968; Kwangtung, February 3, 1968; Liaoning, April 28, 1968; Ninghsia, February 21, 1968; Shensi, February 17, 1968 and Szechuan, May 31, 1968. The population proportions for each reported province were developed by us utilizing the 1964 provincial population estimates provided by the regime and reported in Robert M. Field, "A note on the population," *CQ*, No. 38, April-June 1969, p. 162, column "c."

54. See George P. Jan, loc. cit., p. 33. All the data on the distribution of Mao's writings to the following seven provinces were compiled in Jan's survey of the 1968 editions of *Jen Min Jih Pao*, Peking. The dates on which the data was a particular province or autonomous region appeared in this paper are as follows: Hupei, Anhwei, and Kwangsi, April 11, 1968; Chinghai, May 19, 1968; Yunnan, May 19, 1968; Heilungkiang, June 15, 1968; and Honan, January 28, 1968.

55. "Quarterly chronical and documentation," *CQ*, No. 28, October-December 1966, pp. 186-187.

56. The two exceptions are the following: Chou En-lai, who is a notorious compromiser; and Chu Teh, who was an octogenerian in 1966 and believed not to be an active

politician. The thorough research of Philip Bridgham indicates that Chou En-lai, who retained his third ranking position at the eleventh plenum, gave support to the Maoists throughout the sixties. In October 1960, Chou produced a tribute to TMTT which is recorded in the PLA *Bulletin of Activities* for December 6, 1961. At the enlarged central committee work conference of January 1962, Chou is credited in Red Guard publications of "defending the TMTT and the proletarian revolutionary line represented by Mao." Bridgham also cites evidence that Chou supported Mao's tough line on literature and art at various party meetings in the period following the tenth plenum. In his work report to the third national people's congress in December 1964, Chou publicly denounced a number of emergency policies implemented in the retreat from the Great Leap as the work of "class enemies," namely those approved by Liu and Teng. Thus, in Bridgham's words, "whatever his real views on policy . . . the record suggests that Chou En-lai defended Mao against his critics during this critical period. . . ." See Philip Bridgham, "Factionalism in the central committee," in John W. Lewis, *Party Leadership and Revolutionary Power in China*. Cambridge, Mass.: Cambridge University Press, 1970, p. 228.

On the other hand, Chu Teh, who was demoted from fourth to ninth position at the eleventh plenum, is reliably reported to have supported P'eng Teh-huai and his criticism of the Great Leap at Lushan, an act for which he was condemned by Lin Piao at the enlarged meeting of the Military Affairs Committee shortly thereafter. See Bridgham, op. cit., p. 216.

57. "Press communique of the first plenary session of the ninth central committee of the Communist party of China," *PR*, No. 18, April 30, 1969, pp. 28-29.

58. Philip Bridgham, "Mao's Cultural Revolution: The struggle to consolidate power," *CQ*, No. 41, January-March 1970, p. 16.

59. Ibid.

60. Donald W. Klein and Lois B. Hager, "The ninth central committee," *CQ*, No. 45, January-March 1971, pp. 37-56.

61. Merle Fainsod, *How Russia is Ruled*. Cambridge, Mass.: Harvard University Press, 1963, pp. 195-196, 260-269, and passim.

62. Klein, op. cit., pp. 39-40.

63. Fainsod, op. cit., pp. 477-480.

64. Klein, loc. cit.

65. Lin Piao, "Report to the ninth national congress of the Communist party of China," *PR*, No. 18, April 30, 1969, pp. 12-35.

66. See Stuart Schramm, "Mao Tse-tung and the theory of the permanent revolution," *CQ*, April-June 1971, p. 443.

67. Lin Piao, loc. cit.

68. See Paragraph four in "Constitution of the Communist party of China" (adopted by the ninth national congress of the CCP, April 14, 1969, *PR*, No. 18, April 30, 1969, p. 36.

69. See "Revised draft of the 'Constitution of the People's Republic of China," (adopted September 6, 1970 by the second plenary session of the ninth CC of the CCP), *IAS*, Vol. VII, No. 3, December 1970, pp. 89-93.

Chapter 12

EPILOGUE: Compromised Maoism

I am only a lone monk walking the world with a leaky umbrella.

With these humble words of December 18, 1970 Chairman Mao concluded his interview with his long-time friend and associate from the early days of Yenan, Edgar Snow.[1]

The great leader, great supreme commander, great helmsman, and great teacher of the Great Proletarian Cultural Revolution days, confided just twenty months after the exultant Maoist fanfare of the ninth party congress that he wished to be known simply as a teacher.[2] Mao admitted to Snow that his teachings had been compromised in the conduct of the GPCR: Factions had arisen within the forces of the Revolution; fighting had broken out between them; and opposing groups had lied to each other over the instigation of the coercion. Furthermore, "captives" of the revolutionaries, including many party members, were maltreated and coerced into action where persuasion should have been applied according to the Yenan dictum.[3] Many had waved the red flag to oppose the red flag. Faced with the exigencies of protracted internal turmoil and the Soviet menace on the frontiers, Mao moved toward the middle of the spectrum as the Maoists compromised their policies and compromised their personnel, increasing the prospects for further compromises in Maoism.

Viewed in historical perspective, the stage of Thermidor had at long last overcome Mao's revolution. Ascending to chairman of the politburo of the beleagured Chinese Communist movement on the Long March to Yenan in the midthirties, Mao had set about codifying his ideology which was incorporated into the constitution of the strengthened party at the end of the Yenan era in 1945. The tenet of continuing class struggle explained the severe strains of Chinese society by blaming them on exploiting landlords and imperialists and their representatives. The tenet of dialectical progress guaranteed the eventual historical triumph of the party's proletarian forces over their class enemy. The mass line and omnicompetent worker tenets ensured that the nonantagonistic contradictions within the forces of the Communist movement would not disrupt its growth. By the eighth party congress of 1956, Mao's party had captured control of the mainland and, under a moderate first five year plan, constructed a new government; but bureaucracy had burgeoned under the ensconced party leadership. In 1958 Chairman Mao and the committed Maoists issued the utopian Great Leap prophecy as the panacea for China's problems. The prophecy failed and polarized the party along the lines of prior commitment to Maoist ideology. Reacting to the ideological dissonance of the Great Leap failures, the committed Maoists increased their proselyting for Maoist ideology while rejecting and derogating increased numbers of disbelievers. This ideological polarization erupted in a Maoist "reign of terror and virtue," the Great Proletarian Cultural Revolution, which culminated in a radicalized reimposition of Mao's Yenan ideology at the ninth party congress of 1969. Subsequently, the polarization diminished in compromises of unrealistic Maoist ideals and purges of highly committed Maoist disciples at the moderating tenth party congress of 1973; it finally ended with the death and purge of the remaining highly committed Maoists on the Politburo in 1976.

Compromised Policy

With the convening of the tenth party congress, held from 24 to 28 August, 1973, a number of post-GPCR compromises in Maoist policy became apparent.[4] The compromises impaired the implementation of the central Maoist doctrines of dialectical progress, the continuing class struggle, the mass line and the omnicompetent worker. As shown in Figure 11.3, indicators of each of these Maoist leadership tenets oscillated from Yenan seventh congress highs, through eighth congress lows to new ninth congress highs and down again to tenth congress compromises.

DIALECTICAL PROGRESS

Following Mao's Yenan rectification campaign of 1942-1944, the thought of Mao Tse-tung was inscribed in the party constitution for the first time as a "theoretical basis guiding its thinking." This Maoist guideline was excised from the eighth congress constitution and splendidly replaced at the ninth, following the GPCR. The constitution adopted by the tenth congress retained the phrase but restrained the praise. The seven mentions of TMTT on the ninth congress document were reduced to only three in the tenth, and the four additional personal references to Mao in the ninth had vanished entirely.[5]

Missing were both references to Lin Piao's admonition to "apply Marxism-Leninism-Mao Tse-tung Thought in a living way." Missing was any mention of Lin Piao as "Comrade Mao Tse-tung's close comrade-in-arms and successor." Scrapped was Ch'en Po-ta's modified Yenan formulation that "Comrade Mao Tse-tung has integrated the universal truth of Marxism-Leninism with the concrete practice of revolution, inherited defended and developed Marxism-Leninism and brought it to a higher and completely new stage." Added in their stead were growing concerns of the shrunken Maoists: "Revolutions like this [GPCR] will have to be carried out many times in the future"; the persisting need to train "millions of successors for the cause of proletarian revolution"; the continued need for "unity" and the necessity to oppose the incongruous new U.S.-Soviet alliance, "the hegemonism of the two super powers."[6] For the first time since Yenan, Mao did not address the congress. Maoist dialectics were also on the wane in the nation's press: As shown in Chapter 10 Figure 10.2, mention of Maoist themes in *People's Daily* had declined each year following the GPCR from a 1969 high of .39 to the 1973 low of .29. By the end of autumn 1971, the little red book of Mao's quotations with Lin Piao's introduction had been withdrawn from circulation. Even Chou En-lai's report from the congress deflated the universalistic aspirations of TMTT, asserting that this is still an era of Leninism.[7] Indeed, the seventies were a new era. The Chinese had been busy burrowing beneath their cities constructing a massive tunnel network in defense against the leading socialist brother country of the 1950s as Chairman Mao welcomed the leader of the number one imperialist enemy nation, President Nixon, in 1972. As with other Thermidors before, worldwide utopian proselyting was on the wane as the interests of the nation gained the upper hand.

THE CONTINUING CLASS STRUGGLE

In Mao's pursuit of the egalitarian millenium, the class struggle is viewed as persisting even after the basic socialist transformation of the means of production. Both before and after the Yenan land reforms, Mao strove mightily to bring socialism to the Chinese peasantry as well as to the urban proletariat. The GPCR was to be followed by a great socialist upsurge in the economy. No great leaps have been demonstrated and there is little evidence that the Marxian "three great differences" have been appreciably reduced by the GPCR. A few model communes exist in China, but most remain but skeletons of their short-lived Great Leap grandeur. Within the miniaturized communes, proposals to equalize the incomes of peasant households by returning the basic accounting unit to the more inclusive production brigade level and redistributing income from richer to poorer production teams appears to have been rejected in 1971.[8] This was in keeping with the 1970 decisions to maintain private plots and to continue the system of remuneration based essentially on individual productivity.[9] The agricultural practices of 1972 were very similar to the post-Great Leap recovery policies as spelled out in the sixty articles of 1962 which were still in force! Rural rightists were not castigated, but "ultraleftists," seeking more equality, were.[10] In the cities, the locus of major GPCR impact, the Red Guards had returned to the reopened schools. In industry, efforts after more egalitarian wage differentials between grades of workers and managers in state run factories and enterprises also appear to have been in vain. Despite Maoist efforts in the Great Leap and GPCR to reduce wage differentials, to put reds and experts on comparable material footing, one close observer concludes that there has been very little enduring change since the first five year plan of the early 1950s.[11] In sum, in the 1950s agriculture was collectivized and industry was nationalized in a formerly inegalitarian free enterprise economy, but since then actual egalitarian progress has been hard to discern. Among the masses in the seventies, the class struggle was also muted.

At the higher levels of leadership the class struggle was also played down following the GPCR, and the purge of rightists from the party leadership was curtailed and reversed. Following the Long March, Mao had consolidated his position as chairman of the central committee with the rectification campaign at Yenan. As shown in Figure 11.3, 72 percent of former full members of prior central committees were not reelected to the seventh CC at Yenan. A number were purged and many had died since earlier congresses. The subsequent period of civil war, land reform, and liberation from the class enemy, showed a high degree of consensus within the party; and the government was formed and based on a tolerant four-class bloc formula with nearly 30 percent of its ministers holding membership in eight legitimate minority parties. With the convening of the first and second sessions of the eighth congress in 1956 and 1958, only 16 percent of full members of the former CC were not reelected, the purge of Kao Kang and Jao Shu-shih being the only noteworthy incident of high-level dissensus. The subsequent period from the Great Leap failure through the GPCR was one of increasing polarization in the party leadership. For the first time class enemies were discovered *within* the party leadership, and Maoist policy toward the party's constituency narrowed to a restrictive dictatorship of the proletariat in a Maoist reign of terror and virtue which abolished the minority parties and shook the CCP to its foundations in the name of TMTT. With the convening of the ninth congress in 1969, 62 percent of the full members of the former congress were purged as rightists or otherwise not reelected. The subsequent period to the tenth congress has been one of fractionalized party leadership and it is not at all clear that the 27 percent of the full CC members who were not reelected were rightists. Indeed, over 20 percent of those full CC members purged as rightists at the ninth congress were reinstated at the tenth, an unprecedented event in party history under Mao.[12] Many former castigated heretics of the GPCR were now readmitted to the party ranks in the spirit of amnesty and compromise.

THE MASS LINE

In the exercise of correct party leadership, Mao formulated the mass line principle during the Yenan era. Out of preference for simplified administration and dislike of bureaucracy, Mao advocated a decentralized style of leadership with a high proportion of the central committee leadership dispersed to the provinces. As shown in Figure 11.3, nearly 50 percent of the full CC members were so dispersed around the time of the seventh congress. By the eighth congress, only 20 percent remained peripheral to Peking, and Mao advocated the slashing of central bureaucrats by two-thirds in the massive transfer downward campaign preceding the Great Leap. At the ninth congress the Yenan dispersal ideal of 50 percent was again approached. But the achievement was short-lived: by the tenth congress, the full members of the CC had recentralized and only one-third remained in the provinces. The party bureaucracy was on its way back.

THE OMNICOMPETENT WORKER

Since the Yenan guerrilla days, Mao advocated the practice of interchanging personnel between various tasks of production, warfare, and administration as demanded by the current needs of the revolution. Especially the military, which was then nearly indistinguishable from the growing party organization, was to engage in multiple tasks of production, administration, and fighting in the omnicompetent Yenan spirit of Nanniwan. As shown in Figure 11.3, at the seventh congress 50 percent of the full CC members held their primary positions in the PLA. As the party mission shifted to civil affairs and the government grew following the liberation, Mao still strove to keep the PLA involved in civilian tasks as part of his institutional triad of rule. In 1959, Mao was to cede his formal government, leadership position to Liu Shao-ch'i, but retained his dominance over the military. In the early 1950s, the PLA acted as administrators during the land reform. In the later 1950s, the PLA participated in collectivization and commune formation. But by the eighth congress, their representation among the full CC membership had declined to 37 percent.

With the failure of the Great Leap, in the early 1960s, the PLA under Lin Piao became increasingly active in civil affairs. At the ninth congress, at the end of their heavy involvement in the GPCR, the PLA occupied 47 percent of the full CC positions. But after it was charged in the July 1972 issue of *Red Flag* that "the gun might control the Party," many military men were

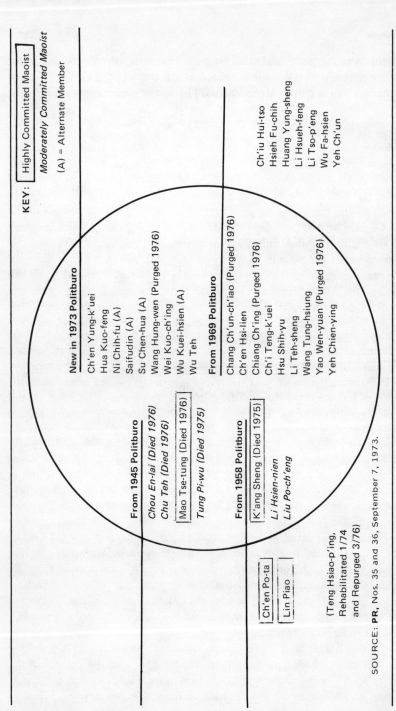

KEY: Highly Committed Maoist
Moderately Committed Maoist
(A) = Alternate Member

New in 1973 Politburo

Ch'en Yung-k'uei
Hua Kuo-feng
Ni Chih-fu (A)
Saifudin (A)
Su Chen-hua (A)
Wang Hung-wen (Purged 1976)
Wei Kuo-ch'ing
Wu Kuei-hsien (A)
Wu Teh

From 1969 Politburo

Chang Ch'un-ch'iao (Purged 1976)
Ch'en Hsi-lien
Chiang Ch'ing (Purged 1976)
Ch'i Teng-k'uei
Hsu Shih-yu
Li Teh-sheng
Wang Tung-hsiung
Yao Wen-yuan (Purged 1976)
Yeh Chien-ying

Ch'iu Hui-tso
Hsieh Fu-chih
Huang Yung-sheng
Li Hsueh-feng
Li Tso-p'eng
Wu Fa-hsien
Yeh Ch'un

From 1945 Politburo

Chou En-lai (Died 1976)
Chu Teh (Died 1976)
Mao Tse-tung (Died 1976)
Tung Pi-wu (Died 1975)

From 1958 Politburo

K'ang Sheng (Died 1975)
Li Hsien-nien
Liu Po-ch'eng

Ch'en Po-ta

Lin Piao

(Teng Hsiao-p'ing,
Rehabilitated 1/74
and Repurged 3/76)

SOURCE: **PR**, Nos. 35 and 36, September 7, 1973.

Figure 12.1: SURVIVAL OF COMMITTED MAOISTS FROM THE EIGHTH CC POLITBURO INTO THE TENTH CC POLITBURO, 1973

purged from the party leadership, and the PLA retained only 31 percent of the membership in the full CC elected at the tenth congress. Thus another prong was plucked from Mao's trident, and skittish cadres swam more freely.

Compromised Personnel

As compromises were made on the prominence of Maoist dialectics, the concepts of the omnicompetent worker-warrior, the mass line, and the intensity of the class struggle, the composition of the politburo was significantly changed between the ninth and tenth congresses. To accommodate the growing needs for order, modernization, and the realities of international politics, the leading group became less Maoist in commitment and less polarized over the issue of Maoism through the purge or elimination of the most extreme Maoists from its leadership. The purging pendulum which had sliced off the most recalcitrant rightists in the GPCR swung back again in the early seventies to lop off the ultraleftists. This resulted in a more moderate, fractionalized collectivity composed of interdependent leaders knit together with multiple cross-cutting interests. Balance was sought between different interests: radical and conservative, military and civilian, central and regional, as well as the special interests of workers, youth, and women.[13]

1971 was a significant year for revolutionaries the world over. It was the centenary of the Paris Commune. In Mao's China the anniversary of this major organizational model for the GPCR went largely unheralded. Instead the most extreme Maoists of the late fifties and sixties were purged. As shown in Figure 12.1, neither Ch'en Po-ta nor Lin Piao managed to survive in the politburo membership elected at the tenth party congress. In this year, beside muffled protests in *Red Flag,* Ch'en Po-ta and the "May 16th" Cultural Revolution group of leaders of radical Red Guards were publicly charged with "ultraleftism." Seeking to achieve communism overnight they were criticized as having engaged in anarchism and violence especially during 1967 and 1968. Ch'en was purged from his high position on the standing committee of the politburo, and the Cultural Revolution group he headed was dissolved as more routinized structures of the party and the youth league began to reappear.

Mao's "close comrade-in-arms" and constitutional "successor" of 1969 was publicly charged with having attempted a political coup against Chairman Mao at the second Lushan plenum in September 1970. A year later, he and his generals were charged with having begun a failed military coup. Lin is reported to have died with his wife, Yeh Ch'un, and a number of generals on September 13, 1971 in a failed escape attempt when their Trident jet crashed in Mongolia.[14] In his fall, Lin Piao carried with him the politburo generals recruited from his old fourth field army power base, Ch'iu Hui-tso, Huang

Yung-sheng, Li Tso-p'eng, and Wu Fa-hsien. Li Hsueh-feng, a politburo alternate, was also purged and security chief, Hsieh Fu-chih, died of disease.

Following the revolutionary extravagancies of the ninth party congress,
Mao was forced to moderate his policies and there was a falling out among
the cultural revolutionaries. In March 1970, Mao decided to eliminate the
post of chairman of the state from the new draft constitution of the People's
Republic of China.[15] This decision confirmed Chou En-lai's position as head
of government, apparently controverted Ch'en Po-ta's wishes, and definitely
downgraded Lin Piao's power as Mao's sole successor. In addition there was
a significant change in the definition of a loyal Maoist following the ninth
congress which left Lin's own 1966 definition appreciably to the left of the
new definition. In August 1966, Lin's three criteria had defined a loyal
Maoist as one who diligently studied Mao thought, attached great importance
to political and ideological work, and was filled with revolutionary zeal; the
July 1, 1970 joint editorial in *People's Daily, Red Flag*, and *Liberation Army
Daily* redefined a loyal Maoist as one who was loyal to Marxism-Leninism-
Mao Tse-tung thought, who trusted the masses and who, after making mistakes, was willing to conduct self-criticism.[16] The latter definition enhanced
the acceptability of the purged experts as opposed to reds.

In October 1970, Mao confirmed his rightward shift when he told Couve
de Murville that he was a "center-leftist" and that he was continuing to attack
the arrogance and complacency of PLA representatives serving in the new
structure of power.[17] In August 1970 at the second Lushan plenum, Lin,
four top military leaders, and Ch'en Po-ta banded together to "launch a
surprise attack" on the moderates.[18] Then Ch'en and Lin became the victims
of a concerted campaign against "ultraleftism," in response to which Lin
allegedly plotted an abortive coup against Mao. Mao and Lin apparently had
disagreed following the congress over the relative roles of the party and the
army during reconstruction from the Cultural Revolution and over the
related general question of the use of coercion in the treatment of party
dissidents.

Back in time and behind the scenes, the extremist leaders of Mao's GPCR
had themselves been forced to compromise Mao's ideals and make concessions to military commanders. In the fall of 1967 following the July mutiny
at Wuhan, Lin Piao had been forced to denounce his leading political commissars, and the radical head of his general political department since Lo
Jung-huan's death, Hsiao Hua, was purged. Hsiao had soared from obscurity
to twenty-sixth rank of the CC of the eleventh plenum in 1966. Just one
year later he returned to obscurity. Subsequently, he was replaced by Li
Teh-sheng, a professional commander from the second field army.[19] Furthermore, Ch'en Po-ta's *Red Flag* temporarily suspended publication in November. Ch'en's Cultural Revolution group was so shot through with factionalism

that two-thirds of its first eighteen members were purged by the end of the year. Especially hard hit in the purge of radicals in the fall of 1967 were editors of *Red Flag* and regional propaganda chiefs.[20] Publicly in the early 1970s, those extremists perceived as perpetrators of Mao's reign of terror were labeled traitors and replaced in rule, as the more moderate men remaining in the middle took charge.

Surviving into the politburo of the tenth CC was a pluralistic mix of sixteen of the prior group of twenty-five. The core group of Mao Tse-tung, Chou En-lai, Chu Teh, and Tung Pi-wu were all members of the new standing committee, being the only members to have survived three decades of purgings in the seventh, eighth, ninth, and tenth party congresses. Chu and Tung were now relatively inactive. K'ang Sheng, a close but quiet associate of Mao from the Yenan days and former advisor to the Cultural Revolution group, also survived as a member of the standing committee. Aiding him in security matters was Wang Tung-hsiung. At the party center in Peking, the military leader, Yeh Chien-ying, was elevated to a position on the new standing committee. The military man at his side was Liu Po-ch'eng of second field army fame. Dealing with civilian politics at the center was Li Hsien-nien, who was formerly associated with the second field army.[21]

In K'o Ch'ing-shih's radical region of Shanghai, from which Mao had launched his Cultural Revolution in the fall of 1965, two leaders of the Cultural Revolution group survived. Chang Ch'un-ch'iao, first party secretary of Shanghai, was now on the standing committee of the politburo and Yao Wen-yuan, author of the 1965 article attacking bourgeois culture, was a full member. Chiang Ch'ing, their close associate in the Cultural Revolution group and Mao's Yenan bride, was also a full member but received no position on the standing committee. From the surrounding Shanghai-Nanking military region Li Teh-sheng of second field army background was given a position on the standing committee and Hsu Shi-yu was granted full membership. In the outlying provinces, the military man Ch'en Hsi-lien of the second field army was granted full membership as was Ch'i Teng-k'uei, party leader in Honan.

The nine new additions to the politburo provided even more balance of interests. The sudden rise of Wang Hung-wen, a 36 year old Cultural Revolution activist from the Shanghai party committee to membership in the standing committee must have encouraged youthful radicals. Wu K'uei-hsien is a female party secretary in Shensi. Ni Chih-fu is a Peking trade union leader. Ch'en Yung-k'uei is a leader of the well-publicized Tachai production brigade. Su Chien-hua is a rehabilitated political commissar from the navy and was formerly associated with the second field army. Wu Teh is the municipal party chief in Peking. Hua Kuo-feng is party chief in Hunan. Wei Kuo-ch'ing and Saifudin are leaders of national minority groups.

The decline of the highly committed Maoists in the new politburo was portentious. Even though new "Maoists" were reared in the course of the 1960s proselyting efforts, the nature of their ideological commitment is likely to be different from the old revolutionaries. The new "Maoists" are much more likely to be opportunists rather than true believers who have truly sacrificed for their ideology. Furthermore, only a small proportion of the new Maoists can be expected to be driven by the sharp prophecy-fails dissonance experienced by Mao, Lin, Ch'en, K'ang and others because the events and the activists of 1959 have now receded in his history and a new specific utopian prophecy is unlikely to be uttered from on high.

The decline of the military in the new politburo was indicative of the factionalism underlying the new balance of interests in the political elite. As Lin Piao strove to implement Mao's GPCR, strong opposition grew inside and outside the PLA, and Lin was forced to rely on his most trusted military comrades from the fourth field army which he had led through the northeast and southeast regions of China during the civil war. Consequently, in contrast to the low military representation on the eighth CC and politburo, which constituted a minority of numbers and contained strong domination by the fourth field army,[22] following the fall of Lin Piao, the tenth CC and politburo not only had less military representation and far fewer from the fourth field army, but also showed the unmistakable dominance of the second field army which the professional commander, Liu Po-ch'eng, had led through the southwest of China.[23] To the chagrin of the ardent proselytizers of TMTT, both the ninth and tenth CCs and politburos showed the clear supercession of the professional military commanders over the red political commissars.[24]

The new twenty-five-man politburo leadership was a fragile balance of cross-cutting interests. Three quarters of the members had entered the leading body since the onset of the GPCR upheaval in which two-thirds of the former ninth CC politburo members were attacked and purged. This purge rate was unprecedented. The earlier purge rate among politburo members between the Yenan congress and the eighth congress had been only 18 percent. Between the end of the GPCR at the ninth party congress and the tenth congress, another 36 percent were purged. The fragility was highlighted by the readmission to the tenth central committee of former prominent politburo members who had been attacked and purged as rightists in the GPCR. These included Li Ching-ch'uan, T'an Ch'en-lin, U Lan-fu, and the "number two capitalist roader," Teng Hsiao-p'ing.

The post-Cultural Revolution government leadership also constituted a compromise of Maoism. Between January 13 and 17, 1975, the first meeting of the national people's congress in nearly a decade was held in Peking.[25] Since the beginning of Mao's Cultural Revolution, a formal reconstitution of the government apparatus had been expected, but the results of the consolidating congress did not constitute a victory for the committed Maoists. The congress continued the policy of compromise of Maoist ideals. These results were apparent in the composition of the new leading members of the two most powerful government organs, the chairman and twenty-two vice-chairmen of the standing committee of the national people's congress and the premier, twelve vice-premiers, and twenty-nine ministers of the new state council.

There were strong indications that the reconstituted leading government bodies were now more consensual but less Maoist in their composition that was the case on the eve of the Cultural Revolution a decade earlier.[26] While the new leaders of the standing committee of the NPC included four rehabilitated Cultural Revolution purge victims, Li Ching-ch'uan, T'an Ch'en-lin, U Lan-fu, and Ch'en Yun, it included only one committed Maoist, K'ang Sheng. The new state council was still led by Chou En-lai, but his first vice-premier was now the rehabilitated "number two capitalist roader," Teng Hsiao-p'ing. Teng was even made chief of staff of the PLA and elevated within the party to deputy chairman and member of the standing committee of the politburo over the heads of the Cultural Revolution radicals, Wang Hung-wen, Chiang Ch'ing, and Chang Ch'un-ch'iao. The former pair received no leading positions on any important government body; only Chang Ch'un-ch'iao received a second vice-premiership on the state council as well as a position as head of the general political department of the PLA. The other Shanghai radical on the current politburo, Yao Wen-yuan, received no leading government position at all. The committed Maoists, Lin Piao and Ch'en Po-ta, had vanished completely.

Even Chairman Mao himself was in apparent eclipse at the congress. Although he retained his position as chairman of the central committee of the party and head of the party's military affairs committee, he received no formal government position at the post-Cultural Revolution congress, gave no address, and was reported absent from the important congressional meeting for the first time in its two-decade history. Instead, the new state constitution reflected Chou En-lai's themes at the congress of unity, consensus, and socialist construction.[27] Contrary to its earlier draft, the new constitution gave no personal mention to Mao. While it did make allusion to Mao's thought, it also explicitly guaranteed private plots and side-line markets to peasants in the countryside—institutionalizing the rural retrogressions from socialism made in the post-Great Leap era a dozen tumultuous years before.

As indicated in Figure 12.2, by the end of 1976 the members retained in the politburo since Great Leap days constituted a small group much less committed to or polarized over Maoist ideology than ever before.[28] Following the national people's congress in 1975, time began to take its own toll on the

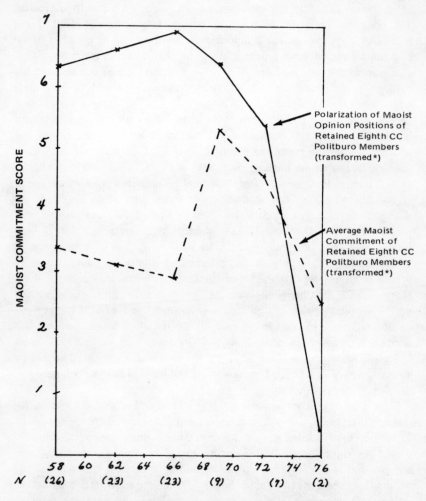

*Transformation of pre-1966 scale positions was obtained by dividing each score by the proportion of 1966 commitment opportunities available up to a given year. Thus 1958 is 0.5 of 1966 maximum; and 1962 is 0.8 of 1966 maximum. See Appendix A for Eighth CC members' scale scores.

Figure 12.2: ESTIMATED AVERAGE MAOIST OPINION AND POLARIZATION OF RETAINED EIGHTH CC POLITBURO MEMBERS, 1958-1976 (Based on members' actions taken up to mid-1966)

old revolutionaries. The venerable warriors, Tung Pi-wu and later in 1976, Chu Teh, died natural deaths and vacated positions on the politburo. In addition, K'ang Sheng was the second of Mao's Yenan coterie to pass away and the third to be removed from the politburo in the seventies; but his death was more natural than Lin Piao's and his vacancy less sought than Ch'en Po-ta's. In 1976 the demise of the Yenan coterie, the committed Maoists of Great Leap and Cultural Revolution days, was completed. The new year began precipitously with the death on January 9 of Premier Chou En-lai followed by radical criticism of his apparent successor, the rehabilitated "capitalist roader," Teng Hsiao-p'ing who was again purged from his high party posts in April. Within weeks of an ominous earthquake, on September 9, the aging chairman himself finally expired in Peking. Following a bare month's mourning, Chiang Ch'ing was viciously attacked in wall posters and purged along with the three Shanghai radicals of the Cultural Revolution days, Chang Ch'un-ch'iao, Wang Hung-wen, and Yao Wen-yuan. The compromise choice, Hua Kuo-feng, ascended the stage as chairman of the central committee of the Chinese Communist party, signifying the rise of a new generation in China after forty-one years of revolutionary Maoist leadership. The strains of the emperor's chorus are must muted now.

Rival Explanations of the Cultural Revolution

Whereas we have set forth one explanation of the Cultural Revolution in terms of the concept of ideological polarization caused by the dissonance reduction activities of committed revolutionaries who experienced a sharp failure of their utopian Great Leap prophecy, other scholars have advanced rival explanations for the GPCR. These explanations have variously viewed the GPCR as a power struggle, an attempt to continue the vitality of the Chinese social revolution, a policy dispute over the fate of people's wars, the resurgence of normative incentives, elite factionalism and a search for revolutionary immortality. Let us briefly examine these different viewpoints.

The rival view that Mao's Cultural Revolution was simply a power struggle has little to recommend it. While this view correctly predicts purging to occur in the GPCR, it is too narrow to encompass the essential phenomena of the GPCR. As documented in Chapter 9, Mao, speaking before the Albanian military delegation on May 1, 1967, explicitly stated the goal of the GPCR was ideological change "to solve the problem of world outlook; it is a question of eradicating the roots of revisionism." He further stated that "to struggle against powerholders who take the capitalist road" is only the "main task," a means to the larger end. The power struggle view leaves open the question of issues and the details of the mass-based development of the GPCR as well as the curious way in which Mao directed the struggle while refusing to violate any of the basic tenets of his ideology in the process. It does not explain why Mao became more radical in his revolutionary Great Leap philosophy following its failure, rather than seeking moderation and compromise as an expedient political tactic. In short, it does not explain why the besieged Chairman refused to cut his losses and instead reemphasized vigorous "class struggle." It explains neither the radical attempts to create "the new Socialist man" in China nor the abortive efforts to revive the Great Leap and commune programs. The power struggle explanation is both post hoc and ad hoc.

A second rival view is broader in scope. Solomon takes the Cultural Revolution as an attempt by Mao to ensure the continued vitality of the Chinese social revolution.[29] In contrast to our view, Solomon sees the extensive proselyting of the 1960s for Mao's thought and the class struggle concept as the expression of Mao's continuing opposition to the passivity and dependency orientation of traditional Chinese political culture based on his personal sensitivity to traditional patterns of authority; the refusal of Liu Shao-ch'i and the party bureaucrats to so proselyte is viewed as stemming from their anxieties about *luan,* traditionally based fears about social conflict and the open expression of aggression.[30] The struggles and purges of the GPCR are seen as Mao's attempt to "isolate" and humiliate his enemies.[31] The extensive claims for Mao's thought and the insistence on publication of Mao's works is seen as derivative of the traditional Confucian concept of the "power of the word." The fact that Mao went outside the party to purge his critics is seen as derivative of Mao's prior practice of "controlled conflict" in the One Hundred Flowers campaign of the 1950s.[32]

The Cultural Revolution certainly displayed signs of Mao's continuing revolution, but this view is historically too broad. The Yenan era, the Great Leap era, as well as the Cultural Revolution can be viewed as attempt by Mao to ensure the continued vitality of the Chinese social revolution, yet they were distinct in their causes and effects. Why did Mao find it necessary to purge two-thirds of the politburo and central committee between 1966 and 1969 whereas no previous purge in search of revolutionary continuity had removed more than a small minority of members? Why the unprecedented publication of the thoughts of Mao Tse-tung between 1966 and 1969 and not between 1957 and 1958? Granted that a large part of Mao's GPCR struggle was to overcome the dependency orientation of the traditional culture as represented by the "four olds," it is true that Mao also waged a titanic struggle against the modern, foreign Soviet model for economic development and socialist transformation. Surely this dangerous activity was more than a ploy to secure domestic political support through the creation of even more external enemies.[33] Surely Mao's argument with Khrushchev and Soviet communism was sincere and rooted in fundamental philosophical disagreement over the fate of Mao's own Great Leap and commune programs.

Solomon's perceptive and well-written account of Mao's revolution is at its
best in laying bare what is uniquely Chinese about the long revolution; it is
less useful when one seeks generalizability to other societies and political
cultures.[34]

A third rival view sees the Cultural Revolution as a policy dispute among
the Chinese Communist party elite in which Mao decided, as Stalin before
him, to make a tabula rasa of all who opposed him. What raised the salience
of the dispute in Schurmann's view was the American escalation in Vietnam
causing non-Maoists to favor a return to collaboration with the "revisionist"
Soviet Union, whereas Mao favored "revolutionary fervor" as China's main
hope of survival in the face of a threatening war.[35] Schurmann's view of the
revolutionary-revisionist issue is most thoughtful, but as we have seen, Mao's
turn to the PLA as his revolutionary vanguard occurred in late 1963, *before*
the American escalation in Vietnam, and his turn to the PLA was not pre-
cipitated by foreign events but by *domestic* foot-dragging in the implementation of Mao's proselyting drive in the Socialist Education movement. At
most, the American escalation in Vietnam combined with the failures experienced by people's wars in 1965-1966 can be seen as triggers to the long
nascent GPCR, and then only when combined with domestic economic and
political events in China taken against the backdrop of the Great Leap failures.

A fourth rival explanation views the Cultural Revolution as the rise of
normative incentives in an adapted tripartite framework of incentives for
achieving compliance with leadership goals. An insightful analysis by Skinner
and Winckler of rural collectivization policy in China suggests that regular
cycles of radicalism-retrenchment are followed here.[36] In simplified form,
the policy cycle begins with emphasis on ideological goals using normative
exhortation to gain commitment from relatively indifferent followers. It
then proceeds to a crisis phase which necessitates concern with order and
the use of coercion, thereby alienating followers. It then moves to concern
with economic goals by means of remunerative appeals, thus returning the
population to a state of indifference. The process then moves again to concerns with ideological goals. In sum, the policy cycle in China moves from
use of normative power to use of coercive power to use of remunerative
power and back to normative power.

Although Skinner's model was carefully developed to account for discernible cycles in rural collectivization policy, it has been argued that it also
applies to larger questions of political norms and values, but with longer
cycles.[37] Between 1949 and 1968, eras of rural radicalism occurred especially during the land reform 1949-1950, during the collectivization 1956-
1960, and during the Cultural Revolution beginning in late 1965, with each
radical phase being interspersed with a single retrenchment phase. At the
larger level of political institutions, it has been argued by Townsend that

radical phases occurred during reconstruction following the liberation, 1949-1953, during the Great Leap, 1958-1960, and during the Cultural Revolution, 1965-1969, with intervening periods of institutional stabilization.[38]

However, in extrapolating the Skinner cyclical model of rural collectivization policy to the broader level of national politics, Townsend obviously found it necessary to make some gross simplifications. Apparently normative and coercive phases were combined to produce a two-part framework, for indeed, the eras of reconstruction, Great Leap, and Cultural Revolution, normative phases all, were historically *preceded* or accompanied not by renumerative phases but by PLA coercion before the land reform and reconstruction, the severe antirightist campaign and paramilitary activity before the Great Leap, and learn from the PLA campaign before the Cultural Revolution. Second, placing reconstruction, Great Leap, and Cultural Revolution all in the same category of normative or radical phases preceded by renumerative or retrenchment phases obscures the real differences between the movements. As Townsend points out, the GPCR was characterized by a *much* higher level of elite conflict and more normative exhortation, both domestic and foreign, than either of the former movements, but he neglects to explain in terms of this model why such was the case.[39]

A fifth view sees the Cultural Revolution as a student-based Maoist attack on the factional party elite. Chinese politics has often followed the typical factional cycle outlined by Nathan in which a crisis leads to a consensus on a policy decision, which itself becomes the focus of renewed conflict, leading ultimately to another crisis.[40] Such cycling is apparent in events leading from the decision to launch the leap through the eleventh plenum of 1966. However, the GPCR itself was not a prime instance of factionalism according to Nathan.[41] The structure of factions is a network articulated from a set of clientalist ties which are nonascriptive, two-person relationships founded on exchange in which well-understood rights and obligations are established between two parties.[42] Since in a factional system, no party will be able to achieve or maintain superior power, a code of civility arises which circumscribes the nature of political conflict, usually eliminating the application of such sanctions as killing or jailing, and furthermore, forces are set up to block the emergence of any strong leader. In terms of the size and shape of factional systems, resources over which factions compete are supposed to be allocated among faction members themselves in accordance with their own rules of conflict; politicians are supposed to compete in expressions of fealty to the constitution or leader; and factional systems are extremely stable, for in no case are outside forces allowed to disrupt the system. Thus, "only continued factionalism can be predicted on the basis of the fact that a system is already factional.[43]

Nathan's explicit model and searching review of CCP history usefully diminishes the myth of a monolithic party organization in postliberation China. However, while many of the characteristics specified by this intriguing general model of factional politics were displayed by the party elite before and after the GPCR, the Cultural Revolution itself was different. As we have seen, the highly committed Maoists, Mao, Lin Piao, Ch'en Po-ta, and K'ang Sheng broke the rules of a factional system and went *outside* the party elite to recruit youthful Red Guards and others to attack many members of the elite, and Mao's bureaucratic opponents also mobilized loyalist Red Guards in defense; and although there was a serious attempt to minimize violence, Liu Shao-ch'i and others were placed under house arrest, and killings did occur during the GPCR; Mao did emerge as a strong leader during the GPCR; hundreds of sought-after high party and government offices were vacated and reassigned to outside GPCR activists; only a small portion of the elite actively participated in expressions of fealty to Chairman Mao and his thought during the early sixties, and some openly or obliquely criticized the Chairman; and finally, the factional system was, in fact, destabilized by the GPCR for years. Thus we are left with the twin conclusions that the GPCR was not primarily an instance of factional politics, and that there is no method endogenous to the factionalism model to predict an episode of non-factionalism like the GPCR.[44]

A sixth rival view sees the Cultural Revolution as a heightened search for revolutionary immortality. Rejecting the view that the GPCR was simply a selfish power struggle, Lifton asserts that its main motive force was a search for "power over death."[45] The sought-after revolutionary immortality, present in all revolutions, is defined as "a shared sense of participating in permanent revolutionary fermentation and of transcending individual death by 'living on' indefinitely within the continuing revolution."[46] A reassertion of this motive is seen as the activist response to symbolic death.[47] When the disparity between Chinese revolutionary vision and experience became manifest, as in the failure of the Great Leap, earlier confidence in China's revolutionary immortality was severely undermined, and *all* those active in the revolution, Mao as well as Liu Shao-ch'i and other "pragmatists," came to feel anxious about the life of the revolution.[48] The GPCR served to reduce this anxiety.

Lifton's view is quite insightful and suggestive. Though expressed in meta-phorical terms, it is potentially generalizable to other revolutions. However, while it captures much of what the committed Maoists, Mao, Lin Piao, Ch'en Po-ta and others wished to accomplish in the GPCR, it fails to capture ade-quately the motives or behavior of Liu Shao-ch'i, Teng Hsiao-p'ing, P'eng Teh-huai and other "pragmatists" in the leadership. To suggest that the latter were motivated by a desire to "participate in permanent revolutionary fer-mentation" within the "continuing revolution" is to obscure some major issues of the Cultural Revolution. Lifton fails to make clear the necessary distinction between the motives of the highly committed Maoist revolutionaries and those of their less committed colleagues in the leadership.

Our own explanation is that Mao's Great Proletarian Cultural Revolution was an instance of the general phenomenon of ideological polarization, a group phenomenon characterized by increased ideological proselyting by highly committed members of a social movement coupled with rejection and derogation of increased numbers of disbelievers. Such ideological polarization is a manifestation of the dissonance reduction activities of highly committed ideologues who are faced with undeniable evidence of the failure of their utopian prophecy. This phenomenon is observable in many historical social movements.

In Communist China, given the prevailing state of commitment to Mao's Great Leap prophecy in 1958, dissonance theory yields a good accounting of many historical facts leading from the failures of the leap announced so forcefully by P'eng Teh-huai at the Lushan plenum in the second half of 1959 through the eruption of the GPCR between 1966 and 1969. It explains why Mao Tse-tung, Lin Piao, Ch'en Po-ta and K'ang Sheng, aided initially by K'o Ch'ing-shih and Lo Jung-huan, began immediately in late 1959 to increase their proselyting for TMTT and for the continued operation of class struggle in China; it explains why the lowly committed Liu Shao-ch'i, Teng Hsiao-p'ing and other politburo members did not so proselyte. It thereby explains the beginning of polarization over Maoist policies on the politburo, and the subsequent increased polarization and extensive purgings are rendered more understandable. It explains why a small cultural revolution broke out in 1960-1961, and why Mao was so intent upon capturing the news media and propoganda apparatus following Lushan and throughout the 1960s until the eruption of the GPCR. It further explains why the ideological and class contents of Ch'en Po-ta's *Red Flag* were out of synchronization with the more pragmatic contents of the party-controlled *People's Daily*. It explains why Mao shifted the targets of his mass campaigns from the bourgeois enemies of the fifties to the potentially more supportive proletarian allies in the early sixties only to attack highly placed purveyors of bourgeois ideology again in the middle sixties.

Dissonance theory also explains why Mao turned from the party to Lin Piao's revolutionized PLA as the prime proselyting vehicle for his dialectics following the party center's promulgation of the relatively repressive version of the double ten articles in late 1963, and why Mao went *outside* the party to seek social support for his ideology and castigation of his "bourgeois" critics, eventuating in the formation of Red Guard contingents from the ranks of previously indoctrinated youths in 1966. It explains why such extreme claims were made for the efficacy of TMTT during the 1960s and why serious attempts were made to create "the new socialist man" in China while spreading Maoist dialectics beyond the party and beyond the Chinese populace to potentially receptive people of the entire world.

In the international arena, prophecy-fails dissonance helps explain why Mao engaged in such a heated dispute with the critical Khrushchev's Soviet party during the 1960s, and why, simultaneously, Mao became so intent upon waging successful people's wars in the developing areas, providing proof of the validity of his ideology. Finally, this theory explains why Mao persisted in his prediction of success for his Great Leap-style plan and commune program and related experiments in China throughout the sixties, and why there was an attempt to revive both during the GPCR.

In predicting increased action attempts to reintroduce a successful Great Leap, our use of dissonance theory is similar to that proposed by the economist Albert Hirschman in analyzing the exit and voice responses of loyalist members of an organization to declines in the quality of production.[49] In addition to attempting to "drown out" the cognition of Great Leap failures by proselytizing for their ideology, the "loyal" Maoists also attempted to reduce their dissonance by changing the implications of that cognition through actually reimposing another Great Leap-style program on China. As Hirschman points out, like the historian Brinton before him, the attempt by the most committed of the revolutionaries to eliminate the gap between the actual and expected state of affairs of the revolution leads to their attempt to change it anew and accounts for the oft-noted generalization that "revolution, like Saturn, devours its own children."[50]

There are, of course, many important events in postliberation China that are beyond the ken of dissonance theory per se. Dissonance theory plays no obvious role in explaining, for example, how economic recovery occurred in China following the Great Leap debacles. Dissonance theory alone deals with motivation, and by itself is little help in predicting which of two competing groups is more capable in power terms. The fact that the Maoists in postliberation China continually had events dissonant with the "mass line," "omnicompetent worker," and "class struggle" precepts thrust upon them in the forms of increasing bureaucratization, specialization, and elitism is not an occurrence derivative of dissonance theory but of Max Weber's theory of social and economic organization which predicts the eventual routinization of charismatic movements.[51] Weber and others have pointed out that a burgeoning division of labor is characteristic of industrializing societies, and the type of undifferentiated charismatic authority so characteristic of Mao's style of rule, is historically a very transitory phenomenon.[52] However, assuming that Weber is basically correct in his social prognoses and that Maoists were highly committed to Mao's Yenan ideology, dissonance theory goes a long way toward explaining the behavior of Mao and the committed Maoists in response to dissonant events in the transformation of postliberation China.

NOTES

1. Edgar Snow, *The Long Revolution.* New York: Vintage, 1971, pp. 174-175.
2. Ibid., p. 169.
3. Ibid., p. 174.
4. See Richard Wich, "The tenth party congress: The power struggle and the succession question," *CQ,* No. 58, April-June 1974, pp. 231-248.
5. For copies of the two party constitutions, see *PR,* No. 18, April 30, 1969, and *PR,* Nos. 35 and 36, September 7, 1973.
6. *PR,* Nos. 35 and 36, September 7, 1973.
7. Richard Wich, op. cit., p. 245. The eighth party congress of 1956 had previously asserted that China was in an era of Leninism. While this chapter surveys some conflicts between Maoism and modernization over the past three decades of Mao's rule, two insightful works have taken an even longer historical perspective and focussed upon the clash between Maoism and traditional political culture in China. See Lucian W. Pye, *The Spirit of Chinese Politics: A Psychological Study of the Authority Crisis in Political Development.* Cambridge, Mass.: MIT Press, 1968. See also Richard H. Solomon, *Mao's Revolution and the Chinese Political Culture.* Berkeley: University of California Press, 1971. For a psychohistory of Mao, see Lucian W. Pye, *Mao Tse-tung: The Man in the Leader.* New York: Basic Books, 1976.
8. Harry Harding, Jr., "China: The fragmentation of power," *Asian Survey,* Vol. XII, No. 1, 1972, p. 5.
9. Ibid., p. 5.
10. Thomas W. Robinson, "China in 1972: Socio-economic progress amidst political uncertainty," *Asian Survey,* Vol. XII, No. 1, 1973, p. 14.
11. Peter Schran, "Institutional continuity and motivational change: The Chinese industrial wages system, 1950-1973," paper presented at Midwest Regional China seminar, University of Chicago, April 1974, p. 16.
12. See Thomas W. Robinson, "China in 1973: 'Renewed leftism threatens the new course,' " *Asian Survey,* Vol. XIV, No. 1, p. 974, p. 4. For historical perspective, see also Robert North with Ithiel de Sola Pool, "Kuomintang and Chinese Communist Elites," in Harold Lasswell and Daniel Lerner, eds., *World Revolutionary Elites.* Cambridge, Mass.: MIT Press, 1966, pp. 319-455.
13. Ibid., pp. 2-6.
14. Philip Bridgham, "The fall of Lin Piao," *CQ,* No. 55, July-September 1973, pp. 427-449.
15. Ibid., p. 433.
16. Ibid.
17. Ibid.
18. Ibid., p. 434.
19. William Whitson, *The Chinese High Command.* New York: Praeger, 1973.
20. See *ARC, The Great Power Struggle in China,* p. 227.
21. Whitson, op. cit., p. 532.
22. Ibid., p. 521. In 1971, 70 percent of the 29 ministers were commanders (p. 549). This contrasts with the moderate period before the Lushan plenum in which 14 of 49 ministers were members of minority parties.
23. Ibid., p. 124, Chart C.
24. Ibid., p. 521.
25. See *PR,* No. 4, January 24, 1975.

26. Analysis of the eighth CC politburo members, listed in Appendix A, who retained, lost, and gained positions as chairman or vice-chairman of the standing committee of the fourth national people's congress or as premier or vice-premier of the 1975 state council as compared with 1965 yields the following results. In NPC K'ang Sheng, Li Ching-ch'uan, Liu Po-ch'eng, and Chu Teh were retained; P'eng Chen was purged; and Tung Pi-wu, Ch'en Yun, T'an Chen-lin, and U Lan-fu were added. Thus the average Maoist commitment score of the NPC members dropped from 3.4 to 2.8, while polarization fell from 4.2 to 3.6. On the state council, Chou En-Lai, Li Hsien-nien, Teng Hsiao-p'ing were retained; Ch'en Yi, Ch'en Yun, Ho Lung, Li Fu-ch'un, Lin Piao, Lu Ting-yi, Po Yi-po, T'an Chen-lin and U Lan-fu were purged and none was added. Thus the average Maoist commitment score dropped from 2.2 to 2.0, while polarization fell from 5.7 to 2.7. Analysis of the Maoist commitment of those who were not eighth CC politburo members but who figured in the 1965 or 1975 NPC or state council is more ambiguous and was not formally carried out.

27. See *PR*, loc. cit.

28. The only two remaining eighth CC politburo members at the end of 1976 were Li Hsien-nien with a commitment score of 2.0 and Liu Po-ch'eng scoring 3.0. See Appendix A1 and Figure 12.1. If the two committed Maoists who died in the early 1960s, K'o Ch'ing-shih and Lo Jung-huan, are added to the 23 others on the 1962 politburo, and if they are realistically considered to have supported Mao's class struggle rationalization in 1959 and 1960 and to have refrained from criticizing Maoist policies in 1962, the expanded 1962 distribution takes on a mean commitment of 3.4 and a polarization figure of 6.8. This expansion does not change the rank ordering of any of the points plotted on Figure 11.3 from 1958 to 1976.

29. See Richard H. Solomon, op. cit., 1971, pp. 248-267, 411-524. See also Richard H. Solomon, "Mao's linking of foreign relations with China's domestic political process," in Ping-ti Ho and Tang Tsou, eds., *China in Crisis.* Chicago: University of Chicago Press, 1968, pp. 570-578.

30. Ibid., p. 524.

31. Ibid., p. 411.

32. Ibid., p. 524.

33. Solomon, op. cit., 1968, p. 578.

34. For one experimental attempt to assess the way in which peculiar national character may modify the general applicability of Western social science theory, see Paul J. Hiniker, "Chinese reactions to forced compliance: Dissonance reduction or national character," *Journal of Social Psychology,* Vol. 77, April 1969, pp. 157-176.

35. Franz Schurmann, "The attack of the Cultural Revolution on ideology and organization," in Ping-ti Ho and Tang Tsou, op. cit., pp. 525-564. See also "Comments by Ezra F. Vogal," Ibid., pp. 564-570.

36. G. William Skinner and Edwin A. Winckler, "Compliance succession in rural Communist China: A cyclical theory," in Amitai Etzioni, ed., *Complex Organizations: A Sociological Reader.* New York: Holt, Rinehart and Winston, 1969, pp. 410-432.

37. Ibid., pp. 426-432.

38. James R. Townsend, *Politics in China.* Boston: Little, Brown, 1974, pp. 145-166. For another analysis of cycles in China, see Paul J. Hiniker and R. Vincent Farace, "Approaches to national development in China: 1949-1958," *Economic Development and Cultural Change,* Vol. 18, No. 1, October 1969, pp. 51-72.

39. Townsend, op. cit., pp. 151, 278. For a somewhat different characterization of policy cycles in Communist China based upon a content analysis of *People's Daily.* See Paul J. Hiniker and Jolanta Perlstein, "Alternation of charismatic and bureaucratic styles

of leadership in Communist China," *Comparative Political Studies*, forthcoming, spring 1978.

40. Andrew J. Nathan, "A factionalism model for CCP politics," *CQ*, No. 53, 1973, pp. 48, 54.

41. Ibid., p. 52.

42. Ibid., p. 37.

43. Ibid., p. 51.

44. See also Tang Tsou's "Prolegomenon to the study of informal groups in CCP politics," and Andrew Nathan's "Reply," *CQ*, No. 65, 1976, pp. 99-117. Professor Tsou also points out that the GPCR violated the characteristic of immobilism in Nathan's model of factionalism, ibid., p. 107.

45. Robert J. Lifton, *Revolutionary Immortality: Mao Tse-tung and the Chinese Cultural Revolution.* New York: W. W. Norton, 1976, p. 8.

46. Ibid., p. 7.

47. Ibid., p. 31.

48. Ibid., p. 22.

49. Albert O. Hirschman, *Exit, Voice, and Loyalty*. Cambridge, Mass.: Harvard University Press, 1970, pp. 93-95.

50. Ibid., p. 95.

51. Max Weber, *The Theory of Social and Economic Organization.* New York: Free Press, 1964, esp. pp. 324-406 on the types of authority.

52. Cyril E. Black, *The Dynamics of Modernization.* New York: Harper and Row, 1966, pp. 1-100. See also Gariel Almond and G. Bingham Powell, *Comparative Politics: A Developmental Approach.* Boston: Little, Brown, 1966. As applied to China, see Benjamin Schwartz, "Modernization and the Maoist vision," in Roderick MacFarquhar, ed., *China Under Mao.* Cambridge, Mass.: MIT Press, 1966, pp. 3-19.

APPENDIX A

Validation of Scale of Commitment to Mao's Thought for Politburo Members Elected by Eighth Central Committee, 1956 and 1958

Frequently politburo members and their policies are characterized as relatively "leftist" or "rightist." Such a characterization implies an underlying scale whose definition is seldom explicit. We have constructed below an explicit scale of the extremity of Maoist commitment for the eighth CC politburo members. It was fashioned from an assemblage of items denoting committing Maoist actions performed by members of China's Communist political elite through the main eras of Mao's rule between 1940 and 1966. In selecting items for the scale it was not necessary for our purposes that every Maoist action be included; it was necessary that every action selected from the total universe of elite activities be relevant to the thought of Mao, indicating at least a dichotomous pro or anti orientation, and that each selected action permit meaningful comparison among members of the elite. Furthermore, in keeping with Kiesler's definition of the concept of commitment, only those Maoist actions were considered which were public, important, and somewhat voluntarily undertaken.

According to these criteria, nine committing action items were selected for inclusion in the scale. Unless otherwise noted, the source of behavioral information on each of the twenty-six politburo members elected by the eighth central committee in 1956 or 1958 is the appropriate alphabetical entry in Don W. Klein and Ann B. Clark, *A Biographic Dictionary of Chinese Communism*. Cambridge, Mass.: Harvard University Press, 1971. Table A.1 shows the pattern of performance of the nine selected actions between the Yenan era and the beginnings of the Cultural Revolution for each of the twenty-six eighth CC politburo members. They are ranked from high to low on total score. The following items were selected for the scale.

(1) Member served as an instructor or administrator of the central party school at Yenan during Mao's first rectification *(cheng feng)* campaign between 1942 and 1944. This involved indoctrinating other party members with Mao's thought, especially in opposition to the returned Moscow student clique headed by Wang Ming.

(2) Member refrained from serving as a top-level bureaucrat in the party-government hierarchy between 1950 and 1957. Top-level bureaucrat positions are defined as ministerial or commission headship positions in the government and/or secretaryship of the party secretariat or chairmanship of a central committee department in the party. The activities associated with such positions are often incompatible with Mao's mass line tenet, especially during the Soviet-modeled first five year plan, 1953-1957.

(3) Member publicly endorsed Mao's concept of rapid agricultural collectivization leading to the Great Leap Forward and communes between 1954-1958. Early public endorsement was important and risky as the politburo was, in Mao's own words, divided on the issue. The sources designating members' positions follow using footnote abbreviations, vide. Mao, *CB*, No. 892, p. 11ff; Lin Piao, *CLG*, Vol. I, No. 4, pp. 15-21; Ch'en Po-ta, *HC*, July 1958; K'ang Sheng, *URS*, Vol. 53, No. 6, pp. 63, 67; Lo Jung-huan, Gittings, *The Role of the Chinese Army*. Oxford: Oxford University Press, 1967, pp. 189, 285, the statements by K'o, T'an, and Liu are to be found in Klein, loc. cit.

(4) Member refrained from publicly opposing Mao's concept of rapid agricultural collectivization between 1954-1958. The opposition of nine politburo members to rapid collectivization is documented in the following sources: Ch'en Yun, Schurmann, *Ideoloty and Organization in Communist China*. Berkeley: University of California Press, 1966, p. 144; Po Yi-po, *URS*, Vol. 53, No. 4, p. 57; P'eng Teh-huai, Philip Bridgham, "Factionalism in the central committee," in John W. Lewis, *Party Leadership and Revolutionary Power in China*. Cambridge: Cambridge University Press, 1970, p. 215; Teng Hsiao-p'ing, *NYT*, 10/21/67; P'eng Chen, *URS*, Vol. 53, No. 7, pp. 80-81; and Li Ching-ch'uan, *URS*, Vol. 53, No. 6, p. 73.

(5) Member publicly supported Mao's class struggle rationalization of the reports of Great Leap failures following the Lushan plenum in 1959. In view of the compelling evidence of economic failings at the time, this action distinguished the commitment of but three other politburo members. The statements by Lin Piao and K'ang Sheng are to be found in *Ten Glorious Years*. Peking: Foreign Languages Press, 1960, pp. 67-89 and pp. 245-254 respectively. Ch'en Po-ta's statement is in *HC*, No. 22, 1959.

(6) Member publicly defended Mao's Great Leap at critical conference of 7,000 cadres in January 1962. In the wake of increased economic hardships wrought by the Great Leap, only three members had the fortitude to continue to argue the merits of Mao's leap before this mass meeting of the political elite. The record is to be found in Bridgham, op. cit., pp. 223, and 228 for Mao, Lin Piao, and Chou En-lai respectively.

(7) Member refrained from opposing Mao's Great Leap at conferences during 1961-1962. The relevant conferences are the 7,000 cadres above, the secret conference held by P'eng Chen in November 1961, and other party conferences on agricultural policy during 1961-1962. Eight politburo members are recorded as having opposed Mao's leap at such conferences during these hard times: Ch'en Yun, Schurmann, op. cit., p. 224; P'eng Chen, Bridgham, op. cit., p. 222; Liu Shao-ch'i, *URS*, Vol. 53, No. 7, pp. 80-84; and T'an Chen-lin, *URS*, Vol. 53, No. 7, pp. 78-82.

(8) Member publicly endorsed martyr Lei Feng and the Lei Feng campaign in 1963 as demonstrating value of Mao's thought. In the context of widespread non-compliance with Mao's tenth plenum call for deepened class struggle, explicitly endorsing Lei Feng as Mao's martyr in the nation's press was a committing action. See *URS*, Vol. 31, No. 24, for the actions of Mao, Lin Piao, Chu Teh and Chou En-lai.

(9) Member sincerely accepted ad hoc assignment from Mao in May 1966 to spread his thought and to criticize his party and nonparty opponents in the Great

Proletarian Cultural Revolution. Giving, accepting, and acting upon such instructions was an important act difficult to undo. For Mao's May 7 letter to Lin Piao, see *CB*, No. 891, pp. 56-57; for the unique assignments of Ch'en Po-ta and K'ang Sheng to the new Cultural Revolution group, see Asia Research Center, *The Great Power Struggle in China*. Hong Kong: Yee Tin Tong Press, 1969, pp. 227, 429-436. All of the above items represent important actions taken by members over the years of his rule and they committed the actors to Mao's thought in the face of opposition.

Once the nine items of the scale were selected, Kiesler's concept of additivity was invoked by considering a member relatively more committed than another member if and only if he performed relatively more of the nine committing actions. Indeed, each item was assigned an equal value of unity yielding a scale running from zero to a maximum of nine points. A short score running from zero to four was also constructed for commitments through 1958. Assuming we have constructed a valid interval scale of Maoist commitment for 8th CC politburo members, the mean scale score of the 8th CC members for any given politburo can be computed according to the formula

$$\overline{X} = \sum_{i=1}^{N} \frac{X_i}{N} ,$$

where X_i is the score of any individual member, yielding a measure of the *average* extremity of group commitment to Mao's thought. The ideological *polarization* of lack of unanimity of the group is measured by summing the squared deviations of the individual members' scores from their group mean according to the formula for the variance,

$$\sigma_x^2 = \sum_{i=1}^{N} \frac{(X_i - \overline{X})^2}{N}.$$

This measure is maximal when no scale scores are actually located at the mean position and all are clustered at the extremes of the distribution.

Finally, the association or covariation between Maoist commitment and some other variable, Y, such as standing in a particular politburo, is measured by the Pearson product-moment *correlation* coefficient,

$$r_{xy} = \sum_{i=1}^{N} \frac{(X_i - \overline{X}) (Y_i - \overline{Y})}{N \sigma_x \sigma_y} , \text{ where } -1.00 \leq r_{xy} \leq +1.00.$$

For rigorous interpretations of these distributional measures and their assumptions, see Quinn McNemar, *Psychological Statistics*. New York: John Wiley, 1965.

The use of each of these measures, X_i, $\overline{X}$, σ_x^2, and r_{xy}, rests upon the technical assumption that we have constructed a valid interval scale of Maoist commitment for politburo members. In addition to the face validity of the behavioral items, there are ways of testing this assumption. First of all, the items must form a unidimensional scale. This implies that the items must all be highly intercorrelated with the total scale score and that they are intercorrelated with each other. Table A.2 shows that this assumption is met with the average item to total scale correlation being .70, homogeneously varying with σ = .10; furthermore, the average interitem correlation is high with ϕ/ϕ max = .69, where ϕ = r for zero-one dummy variables and ϕ max is the maximum possible value for the correlation given the distribution of the marginals. (Correlations between an item and the total score minus the item are only slightly discrepant with the correlations shown.) Thus, the items all share a common variable at the core and those members who score positively on one commitment item are much more likely than chance to score positively on the other items also. Indeed, it is the nature of an ideologue that his actions are highly related to the ideology and highly correlated with each other.

Second, we can further test the assumption that this common core variable is, in fact, Maoist commitment. This may be accomplished by correlating politburo members' commitment scores with some external criterion variable indicative of such commitment. It is generally agreed that the 1958 politburo rankings were less Maoist than the new rankings established at the eleventh plenum in August 1966 during the Cultural Revolution when one's attitude toward Mao's thought was taken as the main criterion in party standing. Hence, if our scale does measure Maoist commitment, then there should be a lower correlation between it and rankings in the 1958 politburo than the correlation between it and rankings in the 1966 politburo. Indeed, as shown in Table A.3, the 1958 correlation is only .16 whereas the 1966 correlation is .69. Furthermore, it is generally agreed that the eighth CC composition of the April 1969 politburo, which consolidated the changes wrought by the Cultural Revolution, was more Maoist than that of the subsequent August 1973 politburo, which made more concessions to socioeconomic exigencies. Accordingly, the correlation between commitment scores and membership in the 1969 politburo is .77, whereas the comparable correlation for the 1973 politburo is only .43. In sum, even though tests of the scale have not *proved* the assumption of empirically equal intervals between scale positions, we have reason to be quite confident of having constructed a valid unidimensional scale of commitment to Mao's thought for members of the political elite elected or reelected to the politburo by the eighth central committee in 1956 or 1958.*

*For research demonstrating the utility and minimal assumptions involved in treating ordinal scales as interval scales, see the following articles which point out the real merits involved: Edward R. Tufte, "Improving data analysis in political science," *World Politics* 21, July 1969, pp. 641-654; for a substantive article demonstrating similar results in using either Spearman rank-order or Pearson product-moment correlation coefficients between indicators, see Norman H. Nie, G. Bingham Powell, Jr., and Kenneth Prewitt, "Social structure and political participation: Developmental relationships, I" *American Political Science Review* Vol. LXIII, No. 2, June 1969, pp. 361-378, esp. p. 375; see also Sanford Labovitz, "Some observations on measurement and statistics," *Social Forces* 46, 1967, pp. 151-160.

Table A.1: Selected Maoist Action Commitments Performed by Politburo Members Elected by Eighth Central Committee, 1956-1958

Action Commitment Items 1958 — Politburo Members	Yenan Central Party School 1940 (1)	Not Minister 1950-1957 (2)	Spoke Pro-Great Leap 1954-1958 (3)	Not Speak Anti-Great Leap 1954-1958 (4)	Short Score 1940-1958 Σ	Spoke Pro-Great Leap, Lushan 1959 (5)	Spoke Pro-Great Leap, 7,000 Cadres 1962 (6)	Not Speak Anti-Great Leap, 7,000 Cadres 1962 (7)	Spoke Pro-Lei Feng Campaign 1963 (8)	Acted Pro-Cultural Revolution 1966 (9)	Total Score 1940-1966 ΣΣ	Rank 1958 Politburo	Rank 1966 Politburo	Member 1969 Politburo	Member 1973 Politburo
Mao Tse-tung	1	1	1	1	4	1	1	1	1	1	9	1	1	1	1
Lin Piao	1	1	1	1	4	1	1	1	1	1	9	7	2	1	1
Ch'en Po-ta	1	1	1	1	4	1	1	1	0	1	7	24	4	1	0
K'ang Sheng	1	1	1	1	4	1	0	1	0	1	7	25	6	1	1
Lo Jung-huan	0	1	1	1	3	D**	D	D	D	D	D	11	D	D	D
Chu Teh	0	1	1	0	2	0	0	1	1	0	4	4	8	1	1
Chou En-lai	0	0	0	1	1	0	1	1	1	0	4	3	3	1	1
Liu Po-ch'eng	0	1	0	1	2	0	0	1	0	0	3	15	13	1	0
Tung Pi-wu	0	1	0	1	2	0	0	1	0	0	3	9	11	1	1
K'o Ch'ing-shih	0	1	1	1	3	0	0	D	D	D	D	18	D	D	D
Lin Po-ch'u	0	1	0	1	2	0	0	0	0	0	2	8	D	D	D
Li Hsien-nien	0	1	0	1	2	0	0	0	0	0	2	17	15	1	1
Li Ching-ch'uan	0	1	0	0	1	0	0	1	0	0	2	19	20	0	0
Ho Lung	0	0	0	1	1	0	0	1	0	0	2	16	14	0	0
Lu Ting-yi	0	1	0	1	2	0	0	0	0	0	2	23	21*	0	0
Ch'en Yi	0	0	0	1	1	0	0	1	0	0	2	12	12	0	0
U Lan-fu	0	0	0	1	1	0	0	1	0	0	2	21	17	0	0
Li Fu-ch'un	0	0	0	1	1	0	0	1	0	0	2	13	9	0	0
T'an Chen-lin	0	1	1	0	2	0	0	0	0	0	2	20	16	0	0
Liu Shao-ch'i	0	0	0	1	1	0	0	0	0	0	1	2	7	0	0
Chang Wen-t'ien	1	0	0	0	1	0	0	0	0	0	1	22	21*	0	0
P'eng Chen	0	0	0	0	0	0	0	0	0	0	0	10	21*	0	0
Teng Hsiao-p'ing	0	0	0	0	0	0	0	0	0	0	0	6	5	0	0
P'eng Teh-huai	0	0	0	0	0	0	0	0	0	0	0	14	21*	0	0
Po Yi-po	0	0	0	0	0	0	0	0	0	0	0	26	18	0	0
Ch'en Yun	0	0	0	0	0	0	0	0	0	0	0	5	10	0	0
TOTAL N = 26	5	14	8	17	44	4	3	15	4	4	66	(26)	(23)	(9)	7

KEY: * = purged, D** = died.

Table A.2: Internal Consistency of Eighth CC Politburo Members' Action Commitments to Mao's Thought, 1940-1966

Politburo Members' Action Commitments to Mao's Thought, 1940-1966	V1	V2	V3	V4	V5	V6	V7	V8	V9	Total ΣV1-V9
					Action Commitments to Mao's Thought, 1940-1966					
V1. Taught at Yenan central party school, 1942	(r)	.26	.52	.15	.87	.31	.16	.37	-.10	.73
	(ϕ/ϕ max)	.57	.71	.42	1.00	.42	.43	.42	-.12	
V2. Not government minister, 1950-1957			.62	.14	.48	.15	.15	.25	.48	.59
			1.00	.17	1.00	.36	.22	.52	1.00	
V3. Spoke pro-Great Leap, 1958				.14	.77	.36	.02	.25	.77	.69
				.28	1.00	.55	.04	.32	1.00	
V4. Not speak anti-Great Leap, 1958					.37	.31	.91	.37	.37	.61
					1.00	1.00	1.00	1.00	1.00	
V5. Spoke pro-class struggle, Lushan 1959						.50	.34	.40	1.00	.88
						.60	1.00	.40	1.00	
V6. Spoke pro-Great Leap, 7,000 cadres, 1962							.28	.84	.50	.65
							1.00	1.00	.60	
V7. Not speak anti-Great Leap, 7,000 cadres, 1962								.34	.34	.60
								1.00	1.00	
V8. Spoke pro-Lei Feng campaign, 1963									.40	.66
									1.00	
V9. Acted pro-Cultural Revolution, 1966										.88
Short score, 1942-1958 ΣV1-V4	.65	.76	.79	.54						

Late score, 1959-1966 ΣV5-V9 → .80

Table A.3: External Validity of Scale of Eighth CC Politburo Members'
Action Commitments to Mao's Thought, 1940-1966, as Determined by
Standing in Politburo, 1958, 1966, 1969 and 1973

Action Commitments to Mao's Thought, 1940-1966	Rank in 1958 Politburo	Rank in 1966 Politburo	Member of 1969 Politburo	Member of 1973 Politburo
V1. Taught at (r) Yenan central (ϕ/ϕ max) party school, 1942	.01	.42	.31 .48	.11 .14
V2. Not government minister, 1950-1957	.04	.30	.55 .65	.31 .47
V3. Spoke pro-Great Leap, 1958	.00	.54	.39 .52	.04 .04
V4. Not speak anti- Great Leap, 1958	.03	.43	.64 1.00	.53 1.00
V5. Spoke pro-class struggle, Lushan 1959	−.04	.61	.52 1.00	.20 .28
V6. Spoke pro-Great Leap, 7,000 cadres, 1962	.50	.59	.48 1.00	−.02 −.11
V7. Not speak anti-Great Leap, 7,000 cadres, 1962	−.16	.08	.48 .81	.48 1.00
V8. Spoke Pro-Lei Feng campaign, 1963	.58	.59	.57 1.00	.44 .64
V9. Acted pro-Cultural Revolution, 1966	−.04	.61	.57 1.00	.20 .28
Short score, 1940-1958 V1-V4	.00	.50	.72	.39
Total Score, 1940-1966 V1-V9	.16	.69	.77	.43

APPENDIX B

Comparison of Communist China (1959) and Soviet Union (1939) on Population Characteristics and Facilities for Popular Mobilization*

Population Characteristics	Communist China (1959)	Soviet Union (1939)
Population	670 million	170 million
Adult population	390 million	110 million
Gross national product per capita	$150	$400
Literacy	37%	89%
Urbanization	12%	33%
Peasantry	57%	44%

Mobilization Facilities (per adult)

Party membership	1/30 (67% peasant)	1/50 (20% peasant)

		Regular Exposure				Regular Exposure		
	Facilities	Adults	Intelligentsia	Peasantry	Facilities	Adults	Intelligentsia	Peasantry
Periodicals	1 copy/30	62%	99%	65%	— —			
Newspapers	2 copy/20	39%	97%	46%	1/3			
Radio	1 receiver/52	58%	90%	53%	1/22	25%	65%	9%
Cinema	10 movies/1	69%	87%	74%	11/1	22%	55%	8%
Political study	— —	59%	81%	56%	— —	12%	24%	10%

*DATA SOURCES: Colin Clark, "Economic growth in Communist China," *China Quarterly* No. 21, January-March 1965, pp. 148-167.

John P. Emerson, *Non-Agricultural Employment in Communist China: 1949-1958.* Washington, D.C.: International Population Statistics Reports, Series P-90, No. 21, U.S. Bureau of the Census, U.S. Government Printing Office, 1965.

Paul Hiniker, *The Effects of Mass Communication in Communist China: The Organization and Distribution of Exposure,* unpublished doctoral dissertation. Cambridge, Mass.: MIT, Department of Political Science, 1966.

Alex Inkeles, *Public Opinion in Soviet Russia.* Cambridge, Mass.: Harvard University Press, 1950, passim.

Alex Inkeles and Raymond Bauer, *The Soviet Citizen.* Cambridge, Mass.: Harvard University Press, 1961, pp. 159-188. Media exposure projections were made from these data employing the following adult population weights derived from the 1939 census: intelligentsia, .0871; white collar, .0735; blue collar, .3998; peasantry, .4396.

APPENDIX C

Estimation of Media Exposure Parameters from Combination of Survey Statistics and Population Weights, 1962

The main data base for our study of media exposure is the survey of 413 mainland refugees previously referred to. Combining this data base with the population coefficients developed in Figure C.1 below, we shall make projections to readership, listenership, and viewership of the media in Communist China for the period circa 1962. The method of our projections involves taking a weighed average of our population subgroups to produce a total population statistic. Thus we hope to gain an estimate of the total number of Chinese exposed to particular media vehicles; further, we will gain a social profile of the population segments exposed to particular vehicles. A rough check on accuracy is provided by making dual estimates from demographic types and occupational roles. In general it will be true that as the number of persons in the sample engaging in a particular media behavior falls much below twenty, the sample error in our estimate will be relatively large and this inaccuracy will be reflected in a divergence between our projections from demographic types and demographic roles. In cases where it is possible, such as the press and film, recent production figures will be analyzed in a form that provides a rough check on our projections for media exposure.

In brief, two models of the adult population of Communist China in 1962 were created, one demographic and one occupational. For both models, census figures required that 59% of the total population of 706 million be considered adults of 15 years of age or older. In the demographic model, these 415 million adults were categorized by three descriptors: sex, with 51% being male; literacy, with 37% knowing the 2,000 characters necessary to read a newspaper; and residence, with 10% living in municipalities or cities of at least 20,000 persons. The latter figure assumes a stricter definition of urban than does the official classification which yielded a national estimate of 14% urban residents in 1957. After removing the 13% of adults who are "cadres," party members (18 million), youth leaguers (33 million), and residual government officials at and above the county level (one million), the remaining 87% of the population was divided into the mutually exclusive and collectively exhaustive demographic types, shown in Table C.1B, permuting the dichotomous descriptors of sex, residence, and literacy. This procedure, when refined, yielded the demographic model for use in making readership projections from our survey.

The occupational model, depicted in Table C.1A, was created by dividing the population into thirteen occupational groups based on manpower statistics for Communist China. Since persons of sixty years or over are not eligible for the "labor force," they are lumped together in the "other" category encompassing 12% of the population. To compose the 64% of the population that are "proletarians," five of these categories were collapsed, namely peasants, fishermen, blue-collar workers, skilled workers, and soldiers. Such a procedure tends to underestimate the proletariat since the "rural proletarians" or peasants (57%) are more heavily represented among the aged "other" category. Assuming that 80% of these "others" are old peasants, would yield a total population classification which is two-thirds peasant and three-fourths proletarian. The original procedure yielded the occupational model for making projections from our sample.

The stratified quota sample of 413 subjects was one-eleventh cadre (9 CCP, 14 YCL, and 11 government cadres), one-half male, two-thirds urban, and three-fourths literate. Three-fourths of the provinces were represented although two-thirds of the sample came from Kwangtung and one-fifth from Shanghai. The refugees arrived in Hong Kong on Macau between 1956 and 1964, with the median time of arrival being 1962 and with 80% of the sample arriving between 1962 and 1964. The median age was 29 and the average 34. Seventy-two percent were married. The median level of education was at least some middle school. Projections from our sample, however, yield an average of 5.7 years of education for the adult mainlander with the average for proletarians being 4.3 years compared with 8.3 years for bourgeois. When making readership projections from the sample, the category definitions and population weights developed in the population models were strictly adhered to.

To clarify our method of making readership projections, it will suffice to go through the procedure for the periodical *Red Flag*. The survey showed that it was read regularly by the following proportions of each occupational group: 64% of professionals, 73% of officials, 61% of students, 50% of businessmen, 70% of white-collar workers, 44% of unemployed, 100% of soldiers, 14% of housewives, 23% of others, 26% of skilled workers, 14% of manual laborers, 8% of peasants, and 7% of fishermen. Multiplying each of these group proportions by the corresponding population weight for that group, depicted in Table C.1A, showed that 18% of the total adult population or 75 million persons were regular readers of *Red Flag*. Combining the readership figures for skilled workers, manual workers, peasants, fishermen and soldiers, showed that 33% of these regular readers were "proletarians." Reclassifying our sample by demographic type and applying the population weights depicted in Table C.1B yielded the same estimate of 18% regular adult readership as composed from the following group proportions provided by the sample: 78% of the cadres, 67% of MUL-S, 67% of MUL-P, 39% of MUL-O, 28% of FUL-H, 35% of FUL-O, 24% of MRL, 23% of FRL, 13% of MUI, 0% of FUI, 7% of MRI, 0% of FRI. Recombining figures for the separate descriptors showed that cadres constituted 56% of the regular readers. The residual readership was composed of 11% females, 97% ruralites and 15% illiterates. The audience profile for *Red Flag* was completed by noting that on the average, our "regular" sample readers estimated that they read two-thirds of the issues of periodical yielding an estimate of 50 million readers per issue. See Hiniker, 1966, cited in Appendix B.

Table C.1: Models of Adult Chinese Population, 1962

A: Proportion of the Adult Population in Occupational Categories, 1962

Population Categories	Percentages	Thousands of Persons	Survey Sample Size (n)
Proletarian (64%)			
Peasants	57.079	236,749	88
Fishermen	.386	1,601	14
Blue collar	2.554	10,593	43
Skilled workers	3.292	13,654	57
Soldiers	.634	2,667	2
Bourgeois (36%)			
Officials	1.813	7,520	11
Professionals	.775	3,214	39
White collar	1.155	4,803	24
Businessmen	.221	917	13
Housewives	13.910	57,695	56
Students	1.928	7,997	44
Unemployed	4.391	18,213	9
Others*	11.850	49,151	13
Total Adult Population	100.000	414,774	413

B: Proportion of the Adult Population in Demographic Categories, 1962

Cadres**	12.771	52,971	36
Male urban literate (student)	.036	149	33
Male urban literate (intelligentsia)	.056	228	31
Male urban literate (others)	.042	174	33
Female urban literate (housewives)	.502	2,078	29
Female urban literate (others)	1.047	4,338	34
Male urban illiterate	1.405	5,823	31
Female urban illiterate	2.957	12,265	32
Male rural literate	22.392	92,880	50
Female rural literate	5.662	23,484	30
Male rural illiterate	15.575	64,605	30
Female rural illiterate	37.555	155,777	44

*See Paul J. Hiniker, 1966, pp. 101-135 (cited in Appendix B). The percentiles are computed on the population of age fifteen and over. The "other" category is composed of those persons who are ineligible for participation in the labor force by virtue of age consisting of males who are sixty years of age or over and females who are fifty-five years of age or older.

**Thirteen percent of the adult population are cadres composed in 1962 of eighteen million party members, thirty-three million youth league members and one million residual government officials. The party contains 80% of proletarian background, 90% males, and 67% ruralites. The adult population is 64% proletarian, 51% male, 90% rural, and 63% illiterate.

APPENDIX D

Estimation of Word-of-Mouth Communications Polarization by Social Class from Survey Statistics, 1956-1966

Time Designation of Sample	ϕ		Normalized Distribution of Political Communications P	B		Number of Respondents	Average Years of Education	Time Respondents Left Mainland (n)
1956	.498	B	12	24	36	n.d.	n.d.	1953 (9), 1954 (234)
		P	53	11	64	n.d.	n.d.	1955 (137), 1956 (371)
			65	35	100	751		
1957	.511	B	10	26	36	n.d.	n.d.	1957 (1,003)
		P	51	13	64	n.d.	n.d.	
			61	39	100	1,003		
1958	.392	B	12	24	36	n.d.	n.d.	1958 (321)
		P	47	17	64	n.d.	n.d.	
			59	41	100	321		
						Σ SORO* = 2,075		
1959	.442	B	4	32	36	60	12.2	1956 (14) 1957 (16)
		P	36	28	64	28	3.2	1958 (10) 1959 (5)
			40	60	100	88		1960 (18) 1961 (25)
1962	.544	B	8	28	36	96	10.1	1962 (193)
		P	50	14	64	97	4.5	
			58	42	100	193		
1964	.586	B	7	29	36	54	11.8	1963 (61) 1964 (71)
		P	51	13	64	78	4.8	
			58	42	100	132		
1966	.623	B	2	34	36	10	12.8	1965 (2) 1966 (10)
		P	45	19	64	10	6.3	1967 (8)
			47	53	100	20		
						Σ Author = 433		
						$\Sigma\Sigma$ Total = 2,508		

KEY: B = Bourgeoisie

P = Proletariat

ϕ = Phi Coefficient of Polarization of Political Communications, e.g.:

$\phi = c - qq'$, where

$$\phi = \frac{c - qq'}{\sqrt{pq \, p'q'}}$$

	B	P		
B	a	b	p	
P	c	d	q	
	q'	p'		

Complete Cleavage

$\phi = 1.00$

	P	B	
B	00	36	36
P	64	00	64
	64	36	100

Complete Integration

$\phi = 0.00$

	P	B	
B	23	13	36
P	41	23	64
	64	36	100

*SORO = Survey of 2,075 mainland refugees conducted on Taiwan in 1958. See Barton Whaley, George Schueller, and John Scott. *PROPIN-China: A Study of Word-of-Mouth Communications in Communist China.* Washington, D.C.: Special Operations Research Office, The American University, 1961. The surveys conducted by the author in Hong Kong and Macau in 1964 (n = 413) and 1967 (n = 20) matched questions and occupational categories to this prior survey. The question asked on both surveys regarding political communications contacts dealt with who were the persons with whom he regularly communicated about what was going on in his locale and in China generally. The respondent then provided an occupational and demographic description of each of these.

ABBREVIATIONS IN NOTES*

ARC   *Asia Research Center*, Hong Kong

CFCP *Chieh Fang Chun Pao* (Liberation Army Daily), Peking.

CB   *Current Background*, Hong Kong: American Consulate General.

CLG   *Chinese Law and Government*, White Plains, N.Y.: International Arts and Sciences Press.

CQ   *China Quarterly*, London: Contemporary China Institute.

CS   *Current Scene*, Hong Kong: American Consulate General.

HC   *Hung Ch'i* (Red Flag), Peking.

IAS   *Issues and Studies*, Taipei: Institute of International Relations.

JMJP *Jen Min Jih Pao* (People's Daily), Peking.

KTTH *Kung-tso T'ung-hsun* (Bulletin of Activities), Palo Alto, Calif.: Hoover Institute Translation.

MISC *Miscellany of Mao Tse-tung Thought (1949-1968)*, Washington, D.C.: Joint Publications Research Service, No. 61269, February 20, 1974.

NCNA *New China News Agency*, Peking.

NYT   *New York Times*, New York.

PR   *Peking Review*, Peking.

SCMM *Selections from China Mainland Magazines*, Hong Kong: American Consulate General.

SCMP *Survey of China Mainland Press*, Hong Kong: American Consulate General.

SW   *Mao Tse-tung's Selected Works*, Peking: Foreign Languages Press.

URS   *Union Research Service*, Hong Kong.

*The first time a source is cited, it is fully listed in the notes; thereafter, only the abbreviation is listed.

ABOUT THE AUTHOR

PAUL J. HINIKER is an Associate Member of the Center for Far Eastern Studies at the University of Chicago. In addition to his Ph.D. (political science, MIT, 1966) he holds an M.A. in social psychology and a certificate in elementary Mandarin Chinese. Dr. Hiniker has held a number of teaching positions in political and social science, and he has been a researcher and consultant with several private and public institutions. In 1964, 1967, and 1969 he did research in Hong Kong. Dr. Hiniker is the author of many scholarly articles, papers, and monographs. Among his recent writings are "Alternation of charismatic and bureaucratic styles of leadership in Communist China," *Comparative Political Studies* (with J. J. Perlstein), forthcoming, Winter 1977-1978; and "Media Exposure in China during the Socialist Education Campaign: Some survey results," in F. Gilbert Chan (ed.), *China Under Communism: Revolutionary and Diplomacy, 1949-1976,* New Viewpoints, forthcoming, Fall 1977.